Praise for *Documentary Storytelling*

"Bernard demonstrates to documentarians how story can be more effectively incorporated into every level of nonfiction filmmaking from conception to development and pre-production, in the field and in the editing room. Her discussions incorporate many examples from contemporary documentaries to illustrate a variety of salient points."

—*Documentary* (International Documentary Association)

"Sheila Curran Bernard's *Documentary Storytelling* is an essential, pragmatic, common-sense approach to making nonfiction films for the student and/or first-time filmmaker, based on the author's deep awareness of documentary film history and theory, and her intimate knowledge of how today's most important documentarians formulate their works."

—Gerald Peary, film critic, *The Boston Phoenix*

"[T]eems with insight and instruction on the documentary craft, from elements of storytelling to divining the story arc of a given topic, as well as more specific script-to-screen information about documentary film production and post-production, and finding a market for your documentary work. . . . Part III is the interviews. There's all kinds of wise and thought-provoking stuff . . . along with great, revealing stories from documentary film production."

—Stephen Nathans-Kelly, *EventDV*

"While documentaries are nonfiction, they are certainly not objective, and even the smallest choices in writing, filming, interviewing, narrating, or scoring can drastically alter the perspective of the film, and in turn, the audience. Bernard is keenly aware of the power of persuasive images, and her insistence on complexity and integrity is a consistent theme throughout the book."

—Alyssa Worsham, *The Independent*

"If you fancy yourself as a documentary film-maker, or simply want to improve your understanding of observational storytelling, buy this book, read it, and apply the ideas contained within."

—Quentin Budworth, *Focus Magazine*

"*Documentary Storytelling*. That's what this book is about. It's about the story, how to convey that story eloquently, effectively, and ethically. . . . This book is absolutely brilliant . . . packed full of interviews with award-winning documentary filmmakers offering up information, advice, and wisdom you'll find interesting and useful."

—Krista Galyen, *AAUG Reviews*

Praise for *Archival Storytelling: A Filmmaker's Guide to Finding, Using, and Licensing Third-Party Visuals and Music* (with Kenn Rabin)

"The excellent new resource, *Archival Storytelling*, is really two books in one: a detailed how-to guide for filmmakers on the process of researching, acquiring, and clearing rights to archival materials; and a deeper exploration of the implications, ethical and creative, of using these materials to tell new stories."
—Grace Lile, *American Archivist* (The Society of American Archivists)

"This book is a great resource because it surveys the entire landscape from ethical/creative considerations to fair use to changes in the digital age, and the focus is always on the importance of telling stories."
—Ingrid Kopp, Shooting People

"I am often asked how to work with archival materials. Now I have an easy answer: Get a copy of *Archival Storytelling* and read it. Everything's there—how to use archival materials, acquire them, and most of all, how to think about them. *Archival Storytelling* is indispensable."
—David Grubin, Filmmaker

"This is it, the book that will save you thousands of dollars and untold hours of frustration. It will be the single best purchase your production company will make. *Archival Storytelling* clearly explains the entire process of researching, acquiring and licensing archival footage and music. Included are time-tested tips and techniques for efficiently managing the work flow and negotiating rights."
—Ann Petrone, Archival Supervisor

"One of the best—and most needed—texts I have seen in a while. The challenge is to keep what is a fairly technical aspect of filmmaking interesting without compromising the quality and depth of information. The authors have done an exceptional job in this regard by the careful interweaving of interviews with researchers, filmmakers, and legal experts through the factual material. There is the strong sense of being in the presence of experienced filmmakers and researchers who accept that while there are standard practices, archival use and intellectual property laws, etc. are contingent fields in which each case must be assessed and dealt with on its merits."
—Bruce Sheridan, Chair, Film & Video Department, Columbia College

"I've been making historical documentaries for many years, yet I learned new things from this book. This is the definitive guide for archival research for documentary filmmakers. An invaluable resource."
—Mark Jonathan Harris, Filmmaker and Distinguished Professor, School of Cinematic Arts, University of Southern California

Documentary Storytelling

Documentary Storytelling has reached filmmakers and filmgoers worldwide with its unique focus on the key ingredient for success in the growing global documentary marketplace: storytelling. This practical guide reveals how today's top filmmakers bring the tools of narrative cinema to the world of nonfiction film and video without sacrificing the rigor and truthfulness that give documentaries their power. The book offers practical advice for producers, directors, editors, cinematographers, writers, and others seeking to make ethical and effective films that merge the strengths of visual and aural media with the power of narrative storytelling.

In this new, updated edition, Emmy Award-winning filmmaker and author Sheila Curran Bernard offers:

- new strategies for analyzing documentary work;
- new conversations with filmmakers including Stanley Nelson (*The Black Panthers*), Kazuhiro Soda (*Mental*), Orlando von Einsiedel (*Virunga*), and Cara Mertes (JustFilms);
- discussions previously held with filmmakers Susan Kim (*Imaginary Witness*), Deborah Scranton (*The War Tapes*), Alex Gibney (*Taxi to the Dark Side*), and James Marsh (*Man on Wire*).

Sheila Curran Bernard's credits include projects for broadcast and theatrical release as well as museum and classroom use. She has taught at Princeton University, Westbrook College, and the University at Albany, State University of New York.

Documentary Storytelling

Creative Nonfiction on Screen

Fourth Edition

Sheila Curran Bernard

Focal Press
Taylor & Francis Group

NEW YORK AND LONDON

Fourth edition published 2016
by Focal Press
711 Third Avenue, New York, NY 10017

and by Focal Press
2 Park Square, Milton Park, Abingdon, Oxon OX 14 4RN

Focal Press is an imprint of the Taylor & Francis Group, an informa business

First edition published by Focal Press 2003

Second edition published by Focal Press 2007

Third edition published by Focal Press 2011

Library of Congress Cataloging in Publication Data
Bernard, Sheila Curran.
   Documentary storytelling: creative nonfiction on screen / Sheila Curran Bernard.—Fourth edition.
      pages cm
   Includes bibliographical references and index.
Includes filmography.
   1. Documentary films—Production and direction.   2. Documentary films—Authorship.   I. Title.
   PN1995.9.D6B394 2016
   070.1'8—dc23
   2015026947

ISBN: 978-1-138-12341-0 (hbk)
ISBN: 978-0-415-84330-0 (pbk)
ISBN: 978-0-203-75631-7 (ebk)

Typeset in Giovanni
by Apex CoVantage, LLC

In memory of Henry Hampton

Contents

Preface to the Fourth Edition

The phrase "documentary storytelling" has become commonplace since this book was first published in 2003. It describes the powerful merging of visual and literary narrative devices to enable media makers to reach and engage audiences with nonfiction content. But the need for "storytelling" is also sometimes used to justify nonfiction work that is overly sentimental or sensational, poorly researched, poorly crafted, or dishonest. That's not what this book is about, and it's not what the filmmakers featured in these pages do.

Instead, good documentary storytelling is an organic process through which a filmmaker approaches a subject, *finds* (as opposed to imposes) a story within that subject, and then uses a wealth of narrative devices—structure, character, questions, point of view, tone, stakes, and more—to tell that story honestly and artfully in order to actively engage an audience. In this way, the documentary filmmaker joins the ranks of other master storytellers, whether they work in fiction or nonfiction. The extraordinary films of today's leading directors—and the teams of producers, writers, editors, cinematographers, and sound recordists with whom they work—continue to set a high bar for those seeking to work in nonfiction media. *Documentary Storytelling*, in this and previous editions, puts the tools used by these filmmakers into the hands of anyone seeking to tell nonfiction stories, whether for broadcast, web, or theatrical release, or for use in educational and community settings.

"Documentary" is a term often broadly used to describe nonfiction (or "unscripted") media, but a closer definition is more useful. For an analogy, consider the nonfiction section of a bookstore or library. There are books with advice on cooking and gardening and pet care; graphic novels and how-to manuals; histories that are scrupulously researched and histories that appeal primarily through images and sentiment; rigorous science alongside pseudoscience. As lifelong readers, we've learned to recognize the differences of quality, purpose, intended audience, format, substance, and form that characterize these works, and make our choices accordingly. This book, *Documentary Storytelling*, most closely aligns with long-form print described as creative (or literary) nonfiction: authored, substantive, creative works.

This fourth edition contains more than 30 percent new material, including an examination of new films, new conversations with award-winning filmmakers (Cara Mertes, Stanley Nelson, Kazuhiro Soda, and Orlando von Einsiedel), and strategies for more closely viewing and analyzing documentary work as a means of learning from the best.

With only a few exceptions, films discussed in this edition can easily be bought, rented, or streamed through legitimate vendors or broadcasters. A complete list of works discussed can be found at the back of the book.

Acknowledgments

My thanks to Focal Press for shepherding four editions of this book into print, and also overseeing its publication in Chinese, Japanese, Korean, Polish, and Portuguese. For this edition, special thanks to Emily McCloskey, Elliana Arons, Mary LaMacchia, Christina Taranto, and Diana Taylor. Thanks also to Johanna Kovitz and Karen Weitzel for their transcriptions.

For all editions and translations, thanks to Elinor Actipis, Michael Ambrosino, Paula Apsell, Steven Ascher, Mhairi Bennett, Ronald Blumer, Liane Brandon, Victoria Bruce, Michał Bukojemski, Ric Burns, Brett Culp, Gail Dolgin, Jon Else, Boyd Estus, Nick Fraser, Susan Froemke, Peter Frumkin, Alex Gibney, Jim Gilmore, Karin Hayes, Sun Hongyun, Ken-Ichi Imamura, Saul Janson, Jeanne Jordan, Susan Kim, JoAnna Baldwin Mallory, James Marsh, Tom Mascaro, Cara Mertes, Muffie Meyer, Frank Moens, Stanley Nelson, Hans Otto Nicolaysen, Richard Panek, Sam Pollard, Kenn Rabin, Per Saari, Deborah Scranton, Tetsuro Shimauchi, Susanne Simpson, Bennett Singer, Kazuhiro Soda, Holly Stadtler, Tracy Heather Strain, Ryoya Terao, Orlando von Einsiedel, Melanie Wallace, Onyekachi Wambu, Renata Warchał, and Ewa Zukrowska. My thanks also to colleagues and students at the University at Albany, State University of New York.

For everything else, as always, my gratitude and love goes to friends and family.

Sheila Curran Bernard
June 2015

Sources and Notes

In most cases, quotations in this book are drawn from conversations I conducted during preparation for each of the four editions. These include talks with Michael Ambrosino, Paula Apsell, Steven Ascher, Ronald Blumer, Liane Brandon, Victoria Bruce, Ric Burns, Brett Culp, Gail Dolgin, Jon Else, Boyd Estus, Nick Fraser, Susan Froemke, Alex Gibney, Jim Gilmore, Karin Hayes, Jeanne Jordan, Susan Kim, James Marsh, Cara Mertes, Muffie Meyer, Stanley Nelson, Hans Otto Nicolaysen, Richard Panek, Sam Pollard, Kenn Rabin, Per Saari, Deborah Scranton, Susanne Simpson, Bennett Singer, Kazuhiro Soda, Holly Stadtler, Tracy Heather Strain, Orlando von Einsiedel, Melanie Wallace, and Onyekachi Wambu. Additional information about films and filmmakers was taken as noted from a range of sources, including information provided by the filmmakers themselves through their official websites and press material and in material included on their DVDs.

Throughout this book (and all previous editions), attention has been paid to effective and also ethical uses of storytelling to enhance the power and appeal of documentary films. In September 2009, the American University Center for Media & Social Impact published *Honest Truths: Documentary Filmmakers on Ethical Challenges in Their Work*, on which I served as an advisor. CSMI is also responsible for the 2005 publication *The Documentary Filmmakers' Statement of Best Practices in Fair Use*. Both documents, and much more, can be found at their website, www.cmsimpact.org.

About the Author

Sheila Curran Bernard is an Emmy and Peabody Award-winning film-maker with credits on nearly 50 hours of theatrical and broadcast programming, in addition to work for classroom, web, and community use. With Kenn Rabin, she is also the author of *Archival Storytelling: A Filmmaker's Guide to Finding, Using, and Licensing Third-Party Visuals and Music*. She has been honored with fellowships at the MacDowell Colony for the Arts and the Virginia Center for the Creative Arts, and in 2005 served as the Anschutz Distinguished Fellow in American Studies at Princeton University. In 2008, she joined the faculty at the University at Albany, State University of New York.

Please visit the author's website, **www.sheilacurranbernard.com**.

CHAPTER 1

Introduction

It's not uncommon for people, including documentary filmmakers, to differentiate the nonfiction films they enjoy (and make) from something they've stereotyped as "documentaries." Documentaries, from the reputation they seem to hold, are the films some of us had to watch during fifth-grade history or eighth-grade science. Sometimes derided as "chalk and talk," these films tended to be dry, heavily narrated, filled with facts, and painful to sit through. So ingrained is this model, it seems, that inexperienced or polemical filmmakers sometimes imitate it, creating films that are little more than illustrated lectures created to "show" or "prove" something through a steady recitation of data. Conversely, nonfiction films that *work*—that grab and hold audiences through creative, innovative storytelling—are often set apart by their makers and audiences as being somehow an exception to the form, rather than high-quality examples of it.

Like their "narrative" (fictional) counterparts, these stand-out films often emphasize character, conflict, rising stakes, a dramatic arc, and a resolution. They bring viewers on a journey, immerse them in new worlds, and explore universal themes. Done well, they compel viewers to consider and even care about topics and subjects they might previously have overlooked. And yet, unlike fictional drama, these movies are based on a single and powerful premise: they're true. The stories are based in the real, factual world.

Done well, documentary storytelling appears easy, almost inevitable. And yet the filmmakers who do it can assure you that it's hard work, a painstaking process that continues through every stage of production, from conception through editing. That process is what this book is about.

DEFINING DOCUMENTARY

Documentaries bring viewers into new worlds and experiences through the presentation of accurate, factual information about real people, places, and events, generally (but not always) portrayed through the use of actual images and artifacts. A performing killer whale turns deadly under the conditions of captivity (*Blackfish*); children in Kolkata are given cameras and inspired to move beyond their limited circumstances (*Born into Brothels*); soldiers on the front lines in Iraq film their own stories of combat (*The War Tapes*). But factuality alone does not define documentary films; it's what the filmmaker does with those factual elements, artfully weaving them into an overall narrative that is often greater than the sum of its parts. "The documentarist has a passion for what he finds in images and sounds—which always seem to him more meaningful than anything he can invent," wrote Erik Barnouw in his 1974 book *Documentary*. "Unlike the fiction artist, he is dedicated to *not* inventing. It is in selecting and arranging his findings that he expresses himself."

Story is the device that describes this arrangement. A story may begin as an idea, hypothesis, or series of questions. It becomes more focused throughout the filmmaking process, until the finished film has a compelling beginning, an unexpected middle, and a satisfying end. Along the way, the better you understand your story, even as it's evolving, the more prepared you'll be to tell it creatively and well. You're likely to identify characters and scout locations more carefully, and the visuals you shoot will be stronger. Perhaps surprisingly, you'll be better prepared to follow the unexpected—to take advantage of the twists and turns that are an inevitable and welcome part of documentary production, and recognize those elements that will make your film even stronger.

Puja running, from *Born into Brothels*.
Photo by Gour, courtesy of Kids with Cameras.

DOCUMENTARY AS A SUBSET OF NONFICTION FILM AND VIDEO

As noted in the preface, the range of film and video categorized loosely as "documentary" is broad and varies widely in quality, in terms of both content and craft. The best documentaries demand viewers' active engagement. When the audience is caught up in a life-and-death struggle to protect Africa's oldest park (*Virunga*), embedded with the filmmakers in Cairo's Tahrir Square (*The Square*), or behind the scenes with some of music's most significant and unheralded backup singers (*20 Feet from Stardom*), there is nothing as powerful as a documentary.

Many documentaries have far-reaching impact. Jeanne Jordan and Steven Ascher learned that their Academy Award-nominated film *Troublesome Creek: A Midwestern*, about the efforts of Jordan's parents to save their Iowa farm from foreclosure, influenced farming policy in Australia. Jon Else's *Cadillac Desert*, the story of water and the transformation of nature in the American West, was screened to inform policy makers on Capitol Hill. Alex Gibney learned that *Taxi to the Dark Side*, his Academy Award-winning look at the U.S. military's treatment of detainees in Iraq and Iran, was viewed by individuals campaigning for the U.S. presidency in 2008 and by the U.S. Army in its training of the Judge Advocate General (JAG) Corps. To achieve this effectiveness, films must not only reach audiences through compelling, nuanced storytelling, but they must also earn their audiences' trust through reliable, honest content.

Although the storytelling tools explored in this book can be applied to other kinds of nonfiction media production, the examples are drawn primarily from longer-form work, including broadcast hours and series and theatrical-length features. As discussed in the preface, these films and their creators have their counterparts in the world of creative nonfiction prose, also sometimes described as literary nonfiction.

CREATIVE NONFICTION ON SCREEN

Consider this list of the "five characteristics" that make nonfiction writing creative, as described by author Philip Gerard in his book *Creative Nonfiction: Researching and Crafting Stories of Real Life*:

- First, it has an apparent subject and a deeper subject . . .
- Second, and partly because of the duality of subject, such nonfiction is released from the usual journalistic requirement of *timeliness* . . .

- Third, creative nonfiction is narrative, it always tells a good story [Gerard cites another writer, Lee Gutkind, in explaining that to do this, the nonfiction writer "takes advantage of such fictional devices as character, plot, and dialogue. . . . It is action-oriented. Most good creative nonfiction is constructed in scenes."] . . .
- Fourth, creative nonfiction contains a sense of *reflection* on the part of the author. . . . It is a *finished* thought . . .
- Fifth, such nonfiction shows serious attention to the craft of writing.

How does this evaluation apply to documentary films?

An Apparent Subject and a Deeper Subject

There may be a deceptively simple story that *organizes* the film, but the story is being told because it reveals something more. *Sound and Fury*, on the surface, is a documentary about a little girl who wants a cochlear implant, an operation that may enable her to hear. But in telling that story, the filmmakers explore the world of Deaf culture, what it means to belong to a family and a community, how language is acquired, and more. *The Donner Party*, at its most basic level, tells the story of pioneers who took an ill-fated shortcut across the Sierra Nevada, became trapped by winter snowfall, and in desperation resorted to cannibalism. But filmmaker Ric Burns chose that story not for its shock value but because he felt that it revealed something about the American character.

Released from the Journalistic Requirement of Timeliness

Even when documentaries are derived from news reports, they are not bound to tell the story while it's still "news." Instead, their creators take time to consider events and put them in more detailed and often layered context. The financial meltdown of Enron; the abuse of prisoners at Bagram, Abu Ghraib, and Guantánamo; the suicide of writer Hunter S. Thompson—all, at one time, were news stories, and all have been used as fodder for enduring, thought-provoking documentaries by director Alex Gibney.

Tells a Good Story

This means that a filmmaker uses the tools of creative writing to *identify* and *shape* a good story, one that accurately represents the truth.

It does not mean inventing or distorting characters or plots or conflicts for the purpose of enhancing a documentary's appeal.

Contains a Sense of Reflection on the Part of the Author

A documentary is not a news report. It is a thoughtful presentation of a subject that has been explored, researched, weighed, considered, and shaped by the filmmaker over a period of time, and then communicated outward in a voice and style that are unique. Who is a film's author? The conventional view is that it is the director, provided the director is principally responsible for the story that is told, from development through editing. Many films, more accurately, have multiple authors, reflecting close relationships between a producer(s), a director, a writer, and an editor, or some combination within that group. But the author is the person or group whose vision, ultimately, is reflected on screen.

Shows Serious Attention to the Craft of Film Storytelling

A filmmaker's palette is different, in many ways, from that of a novelist or playwright, but the underlying considerations remain the same. Craft is about wielding the unique tools of a chosen medium to their full and best advantage. A story told on film has the power to actively engage viewers both emotionally and intellectually by immersing them, visually and aurally, in an on-screen experience.

OBJECTIVITY, SUBJECTIVITY, AND BIAS

The power of documentary films comes from the fact that they are grounded in fact, not fiction. This is not to say that they're "objective." Like any form of communication, whether spoken, written, painted, or photographed, documentary filmmaking involves the communicator in making choices. It's therefore unavoidably subjective, no matter how balanced, neutral, fair, or accurate the presentation seeks to be. Which stories are being told, why, and by whom? What information or material is included or excluded? What choices are made concerning style, tone, point of view, and format? "To be sure, some documentarists claim to be 'objective,'" noted Barnouw, "a term that seems to renounce an interpretive role. The claim may be strategic but is surely meaningless."

Subjectivity is not the opposite of objectivity. All forms of communication are *subjective*. Someone made that film, just as someone painted that picture, took that photograph, or even aimed a surveillance camera in one direction rather than another. Sometimes the subjectivity is less apparent, as when a writer or filmmaker strives for neutrality, working to present the journalistic basics of who, what, where, and when, and in addition, working to ensure that multiple points of view are fairly presented. (This does not mean seeking out "both" sides, if doing so misrepresents the issues.) But a work can also have a point of view and remain journalistically sound, if the author's point of view is transparent and if the evidence that's assembled is fairly chosen and presented truthfully.

A work is subjective whether or not an author or filmmaker is identified. Arguably, it strengthens the integrity of work to reveal the reporters or storytellers. Consider detailed web pages that have no listed author, or a newspaper story with no byline. That writing is not necessarily any more balanced, fair, accurate, or neutral; it's just that viewers/readers have to work harder to evaluate the credibility of the information's source—and should.

Bias

"Bias" is often used to describe the perspective of a news source: people say that a certain network has a conservative bias, or a newspaper has a liberal bias, and so forth. Merriam-Webster defines bias as "a tendency to believe that some people, ideas, etc. are better than others that usually results in treating some people unfairly." A bias may be positive or negative. A professor with a positive bias toward older students might grade them more easily, whether intentionally or not. An employer with a negative bias against workers with young children might find reasons not to hire them.

Everyone has biases. A good journalist, like a good documentary filmmaker, works to overcome them and trusts that the audience, presented with sufficient evidence, is capable of reaching its own conclusions. Bias becomes *distortion*, *falsehood*, *deception*, and such when the author only cherry-picks the record, selecting information and interviews in a way that pushes the audience unfairly toward a conclusion that is false or misleading.

Bias is not the same thing as point of view. Here's an example, drawn from an exercise shared with me by Richard Panek, an award-winning nonfiction writer and educator: Suppose that a dozen students attend a lecture given by a visiting professor of history, an

American in his early thirties who's an expert on modern France. Afterward, they are divided into four groups, and each group is asked to write a brief report about the lecture. The catch is that each group is writing for a specific audience, such as: 1) a university tenure committee; 2) the visiting professor's hometown newspaper; 3) a men's fashion magazine; and 4) a documentary production company that's scouting talent for a TV special on the history of France.

Imagine that once the groups have finished the reports, they're asked to take a bit more time to remove anything in their write-ups that might be construed as bias. They do so. Will the four completed reports be identical? Of course not, because they're created for different audiences. The university tenure committee wants to know about the effectiveness and content of the lecture, for example, and not about the out-of-season Armani blazer the professor wore. The hometown newspaper will be less interested in that day's lecture than in the overall achievements of their former resident. And so on. Each of the reports will emphasize those details that serve its unique audience, and at the same time, each of the reports might still be accurate, fair, and truthful.

Within this example, a *biased* report might result if those writing for the tenure committee already had a preferred candidate, and therefore focused on the few missteps made by the professor without acknowledging that they were not representative of the talk overall or the students' positive reception of it. A rule of thumb, if you're wondering whether your work is biased, is to ask yourself whether a reasonable group of smart people, much like a jury, given not only your report or film but also the overall evidence available, would find your work to be generally accurate and fair in its representation of the known facts.

With documentary films, balance and neutrality are not prerequisites; fairness, accuracy, and transparency should be. Viewers don't need to agree with your documentary or its conclusions. But they should be able to trust that important events happened in a way that the film presents them as happening, and that evidence has not been distorted or withheld in the interest of creating a more convincing (albeit misleading) argument or a more "dramatic" storyline. Once your deception is discovered, the whole film has lost its value, except perhaps to audiences looking for affirmation of pre-existing views, even if those views are, in fact, biased.

Fairness and Balance

A filmmaker striving for journalistic balance will often work to present the story or argument in a way that seeks out and gives a *fair* hearing to a range of viewpoints essential to a true understanding of the issue at hand. This doesn't mean setting up a false dichotomy (pro/con, he said/she said) if that would be misleading. For example, the overwhelming majority of scientists agree that the climate is changing, even if there are differences of thought about causes and solutions. It would be dishonest, therefore, to give the fringe position—climate-change deniers—an equal say to "balance out" climate-change adherents.

A film can be truthful and accurate without being balanced. Suppose you decide to tell the story of a woman's crusade against the use of animals to test cosmetics, from her point of view. You're not representing your film as a neutral look at the issue of animal testing; your film is about this crusader. The main caveat is that false statements by her (or her supporters) can't be allowed to stand uncontested; you'd need to find a way to let viewers know that while these are their views, the facts don't support them.

The other caveat with a narrow point of view is that if you *do* need multiple perspectives, you should get them. A film loses credibility when interviewees are telling us what other people, especially those in opposition, think or feel. If your subjects are talking about a "them"—as in, "they were afraid of us, we had them worried"—you should consider letting "them" speak for themselves. In fact, allowing for contradictory points of view can strengthen a film, not least because it plays to the fact that people like to weigh evidence for themselves and make up their own minds. For example, I was among the producers responsible for the multipart PBS series *Eyes on the Prize*, a history of the American civil rights movement, which covered events from the mid-1950s through the mid-1980s. We did not set out to "show" that the movement was necessary and right, although I doubt any of us felt otherwise. Instead, our task was to explore the history and let it reveal itself—especially to younger viewers, who had not experienced it firsthand—through participants' stories. We were continually reminded by the production executives that our ability to do so, effectively and well, lay in our willingness to let the evidence of history speak for itself, including giving a fair platform to individuals who'd lived through this era and opposed (at least during that time) the movement. Fairness, in this context, meant not judging or sandbagging opponents; it meant allowing them the same right to speak about their experiences as anyone else, and earning their trust that we would do so. The series, and the history it conveys, is stronger and richer because of it.

As another example, look at *Super Size Me*: When starting his 30-day diet, director Morgan Spurlock is critical but also somewhat ambivalent about McDonald's and a lawsuit that blames fast food for the obesity of two teenaged girls. He lays out the basic construction of his experiment on camera and brings in three independent doctors to measure the results. (Some critics have argued that the artificiality of this experiment stacks the deck against McDonald's, but I don't agree. Knowing the setup, the audience can and should bring its own skepticism to the table; the experiment is obviously extreme.) Throughout the film, Spurlock also allows interviewees with whom he might be assumed to be sympathetic—doctors, lawyers, school personnel, people on the street—to paint themselves (at times) as mercenary, misinformed, or ignorant. How difficult is it to understand that 64 ounces of soda contains a lot of sugar? Or to look across a lunchroom and notice that the teens you're feeding are eating nothing but high-fat, high-salt junk food? By the film's end, Spurlock has learned and conveyed a great deal of unflattering evidence against the fast-food industry, but his call for change is directed at consumers.

Selection

Making choices about what to include or exclude in the film also does not constitute bias. (Remember the definition of documentary is *selecting* as well as arranging materials.) Whether you're creating a 30-minute film or a nine-hour series, you can't include everything; there's not enough time, and you'll confuse viewers who are trying to follow your story. Instead, you make choices that help you to focus that story, while remaining careful not to leave out characters or information that is essential to an honest understanding of that chosen story.

For example, *The Boys of Baraka* follows a group of "at risk" boys in the U.S. who are sent to an experimental boarding school in Kenya, in hopes of improving their odds at future success. The film does not offer a menu of other educational options for at-risk Baltimore youth, nor were there critics arguing against programs like the Baraka School—and these alternatives weren't necessary to this story or its honest telling. *Born into Brothels* did not spend screen time telling you how or where Zana Briski learned photography or how she'd chosen the particular cameras the children in Kolkata were using, nor did the filmmakers include voices of people who thought, for example, that Briski shouldn't be interfering in a foreign culture. Even if such concerns existed, filmmaking always involves choices, and those concerns didn't impact the story the filmmakers had chosen to tell.

DOCUMENTARY DECEPTION

Film is a medium that we *experience*, both because of the range of senses involved (we see and hear events unfolding with our own eyes and ears) and the kind of storytelling that engages us both emotionally and intellectually. It is powerful and convincing, and if we are not on guard, we may be deceived by films that deliberately (or naively) distort or mislead, perhaps in the interest of entertainment or advocacy, convincing us of the existence of mermaids, alien spaceships, or unproven conspiracy theories. This is achieved, for example, by:

- asking rhetorical and unmotivated questions that lead the viewer in a false direction;
- presenting facts out of context or in a context designed to mislead. Suppose that I'm trying to convince you that Joe had his wife murdered, and as evidence, I tell you that he paid $25,000 to the killer. That sounds bad, until someone points out that the killer happened to work in a factory that Joe owns, and he earned the money in hourly wages;
- presenting evidence out of context and/or mashed together in a way that creates a false impression;
- creating fake evidence, such as reports that sound like news reports, or documents that appear to be genuine.

It takes a certain amount of media literacy to unravel the strands of a dishonest film. Some approaches:

- Do what you can to determine not only who made the film but also who paid for it, and dig beyond organization names to learn more about their activities and what kinds of work they do or support.
- Consider how and where the film is promoted.
- Find interviews with the filmmakers and/or and go to their websites to learn more about who they are and what other sorts of films they've done. There is diversity in most filmmakers' portfolios, but if someone has made a career out of films that focus on alien abductions and conspiracies, the chances are good that the climate-change film they're producing is not going to be scientifically rigorous.
- Look very closely at what the film presents as evidence. If a newspaper looks odd, find out if it's an actual publication. If documents are presented, do they seem real?
- When statistics are presented, are they anchored by time and specifics?

- When headlines and news reports are offered, are they anchored by time and context?
- Is the film asking unmotivated and leading questions? One example involves questions that are posed to suggest the validity of a hypothesis that simply can't be proven: "Could it be that these tracks were not made by humans or animals, but by the very aliens Dr. Smith claims to have seen?" Another involves questions that are not derived from evidence presented in the film, but serve to advance the thesis the filmmaker is trying to drive home. "Why were analysts so afraid of considering the alternative?" for example, implies that it's an established fact that analysts *were* afraid of considering the alternative, whether or not that is true.

Inaccuracies can (and do) find their way into even the best-researched films, but you don't want them to be there on purpose.

WHO TELLS DOCUMENTARY STORIES?

The range and breadth of documentary filmmaking worldwide is actually quite astonishing. Some documentary filmmakers work within production houses or stations; many more work independently, with varying degrees of financial and technical support from national or local governments, commissioning stations or broadcast venues, and/ or foundations and corporations. Some filmmakers work to reach regional or local audiences, including community groups; others strive for national theatrical or broadcast release and acclaim at prestigious film festivals; a growing number put their work online, reaching virtual communities.

Documentary storytelling does not refer specifically or even primarily to writing, nor is it strictly the province of someone identified as a writer. The tools described in this book are employed by almost anyone involved in documentary production, including producers, directors, editors, cinematographers, sound recordists, and researchers. Storytelling describes the conceptual process that begins at the moment an idea is raised and continues to be applied and reapplied as a project is filmed, edited, and completed. Throughout the process, filmmakers routinely address story issues: "Who are the central characters? What do they want? What are the stakes if they don't get it? Where is the tension? Where is the story going? Why does it matter?" Even if the film is structured as an essay, there should be an escalating sense of urgency, discovery, and relevance as the answers and subsequent questions are revealed. Someone is making those choices, whether or not he or she is credited as writer.

Hunter S. Thompson, in *Gonzo: The Life &
Work of Hunter S. Thompson*, a Magnolia
Pictures release.
Photo courtesy of Magnolia Pictures.

THE "WRITER'S" ROLE

Some have questioned how it's possible to "write" or "script" reality.
The answer is straightforward: documentary filmmaking involves the
selection and arrangement of reality into films and series, and the process by which that happens involves "writerly" choices about story,
structure, character, style, and point of view. Even purely vérité films
are constructed, before and during production and often, more significantly, in the editing room. Even if there is no one on the crew who
takes a writing credit, there is someone—or more likely a few people
(in the case of vérité filmmaking, it's often the editor(s) as well as the
director—making these decisions of story and structure.

The process of writing the film takes place over time. As historical
filmmaker Ric Burns explains:

> You create your first description of what the film is. Sometimes it's
> in the form of a letter to a colleague, sometimes it's in the form of

a two-page proposal to get seed money. But every iteration in some sense is a version of the film, and you try to give that iteration as powerful and intense an articulation as you can. And then, when you move to the next articulation—longer, more detailed, more structured, more intense, hopefully more involving—you don't abandon the previous iteration. You use it as the point of departure.

Ideas become outlines, and outlines may become shooting treatments: flexible enough to allow for inevitable surprises, but detailed enough to enable cost-effective production choices. Even if no writing is involved, something about a situation suggests to a filmmaker that there is content to be captured and shaped into a film. The writing decisions continue throughout editing—sometimes on paper, sometimes not. The film continues to be written, in its broadest sense, throughout postproduction, and a final written script or transcript, if one is produced, reflects this evolution.

Writers and Writing Credit

In the world of Hollywood theatrical dramas, there is a market for "spec" scripts—full screenplays written in advance of production. As noted above, documentary scripts are rarely compiled in this way; the main exception tends to be giant screen films or the portions of films that involve re-enactment. Some filmmakers write much more detailed shooting treatments than others, and as noted, the script evolves over the course of production. A credited film *writer*, whether that person is acting solely as writer or is also a producer or the director, will often be involved in shaping the film's content, story, and structure from idea through editing. (If there is narration, that might be part of the writing, but a writer's role, unless specified, is not limited to scripting narration.)

In recognition of the importance of writing to documentary, the Writers Guild of America, West and the Writers Guild of America, East in 2005 began to offer an annual Documentary Screenplay Award. The script must be for a film that's at least 40 minutes in length, and the film as exhibited "must have had an on-screen writing credit (i.e., a 'written by,' 'story by,' 'screenplay by,' 'documentary script by,' or 'narration written by' credit, as appropriate) related to the writing of the film." Winners to date include *Stories We Tell* (Sarah Polley), *Searching for Sugarman* (Malik Bendjelloul), *Super Size Me* (Morgan Spurlock), *Enron: The Smartest Guys in the Room* (Alex Gibney), *Waltz with Bashir* (Ari Folman), and *The Cove* (Mark Monroe). Of these winners, Monroe is the only writer who did not also direct the nominated film; notably, only some of these films are narrated.

ABOUT THE BOOK

The idea for this book emerged from my experiences as a documentary filmmaker, writer, and consultant on a range of projects, large and small, and from my study of storytelling across genres, including documentary and dramatic films, stage plays, and works in print. It became clear to me that underlying, universal issues of story and structure can generally be applied regardless of a project's style or length. It also became clear that despite the growing popularity of documentary films and filmmaking, discussion of the form was still too often clouded by misinformation and misconceptions. In particular, this book is written to counter two prevailing and false notions: one, that it's better and more "real" to shoot a documentary first and find the story later, and, two, that the need for "story" permits a filmmaker to impose a shallow and external framework on a subject.

INTENDED READERSHIP

Documentary Storytelling is intended for those who have an interest in understanding how story and structure work, and in particular, why some nonfiction films seem to have so much more power than others and whether that power is built on credible content. It's my hope that by understanding the storytelling choices filmmakers make, viewers and filmmakers will become better and more critical consumers of nonfiction programming in general. They'll have a clearer understanding of why something does or does not "ring true," why some films seem to carry greater emotional or intellectual weight, why some programs leave them feeling manipulated or bored, and how shifts in point of view or tone can change the nature of the presentation. In today's media-saturated world, such media literacy is more important than ever.

The stages of filmmaking generally described in this book are research and development, preproduction, production, and editing (assembly, rough cut, fine cut, lock). In most cases, there is not a clear division between steps: Filmmakers may continue fundraising well into editing, for example, and the editing room may be opened while shooting is still under way. Discussions of story and structure, likewise, will continue throughout this process. It's very common for a team in the editing room to revise a preliminary outline (on paper), and even a pitch, to be sure that they can articulate the story as it's evolved during research and production. Surrounded by hours of material—still and motion images, audio interviews, music, archival materials—filmmakers often find that stripping a project back to its bare bones, its narrative structure, is the best and most effective way to begin a project's final and strongest construction.

Examples in this book that are drawn from actual films are identified as such. Otherwise, the examples were created by me for illustration purposes, and any resemblance to actual films, whether produced or proposed, is purely coincidental. At the back of the book, I've included some information on films cited, many of which are now available for purchase, rental, or streaming through legitimate online vendors.

ANALYSIS, NOT FORMULA

Documentary storytelling describes an *organic* editorial approach to making choices about a film's structure, point of view, balance, style, casting, and more, at every stage of a film's creation. Although the book uses language familiar to anyone who has worked on a creative endeavor, the strategies described are in some ways most akin to dramatic screen storytelling. The difference is that documentarians are not free to invent plot points or character arcs and instead must find them in the raw material of real life. Our stories depend not on creative invention but on creative arrangement, and our storytelling must be done without sacrificing journalistic integrity. It's a tall order, which is why this book—the first to comprehensively examine the role of story and structure in nonfiction filmmaking—was written. The information in this book is not prescriptive, but analytical, describing some underlying qualities that many successful documentaries share. Understanding what story is and how it works to your advantage is a step toward finding your own creative and ethical voice as a nonfiction filmmaker.

OBSERVATIONS

In preparing all editions of this book, I screened a wide variety of films and spoke with a range of filmmakers, many of whom raised the same basic points:

- It's not about the technology. Too often, filmmakers (and filmmaking courses) get caught up in the *tools* of storytelling. The best equipment in the world, even the best *shots* in the world, won't save a film from a lack of focus.
- Time is an increasingly rare commodity for filmmakers, especially during preproduction and editing. Yet time is often what

enables a film to have depth, in terms of research, themes, and layers of storytelling; it can enhance creativity. As a group, we need to resist the pressure to turn out documentary products, rather than documentary films.

- Story does not have to mean three-act drama, and it definitely does not mean artificial tension that is imposed from without. Story comes organically from within the material and the ways in which you, the filmmaker, structure it.
- Documentary filmmakers, increasingly, offer a powerful addition to or contradiction of information presented by mainstream media. It is critical that this work be ethical and honest, even as it is also creative and innovative.
- Share the humor. No matter how grim the situation or subject, audiences cannot take a program that is unrelieved misery. Watch any of the top documentaries of the past few years, and notice not only how often you're on the verge of tears, but also, even within the same film, how often you're laughing.
- Think easier. Some of the best documentaries made recently are built on a narrative train that is very basic; that's often what allows for overall complexity.

SOURCES AND NOTES

Recent coverage of the Australian use of *Troublesome Creek* can be found in *The Sydney Morning Herald* (June 7, 2015, written by Paul Byrnes), www.smh.com.au/entertainment/movies/return-to-trouble some-creek-and-a-sydney-film-festival-pick-that-helped-farmers-20150602-gheglt.html. Definition of documentary, in Erik Barnouw, *Documentary: A History of the Non-fiction Film* (New York: Oxford University Press, 1974). Information about creative nonfiction from Philip Gerard's *Creative Nonfiction: Researching and Crafting Stories of Real Life* (Cincinnati: Writer's Digest Books, 1996). For more information about Richard Panek, visit www.lastwordonnothing.com/about-us/richard-panek/. An example of the discussion re writing credits: Tom Rostin's article, "You Say True Life, I Say Scripted/The Rise of Writing Credits in Documentary," *The New York Times*, August 24, 2012 (www.nytimes.com/2012/08/26/movies/the-rise-of-writing-credits-in-doc umentaries.html?_r=0). Information about the WGA documentary screenwriting awards can be found at www.wga.org/wga-awards/rules-documentary-screenplay.aspx.

PART I

Understanding Story

CHAPTER 2

Story Basics

A story is the narrative, or telling, of an event or series of events, crafted in a way to interest the audience members, whether they are readers, listeners, or viewers. At its most basic, a story has a beginning, middle, and end. It has compelling characters (or questions), rising tension, and conflict that reaches some sort of resolution. It engages the audience on an emotional and intellectual level, motivating viewers to want to know what happens next.

Don't be confused by the fact that festivals and film schools commonly use the term *narrative* to describe only works of dramatic fiction. Most documentaries are also narrative, which simply means that they tell stories (whether or not those stories are also narrated is an entirely different issue). How they tell those stories, and which stories they tell, are part of what separates these films into subcategories of genre or style, from cinéma vérité to film noir.

Efforts to articulate the basics of good storytelling are not new. The Greek philosopher Aristotle first set out guidelines for what his analysis revealed as a "well-constructed plot" in 350 BCE, and these have been applied to storytelling—onstage, on the page, and on screen—ever since. Expectations about how storytelling works seem hardwired in audiences, and meeting, confounding, and challenging those expectations is no less important to the documentarian than it is to the dramatist.

SOME STORYTELLING TERMS

Exposition

Exposition is the information that grounds you in a story: who, what, where, when, and why. It gives audience members the tools they need to follow the story that's unfolding and, more importantly, it allows them inside the story. But exposition should not be thought of as something to "get out of the way." Too often, programs are front-loaded with information that audiences don't yet need to know, including backstory. The problem is that when audiences do need this information, they won't remember it, and in the meantime, the film seems dull and didactic.

Films may start with a bit of establishing information, conveyed through narration, interviews, or text on screen (look at the openings of *Control Room* and *Jonestown*, for example). But this information should offer the minimum necessary—just enough to get the story under way. After that, the trick is to reveal exposition when it best serves that story, whether by raising the stakes, advancing our understanding of character, or anticipating and addressing potential confusion.

Good exposition is a way to build suspense and motivate audiences to stay with you. Noted filmmaker Alfred Hitchcock once explained suspense in this way: Suppose audiences are watching a scene in which people are seated at a table, with a clock nearby, talking casually. Suddenly a bomb beneath the table explodes. The viewers are shocked, of course. But suppose that audiences had previously seen a character put a bomb into a briefcase, set it to go off at a specific time, and then place the briefcase under the table. The people sitting and chatting are unaware of the danger, but the audience is tense as it watches the clock, knowing what's coming. In the first scenario, Hitchcock noted, there are several seconds of shock. In the second, there are several minutes of suspense.

Watch films that you enjoy and pay attention not only to what you know, but as importantly, *when* you learn it. This is true of present-day details and of backstory; if the backstory matters, you want to present it when it when the audience is *motivated* to hear it. Also pay attention to the many ways in which filmmakers convey information. Sometimes it's revealed when the people you're filming argue: "Yeah? Well, we wouldn't even be in this mess if you hadn't decided to take your paycheck to Vegas!" Sometimes it's revealed through headlines or other printed material. Good narration can deftly weave exposition into a story, filling in gaps as needed; voice-over material drawn from interviews can sometimes do the same thing. Exposition can also be handled through visuals: an establishing shot of a place or sign; footage of a sheriff nailing an eviction notice on a door (*Roger & Me*); the opening moments of an auction (*Troublesome Creek*). Toys littered on a suburban lawn say "Children live here." Black bunting and a homemade shrine of flowers and cards outside a fire station say "Tragedy has occurred." A long shot of an elegantly-dressed woman in a large, spare office high up in a modern building says "This woman is powerful." A man on a subway car reading an issue of *The Boston Globe* tells us where we are, as would a highway sign or a famous landmark—the Eiffel Tower, for example. Time-lapse photography, title cards, and animation can all be used to convey exposition, sometimes with the added element of humor or surprise—think of the cartoons in *Super Size Me*.

Offered at the right time, exposition enriches our understanding of characters and raises the stakes in their stories. Watch *Daughter from Danang* and pay attention to when we learn that Heidi Bub's birth father was an American soldier, for example; that her birth mother's husband was fighting for the Viet Cong; and that Heidi's adoptive mother has stopped communicating with her. These details add to our understanding of who these characters are and why they do what they do, and the information is effective because of the careful way it's seeded throughout the film.

Theme

In literary terms, theme is the general underlying subject of a specific story, a recurring idea that often illuminates an aspect of the human condition. *Eyes on the Prize*, in 14 hours, tells an overarching story of America's civil rights struggle. The underlying themes include race, poverty, and the power of ordinary people to accomplish extraordinary change. Themes in *The Day after Trinity*, the story of J. Robert Oppenheimer's development of the atomic bomb, include scientific ambition, the quest for power, and efforts to ensure peace and disarmament when it may be too late.

"Theme is the most basic lifeblood of a film," says filmmaker Ric Burns. "Theme tells you the tenor of your story. This is what this thing is about." Burns chose to tell the story of the ill-fated Donner Party and their attempt to take a shortcut to California in 1846 not because the cannibalism they resorted to would appeal to prurient viewers, but because their story illuminated themes and vulnerabilities in the American character. These themes are foreshadowed in the film's opening quote from Alexis de Tocqueville, a French author who toured the United States in 1831. He wrote of the "feverish ardor" with which Americans pursue prosperity, the "shadowy suspicion that they may not have chosen the shortest route to get it," and the way in which they "cleave to the things of this world," even though death steps in, in the end. These words presage the fate of the Donner Party, whose ambitious pursuit of a new life in California will have tragic consequences.

Themes may emerge from the questions that initially drove the filmmaking. On one level, *My Architect* is about a middle-aged filmmaker's quest to know the father he lost at the age of 11, some 30 years before. But among the film's themes are impermanence and legacy. Kahn says in bonus material on the film's DVD:

> You sort of wonder, "After we're gone, what's left?" How much would I really find of my father out there? . . . I know there are buildings. But how much emotion, how much is really left? And I think what really kind of shocked me is how many people are still actively engaged in a relationship with him. They talk to him as if he's still here. They think of him every day. In a way I find that very heartening.

Understanding your theme(s) can help you determine both what and how you shoot. Renowned cinematographer Jon Else explains his thinking as he planned to shoot workers building a trail at Yosemite National Park for his film *Yosemite: The Fate of Heaven*.

> What is this shot or sequence telling us within the developing narrative of this film, and what is this shot or sequence telling us about the world? . . . Are we there with the trail crew and the dynamite because it's dangerous? Are we there because all the dynamite in the world is not going to make a bit of difference in this giant range of mountains, where people are really insignificant? Are we there because these people are underpaid and they're trying to unionize?

Else offers examples of how different answers might change the shooting:

> If the scene was about the camaraderie between the members of the trail crew, all of whom had lived in these mountains together, in camp, for many months by that time, you try to do a lot of shots in which the physical relationship between people shows.

> . . . They weren't trying to unionize, but if, in fact, we had been doing a sequence about the labor conditions for trail workers in Yosemite, we probably would have made it a point to shoot over the course of a long day, to show how long the day was, show them eating three meals on the trail, walking home really bone-tired in the dark. Basically, the more you're aware of what you want these images to convey, the richer the images are going to be.

Filmmaker Sam Pollard (*August Wilson: The Ground on Which I Stand*), a professor at New York University, says that for student filmmakers:

> The biggest pitfall is understanding what their film's about right from the beginning. Before they sit down to write a page of the narration or script, what's the theme? And then on the theme, what's the story that they're going to convey to get across the theme?

Arc

The arc refers to the way or ways in which the events of the story transform your characters. An overworked executive learns that his family should come first; a mousy secretary stands up for himself and takes over the company; a rag-tag group of unlikely kids wins the national chess tournament. In pursuing a goal, protagonists learn something about themselves and their place in the world, and those lessons change them—and may, in fact, change their desire for the goal.

In documentary films, story arcs can be hard to find. Never, simply in the interest of a good story, presume to know what a character is thinking or feeling, or present a transformation that hasn't occurred. If there is change, you will discover it through solid research and multiple strands of verifiable evidence. For example, in *The Day after Trinity*, physicist J. Robert Oppenheimer, a left-leaning intellectual, successfully develops the world's first nuclear weapons and is then horrified by the destructive powers he's helped to unleash. He spends the rest of his life trying to stop the spread of nuclear weapons and in the process falls victim to the Cold War he helped to launch; once hailed as an American hero, he is accused of being a Soviet spy.

In *The Thin Blue Line*, we hear and see multiple versions of a story that begins when Randall Adams's car breaks down on a Saturday night and a teenager named David Harris offers him a ride. Later that night, a police officer is shot and killed by someone driving Harris's car, and Adams is charged with the murder. The deeper we become immersed in the case, the more clearly we see that Adams's imprisonment and subsequent conviction are about politics, not justice. He is transformed from a free man to a convicted felon, and that transformation challenges the viewer's assumptions about justice and the basic notion that individuals are innocent until proven guilty.

In *Murderball*, a documentary about quadriplegic athletes who compete internationally in wheelchair rugby, a few characters undergo transformations that together complement the overall film. There's Joe Soares, a hard-driving American champion now coaching for Canada, whose relationship with his son changes noticeably after he suffers a heart attack. Player Mark Zupan comes to terms with the friend who was at the wheel during the accident in which he was injured. And Keith Cavill, recently injured, adjusts to his new life and even explores wheelchair rugby. All of these transformations occurred over the course of filming, and the filmmakers made sure they had the visual material they needed to show them in a way that felt organic and unforced.

Plot and Character

Films are often described as either plot- or character-driven. A character-driven film is one in which the action of the film emerges from the wants and needs of the characters. In a plot-driven film, the characters are secondary to the events that make up the plot. (Many thrillers and action movies are plot-driven.) In documentary, both types of films exist, and there is a lot of gray area between them. Errol Morris's *The Thin Blue Line* imitates a plot-driven noir thriller in its exploration of the casual encounter that leaves Randall Adams facing the death penalty. Circumstances act upon Adams; he doesn't set the plot in motion except inadvertently, when his car breaks down and he accepts a ride from David Harris. In fact, part of the film's power comes from Adams's inability to alter events, even as it becomes apparent that Harris, not Adams, is likely to be the killer.

Some films are clearly character-driven. *Daughter from Danang*, for example, is driven by the wants of its main character, Heidi Bub, who

From *Waltz with Bashir*.
Photo courtesy Bridget Folman Film Gang.

was born in Vietnam and given up for adoption. Raised in Tennessee and taught to deny her Asian heritage, Bub is now estranged from her adoptive mother. She sets the events of the film in motion when she decides to reunite with her birth mother. Similarly, in *Waltz with Bashir*, Israeli filmmaker Ari Folman sets events in motion when he decides to look back at a past he cannot remember.

As mentioned, the difference between plot- and character-driven films can be subtle, and one often has strong elements of the other. The characters in *The Thin Blue Line* are distinct and memorable; the plot in both *Daughter from Danang* and *Waltz with Bashir* is strong and takes unexpected turns. It's also true that plenty of memorable documentaries are not "driven" at all in the Hollywood sense. *When the Levees Broke*, a four-hour documentary about New Orleans during and after Hurricane Katrina in 2005, generally follows the chronology of events that devastated a city and its people. As described by Sam Pollard, the film's supervising editor and co-producer, there is a narrative arc to each hour and to the series. But the complexity of the four-hour film and its interweaving of dozens of individual stories, rather than a select few, differentiate it from a more traditional form of narrative.

Some shorter films present a "slice of life" portrait of people or places. With longer films, however, there generally needs to be some overarching structure. Frederick Wiseman's documentaries are elegantly structured but not "plotted" in the sense that each sequence makes the next one inevitable, but there is usually an organizing principle behind his work, such as a "year in the life" of an institution. Still other films are driven not by characters or plot but by questions, following an essay-like structure; examples include Michael Moore's *Fahrenheit 9/11* and Daniel Anker's *Imaginary Witness: Hollywood and the Holocaust*, discussed by Susan Kim in Chapter 16. Many films merge styles: *Super Size Me* is built around the filmmaker's 30-day McDonald's diet, but to a large extent the film is actually driven by a series of questions, making it an essay. This combination of journey and essay can also be found in Nathaniel Kahn's *My Architect. Virunga* combines several types of filmmaking, as discussed by Orlando von Einsiedel in Chapter 22.

Point of View

Point of view describes the perspective, or position, from which a story is told. This can be interpreted in a range of ways. For example, point of view may describe the character through whom you're telling a story. Imagine telling the story of Goldilocks and the three bears from the point of view of Goldilocks, and then retelling it from the point of view of Papa Bear. Goldilocks might tell you the story of a perfectly innocent child who was wandering through the woods when she became hungry, ventured into an apparently abandoned house, and found herself under attack by bears. In contrast, Papa Bear might tell you the story of an unwanted intruder.

By offering an unexpected point of view, filmmakers can sometimes force viewers to take a new look at a familiar subject. For example, Jon Else's *Sing Faster: The Stagehands' Ring Cycle* documents a performance by the San Francisco Opera of Richard Wagner's *Ring* cycle from the point of view of the union stagehands behind the scenes.

Point of view can also be used to describe the perspective of the camera, including who's operating it and from what vantage point. Much of Deborah Scranton's *The War Tapes*, for example, was filmed by the soldiers themselves, rather than by camera crews following the soldiers. Point of view can also refer to the perspective of time and the lens through which an event is viewed. As one example, *The War Tapes* looks at the aftermath of a car bombing outside Al Taji through footage of the event as it unfolds (from the camera operated by Sgt. Steve Pink, who was there); an interview with Pink conducted within 24 hours of the event by Spc. Mike Moriarty; audio from an interview Scranton conducted with Pink in the months after he returned to the United States; and Pink in voice-over, reading (after he had returned home) from a journal he kept while he was in Iraq. "So it's all layered in there, this multi-faceted perception of that event," Scranton explains in Chapter 20.

There is also, of course, "point of view" of the filmmaker and/or filmmaking team.

Detail

Detail encompasses a range of things that all have to do with specificity. First, there is what's known as the "telling detail." A full ashtray next to a bedridden man would indicate that either the man or a caregiver is a heavy smoker. The choice of what to smoke, what to drink, when to drink it (whisky for breakfast?), what to wear, how to decorate a home or an office or a car, all provide clues about people. They may be misleading clues: That African artwork may have been left behind by an old boyfriend, rather than chosen by the apartment renter; the expensive suit may have been borrowed for the purpose of the interview. But as storytellers, our ears and eyes should be open to details, the specifics that add layers of texture and meaning. We also need to focus on detail if we write narration. "The organization grew like wildfire" is clichéd and meaningless; better to provide evidence: "Within 10 years, an organization that began in Paris with 20 members had chapters in 12 nations, with more than 2,500 members worldwide."

IN HOLLYWOOD TERMS: A "GOOD STORY WELL TOLD"

In their book, *The Tools of Screenwriting*, authors David Howard and Edward Mabley stress that a story is not simply about somebody experiencing difficulty meeting a goal; it's also "the way in which the audience experiences the story." The elements of a "good story well told," they write, are:

1. This story is about *somebody* with whom we have some empathy.
2. This somebody wants *something* very badly.
3. This something is *difficult*, but possible, to do, get, or achieve.
4. The story is told for maximum *emotional* impact and *audience participation* in the proceedings.
5. The story must come to a *satisfactory ending* (which does not necessarily mean a happy ending).

Although Howard and Mabley's book is directed at dramatic screenwriters, who are free to invent not only characters but also the things that they want and the things that are getting in the way, this list is useful for documentary storytellers. Your particular film subject or situation might not fit neatly within these parameters, however, so further explanation follows.

Who (or What) the Story Is About

The *somebody* is your protagonist, your hero, the entity whose story is being told. Note that your hero can, in fact, be very "unheroic," and the audience might struggle to empathize with him or her. But the character and/or character's mission should be compelling enough that the audience cares about the outcome. In *The Execution of Wanda Jean*, for example, Liz Garbus offers a sympathetic but unsparing portrait of a woman on death row for murder. You also may have multiple protagonists, as was the case in *Spellbound*.

The central character doesn't necessarily need to be a person. In Ric Burns's *New York*, a seven-episode history, the city itself is the protagonist, whose fortunes rise and fall and rise over the course of the series. (Throughout that series, however, individual characters and stories come to the fore.) But often, finding a central person through whom to tell your story can make an otherwise complex topic more manageable and accessible to viewers. For *I'll Make Me a World*, a six-hour history of African-American arts in the twentieth century, producer Denise Greene explored the Black Arts Movement of the 1960s by viewing it through the eyes and experience of Pulitzer Prize-winning poet Gwendolyn Brooks, an established, middle-aged author whose life and work were transformed by her interactions with younger artists responding to the political call for Black Power.

What the Protagonist Wants

The *something* that somebody wants is also referred to as a goal or an objective. In *Blue Vinyl*, filmmaker Judith Helfand sets out, on camera, to convince her parents to remove the new siding from their home. Note that a filmmaker's on-screen presence doesn't necessarily make him or her the protagonist. In Steven Ascher and Jeanne Jordan's *Troublesome Creek: A Midwestern*, the filmmakers travel to Iowa, where Jeanne's family is working to save their farm from foreclosure. Jeanne is the film's narrator and she can be seen in the footage, but the protagonists are her parents, Russel and Mary Jane Jordan. It's their goal—to pay off their debt by auctioning off their belongings—that drives the film's story.

Active versus Passive

Storytellers speak of active versus passive goals and active versus passive heroes. In general, you want a story's goals and heroes to be active, which means that you want your story's protagonist to be in charge of his or her own life: To set a goal and then to go about doing what needs to be done to achieve it. A passive goal is something like this: A secretary wants a raise in order to pay for a trip to Europe. She is passively waiting for the raise, hoping someone will notice that her work merits reward. To be active, she would have to do something to ensure that she gets that raise, or she would have to wage a campaign to raise the extra money she needs for the trip, such as taking a second job.

An exception is when the passivity *is* the story. In *The Thin Blue Line*, for example, Randall Adams, locked up on death row, is a passive protagonist because he can't do anything to free himself, as no one believes him when he claims to be innocent. In general, though, you want your protagonist to be active, and you want him or her to have a goal that's worthy. In the example of the secretary, will an audience really care whether or not she gets the trip? Probably not. If we had a reason to be sympathetic—she is visiting her estranged family, for example—maybe we would care, but it's not a very strong goal. Worthy does not mean a goal has to be noble—it doesn't all have to be about ending world hunger or ensuring world peace. It does have to matter enough to be worth committing significant time and resources to. If you only care a little about your protagonists and what they want, your financiers and audience are likely to care not at all.

Difficulty and Tangibility

The something that is wanted—the goal—must be *difficult* to do or achieve. If something is easy, there's no tension, and without tension, there's little incentive for an audience to keep watching. Tension is the feeling we get when issues or events are unresolved, especially when we want them to be resolved. It's what motivates us to demand, "And then what happens? And what happens after *that*?" We need to know, because it makes us uncomfortable *not* to know. Think of a movie thriller in which you're aware, but the heroine is not, that danger lurks in the cellar. As she heads toward the steps, you feel escalating tension because she is walking *toward* danger. If you didn't know that the bad guy was in the basement, she would just be a girl heading down some stairs. Without tension, a story feels flat; you don't care one way or the other about the outcome.

So where do you find the tension? Sometimes, it's inescapable, as is the case with the National Guardsmen enduring a year-long tour of duty in Iraq, in Deborah Scranton's *The War Tapes*. Sometimes, tension comes from conflict between your protagonist and an opposing force, whether another person (often referred to as the *antagonist* or *opponent*), a force of nature, society, or the individual (i.e., internal conflict). In Barbara Kopple's *Harlan County, U.S.A.*, striking miners are in conflict with mine owners. In Heidi Ewing and Rachel Grady's *The Boys of Baraka*, the tension comes from knowing that the odds of an education, or even a future that doesn't involve prison or death, are stacked against a group of African-American boys from inner-city Baltimore. When a small group of boys is given an opportunity to attend school in Kenya as a means of getting fast-tracked to better high schools in Baltimore, we want them to succeed and are devastated when things seem to fall apart. In *Born into Brothels*, similarly, efforts to save a handful of children are threatened by societal pressures (including not only economic hardship but also the wishes of family members who don't share the filmmakers' commitment to removing children from their unstable homes), and by the fact that the ultimate decision makers, in a few cases, are the children themselves. The audience experiences frustration—and perhaps recognition—as some of these children make choices that in the long run are likely to have significant consequences.

Note that conflict can mean a direct argument between two sides, pro and con (or "he said, she said"). But such an argument sometimes weakens tension, especially if each side is talking past the other or if individuals in conflict have not been properly established to viewers. If we don't know who's fighting or what's at stake for the various sides, we won't care about the outcome. On the other hand, if the audience goes into an argument caring about the individuals involved, especially if they care about *all* the individuals involved, it can lead to powerful emotional storytelling. Near the end of *Daughter from Danang*, for example, the joyful reunion between the American adoptee and her Vietnamese family gives way to feelings of anger and betrayal brought on by the family's request for money. The palpable tension the audience feels stems not from taking one side or another in the argument, but from empathy for all sides.

Weather, illness, war, self-doubt, inexperience, hubris—all of these can pose obstacles as your protagonist strives to achieve his or her goal. And just as it can be useful to find an individual (or individuals) through whom to tell a complex story, it can be useful to personify the opposition. Television viewers in the 1960s, for example, at times seemed better able to understand the injustices of southern segregation when reporters focused on the actions of individuals like Birmingham (Alabama) Police Chief Bull Connor, who turned police dogs and fire hoses on young African Americans as they engaged in peaceful protest.

Worthy Opponent

Just as you want your protagonist to have a worthy goal, you want him or her to have a worthy opponent. A common problem for many filmmakers is that they portray opponents as one-dimensional; if their hero is good, the opponent must be bad. In fact, the most memorable opponent is often not the opposite of the hero, but a complement to him or her. In the film *Sound and Fury*, young Heather's parents oppose her wishes for a cochlear implant not out of malice but out of their deep love for her and their strong commitment to the Deaf culture into which they and their daughter were born. Chicago Mayor Richard Daley was a challenging opponent for Dr. Martin Luther King, Jr., in *Eyes on the Prize* specifically because he wasn't Bull Connor; Daley was a savvy northern politician with close ties to the national Democratic Party and a supporter of the southern-based civil rights movement. The story of his efforts to impede Dr. King's campaign for open housing in Chicago in 1966 proved effective at underscoring the significant differences between using nonviolence as a strategy against *de jure* segregation in the South and using it against *de facto* segregation in the North.

As stated earlier, it's important to understand that you should not in any way be fictionalizing characters who are real human beings. (The rules for documentary are different than those for reality television, where content and characters may be manipulated for entertainment purposes, depending on the releases signed by participants.) With documentary work, you are evaluating a real situation from the perspective of a storyteller, and working with what is actual and defensible. If there is no opponent, you can't manufacture one. Mayor Daley, historically speaking, was an effective opponent. Had he welcomed King with open arms and been little more than an inconvenience to the movement, it would have been dishonest to portray him as a significant obstacle.

Tangible Goal

Although difficult, the goal should be possible to do or achieve, which means that it's best if it's both concrete and realistic. "Fighting racism" or "curing cancer" or "saving the rainforest" may all be worthwhile, but none is specific enough to serve as a story objective. In exploring your ideas for a film, follow your interests, but then seek out a specific story to illuminate them. *The Boys of Baraka* is clearly an indictment of racism and inequality, but it is more specifically the story of a handful of boys and their enrollment in a two-year program at a tiny school in Kenya. *Born into Brothels* illuminates the difficult circumstances facing the children of impoverished sex workers in Kolkata, but the story's goals are more tangible. Initially, we learn that filmmaker Zana Briski, in Kolkata to photograph sex workers, has been drawn to their children. "They wanted to learn how to use the camera," she says in voice-over. "That's when I thought it would be really great to teach them, and to see this world through their eyes." Several minutes later, a larger but still tangible goal emerges: "They have absolutely no opportunity without education," she says. "The question is, can I find a school— a good school—that will take kids that are children of prostitutes?"

This, then, becomes the real goal of the film, one enriched by the children's photography and exposure to broader horizons.

Note also that the goal is not necessarily the most "dramatic" or obvious one. In Kate Davis's *Southern Comfort*, a film about a transgender male dying of ovarian cancer, Robert Eads's goal is not to find a cure; it's to survive long enough to attend the Southern Comfort Conference in Atlanta, a national gathering of transgender people, with his girlfriend, Lola, who is also transgender.

Emotional Impact and Audience Participation

The concept of telling a story for greatest emotional impact and audience participation is perhaps the most difficult. It's often described as "show, don't tell," which means that you want to present the evidence or information that allows viewers to experience the story for themselves, anticipating twists and turns and following the story line in a way that's active rather than passive. Too often, films tell us what we're supposed to think through the use of heavy-handed narration, loaded graphics, or a stacked deck of interviews.

Think about the experience of being completely held by a good mystery. You aren't watching characters on screen; you're right there with them, bringing the clues you've seen so far to the story as it unfolds. You lose track of time as you try to anticipate what happens next, who will do what, and what will be learned. It's human nature to try to make sense of the events we're confronted with, and it's human nature to enjoy being stumped or surprised. In *Enron: The Smartest Guys in the Room*, you think Enron's hit bottom, that all the price manipulation has finally caught up with them and they'll be buried in debt—until someone at Enron realizes that there's gold in California's power grid.

Telling a story for emotional impact means that the filmmaker is structuring the story so that the moments of conflict, climax, and resolution—moments of achievement, loss, reversal, etc.—adhere as well as possible to the internal rhythms of storytelling. Audiences expect that the tension in a story will escalate as the story moves toward its conclusion; scenes tend to get shorter, action tighter, the stakes higher. As we get to know the characters and understand their wants and needs, we care more about what happens to them; we become invested in their stories. Much of this structuring takes place in the editing room. But to some extent, it also takes place as you film, and planning for it can make a difference. Knowing that as Heidi Bub got off the airplane in Danang she'd be greeted by a birth mother she hadn't seen in 20 years, what preparations did the filmmakers need to make to be sure they got that moment on film? What might they shoot if they wanted to build up to that moment, either before or after it actually occurred? (They shot an interview with Heidi and filmed her, a "fish out of water," as she spent a bit of time in Vietnam before meeting with her mother.) In the edited film, by the time Heidi sees her mother, we realize (before she does) how fully Americanized she's become and how foreign her family will seem. We also know that the expectations both she and her birth mother have for this meeting are very high.

Mai Thi Kim and her daughter, Heidi Bub, in *Daughter from Danang.*
Photo courtesy of the filmmakers.

You want to avoid creating unnecessary drama—turning a perfectly good story into a soap opera. There's no reason to pull in additional details, however sad or frightening, when they aren't relevant. If you're telling the story of a scientist unlocking the genetic code to a certain mental illness, for example, it's not necessarily relevant that she's also engaged in a custody battle with her former husband, even if this detail seems to spice up the drama or, you hope, make the character more "sympathetic." If the custody battle is influenced by her husband's mental illness and her concerns that the children may have inherited the disease, there is a link that could serve the film well. Otherwise, you risk adding a layer of detail that detracts, rather than adds.

False emotion—hyped-up music and sound effects and narration that warns of danger around every corner—is a common problem, especially on television. As in the story of the boy who cried wolf, at some point it all washes over the viewer like so much noise. If the danger is real, it will have the greatest storytelling impact if it emerges organically from the material.

Raising the Stakes

Another tool of emotional storytelling is to have something at stake and to raise the stakes until the very end. Look at the beginning of *Control Room*. The film intercuts story cards (text on screen) with images of everyday life. The cards read: *March 2003 / The United States and Iraq are on the brink of war. / Al Jazeera Satellite Channel will broadcast the war . . . / to forty million Arab viewers. / The Arab world watches . . . / and waits. / CONTROL ROOM*. Clearly, these stakes are high.

In the hands of a good storyteller, even small or very personal stakes can be made large when their importance to those in the story is conveyed. For example, how many people in the United States—or beyond, for that matter—really care who wins or loses the National Spelling Bee, held each year in Washington, D.C.? But to the handful of children competing in *Spellbound*, and to their families and communities, the contest is all-important. Through skillful storytelling, the filmmakers make us care not only about these kids but about the competition, and as the field narrows, we can't turn away.

Stakes may rise because (genuine) danger is increasing or time is running out. In *Sound and Fury*, for example, the stakes rise as time passes, because for a child born deaf, a cochlear implant is most effective if implanted while language skills are being developed. How do the filmmakers convey this? We see Heather's much younger cousin get the implant and begin to acquire spoken-language skills; we also learn that Heather's mother, born deaf, might now get little benefit from the device. As Heather enrolls in a school for the deaf without getting an implant, we understand that the decision has lifelong implications.

In terms of your role as the storyteller, stakes also rise because of the way you structure and organize your film: What people know, and when they know it, what the stakes of a story mean *to your characters* and how well you convey that—all of these play a role in how invested the audience becomes in wanting or even needing to know the outcome of your film.

A Satisfactory Ending

A *satisfactory ending*, or resolution, is often one that feels both unexpected and inevitable. It must resolve the one story you set out to tell.

Say you start the film with a problem: A little girl has a life-threatening heart condition for which there is no known surgical treatment. Your film then goes into the world of experimental surgery, where you find a charismatic doctor whose efforts to solve a very different medical problem have led him to create a surgical solution that might work in the little girl's situation. To end on this surgical breakthrough, however, won't be satisfactory. Audiences were drawn into the story of the little girl, and this surgeon's work must ultimately be related to that story. Can his work make a difference in her case? You need to complete the story with which the film began. With that said, there is never just one correct ending.

Suppose, for example, that your film is due to be aired months before the approval is granted that will allow doctors to try the experimental surgery on the girl. Make that your ending, and leave the audience with the knowledge that everyone is working to ensure that she will survive until then. Or perhaps the surgery is possible, but at the last minute the parents decide it's too risky. Or they take that risk, and the outcome is positive. Or negative. Or perhaps the doctor's breakthrough simply comes too late for this one child but may make a difference for hundreds of others. Any of these would be a satisfactory ending, provided it is factual. It would be unethical to manipulate the facts to imply a "stronger" or more emotional ending that misrepresents what you know the outcome to be. Suppose, for example, that the parents have already decided that no matter how much success the experimental work is having, they will not allow their daughter to undergo any further operations. You cannot imply that this remains an open question (e.g., with a teaser such as "Whether the operation will save the life of little Candy is yet to be seen.").

Ending a film in a way that's satisfying does not necessitate wrapping up all loose ends or resolving things in a way that's upbeat. The end of *Daughter from Danang* is powerful precisely because things remain unsettled; Heidi Bub has achieved the goal of meeting her birth mother, but even two years after her visit, she remains deeply ambivalent about continued contact. At the end of *The Thin Blue Line*, Randall Adams remains a convicted murderer on death row, even as filmmaker Errol Morris erases any lingering doubts the audience might have as to his innocence.

SOURCES AND NOTES

There are various versions of this Alfred Hitchcock story distinguishing shock and suspense, including a discussion at the American Film

Institute in 1972, http://the.hitchcock.zone/wiki/Alfred_Hitchcock_ at_the_AFI_Seminar_roundtable(18/Aug/1972). Story elements from David Howard and Edward Mabley, *The Tools of Screenwriting* (New York: St. Martin's Press, 1993). As described in a follow-up film, *Sound and Fury: Six Years Later*, Heather Artinian eventually received the cochlear device. Information about her work as an advocate for the hearing impaired can be found online. *The Thin Blue Line*'s Randall Adams was released in 1989, following the film's release. Information about his case can be found online.

CHAPTER 3

Finding the Story

Armed with an understanding of story, how do you find one within a chosen *subject* for a documentary? Suppose, for example, that you're thinking of doing a film about Elvis Presley, a bakery in your home town, or something about labor in the high-tech industry. Something about the topic has caught your interest, and you think you want to take it to the next level.

First, ask yourself what it is about the topic that grabs you. As the initial audience for your film, your gut reaction to the subject is important. Chances are it wasn't a sweeping notion of Elvis Presley that caught your attention, but an account, perhaps, of his time in the military. It's not the fact that there's a bakery in your home town, but that rising taxes and a dwindling customer base have left the owners open to offers from developers looking to build a mall despite significant local opposition. Your interest in the high-tech industry comes from stories you've read about global labor, worker exploitation, or the industry's impact on the environment.

We're surrounded by subjects that offer potential for documentary storytelling. Current events may trigger ideas, or an afternoon spent browsing the shelves at a local library or bookstore. Some filmmakers find stories within their own families. Alan Berliner made *Nobody's Business* about his father, Oscar; Deborah Hoffman made *Confessions of a Dutiful Daughter* about her mother's battle with Alzheimer's. Even when you're very close to a subject, however, you'll need to take an impartial view as you determine whether or not it would make a film that audiences will want to see. This is also true when you adapt documentaries from printed sources. In making the series *Cadillac Desert*, drawn from Marc Reisner's book of the same name, producer Jon Else chose three of the roughly 40 stories in Reisner's book; Else and his team then conducted their own research and determined the best way to tell those stories on film.

STORY RIGHTS

In general, if you're using a range of books and magazines solely for research purposes, you don't need to obtain any of the underlying rights. When the film is indelibly linked to a book, however, as was the case with *Enron: The Smartest Guys in the Room* (directed by Alex Gibney, based on the book by Bethany McLean and Peter Elkind), *A Brief History of Time* (directed by Errol Morris, based on the book by Stephen Hawking), or *Slavery by Another Name* (directed by Sam Pollard, based on the book by Douglas A. Blackmon), you will need to come to a legal arrangement with the author or copyright holder. (Don't confuse this with companion books that are written during or after production, such as the companion book to the first season of *Eyes on the Prize*. This book was written by the Blackside publishing staff and journalist Juan Williams during postproduction, and drew on the production teams' research and interviews. In other words, companion books are based on the documentaries, rather than vice versa.)

Note that when you are negotiating for the rights to a story, you will want to retain creative control over your film. The author may be an expert on the subject, but you are an expert on translating it on film to a general audience. You don't need a degree in science to make an extraordinary science documentary or a degree in social work to create a compelling portrait of runaway teens. What you need are intelligence, curiosity, an ability to learn fast, and a readiness to consult with people who *are* experts in those fields. Ideally, there is a positive collaboration between expert and filmmaker that serves to enrich the film.

"FINDING" THE STORY DURING PRODUCTION

One of the biggest misconceptions about documentary filmmaking is that it happens spontaneously. In fact, it's fairly common to hear filmmakers talk about the story revealing itself over the course of the production or even in the editing room. With experienced filmmakers, however, this tends *not* to mean that a filmmaker has simply shot material without any story in mind, but instead that he or she adjusts the story's focus or, more likely, its *structure* during production and postproduction. Even vérité projects, which are significantly crafted in the editing room, are generally not shot until filmmakers have some confidence that a story will unfold over the course of filming. You can't know where real life will take you, but you can anticipate a range of outcomes and determine whether or not a subject holds sufficient promise.

Sometimes an opportunity comes along that precludes extensive planning. Filmmakers Gail Dolgin and Vicente Franco had just days to decide whether or not to travel to Vietnam after they learned about an upcoming reunion between Heidi Bub and the birth mother who'd given her up years earlier, during "Operation Babylift" in 1975. Dolgin says:

> We all really believed that we were going into a happy reunion, and we had no idea whether we would come back with anything more than that. It just grabbed us with the possibilities of raw emotion and passion, and those are great elements for a documentary. And we're also drawn to films where we don't know what's going to happen—we have a concept and we go with it.

At a minimum, the filmmakers had a basic, straightforward narrative of an adoptee returning to her homeland, although whether or not that could be turned into a documentary remained to be seen. Dolgin says:

> Maybe there would be a film that would explore what happens when you lose your birthplace identity. Heidi grew up in southern Tennessee, and we imagined going back with her and having her rediscover her roots in some way. But we had no idea, truly. We just went. And of course as soon as we got there it became clear that what we had anticipated was going to go in a different direction.

In Vietnam, the filmmakers found themselves immersed in the complex story they told in *Daughter from Danang*. Similarly, New York-based filmmaker Kazuhiro Soda was surprised to learn that a college friend was running to fill a vacant political seat, and hurried to Japan to start shooting the film that became *Campaign*, as he describes in Chapter 21.

Frederick Wiseman, renowned for his exploration of American institutions (*Hospital*, *Basic Training*, *Welfare*, *Public Housing*, *Domestic Violence*), has told interviewers that once he is given permission to film, he moves quickly, spending weeks shooting and then finding his themes and point of view over the course of several months of editing. But note that there is an inherent structure to Wiseman's work—the rhythms of daily life and of the individual stories he picks up over the course of filming—and a distinctive style that he brings to his films. For an interview (published in *The Boston Phoenix*) about the film *Public Housing*, writer and filmmaker Gerald Peary asked Wiseman if he looked for "drama" while shooting. "The first thought: I'm trying to make a movie," Wiseman responded. "A movie has to have dramatic sequences and structure. . . . So yes, I am looking for drama, though I'm not necessarily looking for people beating each other up, shooting each other. There's a lot of drama in ordinary experiences." It's also worth noting that Wiseman's style of shooting almost invariably necessitates a high shooting ratio (footage filmed versus footage that ends up on screen) and a lengthy editing period.

Kazuhiko "Yama-san" Yamauchi, in *Campaign*.
Photo courtesy of the filmmaker.

SERENDIPITY

It's not unusual for filmmakers to begin one project, only to be drawn by the characters and situations they encounter toward a film that is both different and stronger than they anticipated. In publicity material for the film *Sound and Fury*, director Josh Aronson says that he initially intended to film five deaf individuals whose experience covered a range of viewpoints on deafness. But in his research, he discovered the Artinians, a family in which two brothers—one hearing, one not—each had a deaf child. This created an opportunity to explore conflict within an extended family over how to raise deaf children. More recently, British filmmaker Orlando von Einsiedel went to Virunga National Park in Congo to tell a "positive story about the rebirth of the region," he says, in Chapter 22, only to be confronted by a much more complex narrative, which he and his team wove together as *Virunga*.

Knowing that the story may change, or is even *likely* to change, doesn't mean that you shouldn't approach a general idea by looking first for the best story you can, given the subject as you then understand it. Knowing at least your baseline story helps you to anticipate, at minimum, what you'll need to make the film, including characters and location setups. When he worked with emerging documentary filmmakers at the University of California, Berkeley, Jon Else said he would require that they head out "with some bomb-proof fallback plan," so that even if everything on the shoot went wrong, they would still come back with something.

EVALUATING STORY IDEAS

Beyond the conviction that a story you're developing will work well as a film, the following important practical considerations may be helpful to consider.

Access and Feasibility

Does your film provide an entrée into new or interesting worlds, and can you obtain access to those worlds? Over the years, documentary filmmakers have taken audiences behind the scenes with Cuban immigrants as they arrive and settle in the United States (*Balseros*); with high school basketball stars as they follow their dreams of professional sports careers amid hardship in Chicago (*Hoop Dreams*); with a billionaire couple whose dream of constructing the largest privately-owned home in the United States is interrupted by economic crisis (*The Queen of Versailles*); with workers engaged in hazardous labor—as coal miners, sulfur carriers, welders, and more—in Ukraine, Indonesia, China, Pakistan, and Norway (*Workingman's Death*).

Aside from exclusive or extraordinary access, any film, even one shot in your grandparents' home, depends on some kind of access being granted, whether it be personal (your grandparents), location (permission to bring your equipment into their home), or archival (access to family photo albums, personal letters and such). Sometimes, *lack* of access may be part of the story, as with Michael Moore's pursuit of General Motors chairman Roger Smith, in *Roger & Me*.

As you develop your idea, you need to determine whether the elements needed for production are really available to you. Can you get inside a cyclotron to film? Will that Pulitzer Prize-winning author grant you an interview? Will you be allowed to follow a third-grade student during that spelling bee? Several years ago, I worked on a science documentary for which we wanted to film cyclists in the Tour de France to illustrate the conservation of mass and energy. The success of a good portion of that film depended on access to the Tour and to exclusive CBS Sports coverage of it. Had we not been able to arrange these, we would have had to find a different illustration.

As an additional note, gaining access usually means establishing a relationship and building trust with the people who can grant it. This is a professional relationship, although filmmakers often grow very close to their subjects. It's important to respect that trust, so be truthful about yourself and your project from the start. You can generally get people to talk to you even if they know that you don't agree with their position, as long as you make it very clear that they will be given a fair hearing and that you value their point of view. (There are exceptions. Filmmakers such as Nick Broomfield [*Kurt & Courtney*] and Michael Moore may push the boundaries of access as a matter of style; they may show up with the cameras rolling deliberately to put their subjects on edge.)

Affordability

In terms of budget and schedule, is it realistic to think that you can afford to tell the story you want to tell, in the way you want to tell it? Even if digital technology can put a relatively inexpensive camera into your hands, getting your film shot, edited, and technically ready for broadcast or theatrical release will still be very expensive. Even celebrated filmmakers have trouble raising money these days. Have you set your sights too high? Don't think small, just realistically. Know that some types of documentaries are costlier to produce than others, and that "extras," such as the rights to use a clip of archival film from a private collection or a short piece of music from your favorite album, can set you back thousands of dollars.

Passion and Curiosity

Do you care deeply about the subject? Passion is going to be your best weapon against discouragement, boredom, frustration, and confusion. Passion is not the unwavering conviction that you are right and the whole world must be made to agree with you. Instead, it is a commitment to the notion that this idea is exciting, relevant, and meaningful, and perhaps more importantly, that it's something you can look forward to exploring in the months or even years to come.

Passion is also an ingredient that commissioning editors and funders want to see when filmmakers approach them for support.

Filmmaker Hans Otto Nicolaysen used to review proposals for short and documentary films on behalf of Filmkontakt Nord (FkN) in Norway, which he helped to found. His first criteria for making a grant? "Passion," he says. "I always start with the question, 'Why are you telling me this story now?'" Nicolaysen says a proposal should convey not only the filmmaker's skill but also his or her connection to the material.

Passion must come with curiosity, or you risk creating a one-sided diatribe. Few people like being lectured at or told what to think, which is what may happen if you start a project with the conclusion, such as: "I want to show that animal testing is bad." Furthermore, if you already know what you think, why devote months or even years of your life to the film? As you think about issues that you feel strongly about, can you find questions that you'd like to explore? For example, you may think that you can't imagine a single scenario in which animal testing is justified. Are you willing to test that conviction by seeking out, and genuinely listening to, a range of people (scientists, patients, animal rights advocates, and others) who may share your point of view, strongly disagree with it, or more likely fall somewhere in between? If you find the debate of interest, or you come across stories in your research that merit digging deeper, your passion might lead to a viable project. You don't necessarily need to include all or even most of the research you've done on screen. You just need to do your homework, so that whatever story you end up telling contains the complexity it demands and draws viewers in, allowing them to reach their own conclusions based on honestly presented evidence.

Audience

Who is your intended audience? Many documentaries, whether produced independently or in-house, are created with an audience in mind. Even though you may end up reaching a different audience than expected—maybe the project you thought would only play regionally winds up being a national success—it can help to start with some idea of whom you're targeting: age, geographic area, educational level and so on. Are you creating science programming for grade schoolers, or an older audience? Are you hoping your political documentary catches the attention of HBO, or the executives at the PBS series *Frontline*, or audiences at independent art houses? Is your film intended not for broadcast but for use by community or educational groups? Do you hope to release your film theatrically? These questions are worth thinking about early on, because they may affect not only how you research and craft the film but also how and from where you might fund it.

It's also true that some filmmakers begin to work before worrying too much about these questions—the topic is too urgent or the opportunity too fleeting. This was the case with *The Kidnapping of Ingrid Betancourt*, produced and directed by Victoria Bruce and Karin Hayes. In January 2002, they were finalizing plans to film Colombian senator Ingrid Betancourt while she campaigned for the presidency, when they saw on CNN that she'd been kidnapped by the Revolutionary Armed Forces of Colombia (FARC). "When she was kidnapped, we just went into Plan B," remembers Bruce, who headed to Colombia almost immediately. That first shoot lasted 16 days, and two months later, a second shoot lasted 10 days.

"In between that time, we thought, okay, March/April, we're going to cut a trailer together, and we're going to get funding, we're going to get grants," Hayes says—but that didn't happen. Bruce's former boyfriend lent them $15,000, and the pair paid for the rest with their own savings and with credit cards. They taught themselves to edit, still without funding or any guarantee of an audience. But, Hayes notes, "From the very beginning, when I was imagining where did I want my film to be, and what style did it need to be, I was thinking HBO." That fall, their hopes were realized. At an industry gathering featuring commissioning editors, including one from HBO, Bruce pitched the film, motivating the HBO editor to follow up, attend a screening at Slamdance, and acquire the film [then called *Missing Peace*], with a caveat: It still wasn't ready for HBO.

"They wanted to do some re-editing, and we worked on it for another two months with their editor, Geof Bartz," explains Bruce. "The most important thing they changed was that they wanted you to know that Ingrid was kidnapped up front. We had a slow build of getting to know this woman. And Sheila Nevins [President of HBO Documentaries] said that you will care so much more about her time with her kids in the home video if you know she's going to be gone soon. It's brilliant."

There is no single road from idea to audience. Sometimes events and opportunities necessitate working quickly, before too much is known. Sometimes the subject may seem too obscure or too personal to seek sponsorship early on. In some cases, filmmakers nearly complete their films before submitting them to "open calls" for program slots or festival competition, and in that way they gradually find an audience and possibly funds for completion. But as all of these examples illustrate, at some point in the process, you need to identify whom you're trying to reach, and may want to adjust the storytelling accordingly.

Juan Carlos Lecompte and cardboard figure of his wife, from *The Kidnapping of Ingrid Betancourt*.
Photo by Ana Maria Garcia Rojas, courtesy of the filmmakers.

Relevance

Will anybody care about your film, or can you make them care? This can be a tough one. You may be passionate about fourteenth-century Chinese art or the use of mushrooms in gourmet cuisine, but can you find a compelling story that will be worth others not only funding but watching? It's possible to make people care about all sorts of things, but it usually takes the right approach. For more on this, see Chapter 6.

Timeliness

One aspect of relevance, though not always the most important one, is timeliness, which is not to be confused with the timeline of news reporting. In this context, it means that television executives, for example, may hope to plan documentary programming to coincide with an event, such as a historical anniversary or a high-profile motion-picture release on a related topic. The fact that a subject is or may become topical, however, is not by itself a reason to pursue it, because by the time you finish the film, interest in that issue may have passed. In fact, the quality of being "evergreen," meaning the film will have a shelf-life of many years as opposed to many months, can be a positive selling point. A film on elephant behavior or the American electoral process in general may be evergreen, whereas a film that specifically explores a particular environmental campaign or issues in the American presidential campaign of 2016 may not be.

Visualization

Is the story visual, and if not, can you make it visual? This is an important question whether you're telling a modern-day story that involves a lot of technology or bureaucracy, or you're drawn to a historical story that predates the invention of still or motion picture photography. A film subject that doesn't have obvious visuals requires additional foresight on the part of the filmmaker; you'll need to anticipate exactly *how* you plan to tell the story on film. The opposite may also be true: a subject can be inherently visual—it takes place in a spectacular location or involves state-of-the-art microscopic photography, for example— but you'll still need to find a narrative thread, if that's the style of film you're choosing to make.

Hook

Another question to ask as you evaluate the story is, does it have a hook? In its simplest form, the hook is what got you interested in the subject in the first place. It's that bit of information that reveals the essence of the story and its characters, encapsulating the drama that's about to unfold. *Sound and Fury*, for example, is the story of a little girl who wants a cochlear implant. The hook is not that she wants this operation, nor that the implant is a major feat of medical technology. The hook is that the little girl's parents, contrary to what many in the audience might expect, aren't sure they want her to have the operation. It's the part of the story that makes people want to know more.

Jonestown: The Life and Death of Peoples Temple, does not hook audiences with the horror of a mass suicide/murder that took place in 1978, even though the film opens with text on screen announcing the event. Instead, the film's hook is that it promises viewers an insider's look at what it means to join a community, only to be drawn inexorably into a terrifying, downward spiral. As discussed especially in

Chapter 7, the hook is often the last piece of the film to come together, as the themes, characters, and story come more clearly into focus and are distilled into the promise you make to the viewers: *This* is what this movie is; *this* is why it's worth your time; *this* is why this story needs to be told and demands your attention.

Existing Projects

What other films or series have been done on the topic, and when? This is useful to know, in part because it may simply inform your own storytelling. What worked or didn't work about what a previous film-maker did? How will your project be different and/or add to the subject? It's not that you can't tackle a subject that's been covered; look at the range of projects on the American civil rights movement, the threat of nuclear war, or dinosaurs. But knowing as much as you can about your subject also means knowing how else it's been treated on film, not only for the sake of the film but also to bolster your ability to defend the idea to potential funders and distributors.

Is This a Film You'd Want to See?

Given an assignment to research, write, or even make a short documentary on a subject of their choosing, students often seem to go first to "important" topics and the kinds of films that mimic the stereotype of what documentaries are. The initial pitches tend to be for films that are dutiful, critical of the injustice in the world, and in all likelihood nothing like the films they would seek out for entertainment.

Why not think backward? First, it's important to consider what's possible on a fixed schedule and budget (including a time budget); this will likely mean a simpler approach even to a relatively complex issue. But thinking backward also means putting yourself in the position of both filmmaker and audience, and thinking in terms of choice and enjoyment: What sort of film would you enjoy making and, perhaps more importantly, watching? Which filmmakers, films, and subjects are you most drawn to?

DEVELOPING THE STORY

Once you've decided that your idea is worth pursuing, you'll need to start refining the story and planning how you'll tell it. There's no single way to do this, and furthermore, it's a process that tends to continue from the moment an idea strikes you until the final days of postproduction. In general, though, depending on the needs of the project, the budget, and the schedule, you are likely to at least write some form of outline or treatment, so that you know—before you spend a lot of time and money shooting—that you have a story that works, and can plan not only what you need to shoot but also why.

IF YOU ALREADY KNOW THE STORY, HOW CAN THE FILM NOT BE BIASED OR DIDACTIC?

Knowing your story (or at least the germ of it) at the start of a project is not the same thing as knowing exactly what you want to say and how. It simply means having an idea of the narrative spine on which you could hang your subject and having at least some idea of themes you want to explore. From there, you need to research, develop, and shoot your story with questions and an open mind. Building on an earlier example, as sympathetic to the bakery owners as you may feel at the start of your project, you might come to find yourself sympathizing with developers, or discovering that a third solution, while meaning the end of the bakery, is best for the town.

Every film is different. With a historical film, you know the event itself, and finding the story means figuring out which part of the event you want to explore and what the parameters of that story are—in other words, where you enter and where you exit, which is determined to a large degree by what *story* you're choosing to tell. "You have to draw limits on when the story begins and ends," filmmaker Stanley Nelson explains (Chapter 19). "Sometimes it happens on paper before we start. Sometimes it happens in the edit room, and those are sometimes the hardest decisions to make."

For example, imagine a commission to make a film about Prince Charles and Lady Diana. Well, what about them, what piece of their lives together (or apart) are you choosing to tell? Is it a story of their courtship, marriage, and divorce? Is it a critique of the economics of twentieth-century monarchy? Is it about Diana's activism on behalf of HIV/AIDS, and how that may or may not have affected her standing at home? As noted, your story may shift over the course of making the film, but think about how different your production will be if your narrative spine is their wedding rather than a story of Diana's activism.

As noted, even films that end up advocating a position or idea—that these chemicals shouldn't have been dumped, that law enforcement used too much force, that laws are being broken—will be stronger if those creating them remain open to new and even conflicting information. The more effectively and truthfully you can present your case and trust your audience's intelligence, the more likely it is that the resulting film will stand up to scrutiny.

TELLING AN ACTIVE STORY

A significant percentage of the documentaries on television these days are about events that are over and done with. You still generally want to craft a narrative that unfolds over the course of the film, so that the outcome appears to be uncertain. One way of doing this is to keep the storytelling (and interviews) in the moment. This means, for example, that witnesses who are interviewed don't say: "I found out later he was fine, but at this point I got a call from somebody, Andy I think it was, he later became mayor, and Andy told me that my boy Jimmy was down the well." Instead, ask your storytellers to stick to what is known at this point in your narrative, moment to moment, such as, "I got a call that Jimmy was in the well. I ran screaming for help."

Telling an active story allows the viewer to come with you through an experience. It builds tension and leaves the ending a surprise. (This works even when the outcome is already known. A good storyteller can get an audience to suspend disbelief and somehow hope with their hearts for an outcome that their heads know is not possible.) If you or an interviewee begin a story by telling us the outcome, you've let all of the suspense out of your story. Surprisingly, this is a common mistake, not only in interviews but in scripted narration. People will write, "Although he wasn't badly hurt, Jimmy had fallen down a deep well."

Does staying in the moment mean that you can't offer interpretations of the past? No. For example, an expert witness might be interviewed saying, "People complain about over-regulation, that there's too much of it. But there are laws that should have made the contractors responsible for sealing that well up. Instead, they left it open, and a little boy fell in." The expert hasn't yet said when or how the boy got out, but he has put this accident into a broader context.

Sometimes, it will seem that a film's subject just doesn't lend itself to a forward-moving story. For example, suppose that members of the local historical society want you to make a film about their town's founding in 1727, and they want to fold in some material about the origins of some of the wonderful old architecture that still survives. They're excited by the fact that many of the local families are descended from early residents, so they have access to a decent collection of old oil portraits as well as photographs and even some letters. What does it add up to? Not much that will interest anyone who's not a direct relative of the folks on camera, because there's no story being told on screen—yet. When Ken Burns, Ric Burns, and Geoffrey Ward used artifacts and images from the nineteenth century in *The Civil War*, they used them in the service of a powerful story—the North against the South. What's the *story* of this town's history?

In the search for narrative, some filmmakers find a "guide" to the past, such as the town's mayor, who might say, "Let's set out to see where this great city came from," and off he or she goes. But there are often more creative devices, and it can be useful to find a present-day story that would motivate a look back. For example, what if students from the local middle school are researching the town's history in order to write a play that they will perform later that year? That's a possible framework. What if a local builder is trying to restore the town's oldest house, which has been renovated repeatedly over the years? In order to do so he's got to peel back the layers one by one, offering a reason to explore the town's architectural history while also giving us a chance to follow the kind of home building renovation that audiences enjoy. These aren't earth-shattering ideas, but they demonstrate ways to consider a subject that might not seem, at first glance, to have much potential as a film.

"When approaching a film, I always try to find at least two stories that unfold simultaneously," says filmmaker Jon Else. "One of them almost always is a very simple, straight-ahead, forward motion through

Ken "Spike" Kirkland, in *Sing Faster: The Stagehands' Ring Cycle*.
Photo courtesy of Jon Else.

time. For instance, in *Sing Faster*, the forward motion is just the simple story that is told in Wagner's *Ring* cycle, in the operas. It's this crazy soap opera about the gods fighting, a giant Aristotelian drama with characters and rising conflict and resolution and all that. And then parallel to that is the much less linear story of the stagehands preparing this production for opening night."

WORK BACKWARD, EMBRACE LIMITS

This one piece of advice touches on everything else in this chapter, but goes a step farther. First, understand that limitations can be enormously helpful in sparking creativity, while too much freedom can have the opposite effect. Second, be honest about what your limitations are, in terms of experience, access to equipment or personnel, and the level of resources available to you (including not only money but also time). Without substantial resources, you cannot create a comprehensive film history of World War II. Instead, play to your strengths. Find one local World War II veteran, or a group of them who meet weekly to play darts, that sort of thing.

Think about what your end product is going to be and what it will take to get there in terms of your schedule and budget. Be sure to factor in all the costs of finishing the film, especially if you'll need to produce masters and clear rights. Especially, consider your time frame. If you don't have a lot of time to edit, you don't want to go overboard in shooting—you want to shoot less and shoot smarter. And if the overall length of the finished film is limited—in other words, you don't have a lot of *screen time*—that also presents limits, and working backward to incorporate that limit can be useful. Here's an example of this, from Boston-based filmmaker Tracy Heather Strain, whose credits include commissioned films for the PBS series *American Masters* and *Race: The Power of an Illusion*. Earlier in her career, she was talking to a series producer about everything she wanted to include in an hour-long film she was making and where she wanted the story to go. The series producer reminded her that with credits, her film would only run about 55 minutes. Strain says:

> It hit me to think about it. All the things I want to say are not going to fit in a 55-minute film. And so one of the first things I do now is look at how long I have [on screen] and I sketch out a little three-act, minute breakdown.

With classic three-act structure (Chapter 4), for example, the first and third acts are roughly a quarter of the film, with the second act roughly half. A 20-minute film, therefore, needs to get a story going within five or six minutes, with the tension ratcheting up through the second and third acts—a total of maybe 10 to 12 minutes—before reaching a quick resolution. The more focused the story, the better the chances of accomplishing this.

SUMMARY

Going into production with the story in mind, even knowing that the focus is likely to shift, is generally far more effective than just heading out to cover a vaguely defined subject. Jon Else says:

> Films don't go over budget because you paid a sound guy too much and put the crew in a hotel for an extra day. They go over budget because people waste two months of editorial time figuring out what the story is. If you're talking about doing inexpensive work, that's the single most important thing, finding a story that comes with a ready-made through line. It's much more cost-efficient to figure out the story beforehand.

The downside, Else notes, is that "it's very, very tough to do any kind of cinema vérité film—which involves really discovering the story—inexpensively." Even when filmmakers carefully select a subject for the strength of its characters and the potential of a strong narrative line, the films, such as *Salesman* or *Control Room*, are built on an observational approach that takes considerable time to shape in an editing room.

SOURCES AND NOTES

Transcripts and additional information about *Daughter from Danang* can be found at the *American Experience* website, www.pbs.org/wgbh/amex/daughter/filmmore/pt.html; also see the film website, www.daughterfromdanang.com. Gerald Peary's interview with Frederick Wiseman (*Boston Phoenix*, March 1998) can be found at www.geraldpeary.com/interviews/wxyz/wiseman.html. Additional information on Frederick Wiseman and his films can be found at his website, www.zipporah.com. Information on *Sound and Fury* available at www.nextwavefilms.com/sf/joshnotes.html.

CHAPTER 4

Story Structure

A good way to gauge the status of a film in progress is to ask the film-maker to tell you the story of the film in a brief, one- or two-paragraph pitch. If he or she immediately launches into a lengthy description of the opening shot or an amazing scene, the film might be in trouble. Visuals *serve* a story; they are not the story. Along the same lines, if the filmmaker starts to talk about the subject in broad terms—the film is about a soccer team, or World War II, or a famous author—there may also be a problem. To really get to the heart of the story, you need to have a sharper focus: What *about* World War II or that author or team? Given that subject, what story are you telling and how are you telling it?

This is where structure comes in. Think about the times when you've tried and failed to effectively tell a joke. A good joke needs structure: a setup, followed by complications/escalation, followed by a completely unexpected—but in hindsight, inevitable—punchline. If the joke teller gives the punchline away, or interrupts the joke with too many unnecessary details or asides, the joke loses its power.

Narrative structure tends to work in the same way. If your pitch sounds like a grab bag of ideas and explanations, chances are you're missing the structure, whether the project is still at the treatment stage or you think you're nearly finished editing. Lack of structure is evident when a film is strung together with a series of "and then this happened, and then this, and then this," or when it's a jumble of ideas and scenes that feels disorganized and repetitive, with no variation in rhythm and no real build of ideas or argument.

Structure is the foundation of narrative storytelling; it's what gives it a beginning, middle, and end. It puts the filmmaker(s) in the author's seat, driving the film forward in a way that compels the viewer to want to come along to find out what happens next. Perhaps counter-intuitively, *simplicity* of structure is what allows for complexity in the overall film. If you have a strong narrative spine, you can hang a tremendous amount of content onto it and audiences will stay with you. This strategy is a big part of what distinguishes and defines the best of creative nonfiction film.

THE NARRATIVE SPINE, OR TRAIN

Films move forward in time, taking audiences with them. You want the storytelling to move forward, too, and to motivate viewers to be curious about the information you're giving them. The train is the single thread—either an action or a question/argument, generally—that drives your film forward, from beginning to end. The narrative spine, the base-line story, is what you pitch in order to encapsulate what your film is and allow others to imagine it as a story on screen, rather than a subject. It is your narrative framework, and the way it's stated suggests a possible outcome.

- The train for *Super Size Me* might be stated as: *To test whether or not fast food is really as bad for your health as people claim it is, a filmmaker sets out to eat only what is offered at McDonald's for 30 days, measuring his health with the aid of doctors.* Possible outcomes: Either the McDiet will harm the filmmaker or it won't.
- The train for *Daughter from Danang* might be stated as*: A young Amerasian woman returns to Vietnam to meet the birth mother who gave her up for adoption 22 years earlier, in 1975, as Saigon was evacuated.* Possible outcomes: Either the reunion will go well or it won't.

Get a good train going, and you can make detours as needed for exposition, complex theory, additional characters, backstory—whatever you need. Because this is a foundational device, the train does not need to be present at every moment in your film; in fact, in many films the actual screen time devoted to the train is quite small. But you must return to the train periodically throughout, and the train that began the film needs to be resolved as you end the film. All along the way, even as you detour, you must remember to ask yourself, *what does this detour mean for my train, how does it advance or complicate it?* These detours aren't there just as distractions; they add depth and tension to the forward moving narrative.

Identifying the Train

Identifying and articulating a film's train, whether the film is still at the idea stage or has already been produced, can be difficult. One of the key strategies is to think simpler. In the classroom, student filmmakers often struggle with the train because they get caught up in details of the plot rather than thinking in basic terms about something on which to hang that plot. Try to strip the film's structure to its core question or action. Michael Moore's *Roger & Me* follows a lot of issues and characters, but at its core is a very simple device: Moore sets himself up as the protagonist, trying to get a meeting with Roger Smith, CEO of General Motors. That device enables Moore to string together otherwise difficult-to-connect material. As complex as *Sound and Fury* is, the spine is built on one question: Will Heather Artinian be given a cochlear implant?

Look at Maysles Films' *Gimme Shelter*, the 1970 film that follows the Rolling Stones through the end of a 1969 tour, focusing heavily on their efforts to organize and then perform at a free concert at the Altamont Speedway in northern California, where events spiral dangerously out of control. The film's narrative device is not the concert or the stabbing death that occurred there; it's the Stones *watching* the concert on a flatbed editing machine (Steenbeck), in part to see the stabbing that had not been apparent to them from the stage. "This gives us the freedom, all you guys watching this," filmmaker David Maysles explains to the Stones as they sit around the Steenbeck. (The film is directed by David Maysles, who's seen recording sound; his brother Albert, unseen, who's shooting; and editor Charlotte Zwerin, who's operating the Steenbeck.) "We may only be on you for a minute," he continues, "and then we can go to almost anything."

The device allows the Maysles to set up the mysteries of the film—what happened, what was the involvement of the Hell's Angels, did the Stones have any idea what was happening?—and launches the film. By periodically cutting to Mick Jagger and Charlie Watts watching and reacting to the footage that we (the film audience) are watching, the filmmakers are more free to cut between scenes and sequences that are otherwise somewhat disconnected: Footage from concerts that preceded the one at Altamont; scenes showing the complication and risk of trying to organize the free concert and find a venue for it; scenes of chaos in the hours before and during the concert, scenes of performances by Grace Slick, Tina Turner, and others. And at the end of the film, they return again to the editing room, as the Stones ask them to rewind and replay the images captured by one of the cameras, freezing on a gun in the hands of the man who was stabbed. With their responses, the film is essentially over.

The Train Conveys One Story

The train of the film is its core story, its foundation. You will likely be able to identify the train within the opening sequence (whether it runs two minutes or ten; it depends on the film), and if you're right, you would expect to see the film return to the train periodically throughout and then conclusively at the end. This doesn't mean it should be an easy journey to get to that ending, nor should the ending be entirely predictable. It just has to connect to the story you promised when the film opened. If, during production, the film takes a detour and ends up with a powerful end to a different story, it's probable that you and your team will need to rethink how the film opens and what the actual spine of the film is.

Each Film's Train Is Unique

The narrative spine is part of what differentiates your film from someone else's. For example, the website for Firelight Media offers a three-paragraph description of *Jonestown: The Life and Death of Peoples Temple*, directed by Stanley Nelson. The third paragraph suggests the structure of the film: "On November 18, 1978, over 900 members of Peoples Temple died in the largest mass suicide/murder in history. Using never-before-seen archival footage and survivor interviews, *Jonestown: The Life and Death of Peoples Temple* tells the story of the people who followed Jim Jones from Indiana to California and finally to the remote jungles of Guyana, South America in a misbegotten quest to build an ideal society." The journey is implied in the title and this description.

In contrast, another filmmaker drawing on the same history might make a film called *Massacre at Jonestown*, which might have as its train the final days in Guyana. Someone else might make *Jonestown Survivor*, which might tell the story of an individual's journey from that fateful day to a new life. Nelson's film, bookended by the massacre, follows the temple and its members on a harrowing journey that seemed to begin with free choice and ends with entrapment, brutality, and death.

Sometimes, you can confirm your hunch about a train by looking at the DVD box: *Waltz with Bashir*, for example, "chronicles one man's descent into his own half-forgotten past." (If you are pitching it as a train, you'll likely want to add specifics: an *Israeli* man's descent; half-forgotten past *as a soldier in Lebanon*.) *Man on Wire* shows how Philippe Petit "overcame seemingly insurmountable challenges to achieve the artistic crime of the century." Alex Gibney's *Taxi to the Dark Side* "investigates the torture and killing of an innocent Afghani taxi driver in this gripping probe into reckless abuses of government power." As Gibney discusses in Chapter 15, the story of the young taxi driver's murder provided a narrative framework for a subject he'd been struggling with: "I was approached to do a film about torture, and initially reluctant because it was a very difficult subject and I wasn't sure the subject would be a film. And so I looked for a story . . ."

Remember, though, that the train may not be neatly articulated on the box, and that in fact there may not be a clear-cut train. Eugene Jarecki's *Why We Fight* is a well-structured and complex film, but the description on the box ("an unflinching look at the anatomy of American war-making") doesn't describe the train; instead, it talks generally about the film. *Why We Fight* is an interesting example, however, because the film uses the arc of a grieving father, retired police officer Wilton Sekzer, as a narrative *framing device*. Having lost his son in the 9/11 attack on the World Trade Center, Sekzer wants revenge and believes the U.S. government's argument that the target should be Iraq. By the end of the film, his views have changed. Sekzer is not an active protagonist, and his story is not the train, because he does not have a goal that propels the film forward. But his presence and arc helps to give the film's overall essay a coherent and satisfying shape.

A Train Is Both Universal and Specific

Films generally appeal to our emotions before they appeal to our heads. In fact, the reason to tell a story for maximum (genuine) emotional impact is so that you *can* appeal to people's heads. Think about the documentaries and even the fictional dramas that appeal to you. At their most basic level, the questions they raise are: Will the guy get the girl? Will the outbreak be stopped? Will the town/puppy/hostage be saved? Will the team/first grader/unemployed father win the competition?

The train is the device that gets to the heart of your film, whether it's a story of competition or a question that demands an answer. Here's an example. I am not naturally drawn to space exploration. I understand that it's complex and important, but when people start going into details about lunar modules and orbits and heat shields, my eyes glaze over. There are, of course, people who will buy any book or video that comes out about the space program, people who know everything there is to know about Sputnik and Goddard and the Sea of Tranquility. So the question is, how do you make a film that will appeal to both groups? You don't want to make it so superficial that you bore the aficionados, or so dry that you will never attract audiences like me. (Note that I did not say "so technical," because if you get a good train going, you can be surprisingly technical and people will want to follow you.) A student of mine came up with a solution that I thought worked well.

The assignment was to write a treatment for a historical documentary on any U.S. subject. He chose the tragic Apollo 1 mission. (In 1967, a month before they were to become the first men to land on the moon, three U.S. astronauts died in a fire during a routine test.) One possible train that he considered was the government investigation that followed the fire, but it quickly became apparent that this would mire the film in bureaucracy—committees and reports and testimony—and lose anyone not interested in the details. Instead, he used the day of the fire as his train, moving the events forward in a way that motivated a look into the history and politics of space research and the lives of the astronauts involved. Since he presented the story from the point of view of those with something at stake in its outcome, he was able to bring the "initially disinterested" audience members along, giving us a reason to care and want to learn more.

Thinking about the "initially disinterested" is a good strategy in general. It's very easy for your own knowledge of or passion for a subject to get in the way of good storytelling. Assume that a big portion of the people you hope to reach don't know (or perhaps don't care) about something that you know every detail of. As you think about the story you want to tell about these topics, what are the key points that most fascinate you? How might you pitch the film at a family event, or in an elevator should you bump into a commissioning executive? What are the three to five "bullet points" you might fold into a pitch that will not only get people to pay attention, but might prompt them to ask you for details?

BUILDING ON THE NARRATIVE FRAME

The train, or spine, summarizes the film's structure at its most basic. Now you need to build a film that will hold an audience's attention, whether it's for 20 minutes or two hours or more. We've all sat through documentaries that seemed pointless and meandering. Maybe they had great beginnings, but then they seemed to start again, and again, and again. The film seemed to be about one thing, but the rousing conclusion was about something altogether different. The story started in the present, and then quickly plunged into background and never resurfaced. Or the situation and characters were so weakly developed that we found ourselves caring little about the outcome. These are often problems of structure.

Structure works in response to the audience's built-in expectations. It's human nature to try to make sense of patterns and arrangements, to work at filling in the blanks and guessing what happens next. Film-makers can heighten or confound those expectations, thereby increasing the viewer's involvement in a story and investment in its outcome. There's no such thing as a lack of structure; even in an experimental film, something is stringing those images together. That something, for better or worse, is structure.

The building blocks of a film's structure are shots, scenes, sequences, and, in some but not all cases, acts. Because these are commonly used words that at times have conflicting meanings, the following definitions clarify how they're being used here.

Shot

A shot is a single "take" on an image. There may be camera movement during the shot, or it may be static. It may be a close-up, a wide shot, a pan, or a tilt. But it begins and ends with the action of the cinematographer turning on and off the camera; later, the editor will further refine the shot by selecting from within it, giving it a new beginning and end point. Individual shots can convey a great deal of storytelling information: point of view, time of day, mood, emotion, character, rhythm, theme. A single shot may also include a "reversal," which is a twist in the plot, sometimes described as a change in values from one state to another. An example of a shot that contains a reversal can be found in *Yosemite: The Fate of Heaven*. We follow a cascading waterfall down through what appears to be pristine wilderness—until we land in a crowded tram full of noisy tourists. The reversal is from isolation to crowds, nature to humankind, pristine to polluted.

Scene

A scene is a consecutive group of shots within a single location. You might have a "scene at the courthouse" or a "scene on the boat." A scene is usually more than simply a snapshot of a location, however; it's a subset of the overall action. A scene is made up of a series of *beats*. In *Born into Brothels*, the scene "The children ride a bus to the beach" might be broken down like this:

- A few shots (interior, then exterior) show the children's excitement that a bus has arrived and is waiting.
- From inside the bus, we see a child ask if she can sit by a window, because she wants to take pictures. Everyone's on board; another

quick shot, and then filmmaker Zana Briski makes sure the children all have their cameras.

- With a honk, we see the driver's point of view (POV) as the trip gets under way. From inside and outside the bus, we see a range of shots: children looking, taking pictures, their point of view as they look out; the bus moving forward.
- Inside the bus, the children eat and begin to sing (various shots).
- One child is sick.
- The music shifts as the bus gets into a more rural area (seen from various points of view).
- Inside the bus, several of the children have fallen asleep (various shots), intercut with more traveling shots, as the landscape becomes more rural.
- The bus has stopped; the children gather their things and look out at the ocean.

In other words, the scene started with the excited shout, "Hurry up, the bus is here," and ended with "Look at the water!" Like shots, sequences, and acts, scenes like this contain a beginning, middle, and end, and often, they culminate in a reversal, called a turning point, that motivates a shift in action of the overall story. Here, the reversal ties in with some of the film's themes. Boarding a bus in a congested, dirty city, the children arrive at the bright, open seaside. This reversal motivates the next scene—enjoying and photographing the beach.

To be satisfying, a scene should feel complete, which means that those filming the scene need to remain aware that events being witnessed will need to be condensed in the editing room, and shot accordingly. Filmmaker Steven Ascher (*Troublesome Creek*) explains, "Filming real life is a constant struggle to distill reality into a meaningful subset of itself . . . the telling moments, the telling gestures, the lines of dialogue that will suggest the rest of the scene without actually having to see the rest of the scene."

Sequence

A sequence is a collection of shots and scenes that together tell a more or less continuous story of an event that's a piece of your bigger story. Like a book's chapter, a sequence has a beginning, middle, and end. And, like a book's chapter, your sequences should be different from each other; each should have a unique job to do in the overall storytelling, while also moving the film's train—its underlying plot, or narrative—forward. It can be helpful to think of titles for your sequences, whether or not they end up on screen (they probably won't). A title will help you differentiate the "Frankie goes to the prom" sequence, to use an example from an imaginary vérité film, from a sequence in which "Frankie retakes her college admissions test" (SAT).

The sequence in which Frankie goes to the prom might begin with Frankie rushing home from her job at the mall and continue with her emerging from her bedroom in a long white gown, dancing with her boyfriend, crying in the ladies' room because she's been dumped, and then arriving home, where she collapses into her mother's arms. The sequence you're thinking of as *Frankie retakes her SATs* might begin with Frankie hiring a private tutor and continue with a montage of her studying late at night and on Saturdays, getting ready to take the test, and entering the test room; it might end with her nervously taking the envelope, with her results, out of the mailbox.

But you're not yet done with how you think about these as sequences. What's the overall story of this film, and how do the sequences serve the story? If the film is about a high-school student's struggle to earn a college scholarship, and that's your spine, your sequences need to link to that spine. That means that you need to think about the spine either as you're planning the shoot or as you're editing the film. What is the minimum score she needs to get on her SAT to qualify for the scholarship she is pursuing? How does attending the prom affect the story, if at all? You never want to force it, so if you can't find (not impose, find) a connection, you may end up dropping a sequence.

For example, if the point of your film is actually to look at the obstacles that stand between a student and college, the scholarship may be one focus, but your bigger spine would be *affording college*. In that case, you'd want to find out, through your research, what steps this student is taking to afford college, and decide what is *necessary* to honestly tell the story. If she's had a part time job all the way through high school, that's probably necessary. The prom sequence may not be relevant to the story about "getting a scholarship," but the cost of going could be part of a story about "affording college."

Each sequence, like each chapter in a book, should feel unique. As filmmaker Ric Burns explained, describing the creation of *The Center of the World*, a two-hour history of the World Trade Center and the final episode of his acclaimed series *New York: A Documentary Film*, "Every step along the way you ask, 'What's absolutely crucial to telling the story? What advances the story?'" Burns describes applying a:

> basic narrative yardstick, which is: try not to tell any story [in this case, meaning sequences within the overall story] more than once. So there's only one riot. There's only one fire. There's only one burst of skyscrapers. There's only one war. In other words, always find that moment where the nature of the particular story you're telling is caught at its highest arc.

Going back to the example of *Born into Brothels*, we can see how the bus *scene* fits into a bigger *sequence*, which might be called "the day at the beach." The sequence begins with two quick exterior shots before the girl announces the bus's arrival, and continues through the bus ride and into a long scene of the children at the beach, discovering the ocean, playing in the waves, doing cartwheels, and taking pictures. And then it's night, and they're dancing on the bus as it heads back to Kolkata. It arrives, and we see the children make their way up the street, past "the line" of sex workers, and into the narrow passages to their homes. (The entire sequence runs from a fade-in at 36:48, timed from the film's first frame of action, to a fade-out at 43:53.)

This sequence achieves a number of things that serve the overall film. It shows the children interacting as a group and as independent, lively, spirited people. The pictures, especially Avijit's "Bucket," will be featured later in the film. Furthermore, the joy of the scene is immediately contrasted by the next scene, in which we see one of the children being beaten, and his mother (and possibly grandmother) screaming obscenities at him and at neighbors. In the scene after that, we see some of the children in a car and hear Briski's voice-over: "I'm not a social worker, I'm not a teacher, even. That's my fear, you know, that I really can't do anything and that even helping them to get an education's not going to do anything. But without help, they're doomed." Having seen them in a brief day's escape, we want more than ever for her to succeed. (Had there been another sequence that achieved most of the same things as this one, a choice would have been made about which was stronger, and only one of them used.)

Scenes and sequences are a big part of how you establish and vary the rhythm of a film. If it all feels the same, and there's no change of tone, mood, pace, or even content throughout, the film is going to get tedious very quickly. A scene stays in one location; a sequence conveys one important (overall) idea, theme, event. There will likely be a turning point at the end of a scene, and an even bigger one at the end of a sequence. (Story expert Robert McKee says that ideally, each scene creates a shift or reversal that is at least minor; each sequence, a change that is moderate; and each act, a change that is major.) Even if your film does not have acts, each sequence should advance your overall argument or story. Think about the information you need and when you most need it.

The only real way to understand sequences is by discovering and analyzing them yourself, through close viewing of others' films and by trying to organize your own films into sequences. For more on this, see Chapter 7.

Act

First, not all films use act structure; many don't. "Act" is a term borrowed from dramatic storytelling (playwriting, screenwriting). An act is a series of sequences that drives to a major turning point—a climactic moment that springs directly from the story and makes necessary the next series of sequences in the act that follows. Each act plays a role in the overall storytelling, and the tension and momentum within each should be increasing.

In traditional three-act (also known as dramatic) structure, the first act covers the bulk of the story's exposition and, to paraphrase the late showman and writer George M. Cohan, gets your hero up a tree. In the second act, you throw rocks at him, forcing him higher up in the tree. In the third act, you force him to the edge of a branch that looks as if it might break at any moment . . . and then you turn the corner to your story's resolution, and let your hero climb down.

There are three important things to know about acts. The first is that there is something about dramatic structure that seems built into the way we receive and enjoy stories, and even jokes. The second is that many documentaries do not fit neatly into what might be described as formal dramatic structure, even if they employ an approximation of it. Third, there are many ways to create a compelling structural throughline—what fiction writer Madison Smartt Bell describes as "narrative design"—in a documentary without going anywhere near dramatic structure. The film still needs to have compelling characters and rising tension, each scene should move the narrative forward, and the film should satisfactorily conclude the story (or mission, essay, journey, etc.) with which it began. But it doesn't have to do it in three acts.

Before we move into some specifics of act structure, here are a few other useful terms.

Jeanne Jordan and family in 1960, from *Troublesome Creek: A Midwestern*.
Photo courtesy of the filmmakers.

Inciting Incident

The inciting incident is the event that sets into motion the action of the story (the actions that relate to the train, not the subject). It may be something that's occurred before you start filming. In *Troublesome Creek*, for example, it's the decision of the Jordan family to keep their 450-acre Iowa farm running for one final year. Filmmakers Jeannie Jordan and Steve Ascher began the film after Jeannie's father, Russ, told them of the plan. Ascher says:

> Russ called and said he thought this would be his last year of farming. To be able to do a story like this, to have that kind of access— I thought of it as both an opportunity to tell this story and also for Jeannie to be able to tell some of the wonderful stories she'd been telling around the dinner table for years about growing up in Iowa.

The plan was to spend one final year planting and harvesting, after which the Jordans would auction off their livestock, equipment, and personal belongings in order to pay off their debts and keep the land itself, 450 acres. Ascher explains:

> That gave us the possibility of a narrative spine. It would have been much harder, if not impossible, to just make a film about day-to-day life on the farm and be able to get into the kinds of issues that we did. We filmed four times over the course of about a year and a half.

The resulting film, *Troublesome Creek: A Midwestern*, was nominated for an Academy Award, among other honors.

In *Spellbound*, the inciting incident for each of the competitors we meet is that they are qualifying, or have qualified, to compete in the National Spelling Bee. In *Super Size Me*, the inciting incident, arguably, occurs when filmmaker Morgan Spurlock first learns of the lawsuit against McDonald's, and comes up with the notion of filming a 30-day McDiet. In *Waltz with Bashir*, a conversation with an old friend sparks an unexpected flashback, and sets the filmmaker on a journey to recover memories of his time on an Israeli Army mission in Lebanon.

Note: The inciting incident relates specifically to the film's train, not to the underlying history. It's the incident that sets the film's train in motion.

Point of Attack

Not to be confused with the inciting incident, the point of attack is where you, as the filmmaker, enter the film: the first frames of action. It's generally agreed that this is one of the hardest decisions to make over the course of production. In fact, it's often made and unmade many times before the right point of attack is found and you can't imagine why you ever tried anything else.

The point of attack ushers the viewer into the world of your film and its themes and characters. Discussing the opening visuals of his film *The City and the World*, episode seven of *New York*, Ric Burns says:

> It wasn't until fairly late in the editing process that we realized the beginning of the film was a moment in 1944 when Helen Leavitt borrows a 16mm movie camera and takes it up to the streets of East Harlem, and with a couple of friends, including James Agee, begins to shoot the footage that becomes her extraordinary film,

In the Streets. That scene is absolutely, in my view, the best way to start that film, and it seems so completely inevitable—but it wasn't inevitable in the sense that we knew it from the beginning.

Where you begin your film is a critical decision. The first frames may—but don't always—set the train in motion (generally, though, the train or story of your film will be under way by the end of the opening sequence). The film open also is your first chance to draw the audience into your subject and themes. As noted, your point of attack is very likely to change as you grow closer to your material; simply start with the best opening you have at that time and let it evolve from there.

Backstory

Backstory is a form of exposition, but the two terms are not always synonymous. The backstory includes the events that happened before (sometimes long before) the main story being told; it often includes material a filmmaker thinks is critical for the audiences to understand in order to "get" the story.

Backstory can be conveyed in a number of ways, including title cards (text on screen), interviews, narration, and conversation. To some extent, backstory involves the details of exposition that are revealed over the course of the film and add complexity to the story and its characters. Far along in *Grizzly Man*, for example, we learn that Timothy Treadwell very nearly won the role in the television series *Cheers* that went to actor Woody Harrelson. It is backstory—part of the complex journey that led Treadwell to live dangerously close to bears in the Alaskan wilderness. Placed where it is in the film, the detail adds a further layer of complexity to our understanding, and the filmmaker's, of the forces that led to Treadwell's death.

Often, and sometimes painfully, backstory gets dropped in the cutting room because the story itself has become so compelling and the themes so evident that the backstory is more of an interruption than a necessity. Filmmaker Stanley Nelson, for example, describes having to lose historical context of Gandhi and his struggles in India while editing *Freedom Riders* (Chapter 19). Backstory is most likely to stay in if it directly enhances and enriches the story unfolding on screen, adding depth to a character's motivation, illuminating themes and issues, or underscoring irony or historical continuity. A little goes a long way, however. If the backstory starts taking over your film, you might need to rethink which story, past or present, you really want to tell.

You may also need to look at where it's placed. In *When the Levees Broke*, a segment that presents the backstory of New Orleans's history doesn't appear until the third hour of the film. That hour "deals with the whole notion of coming back or staying—are people going to go back to New Orleans or stay where they are, are their lives better now in other places?" explains co-producer Sam Pollard. In other words, the film doesn't go into the history of New Orleans until questions and ideas in the film *motivate* a look back.

THREE-ACT DRAMATIC STRUCTURE

Three-act dramatic structure is a staple of the Hollywood system, but as noted elsewhere, it was first articulated by Aristotle, to *describe* (not prescribe) what he was seeing. Dramatic structure encompasses the basic way that many humans tell and anticipate stories: a setup, complications, resolution. "I think that's just the way we as humans are neurologically and culturally structured," says writer Susan Kim (Chapter 16), noting, for example, that the mind constructs narratives even as we sleep. "I think there is something inherent in the dramatic form that's really powerful. And I think that's why, as storytellers, as people who want to make documentary or write plays, it behooves us to understand the potential of that structure."

There are many books that describe three-act structure, but the best way to learn it is to take films apart and analyze them. Which story (or spine, or train) is *driving* the act structure? Where do the act breaks come, and how are they connected to the train? How do sequences fit into the acts, and how does each play a role in driving the overall story forward? You may not be able to really "see" the act structure until you're all the way through the film, but what you'll tend to find is that it roughly divides as follows.

Act One

The first act generally runs about one-quarter the length of the story. In this act, you introduce your characters and the problem or conflict (in other words, this act will contain some of your important exposition). Act One often contains the "inciting incident"—the event that gets everything rolling—although this event sometimes has already occurred when the story begins. There tends to be a "first turning point," which is somewhat smaller than the turning point that ends the act. By the end of Act One, the audience knows who and what your story is about and, at least initially, what's at stake. The first act drives to an emotional peak, the highest in the film so far, necessitating the action that launches the second act.

Act Two

The second act is the longest in the film, about one-half the length of the story. The stage has been set in Act One and the conflict introduced. In the second act, the story's pace increases as complications emerge, unexpected twists and reversals take place, and the stakes continue to rise. The second act can be difficult, because there is a risk that the story will bog down or become a succession of "and then this happened, and then this." You need your second act to continue to build as new information and new stakes are woven into your story. The second act drives to an emotional peak even greater than at the end of Act One, necessitating the action that launches the third act.

Act Three

The third act is usually slightly less than one-quarter the length of the overall film. As this act unfolds, the character is approaching defeat; he or she will reach the darkest moment just as the third act comes to a close. It's a common misperception that your third act resolves the story, but it doesn't. It intensifies it; the tension at the end of the third act should be even greater than the tension at the end of Act Two. That tension then pushes you into the resolution, those last moments where you resolve the story, tie up loose ends as necessary, and let your hero out of the tree.

STRUCTURING MULTIPLE STORY LINES

Although you can tell only one primary story, it's possible to follow two or even three story lines within that story. In Hollywood terms, these are "A" stories, "B" stories, and possibly even "C" stories. The "A" story carries the primary weight and is the story around which the piece is structured, but the other stories should also have emotional peaks and valleys.

Most importantly, the stories should inform each other, meaning that at some point they should connect to form a coherent whole and advance a single overall story line. *Yosemite: The Fate of Heaven*, for example, contrasts the primeval Yosemite that survived until the nineteenth century with the national park that today accommodates several million visitors a year. The filmmakers interweave two stories, one more clearly narrative than the other. The first is built around an 1854 diary kept by Lafayette Bunnell, who was part of a battalion that entered Yosemite on an Indian raid. The second is a more impressionistic look at the ongoing, day-to-day struggle to balance use of the park by those who love it with the needs of those who maintain it and are working to preserve it for the future.

The use of multiple story lines often enables filmmakers to create films that are more complex than would be possible with a strictly linear approach. Rather than tell everything in the order in which it occurred, they select an event and use that to focus the primary film narrative, which frees them to look back into the past or even ahead into the future as needed. This can be seen in the *Daughter from Danang*, for example, as well as *Murderball*.

WHAT THREE-ACT STRUCTURE IS NOT

Three-act structure does not mean taking a film and dividing it into three parts and calling each part an act. An act can only be considered as such if it advances the one overall story (or essay) that you set out to tell. For example, a film that looks at early settlements in the United States can't be structured, "Act One, Jamestown, Virginia; Act Two, New York, New York; Act Three, Plymouth, Massachusetts." There is no common story there; there may be common themes and this may work as an organizational construct for a film, but these aren't acts. On the other hand, you could tell three individual dramatic stories within that structure, one within each location that you then combine into a film.

Three Acts in Five or One or Two

Whether your film is described as having five acts or one, it can still follow dramatic (three-act) structure. There are many practical reasons to divide a story, including breaks for commercials (television) or audience intermission (theater). But "one-act" plays and "five-act" television specials can often still be divided into three acts. For example, even though David Auburn wrote *Proof* as a fictional, two-act stage play, the action can easily be broken into three-act dramatic structure. Auburn's "first act" contains all of his Act One and the first half of Act Two; his "second act" contains the balance of Act Two and all of Act Three. Where you break a story for reasons like commercials or intermissions is part of the structural discussion, but does not necessarily interfere with your use of dramatic storytelling.

Conversely, simply because a story is divided up for commercial breaks doesn't mean it's divided into acts. Many commercial documentaries are described as having four or five "acts," which may accommodate the points at which there is an interruption for advertising. These breaks come at dramatic moments, but that does not describe the overall structure. (For example, many commercial biographies present a fairly chronological portrayal of a person's life, driving to key moments, without being shaped by three-act structure.)

If you are working on a film that is not going to be interrupted with commercials, but your editor is insisting that your film requires four or even five acts or more, I would strongly suggest that you do a barebones outline of each of the acts. Where does it start, what does it drive to, and how does it relate to your underlying train? While it's possible to structure an interesting film in four or more parts, they may not be acts—or if they are acts, they are likely covering the same ground a few times too many.

APPLYING FILM STRUCTURE

Some documentary filmmakers think about structure over the course of production but don't focus on it until they're editing. Others play with structure from the start, sketching outlines that they return to during production and postproduction, revising them and reshaping them as needed.

In projects where an outline and/or treatment is needed prior to filming, whether to get a greenlight from commissioning editors or to get production funds from a public or private source, you may try to anticipate an act structure that you think will work. This is often the case, for example, with historical films, and can also work with films where the outcome is unknown but can generally be anticipated because of the train. In other words, by the time a filmmaker is seeking support for a film about something with an inherent arc—a competition (for example, an athletic event or a spelling bee), a time-limited event (a state fair, a school prom), a political campaign, even a day in the life—that filmmaker will also, in all likelihood, have a sense of the characters, issues, and themes that have drawn him or her to the story, and can *anticipate* an act structure, even if it ends up changing.

Finding an Act Structure in the Edit Room

In some cases, filmmakers will shoot a story that offers a basic narrative arc but wait until they're editing to specifically consider structure.

This usually means a considerably longer editing period. For example, Susan Froemke describes working with editor Deborah Dickson on the Academy Award-nominated *Lalee's Kin: The Legacy of Cotton*, produced for HBO. Maysles Films had been commissioned by HBO to explore the subject of poverty at the end of the twentieth century, and the company spent months researching the issue and seeking out stories that would illuminate it. They chose two related stories: that of Reggie Barnes, a superintendent of schools in the Mississippi Delta seeking to get an impoverished school system off of academic probation (one narrative arc), and Lalee Wallace, a matriarch struggling to educate the grandchildren and great-grandchildren left in her care (the arc of the school year).

The filmmakers were based in New York, and traveled to Mississippi periodically over a period of several months, shooting about 42 days in all. Their footage ratio was relatively conservative, about 70:1 (meaning that 70 hours of film were shot for each hour that ended up on screen; the film runs 90 minutes). They began to edit about a year and a half into the filming, before production was over. Froemke notes that it's better to have completed shooting before editing starts, because you can build to the end of the film, its climax. With *Lalee's Kin*, they instead began by editing scenes. She says:

> Let's say that there are 10 moments, or maybe 20, that we think really could make great scenes, so we cut those together. And then we do a very rough assembly, like four hours long. And you see how the scenes play against each other. . . . Right away you start to see which story lines are working and which ones are weak. And you keep editing down, you keep sculpting, down and down.

Part of that sculpting involves deciding which job a particular scene or sequence does in moving the story forward. Scenes that reveal character or backstory, for example, could be used in a variety of ways (provided that each use is truthful), or a scene may contain two or three key points, only one of which will be the focus for now. "Often you try to assign a value to the scene," Froemke says. "For example, 'This scene is going to tell Lalee's backstory, her family upbringing.' Or, 'This scene is going to explain what Reggie's dilemma is.' Or, 'This scene, you're going to understand Granny's despair.'"

Froemke says that act structure is part of how this work is organized:

> We often call it Act One, Act Two, Act Three. We'll say, when we're screening, "This is Act One information"—it's setting up the situation. We don't yet know where it's going to appear in Act One, but

we put it in that section. And then Act Two and Act Three. Act Two is always the hardest in vérité, it's the hardest part of the film not to sag. You've got to get a few of your feisty scenes into Act Two.

Another issue she notes is that special attention must be paid to those scenes that move the plot forward; with vérité, there often aren't many of them, so care must be taken in how they're placed.

Lalee's Kin ended up taking a bit less than two years to edit. An earlier Maysles production, *Grey Gardens*, took two and a half years, Froemke says:

> It took a whole year just to figure out what you had in the footage and what story line you were going to go for. Nothing happens in that house in *Grey Gardens*. So how do you structure a film about it? It took a long time to figure out that there was a balance of power between Little and Big Edie [Edie Beale and her mother, Edith Bouvier Beale, reclusive relatives of Jacqueline Kennedy Onassis].

Revising an Act Structure in the Edit Room

Rather than fully discovering a film's structure in the editing room, it's more likely you'll be *revising* the structure that suggested itself to you over the course of research, development, and production. Be careful when making changes that you are not bending your footage to satisfy a story it doesn't represent. This is most likely to happen when filmmakers shoot one story (or no story, just a lot of footage) and then stumble on a story that might work, late in the process of editing.

ANALYZING DOCUMENTARIES USING ACT STRUCTURE

Three-act structure can offer a grid that allows you to anticipate and critique the rhythms of your storytelling. You should map out your film at rough cut or fine cut and try to analyze it the same way you've been analyzing completed films (try to see your film as if for the first time). What story do you think is being told? Where are the turning points? Do the act breaks relate to the specific story (the train)? Does the film bring a satisfying end to the story with which it began?

What's interesting is how many successful documentaries, even those that seem vastly different in style and approach (including essay films), can be analyzed in terms of acts. But act structure or not, the important thing to keep in mind is that if your film is working—even if the charts and stopwatches say it shouldn't be—leave it alone. Storytelling is an art, not a science. Go with your gut. If the film's great, who cares what "rules" you broke?

Sulfur gatherers in East Java, Indonesia, from *Workingman's Death*.
Photo © M. Iqbal, courtesy of Michael Glawogger/Lotus Film.

OTHER STRUCTURES

There are plenty of examples of successful, interesting documentaries that do not tell character-driven dramatic stories. Look, for example, at Austrian filmmaker Michael Glawogger's *Workingman's Death*, a two-hour film that *The New York Times* aptly described as having "the structure and tone of an epic historical poem." It is nonfiction and it is literary—in other words, creative nonfiction—but the filmmaker has created a structure that is unique to this project. The film won the British Film Institute's Grierson Award and the Jury Award at the Gijon Film Festival, among many other honors. Glawogger set out to show *work*: "I wanted to make a movie where you sit in the cinema and actually feel the weight on your back," he said in a 2005 interview. The film offers five portraits of heavy manual labor that is all but invisible to many people these days: *Heroes* visits coal miners of Krasni Lutsch, Ukraine; *Ghosts* looks at men hauling tremendous loads of sulfur from the top of a mountain in East Java, Indonesia, to the valley below; *Lions* keeps up with the workers in Port Harcourt, Nigeria, as they process live goats and bulls into meat for sale; *Brothers* stays with workers in Gaddani, Pakistan, as they risk their lives to convert massive rusted tankers into scrap metal; and *Future*, a much shorter segment, looks at steel workers and industrial progress in the Chinese province of Liaoning. In the film's epilogue, we visit the Duisburg-Nord Country Park in Germany, a recreational facility in what was once the Duisburg-Meiderich Steelworks.

German director Eva Weber's *City of Cranes*, originally produced for Channel 4 and awarded Best Documentary Short at the Los Angeles Film Festival (among numerous honors), is another example of a chaptered approach to structure. Unlike the Glawogger film, all four chapters have the same subject: this 14-minute film brings viewers into the world of crane drivers, who climb up into tiny cages to spend their days working hundreds of feet above the ground. Each of the four chapters is thematically titled: "The City Above," "The Last Topman," "Ballet of Cranes," and "Solitary." The film has a sort of overarching structure as well—the first shot is of a man climbing up into a crane, at the start of the day; it ends on a contemplative note at dusk, from the vantage point of a driver high above the city.

U.S. filmmaker Liane Brandon's 1972 film *Betty Tells Her Story* consists of two 10-minute interviews, played in sequence. Brandon had met the film's subject when both were consulting for the Massachusetts Department of Education, and was drawn to a story Betty told

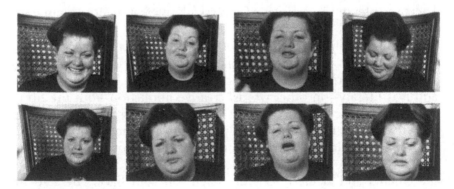

Betty, from *Betty Tells Her Story.*
Photo courtesy of Liane Brandon.

about buying a dress and then losing it before she had a chance to wear it. "I borrowed Ricky Leacock's camera, and John Terry, who worked with Ricky at M.I.T., volunteered to do sound," Brandon says. At Betty's house, the crew loaded the first of three 10-minute black-and-white film magazines, and Brandon asked Betty simply to tell her story. "The first version that you see in the film is the first take that we did. I never told her how long a magazine was, but somehow she ended the story just before we ran out of film." It was basically the story as Betty had first told it to Brandon: a witty anecdote about a dress she'd found that was just perfect—and how she never got to wear it.

A second take was interrupted by a truck. In the third take, Brandon asked Betty to try telling the story as she felt about it while it was happening, rather than as she remembered it. "Everything changed: body language, eye contact," Brandon says. "I don't think she'd ever told or even thought about the story that way." Told from within rather than without, the story is no longer a humorous anecdote; it's the painful memory of a plain, overweight woman who found a dress that made her feel beautiful, then lost it before she ever had a chance to wear it.

In the final film, the first and third takes are run consecutively, with some black leader in between that reads, "Later that day, the filmmaker asked Betty to tell her story again." The contrast between the two takes is what gives this film its power.

SOURCES AND NOTES

Jonestown's website is http://firelightmedia.tv/movies/jonestown-the-life-and-death-of-peoples-temple/; there is also a website at www.pbs.org/wgbh/americanexperience/films/jonestown/. Reference to Robert McKee, *Story* (New York: HarperCollins, 1997). George M. Cohan reference in Wells Root, *Writing the Script* (New York: Holt, Rinehart & Winston, 1987). Reference to Madison Smart Bell, *Narrative Design* (New York: W.W. Norton & Co., 1997). David Mamet, *On Directing Film*, pages xiv, xv (New York: Penguin Books, 1991). *Lalee's Kin* is available through Films Media Group, http://ffh.films.com/search.aspx?q=Lalee. The interview with Michael Glawogger was conducted at the Venice Film Festival on September 4, 2005 by Ginu Kamani, and is reproduced in the film's online press materials at www.workingmansdeath.at/main_interview_en.html. Information on *City of Cranes* can be found at www.pbs.org/pov/cityofcranes/. The film's official website is www.cityofcranes.com/. More information about *Betty Tells Her Story* can be found at www.newday.com/film/betty-tells-her-story.

CHAPTER 5

Time on Screen

In the previous chapters, we looked at the basics of storytelling and the importance of structure. A key element in structure is how the storyteller arranges the presentation of chronological time, without altering cause and effect. Most of us have grown up with storytelling that does this. A television show may start with strangers discovering a body, for example, move forward as detectives arrive on the scene, and then move back in time to the events leading up to the murder as the detectives piece it together. Some stories, for sure, are told entirely in chronological order. Others, more rarely, are told in *reverse* chronological order, from the end to the beginning. In the fictional world, this is how playwright Harold Pinter structured *Betrayal*, and how screenwriter Christopher Nolan, working off a short story by Jonathan Nolan, structured the dramatic feature *Memento*.

The treatment of time on screen is important because of the way we experience movies: Film is a linear medium. People watch it from beginning to end, with one shot following another, one sequence following another, until the film is over. "I've never seen an even vaguely successful documentary film that does not move forward through time," says filmmaker Jon Else. He cites some examples:

> "*Night and Fog* has an absolutely traditional, very simple forward chronological motion through the late 1930s to the end of World War II. *Tongues Untied*, Marlon Riggs's film, appears to be a non-linear rumination about what it means to be young and gay and black in America in the 1980s, but in fact it moves through his life. Even Chris Marker's *Sans Soleil*, which is often described as being nonlinear, moves forward through time. This whole business of a plot moving forward, I think, is just so inextricably embedded in our cultural DNA.

As is already probably clear by the discussion of structure, moving a story forward through time does not necessitate resorting to a plodding narrative that is strictly a chronological recitation of events in the order that they occurred. Instead, and often, it involves the interweaving of chronological and non-chronological elements in and out of order to form a cohesive and satisfying whole. *Daughter from Danang* selects an event within the chronology of Heidi Bub's life—her trip to Vietnam in 1997 to meet her birth mother—as the framework, or train, through which to explore issues and events that cover the entire span of her life, including her birth in 1968 and, especially, her mother's decision to give her up for adoption in 1975. *Jonestown: The Life and Death of Peoples Temple* begins with a title card describing an event that occurred on November 18, 1978, continues through a scene that is not specifically grounded in time, and then moves back to the 1930s and generally follows chronological order back to that day in 1978.

There is one very important caveat. You may not distort or falsify chronology. What we are discussing is the order in which you *tell* the story, not the order in which you are saying the story occurred.

TELLING A CHRONOLOGICAL STORY, BUT NOT CHRONOLOGICALLY

As a documentary storyteller, you decide where to begin and end the story. You can begin in the middle, go back to the beginning, catch up with your story, and then move ahead to the end. You can start at the end before moving to the beginning to ask, "How did we get here?" You can flash forward or back. The only thing you can't do, in a documentary that's driven by a narrative sequence of events, is change the important facts of the main underlying chronology.

Suppose you've unearthed a story in the archives of your local historical society. The following are the events in chronological order:

- A young man becomes engaged.
- His older brother enlists to fight in World War II.
- The young man also enlists.
- Their father dies.
- The young man is shipped overseas.
- He learns that his brother has been killed.
- His fiancée sends a letter, breaking off their engagement.

These events haven't happened in an order that's particularly dramatic, and there's no way to tell, on the surface, which events are linked by cause and effect. It may be that because his brother enlisted, the young man also felt obligated, but there could be other reasons. If you can verify your characters' motivations, whether through records or eyewitnesses, you can state them; otherwise, present the facts and let the audience draw its own conclusions. By the same token, you may not rearrange the underlying chronology to imply a more interesting cause and effect. For example, based on the previous chronology, you might be tempted to:

- show the two sons enlisting after their father's death, to create the impression that they enlisted in his honor;
- film a recreation in which the young man, already in uniform, proposes marriage;
- present the fiancée's letter in voice-over as the young man enlists, implying that he's enlisting in reaction to the breakup.

Each of these might be dramatic, but they all lead the audience to a false understanding of cause and effect. But respecting cause and effect, there are still some more dramatic choices. Start with the young man's rejection by his fiancée, for example, and then reveal that this is another in a string of losses. Leave the father and fiancée out of the story and focus on the two brothers at war. Tell the story of the young man going to war, and then go back to follow the story of his engagement. There's plenty of room for creativity.

An example of a documentary that creates a false impression of chronology, to the detriment of an otherwise powerful argument and film, is Michael Moore's *Roger & Me*. Critic Harlan Jacobson published a detailed review of this film in *Film Comment*, outlining some of the problems. The film's present-day narrative begins in late 1986, when, according to Moore, General Motors chairman Roger Smith closed 11 plants in Flint, Michigan, leaving 30,000 people jobless and sending the city on a downward spiral.

Moore then presents a series of events, including these, in this order:

- Eleven GM plants are opened in Mexico, where, Moore says, workers can be paid 70 cents an hour.
- The last vehicle rolls off the assembly line in Flint.
- Ronald Reagan visits Flint; over archival news footage, Moore narrates, *Just when things were beginning to look bleak, Ronald Reagan arrived in Flint.* At the end of the scene, Moore says someone *borrowed the cash register on his way out the door.*
- A parade is held in Flint, and Moore interviews Miss Michigan shortly before she'll compete to be Miss America.
- Evangelist Robert Schuller comes to Flint to cheer people up.
- As Moore presents an abandoned and decaying Flint, he says, *The city had become the unemployment capital of the country. . . . Just*

when it looked like all was lost, the city fathers came up with one last great idea. This plan includes the building of a Hyatt Regency hotel downtown; the Water Street Pavilion, a new shopping center; and the opening of Auto World.

Remember that the film began with the closing of 11 plants in Flint, late in 1986. From Harlan Jacobson's article, here is the actual chronology of the events:

- In 1980, Ronald Reagan arrives in town as a presidential candidate and buys folks pizza. Two days before his visit, the cash register was stolen.
- In 1982, Reverend Schuller comes to Flint and the Hyatt Regency is opened.
- Auto World opens in mid-1984 and closes in early 1985.
- In 1986, the Water Street Pavilion opens, the result of a plan that may have been under way since the early 1970s. Also in 1986, the number of layoffs at GM do not total 30,000 but about 10,000, according to Jacobson. The real "watershed" of layoffs had occurred much earlier, in 1974. The net loss of jobs since 1974 was about 32,000.
- In the fall of 1988, shortly after the parade, Miss Michigan is crowned Miss America.

In other words, many of the events presented by the filmmaker as the efforts of the powers-that-be to staunch the bleeding from the 1986 layoffs actually occurred or were under way long before those layoffs took place. Jacobson's article includes an interview with Moore, in which he asks the filmmaker about these issues. "The movie is about essentially what happened to this town during the 1980s," Moore responded. "As far as I'm concerned, a period of seven or eight years . . . is pretty immediate and pretty devastating" [ellipses in the original]. Moore argued that he was trying to:

tell a documentary in a way they don't usually get told. The reason why people don't watch documentaries is they are so bogged down with "Now in 1980 . . . then in '82 five thousand were called back . . . in '84 ten thousand were laid off . . . but then in '86 three thousand were called back but later in '86 ten thousand more were laid off."

In fact, telling an accurate story doesn't have to mean getting bogged down in detail or needing to tell the story sequentially. Arguably, you could leave the edit of *Roger & Me* exactly as it is and simply rewrite

Moore's narration. For example, there's nothing to stop your use of footage of candidate Reagan stumping through Flint years before the plant closings; you simply write into it in a way that acknowledges the time shift. Here's Moore's narration, building on the aftermath of the 1986 layoff: *Just when things were beginning to look bleak, Ronald Reagan arrived in Flint and took a dozen unemployed workers out for a pizza. He told them he had come up with a great idea, and if they tried it they'd all be working again.* (In archival footage, a woman then explains that Reagan suggested they move to another state to find work.)

Alternative narration: *People had been trying to help the unemployed in Flint for years. As a candidate in 1980, future president Ronald Reagan took a dozen workers out for some pizza and inspiration.*

The narration needs to keep track of where you are in the film's present—in this case, somewhere between 1986 and 1988—while letting us know that what we're seeing is from the past, and how it informs the present. What to do about the cash register theft? This sounds like one of those facts that is "too good to check," but it must be done. If you know that the theft occurred two days before Reagan's visit, and you really want to use it, you have to be a bit creative.

Moore's words: *None of Reagan's luncheon guests got back into the factories in the ensuing years, and the only bright spot to come out of the whole affair was the individual who borrowed the cash register on his way out the door.*

It's unclear whether these luncheon guests were already laid off before Reagan arrived (and stayed that way) or if they were employed between Reagan's visit and the layoffs later in the 1980s. In any case (or if you can't find out the specifics about the individuals in this footage), you could say something more general, such as: *In the years to come, Reagan's luncheon guests may have wished that instead of listening to the candidate, they'd taken a cue from the guy who'd robbed the pizza parlor two days earlier and made off with the cash register.*

While mine is not brilliant voice-over, it's a quick example of how you can tell a story out of order, with as much irreverence as you want, without building a case that has a weak or inaccurate foundation. To imply that the visits of Reverend Schuller and Ronald Reagan and the opening of the Hyatt Regency and Auto World occurred both after and because of a plant closing in 1986 is simply inaccurate. In his defense, Moore told Jacobson that *Roger & Me* isn't a documentary but "an entertaining movie that hopefully will get people to think a little bit about what is going on." (To be fair, it was his first major film, released in 1989; he has made several blockbuster documentaries since.) However, audiences and critics received the film as a documentary, and it's highly regarded as such. The power of documentaries comes from their veracity, and it's undermined if people discover that in the interest of a compelling argument, they've been misled.

Not all documentaries, or sequences within them, need to adhere to a strict chronology; filmmakers may rearrange filmed sequences if they are typical but not necessarily specific to a timeline, such as routine events (skateboard practice, Sunday church, an annual holiday). Where you place this material in the film, regardless of when it was shot, is generally up to you. If you're following a group of people—residents in an assisted living center, for example—your choice of which scenes and stories to present and when may be driven by the emotional argument you're building, rather than any specific chronology or the order in which stories were filmed. (Within each story, however, rules of cause and effect still apply. If a woman suffers a heart attack, recovers, and then dances with her husband at a formal dinner, it would be dishonest to edit the sequence to imply that the dancing led to the heart attack.)

Material filmed for thematic reasons may also stand apart from the chronological sequence. An example of this can be found in *Troublesome Creek: A Midwestern*. The chronology is built on the Jordans's efforts to pay off a bank debt by auctioning off their belongings. For thematic reasons, the filmmakers asked the Jordans to return to a farm they'd rented for many years before moving to the farm they're now at risk of losing. The scene's exact placement in the film, other than sometime before the auction, isn't specific. Filmmaker Jeanne Jordan's voice-over simply says, "Early one morning we took a trip to Rolfe to visit the farm I grew up on." Jordan's parents are upset to discover that the old place is abandoned, but their visit doesn't motivate any action. Instead, it serves a filmmaking purpose—shedding light on the historical context of the overall film and on themes of change and loss.

COLLAPSING AND EXPANDING TIME

Filmmaking, from shooting through editing, is a process of expanding and/or collapsing real time. The event needs to be covered with the editor in mind, so that there is enough variety of shots, cutaways, and transitional material to make a creative edit possible.

For the most part, simple editing can imply a passage of time. Your characters are at home, seated around the breakfast table, and then they're on the school basketball court; or your character is trying on a tux for the prom, and then he's at the prom. If the story has been taking place in the summertime, and you cut to children playing in the snow, the season has changed. Sometimes, filmmakers emphasize passage of time with dissolves, time-lapse photography, an interlude with music, or a montage. If the passage of time is part of the story, the filmmaker might comment on that visually. Errol Morris used a clock to mark the hours that passed while Randall Adams was being pressured to confess in *The Thin Blue Line*.

Some scenes may be granted more or less emotional weight than others through the length of time you devote to them. For example, you might spend two minutes of screen time bringing the audience up to date on 10 years of history prior to a candidate's decision to run for office, and then spend the next 45 minutes on an eight-month campaign; you've collapsed the first part of the chronological story in order to focus more time on the campaign itself. And sometimes you expand time because you've built to an emotional moment and you need to let it play, as was true at the end of *Bridge to Freedom*, in the last episode of the first season of the series *Eyes on the Prize*.

FILMING OVER TIME

In some cases, a documentary's complexity comes not only from its immediate story but from an opportunity to check in on characters months or even years later. An example of this is the Spanish film *Balseros*. The film begins in 1994 and follows a handful of determined emigrants from Cuba who risk their lives in order to reach the shores of the United States, traveling on dangerous, makeshift rafts. Some don't make it far offshore; others are picked up by the U.S. Coast Guard and held in detention at Guantánamo for many months. Eventually, though, each makes his or her way to the United States, and we see them settling down in small towns and big cities throughout the country. The filmmakers check in on them nine months later to see how they're doing, and then they check in on them again five years later. The result is a look at immigration and the American dream, at opportunities seized and squandered, and at choices and mistakes that can have a lasting impact.

Another noted example is British filmmaker Michael Apted's *Up* series. In the 1960s, Apted worked on *Seven Up!*, a documentary in which 14 seven-year-olds of various economic backgrounds were interviewed about their lives and hopes for the future. Apted, who is also known as a feature-film director (*Coal Miner's Daughter, The World Is Not Enough*), assumed direction of the project, returning in seven-year intervals to see how the children and their dreams were holding up at ages 14, 21, 28, 35, 42, 49, and most recently 56. A few of the original subjects have dropped out of the project over the years, but most continue to participate, and in their achievements and frustrations audiences get a profound look at what it means to live ordinary, extraordinary lives.

COLLAPSING INTERVIEWS

There are two primary reasons to edit an interview: to focus information and to shorten the time it takes to convey that information. A person will talk to you for 10 minutes, an hour, maybe two or three hours, and you'll usually end up using only a few bites, unless the entire film is "a conversation with." You must condense the interview material in a way that does not alter its initial meaning and remains true to the intent of the speaker. For example, here's the (fictional) raw transcript of a witness describing your character, Sanders:

> CHARLIE: Sanders wasn't a bad man, in fact I'd have to say he was a pretty good guy, overall, which is why nobody could figure out—at least I couldn't figure out—uh, what the, what he was doing even thinking about embezzlement. I don't know, but I think, I mean, who knows, but in my opinion, he was just panicked about money. I mean for crying out loud, this guy's got three, uh, three, uh, you know, he's got three kids and another one on the uh, on the way—maybe it got to him, I don't know, maybe he just couldn't figure out how he was going to support all these little ones or whatever, you know? He was selling auto parts, used auto parts. Besides, embezzlement's a white-collar crime, he's a blue-collar guy—well, not really, he's not working with the auto parts, he's more the manager of the store, driving to work in his, oh, what was it, Tercel, his blue Tercel, shirt and tie and all the while I guess he's thinking nobody above him would miss that thirty thou. Arrogance, I guess. Yeah. Arrogance.

What can't you use? No matter how catchy it sounds, I wouldn't use, "embezzlement's a white-collar crime, he's a blue-collar guy" for two reasons. Sanders is not, in fact, blue collar, and furthermore, the witness himself corrects this statement.

In terms of editing for time, however, condensing the essence of this paragraph, you could do any number of cuts depending on the point you want Charlie to make and where it will be used in the film. What material is the interview bite following? What will it precede? One of the ways to see this before trying it in the editing room is to make the cut on paper, which you can then give to the editor.

Two things to remember. First, don't make the editor crazy by cutting out every third word and expecting him or her to construct a sentence or a paragraph out of the bits and pieces. This is very difficult and very time-consuming, and furthermore, any interview material that's hacked to bits will have to be used as a voice-over. In any case, if you're hacking an interview to bits, chances are good that either you've interviewed the wrong person or you're asking this interview to do a job in the film that it wasn't meant to do, and you should probably look for other solutions.

The second thing to remember is that a cut on paper may not work on film. The way people speak often reads differently than it sounds. People end sentences with a question, or they run two sentences together, or they burp or sigh, or a plane flies overhead, or their energy level shifts so much that you can't cut between two bites. You do the best you can to note the big issues when you're watching rushes (the raw footage) with the transcripts in hand, but there will still be times when something that should work just doesn't.

With that said, there are a few tricks to increasing the odds that your paper cut will work. It's generally easier to cut into a hard consonant, such as b, t, or v. Words that begin with soft consonants, such as s or h, can be more difficult. Note that just because you cut the "Well" from "Well, I think it started" doesn't mean that the editor can make the excision. Usually, though, if one bite or cut doesn't work, there will be something else available that's close enough.

Whether or not you "cover" the edits with cutaways is a stylistic choice. When you cut from two different parts of an interview, especially when the focal length (e.g., close-up, medium shot) hasn't changed, the cut—known as a jump cut—can be jarring. Some filmmakers find an elegance or at least an honesty in a jump cut; there is no disguising that the material has been edited. Others "cover" the edit with a cutaway, so that the soundtrack continues, apparently seamlessly. (For example, you're on someone's face as they talk; while they're still talking, the film cuts to the person's hands, fidgeting; then to a neighbor, listening from a nearby chair; then to a clock on the wall; and then back to the speaker's face.) How long you cut away from someone before you need to see them speaking again is a matter of taste, as is the decision about how long you can hear someone's voice "over" before you show who is speaking. Sometimes, you let an interview play simply because you don't want to interrupt the answer. And sometimes, the entire interview will be voice-over (v/o), especially if the footage is all of one person and/or it's very obvious who is speaking. Effective portraits of people at work—a zookeeper, an underwater explorer—have been done this way.

Of course, editing within an interview is only one solution. You can also synthesize a story by using multiple storytellers and cutting between them, or using narration to reduce the amount of interview needed or to state concisely something with which the interviewee struggled. For this chapter, the focus is on reducing the length of the interview in a way that is consistent with generally accepted principles of documentary ethics. For example, here are some ways to shorten the interview in which Charlie discusses his friend, Sanders:

> CHARLIE: *Sanders wasn't a bad man, in fact I'd have to say he was a pretty good guy, overall, which is why nobody could figure out—~~at least I couldn't figure out—uh, what the,~~ what he was doing even thinking about embezzlement. Arrogance, I guess. Yeah. Arrogance.*

> CHARLIE: *(beginning v/o) he was just panicked about money. ~~I mean for crying out loud, this guy's got three, uh, you know,~~ (now, possibly on camera) he's got three kids and another one on the uh, on the way—maybe it got to him, I don't know, maybe he just couldn't figure out how he was going to support all these little ones or whatever, you know?*

> CHARLIE: *(beginning v/o) He was selling auto parts, used auto parts. ~~Besides, embezzlement's a white collar crime, he's a blue collar guy—well, not really, he's not working with the auto parts, he's more the manager of the store,~~ driving to work in his, oh, what was it, Tercel, his blue Tercel, shirt and tie and all the while I guess he's thinking nobody above him would miss that thirty thou.*

Depending on what your story is and where you're going with it, each of these edits might work. The first gets to the root of why Sanders did it, at least in Charlie's opinion—arrogance. The second explores a more sympathetic reason behind the crime. And the third paints a picture and gives some specific information about Sanders and his job. If you already have Sanders's wife describing him staying up late at night panicked by bills, you might not want to use version #2. If in fact he was not at all arrogant, just blindly panicked, you might not use #1. And if you find out that he drove a used BMW, you can't use #3 because it's not accurate. Your talking heads must be fact checked, and errors can't be left in simply because you, the filmmaker, didn't say it. By leaving it in, you are saying it. Note that a significant exception is when the falsehood is part of the story, as was the case with the "eyewitnesses" rounded up by law enforcement personnel in *The Thin Blue Line.*

Another problem to watch out for when condensing interview material (or any sync material, which includes footage of people talking to others on camera) is that out of context, something may honestly seem to mean one thing, but those who were on the shoot know that it meant something else. This is why it's important that someone connected with the original shooting be involved in the edit, or at least given a chance to sign off on it. Usually, the director and/or producer maintain this oversight, but cost cutting has led some venues to farm out bits of production and effectively separate the editing and packaging of a documentary from the shooting of it. When that happens, all editorial decisions are made by people with no direct connection to those filmed, which can be risky. (For the same reason, a writer or consultant who begins work on a film late in the process of editing should refer back to original transcripts and unedited footage.)

Throughout the editing process, and perhaps especially when collapsing interviews, filmmakers need to be careful to maintain accuracy. Something as simple as taking a sentence from late in the interview and putting it at the beginning might make sense for the overall film argument, but if it distorts the meaning of the specific interview, you can't do it. "You've always got to try to know when to back away from that stuff," says filmmaker Sam Pollard (*When the Levees Broke*), "not to manipulate it to such a degree that it's like a lie."

SOURCES AND NOTES

Harlan Jacobson, "Michael & Me," *Film Comment*, Nov/Dec 1989.

CHAPTER 6

Creative Approach

Give any group of filmmakers the same general *subject*—even the same general *story*—and you'll still end up with films that are very different in style, tone, point of view, focus, and more. These differences describe the *approach*: how a story is presented on screen. Is it a half-hour special or a 10-hour series? Is the tone humorous? What production elements are used, such as live shooting, recreations, a narrator, time-lapse photography, music, sound effects, or animation? Is the program produced quickly and inexpensively, or does it take a more considered approach to both content and the craft of storytelling?

Even within a subset of films, such as high-end features intended for theatrical release, the range of approaches is considerable. Consider, for example, the numerous, award-winning theatrical documentaries that explore the U.S. involvement in Iraq and Afghanistan since 2001. These include *Iraq for Sale* (Robert Greenwald), *Standard Operating Procedure* (Errol Morris), *Control Room* (Jehane Noujaim), *Taxi to the Dark Side* (Alex Gibney), *Why We Fight* (Eugene Jarecki), *The Way We Get By* (Aron Gaudet), and *The War Tapes* (Deborah Scranton).

Even when films have a similar focus (such as the Gibney and Morris films, which both look at the issue of detainee abuse), their approach may be completely different. Morris focuses on the story behind the infamous photographs at Abu Ghraib, while Gibney untangles policies and procedures that led to the death of an innocent taxi driver at Bagram. For *Control Room*, Jehane Noujaim embedded herself, essentially, inside the Al Jazeera satellite network to get a different perspective on the war than that offered by U.S. networks. For *The War Tapes*, Deborah Scranton "virtually embedded" herself in Iraq by putting cameras in the hands of National Guardsmen headed there and staying in touch through emails and instant messages. Jarecki and Greenwald both set out to look at the military-industrial complex and the dangers of war profiteering, but Greenwald's film is rapid-paced and filled with data that lacks context, resulting in an argument that seems more emotional than substantive; Jarecki's, on the other hand, feels more considered and balanced. And so on.

SGT Zack Bazzi on a radio in a Humvee, in *The War Tapes*.
Photo credit: SenArt Films/Scranton/Lacy Films.

WHEN TO THINK ABOUT APPROACH

It's helpful to begin thinking about your approach almost as soon as you come up with a subject or story that interests you. If you've become passionately interested in an eighteenth-century battle, for example, you'll need to think about how to visualize a story that occurred before the invention of photography. (Peter Watkins's *Culloden*, for example, used the style of a 1950s black-and-white television documentary to recreate and report on the 1746 Battle of Culloden.) If you want to film residents of a local group home, it's important to know what it is about the residents that interests you: following them on a week-long trip to Jerusalem is very different than filming them at home, over the course of a year, as neighbors seek their eviction. Your approach will evolve as your knowledge of the material increases and you have a better sense of what's practical, but it's good to start off with some ideas.

One way to begin the process is to screen many films and talk with your collaborators about which elements you like or don't like, and which might best serve the project at hand. Do you want to create an intimate portrait or a stylized whodunit? A historical film that uses archival footage, or one that uses recreations (or both)? Watching several films by the same filmmaker can also help you to get a sense of how style and approach change depending on the project. Conversely, you'll notice how some filmmakers bring a fairly established style to subjects chosen, in part, because they are suited to that style.

Approach involves the essence of the film itself. Suppose, for example, that you're drawn to the issue of abused, abandoned, and stray pets and what happens to them in shelters. You might decide to:

- create a journalistic piece on animal welfare that uses experts and news-style footage to explore controversial issues such as unethical breeding, the culture of "fight dogs," and the issue of euthanasia;
- create a vérité portrait of one shelter and its staff for whom these issues are part of a day-to-day struggle, as Cynthia Wade and Heidi Reinberg did in the feature-length documentary *Shelter Dogs*;
- script and narrate a film that involves a family reenacting their search in local shelters for a dog to bring into their home, and then film the process by which experts can rebuild trust and calm aggression in dogs that have been abused; or
- put yourself in the picture, with the "train" being your search in local shelters for the perfect dog, a journey that allows you to take side trips and find out more about how the dogs came to be there, how many are in shelters nationwide, and what fate they face if they aren't adopted. In the end, you either find or don't find the dog of your dreams.

As another example, suppose you know what elements you want to use for a historical film, but not how to use them. You have a collection of diaries, letters, and newspaper clips pertaining to your story, which is set in the past. You might do the following:

- Have actors read this material in voice-over as you present archival stills or footage, perhaps complemented with evocative modern-day footage.
- Have actors in period costume embody the authors of this archival material, speaking the words on camera as if in an interview. This approach can be seen in the work of Middlemarch Films, such as their production of *Liberty! The American Revolution*.
- Have actors perform the words in period documents on camera, but without costumes or makeup. This was the approach taken for the HBO film *Unchained Memories*, in which actors read the words of elderly former slaves, as documented by workers for the Works Progress Administration.

Another example: Who will tell the stories in your film? What will drive the narrative?

- In *Grizzly Man*, the narrative is driven by filmmaker Werner Herzog's quest to understand the life and work of naturalist Timothy Treadwell. In his voice-over narration and his appearances on camera, Herzog makes his presence known and at times argues against Treadwell's views about the natural world.
- In *Enron: The Smartest Guys in the Room*, the point of view is omniscient, although it's derived to some extent from the book of the same title by Peter Elkind and Bethany McLean, both of whom are interviewed on camera. The narration, read by actor Peter Coyote, is anonymous and informational. This style is the most "traditional" for television documentaries. But the use of an omniscient narrator in this film makes a lot of sense: A few title cards could never have provided the kind of detail needed for audiences to follow the enormously complex story unfolding on screen. And while the filmmaker might have cast himself as a storyteller, there is no obvious reason to do so, and a number of reasons not to. (For one, the cast of characters is already quite large: three top Enron executives, the Enron traders, various whistle-blowers, and the two journalist/book authors.)
- In the Academy Award-winning *Born into Brothels*, filmmaker Zana Briski appears on camera and speaks the voice-over narration, but she's also playing an active role in the story unfolding on screen, whose outcome she does not know when the filmmaking begins. The same setup is also true of the 2015 Academy Award-winning *Citizenfour*, as filmmaker Laura Poitras and journalist Glenn Greenwald are drawn into the events surrounding Edward Snowden's decision to leak classified documents obtained from the U.S. National Security Agency.
- *Murderball* is an example of a film that, like many documentaries, is a hybrid of vérité and other filmmaking styles. Although there is no narrator, the film is "narrated" in a few ways, including interviews (seen on screen and heard in voice-over) and text on screen (e.g., *For the first time, Joe will face his former U.S.A. teammates*). The filmmakers follow an ongoing rivalry between quadriplegic rugby teams representing the United States and Canada; they create intimate portraits of key players on the American team and of the American coach of the Canadian team; they combine footage of these top athletes in action with everyday footage— dressing, driving, dating—that rounds out our sense of them as characters; and they contrast these athletes, who have already been through physical and emotional rehabilitation following

devastating injury or illness, with a young man for whom the shock of disability is still new, so that we can appreciate the distance the players have come. There is a "no limits" sense to this film's style, including its soundtrack, and that carries through to participants' willingness to share private moments. The filmmakers play no observable role on screen.

- In some of the more popular biography series on television, the focus is less on storytelling and more on a sort of narrated "scrapbook" approach to a celebrity's life, telling the key events in chronological order and building to emotional highs and lows, such as illness, marriage, or scandal. That these films work is less a tribute to storytelling than to the audience's interest in the subject. Like family photos (which generally fascinate the immediate family but no one else), they're of interest mostly because viewers care about the celebrities on screen, not because there's a particularly strong story being told.

The decision to even *tell* stories is one of approach, along with how to tell them. Michael Ambrosino, who created the long-running PBS science series *Nova* in 1973 (which was inspired by the BBC series *Horizon*), says, "We conceived *Nova* as a series that would explore and explain the way the world worked. We would use science as a tool, but we would primarily think of ourselves as journalists looking for the stories of science." The reason for the stories? "It's not possible to make a film about the crab nebula and have you be interested in it or understand it," Ambrosino says. "It *is* possible to tell the story of the dozen or so men and women who are trying to find out what was the core of the crab nebula. And in telling their story of discovery, you had a story that was understandable."

Some films contrive situations that then unfold on screen, becoming observational. For example, Alan Berliner invited a dozen other people named "Alan Berliner" to dinner at his New York City apartment, and included footage of the event in his film *The Sweetest Sound*. Perhaps you want to include a demonstration of some sort. For a science series called *The Ring of Truth*, I was involved in arranging a sequence in which we drove a yellow rental truck 183 miles due south and charted the path of Antares at the start and end of our journey, in order to do a modern-day version of an ancient measurement of the Earth's circumference. Errol Morris filmed a teacup shattering for *A Brief History of Time*, so that he could play with the notion of it *un*shattering. (Morris also set up and filmed dominoes cascading to use as a recurring motif in *The Fog of War*. This stylized means of visualizing themes and concepts has become increasingly popular; it can be seen, for example, in the casino footage and magic act cut into *Enron*.)

There is an approach to consider for almost every aspect of your filmmaking. Will you interview people alone, together, inside, outside, formally or informally? Will the interviewer be on camera or off screen? If off screen, will the questions be heard by the viewers? Not every detail needs to be considered right up front, but, for example, if you're telling the story of a particular military unit, rather than interview members separately, there might be value in bringing them together and filming their interaction, provided it can be done in a way that feels natural. Nobody wants to see films in which one character interviews another about something they both already know: "Well, Jim, wasn't it a good thing that we invented that breathing apparatus?" "Yes, Pete; without it, many more lives might have been lost."

Former Enron CFO Andy Fastow, in *Enron: The Smartest Guys in the Room*, a Magnolia Pictures release.
Photo credit: AP Worldwide.

ARCHIVAL FILMMAKING

Say "archival films" and most people think of Ken Burns and *The Civil War*. Even though this is a great example of archival filmmaking, there are plenty of other films that use archival (or simply stock or third-party) footage and stills. Used specifically, *archival* and *stock* refer to material available from public or private archives and/or commercial vendors. Used more generally, however, these words (and the term *third-party*) describe any imagery the filmmakers didn't create themselves. Home movies, amateur videos, surveillance tapes, and footage shot for public relations, news, education, or training, for example, might generally be described as stock footage.

Third-party footage (and sound) shows up in a wide range of documentaries. *Grizzly Man* wouldn't have been possible without the footage created by Timothy Treadwell himself. *Enron* includes pivotal audio recordings of Enron traders manipulating the power grid in California, sound the filmmakers discovered in the archives of a power company in Washington State. Alan Berliner has been collecting others' family photos and home movies for years, the visual history of people whose identities are unknown to him, and he uses these eloquently in films such as *Nobody's Business* and *The Sweetest Sound*. The archival imagery in Jay Rosenblatt's *Human Remains* was selected not to tell any particular story, but because the men it captures on screen— including Mao, Hitler, and Stalin, known to history for the atrocities they committed—are seen doing disturbingly ordinary things, such as eating or playing with dogs and children.

How you use the archival material is also important. *The Civil War* used archival imagery (mostly still photographs) to illustrate and advance a powerful and thematically rich narrative. That series has also spawned a wealth of knockoffs. Take two parts archival material, the thinking seems to go, add one part emotional music and a dash of brand-name actors in voice-over, and you've got a film. The missing element, too often, is story.

With archival films, the story is often driven by narration, with visuals playing a supporting role. In rare cases, however, where sufficient archival resources exist, the visuals may drive the storytelling. This was the case with two public television histories, *Vietnam: A Television History* (about the Vietnam War) and *Eyes on the Prize* (about the American civil rights movement). Both series covered events for which extensive news footage existed, with stories covered in depth and over a significant period of time. In developing *Eyes on the Prize*, executive producer Henry Hampton and his team decided that rather than present a survey of the civil rights struggle between the 1950s and 1980s, they wanted to feature a selection of stories from within that period and let them unfold as dramas on screen. Editors on *Eyes* often had sufficient archival footage to craft complete scenes that could then be augmented with modern-day interviews (conducted by the *Eyes* producers). Narration occurred only where it was needed to seam together other elements.

Producers of *Vietnam* and *Eyes* also followed rigorous rules for the use of this archival material. An image could not "stand in" for something else, and the rules of chronology and fact-checking applied to footage just as they did to interviews and narration. This meant that if you were telling the story of rioting in Detroit in 1967, you couldn't use a great scene that you knew had been shot on a Thursday if your narrative was still discussing events on Tuesday. Care was also taken with sound effects and the layering of sound onto otherwise silent film footage. "We sent all our silent archival footage to the Imperial War Museum in London, and they matched sound effects," says Kenn Rabin, describing his work as an archivist on *Vietnam*. If the footage showed a particular helicopter or a particular weapon firing, the sound effect would be of that model helicopter or that model weapon. "We were very careful not to add anything that would editorialize," Rabin adds. "For example, we never added a scream or a baby crying," unless you could see that action on screen.

When historical stills and motion picture are used, how important is it that the images represent what they're being used to portray? This is a subject of some debate among filmmakers and historians. Producers of *The Civil War* grappled with this issue in making their series because the photographic record for their story was extremely limited. At a conference in 1993 ("Telling the Story: The Media, The Public, and American History"), Ken Burns presented a clip from *The Civil War* and then said that, with two exceptions, none of the "illustrative pictures" actually depicted what the narrative implied. "There is a street scene taken in the 1850s of a small Connecticut town, which is used to illustrate Horace Greeley's 1864 lament about the bloodshed of the Civil War," Burns offered. "There are Southern quotes over pictures of Northern soldiers. None of the hospitals specifically mentioned are actually shown, particularly Chimborazo in Richmond. . . . The picture of Walt Whitman is, in fact, several years too old, as is the illustration for Dix." Burns added, "There's not one photograph of action or battle during the Civil War, and yet nearly 40 percent of the series takes place while guns are actually going off. What do you do? What are the kind of licenses that you take?"

His question is an interesting one and still not sufficiently explored by filmmakers or the public. In the skilled hands of filmmakers who have the resources and commitment to work with a stellar group of media and academic personnel, the storytelling may override the limited imagery. But too often, substitutions are made not for historical or storytelling reasons, but because schedules and budgets mandate shortcuts. Not every image needs to be specific to time and place, of course. But if you're using archival stills or motion-picture footage as visual evidence of the past, the images you select matter.

Another problem that filmmakers encounter is that the cost to use commercial archival images (and prerecorded music, especially popular music) is often extremely high. In some cases, copyrighted music and images may be added by the filmmakers and featured in the soundtrack or on screen. But at times, music is naturally present in a scene being documented—you're filming a character as he's arrested and a radio in a nearby car is blaring the latest hit, for example. These are very different uses of music, and the rights involved are also different. Some uses are covered under the "fair use" exception to U.S. copyright law (or similar exceptions that may exist elsewhere). For more information on fair use, see American University's Center for Social Media and its November 2005 report *Documentary Filmmakers' Statement of Best Practices in Fair Use*, available online.

Lastly, there are situations in which filmmakers "create" archival materials—fake footage that seems to be news footage of the civil rights movement, or home movies of the family whose story you're telling, or promotional materials for a company or college. This is done in a number of ways, such as shooting with old equipment using old film or video stock, and/or degrading imagery so that it looks old and worn. The issue here is one of transparency. If it serves the film's story without deceiving the audience in important ways, the ethical issues raised may be answerable. Problems may arise if audiences are led to believe that what they are seeing is genuine, and therefore valid as archival historical evidence.

RECREATIONS AND DOCUDRAMA

Many filmmakers use what are known as recreations (or reenactments) to visualize events, either to augment a sparse visual record or because the recreations better serve their storytelling (and at times, budgetary) needs. There are many ways to film recreations; it's a good idea to watch a range of styles to decide which works best for your film or determine an innovative new approach. You may choose to shoot partial or impressionistic reenactments—a hand here, legs marching, a wagon wheel. Human figures may be kept in the distance, as silhouettes against a skyline, or people may be filmed close up and asked to convey emotions. Entire scenes might be played out, whether by individuals who specialize in staging actual battles from the past or by actors hired to perform for the film. Some reenactments, as discussed above, are shot in a way that makes them appear to be archival (filmed with old cameras and stock, for example). Will your actors speak, and if so, will they be limited to words derived from actual documents (such as diaries, letters, newspaper accounts, and court transcripts), or do you plan to script words—in other words, invent dialogue—for those actors? The farther the reenactment veers into invention, the closer the film moves from documentary to docudrama to fiction.

It's worth considering that if one version of an event is reenacted, the filmmakers are making a choice. A director may have actors play out a murder scene, for example, meaning that the director is portraying a single version of the event, even when other versions may be possible or the chosen version is contested. Along the same lines, whether actors are portraying Roman guards or Chinese warriors, they are standing in for the real thing, and present a compelling *visual* argument that this is how things were.

In some cases, filmmakers use reenactments not only to provide visuals but also to highlight important themes and ideas. In Errol Morris's *The Thin Blue Line*, for example, highly stylized reenactments visit and re-visit the scene of a crime in order to visually underscore the conflicting and at times self-serving testimony of purported eyewitnesses. Filmmaker Ari Folman states, in his film's official press release, that *Waltz with Bashir* was always intended to be animated. In part this was because there was limited archival footage to support the stories, but in addition, he decided that the film "could be done only in animation with fantastic drawings. War is so surreal, and memory is so tricky that I thought I'd better go all along the memory journey with the help of some very fine illustrators." In *Taxi to the Dark Side*, Alex Gibney included a highly stylized scene to depict the interrogation of Mohamed al-Qahtani, with the methods documented in a 65-page log. The scene is included in a sequence that explores the history and science of torture strategies, and forces the audience to confront the bizarre methods applied to al-Qahtani. It's shot in a way that leaves no doubt that it was created by the filmmaker for the purpose of illustration or imagination; there is no mistaking it for actual footage of the interrogation.

SOURCES AND NOTES

Information on *The Sweetest Sound* can be found at www.alanberliner.com. Information about *The Fog of War* is available at www.sonyclassics.com/fogofwar/_media/pdf/pressReleaseFOG.pdf. Discussion of *Eyes on the Prize* comes in part from my own involvement as a producer/director/writer. Ken Burns' comments on *The Civil War* in Sean B. Dolan, ed. *Telling the Story: The Media, The Public and American History* (Boston: New England Foundation for the Humanities, 1994).

Information about Maysles Films is available at www.mayslesfilms.com. Errol Morris discusses his re-enactments in "Play It Again, Sam (Re-enactments, Part One)," *The New York Times*, April 3, 2008, http://opinionator.blogs.nytimes.com/2008/04/03/play-it-again-sam-re-enactments-part-one/. The press kit for *Waltz with Bashir* is available online, at www.sonyclassics.com/waltzwithbashir/pdf/waltzwithbashir_presskit.pdf. The extras on *Waltz with Bashir* DVD include a 12-minute film, "Surreal Soldiers: Making Waltz with Bashir," which shows the process behind the film's creation.

CHAPTER 7

Close Viewing

Audiences often respond to documentary work primarily in terms of its content or issues raised. In some ways, this is a mark of success, in the same way that people binge-watching a television drama may not take the time to notice how carefully the various subplots were constructed over an entire season, or how readers of a terrific mystery novel race through the pages to find out who did it. Done well, craft should feel inevitable, seamless, and invisible. Characters are simply alive; the flow of ideas and plot feels organic; the argument seems well-built and earned.

But people who want to write novels or episodic television or documentaries need to figure out *how* that success was achieved. This chapter offers several ways to analyze documentary films as a way of letting those films' creators—the team of people behind their production—teach you themselves.

WATCHING THE FILM

What follows are some exercises for watching the film closely. You can either watch the film all the way through without stopping and then go back and start to watch more closely from the beginning, *or* you can watch closely from the start. (You'll need to view the film on a device that allows you to pause and to keep track of running time.) The benefit of starting and stopping on the first time through is that you have no preconceived notions as you pause at various points to ask questions such as: *At this point in the film, what do I think it's about? Who or what am I concerned for? What's at stake? Where do I think the story is headed?*

If instead you watch the film first without interruptions, be sure to take a moment before starting again to ask yourself some general questions such as: *What was the film's train? How did the film begin? Did parts of this film drag or seem particularly strong? What's the film's central argument?* Then, when you watch the film again more slowly, you'll have a sense of how your impressions align with or contradict what you're discovering about the film's story and structure.

The Opening Sequence

The opening sequence, beginning with the film's first frame, may be as short as a minute or as long as 10 minutes; each film is different. But in general, this opening sequence contains the DNA of the entire film to come. It sets out the promise between filmmaker and audience, making clear at least some of the film's rules of engagement, such as what the film is about, how the story will be told, with what elements the story will be told, and why it matters—why this film is worth an audience's time and attention.

The opening sequence is the first full sequence in the film, starting from the first frame. After you've watched this sequence, ask yourself some questions, such as:

- What do I think this film is about?
- Where do I think this film is headed?
- What would I say are the top three to five "bullet points" that the filmmaker has used to grab my attention and immerse me in the film, making me want to watch?

Looking at a range of opening sequences can be very useful: first, because there are common storytelling strategies achieved in the way a film opens; and second, because despite this, they can still be very different from each other, each uniquely creative.

Virunga

At the first frame of action, we enter with a group of men in uniform; it's revealed that they are part of a funeral procession. The scene is vérité; there is no text or voice-over to place us. At the graveside, a man speaks: "Protect us, and help us to account for each day of our lives." In voice-over, we hear another man: "Oh, Congo. Our dear Ranger Kaserka died trying to rebuild this country." As we leave the gravesite, the unaccompanied singing of the mourners gives way to recorded music and the film cuts (about 1:25) to aerial footage traveling low along a river. This image becomes black and white, giving way to carefully selected archival imagery, including footage, a map, and stills. Over these visuals, with the theme song continuing, the filmmakers add 13 blocks of text that gives the viewer historical and thematic context. These bring us from 1885 (*"Africa carved into colonies ruled by European nations"*) to 2003 (*"First democratic elections in 40 years."*)

At about 3:40, over a shot of people lined up to vote, the film dissolves back to an aerial over water, then tilts up to reveal mountains. A new series of lower thirds begins, over present-day footage:

- *2010: Oil discovery claimed in eastern Congo under Lake Edward in Virunga National Park.*
- *A home to thousands of people and the last mountain gorillas.*
- *2012: Instability returns.*

At about 4:40, another aerial follows a small plane over a field in which we see rangers patrolling. (The film title comes up, and then the opening sequence, including the music, ends.) The film moves into a new, second sequence.

To summarize: In less than five minutes, the opening of *Virunga* has set forth where we are, why we're there, what the problem is, and its deep historical precedent. We don't know everything, and that's as it should be. *Virunga*, like any good film, unfolds over time. It asks the audience to work as they watch, making connections, seeing irony, coming to realizations. We've seen a range of compelling, disturbing, and breathtaking footage.

In terms of film storytelling, it's useful to note that the film did not start "the beginning," with archival images and data about 1885—that would have been dull, because we're not motivated to care. It started with vérité footage of a funeral, a decision director Orlando von Einsiedel discusses in Chapter 22. The scene lasts about a minute and a half, and raises questions: In Congo, a man has died "trying to rebuild this country." Why does it need rebuilding? Why are people being killed for their efforts? Who are these men in their uniforms, carrying guns?

The aerial along the water breaks us out of the funeral scene and brings us into the historical montage, which as noted runs from 1885 to the elections in 2006. Another aerial breaks this up, which has the effect of drawing additional attention to a newer, current threat (which will turn out to be a focus of this film): the discovery of oil under Lake Edward. The montage continues, but it's more localized now, and we move closer to the communities at risk, and learn that instability has returned. This is the film's launching point.

Super Size Me

Like *Virunga*, Morgan Spurlock's *Super Size Me* packs a lot of basic exposition into the film's opening sequence, but the films are, of course, very different. In this film, at the first frame of action we see a group of children singing a song that invokes the names of fast-food restaurants, to humorous effect. For the purpose of analysis, I've broken what follows into a series of "idea" beats:

- Following a text-on-screen quote from McDonald's founder Ray Kroc, a professional-sounding narrator (who turns out to be Morgan Spurlock) tells us that "everything's bigger in America."
- In a fast-paced, fact-filled setup, he defines the problem: "Nearly 100 million Americans are today either overweight or obese. That's more than 60 percent of all U.S. adults."
- He suggests a cause: When he was growing up, his mother cooked dinner every single day. Now, he says, families eat out all the time, and pay for it with their wallets and waistlines.
- He notes a cost: "Obesity is now second only to smoking as a major cause of preventable death in America."
- About 2:00 in, Spurlock moves on to the lawsuit that inspired the film: "In 2002, a few Americans got fed up with being overweight, and did what we do best: They sued the bastards." Using a magazine cover and animation, he lays out the basics of the case, which was filed on behalf of two teenaged girls: a 14-year-old, who was 4 feet 10 inches and weighed 170 pounds, and a 19-year-old, 5 feet 6 inches, who weighed 270 pounds. Sounding astounded, Spurlock says the "unthinkable" was happening: People were suing McDonald's "for selling them food that most of us know isn't good for you to begin with."
- He then offers evidence to show that we eat it anyway, millions of us worldwide.
- Returning to the lawsuit, he highlights a statement by the judge, which he paraphrases: "If lawyers for the teens could show that McDonald's intends for people to eat its food for every meal of every day, and that doing so would be unreasonably dangerous, they may be able to state a claim."
- Spurlock seizes on this challenge but also notes a question, a theme that will inform the entire film: "Where does personal responsibility stop and corporate responsibility begin? Is fast food really that bad for you?"

At about 4:00, we see Spurlock for the first time on camera as he sets out the design of his experiment: "I mean, what would happen if I ate nothing but McDonald's for 30 days straight? Would I suddenly be on the fast track to becoming an obese American? Would it be unreasonably dangerous? Let's find out. I'm ready. Super size me." With these words, the title sequence begins, with music. A minute later, as the music winds down, the film's second sequence gets under way.

To summarize: The opening of *Super Size Me* has introduced the film's train (eating only McDonald's for 30 days), although Spurlock will lay out the specific rules as the film moves forward. It's set a visual style that's fast-paced, brightly colored, a combination of animation and live action, with Spurlock on camera as participant and voice-over as narrator. It's set up the *why* of the film: an epidemic of obesity in the midst of a world increasingly filled with fast-food offerings. At the same time, it's set up a thematic question about personal versus corporate responsibility. Is McDonald's at fault for selling unhealthy food, or are people at fault for eating it? And it asks a basic consumer's question: Is it really that bad for you, after all? The filmmaker has promised to take us on a journey and has made it clear that he doesn't have all the answers: He wants to find out, and because of the skillful way he's gotten this film going, the audience wants to find out, too.

Jonestown: The Life and Death of Peoples Temple

The opening sequence of Stanley Nelson's *Jonestown* lasts just under 2.5 minutes. The first frame we see is a fade up to a card, with white text appearing on a black background. All of the following appears on one card, but the phrases are added sequentially: *On November 18, 1978/in Jonestown, Guyana,/909 members of Peoples Temple died in what has been called the largest mass suicide in modern history.* The image fades, and the film dissolves to a small crowd, clustered together and smiling. A series of interviews are then intercut with archival footage. (The speakers are identified on screen later in the film, but not in the opening sequence, so I haven't identified them here.)

- Woman: Nobody joins a cult. Nobody joins something they think is going to hurt them. You join a religious organization, you join a political movement, and you join with people that you really like.
- Man: I think in everything that I tell you about Jim Jones, there is going to be a paradox. Having this vision to change the world, but having this whole undercurrent of dysfunction that was underneath that vision.
- Jim Jones (archival): Some people see a great deal of God in my body. They see Christ in me, a hope of glory.
- Man 2: He said, "If you see me as your friend, I'll be your friend. As you see me as your father, I'll be your father." He said, "If you see me as your God, I'll be your God."
- Woman 2: Jim Jones talked about going to the Promised Land and then, pretty soon, we were seeing film footage of Jonestown.

[Jim Jones (archival): Rice, black-eyed peas, Kool-Aid.] We all wanted to go. I wanted to go.

- Woman 3: Peoples Temple truly had the potential to be something big and powerful and great, and yet for whatever reason, Jim took the other road.
- Woman 4: On the night of the 17th, it was still a vibrant community. I would never have imagined that 24 hours later, they would all be dead.
- Jim Jones (v/o archival, also subtitled): Die with a degree of dignity! Don't lay down with tears and agony! It's nothing to death. It's just stepping over into another plane. Don't, don't be this way." The film's title comes up, and the opening sequence ends.

To summarize: This opening, like the others, sets out the promise, point of view, and style of the film to come. The opening title card is attention-grabbing, but it does something more: The film was released in 2007, which meant that for many viewers, the word "Jonestown" would immediately be a distraction as they tried to remember the details they knew about it. The text on screen helps to get that out of the way, putting a date to the event and reminding viewers of just how enormous it was. It also sets the event apart: it was the largest mass suicide in history; it's an event to be understood.

In the first interview, a woman says, "Nobody joins a cult." Other than the last speaker (an aide to Congressman Leo Ryan, who was in

Virunga National Park, from Virunga.
Photo © Franklin Dow, used by permission of the filmmakers.

Guyana to rescue church members and was killed in the violence that ensued), all of the interviewees in the film's opening sequence are former members; one is also a son of Jim Jones. Their words focus not on the mass suicide, but on the contradictions that Peoples Temple held for them, their belief in its promise and their regrets for what was lost. The opening is capped with archival audio from that last fateful day, but what lingers are questions in the audience's mind about what happened and why.

Delivering on the Promise

Now you're going to go through the entire film, slowly. The main things you're looking out for are the elements discussed throughout this book:

- What is the *central argument* being made by the filmmaker(s)?
- What *evidence* do the filmmaker(s) offer in support of the argument? Does any of it seem more or less effective?
- How is this story told? Do you see a *central narrative*—a forward moving story, or train, that makes you want to keep watching? If so, what seems to be the goal or question that's pulling you through the film, what is it you want to find out?
- Once you've identified the train, where and in what context does it return? Is it there at the film's end? Does the film satisfactorily conclude the story it promised in the opening?
- Who are the people in the film, what role does each play in the overall story? Do some people seem more or less credible than others?
- What other elements stand out in this film? For example, does something stand out in terms of lighting, editing, music, cinematography, special effects, motifs, reenactments, etc.?
- Can you identify individual sequences (akin to chapters), that have a unique focus and a clear beginning, middle, and end?
- Do you see how the ordering of these sequences also advances the overall narrative?
- Does the film's pacing feel slow to you? Does it feel dense with information? Just right?

Make some general notes, responding to the film in the way you'd respond to any movie. If it feels like it ends two or three times, note that. If it feels like it has two or three beginnings, note that. If a character feels superfluous, think about why. Do you find yourself engaged by the film, and if so, at what point(s) in particular, and why?

Identifying the Central Argument

This exercise is not unlike being asked to identify the central argument in a nonfiction article or book. This should be a sentence, rather than just a concept, and it's helpful if it's a bit specific. The central argument is akin to the theme; it's the *why* of the film. (A film may have multiple themes and argue a few points, but there will likely be one central one.)

It's possible that what you identify and articulate as the central argument may be different than what someone else sees; you just need to be able to offer specific reasons, from within the film, that you've made the choice you made. Even in the two examples below, my interpretation of the central argument may be different from that of the films' directors.

Slavery by Another Name

This is a 90-minute film that I wrote, based on the Pulitzer Prize-winning book by Douglas A. Blackmon. Produced and directed by Sam Pollard, the film looks at various forms of forced labor (peonage, convict leasing, sharecropping) that were used in the U.S. South as a means of keeping newly freed blacks subjugated after the Civil War and the end of slavery. That's the *subject* of the film. (The train was built around the presence, absence, inaction, and action of the federal government in response to this brutality.)

The film's central argument is not sufficiently described as "racism" or even "racism is bad." Better to be a bit more specific. The central argument might be articulated as: *Legally sanctioned racial oppression and the coercion of black labor in the U.S. South in the decades after emancipation brutally curtailed black advancement while allowing white southerners to make unprecedented economic gains.*

Taxi to the Dark Side

Here is an excerpt of the film description on Jigsaw Production's website: "A documentary murder mystery that examines the death of an Afghan taxi driver at Bagram Air Base, the film exposes a worldwide policy of detention and interrogation that condones torture and the abrogation of human rights." That's what the film *does*.

But the central argument of the film, I think, moves beyond this statement. In film press materials, director Alex Gibney shares a lesson learned from his father,

> that torture is like a virulent virus ... that infects everything in its path. It haunts the psyche of the soldier who administers it; it

corrupts the officials who look the other way; it discredits the information obtained from it; it weakens the evidence in a search for justice, and it strengthens a despotic strain that takes hold in men and women who run hot with a peculiar patriotic fever: believing that, because they are "pure of heart," they are entitled to be above the law.

Building on this, one version of this film's argument might be: *A global policy that condones torture and the abrogation of human rights, as evidenced by events at Bagram and Abu Ghraib, gives lie to and threatens the values of freedom and individual rights that the policy is alleged to defend.*

This isn't an easy exercise. It's worth trying to come up with the argument on your own, and then possibly comparing your argument with that of others who've seen the film, and then check out interviews or statements from the filmmakers, to see how your analysis lines up with theirs.

Identifying Sequences

In some ways, sequences are one of the most challenging aspects of documentary storytelling. The single best way to understand them is to try to identify them over the course of an entire film (or even better, several films). As discussed in Chapter 2, it might be useful to give the sequences you find a name that encompasses the unique *job* they do, as discrete chapters in the overall film. (Again, this is interpretive work; my description of what a sequence achieves may be different from someone else's.) Also, it's likely that the sequences will be easier to see and the breaks between them more clear-cut earlier in the film; once a story's well under way, sequences may be interwoven as part of an overall speed-up in the film's pacing.

As you look at sequences, consider also how the filmmaker transitions between them, whether it's through a transitional line of narration, a music or sound sting, a fade into and out of black, or something else.

Examples of Sequences

Immediately after the opening sequence of *Virunga*, there is a sequence that we might think of as "Meeting Rodrigue Katembo." The sequence follows him and others on what lower thirds describe as "routine ranger patrol, Virunga National Park, present day." They encounter gunfire, discover an illegal settlement, arrest a poacher, and set fire to the hut the poacher's been using. After a brief interlude—a shot of a gorilla, a shot of two hippos, a beautiful view of the park at dusk—the filmmakers talk with Katembo as he works on his rifle. (Watch how they intercut the footage of him with the archival imagery of child soldiers, giving us a sense that he is pointing a gun at what he is seeing, and later, as he talks about his older brother, that he is haunted by what he is seeing.) In sync and in voice-over, Katembo tells us about being recruited as a child solder; about his brother's death; about his mother's insistence that he escape to save his life. "So then I escaped the army to dedicate my life to the National Park," he says. The sequence ends about eight minutes into the film; there is transitional nature footage, and then the next sequence begins, one that we might think of as "Meeting Andre Bauma and the orphaned gorillas." And so on. In this one sequence, we've learned a bit more of the history, but we've also come to understand the backstory of a central character and to see what motivates him as he takes risks on behalf of this park.

The first sequence of *Jonestown: The Life and Death of Peoples Temple* is the opening described above. Sequence 2 is very brief (2:20–3:10), and it's just a story about Jim Jones which reveals, as the speaker says, "everything was plausible, except in retrospect, the whole thing seems absolutely bizarre." The sequence is thematic; it establishes the idea that definitions of "normal" may be fluid. The next sequence (3:10–7:08) presents the Peoples Temple in its heyday; it is a church full of song and success, offering insight into the positive community that members initially joined. From there, the music takes a somber turn, and the film moves back in time. Sequence four (7:08–13:28) is titled onscreen "Indiana, 1931–1965." The sequence moves Jim Jones from childhood to adulthood, revealing frightening character traits; it shows his discovery of the kind of religious workshop he comes to emulate; it launches a pattern of isolation, as we see his church moving to rural California to escape Indiana's opposition to integrated membership, *and* as we see Jones beginning to pull family members away from families. The next sequence begins, with the title "Ukiah, 1965–1974."

As noted, it's useful to chart sequences throughout an entire film, giving them names if possible. Keep track of how long each sequence is, and how "complete" it feels—if there is some sort of beginning, middle, and end to it. What do you learn in the sequence that you didn't previously know? What job does the sequence do? How does it change or advance your understanding of the film's overall narrative— the sequences that came before, and those to follow?

COMPARE AND CONTRAST

Another exercise that's useful is a "compare and contrast" between two or more films on the same general subject. This exercise is about really *seeing* how these films are constructed, as opposed to just deciding if you prefer one to the other. Does one version talk *at* you and the other engage you, and if so, why? Does one leave the audience with more parts of the puzzle to solve, and is that process satisfying? Does one feel more or less honest or manipulative, and if so, why? In thinking about the answers, consider also the experience of the filmmakers, the purpose for which the film was made, and the audience the film eventually reached.

WRITE A CLOSE ANALYSIS OF ONE ASPECT OF THE FILM

The MFA program I attended at Goddard College required us to write annotations of numerous creative works. These were short (just two to three pages, double-spaced) papers in which we were to make and support a focused argument about a specific element in whatever we were studying, such as a play or a novel. I found this exercise very useful, and now assign something similar to students of documentary. They provide a disciplined way to closely watch movies, and can be especially useful when it comes to documentary, where the temptation is often to respond to a film's subject matter. (After viewing *Blackfish*, for examples, students may want to write about SeaWorld or its trainers. But a film analysis requires that they respond to something about the craft; how the filmmakers presented this content.)

A good film analysis asks the viewer to consider *one* aspect of the craft, studying the film closely in order to make and support an argument about that one aspect, with evidence. You might want to figure out how a filmmaker did something that you found particularly effective, or you might want to figure out why something confused or annoyed you. You might look at a particular idea or thread that runs through a film, teasing it apart to see where and how it appears and with what overall effect.

You want to avoid writing a plot synopsis, film review (avoid adjectives and judgment), opinion piece, or film "report" (like a book report), that merely observes. For example, a *report* on Errol Morris's *The Thin Blue Line* might include observations such as: "Here, the film intercuts between the two main subjects before moving on to show a reenactment of the officer being shot. After this, the film brings viewers through the journey to discover which of the two subjects did the shooting. . . . Errol Morris presents evidence including court papers, photographs, and newspapers stories. Interviewees including police officers describe the events and the suspects." That's not analysis.

Similarly, a *review* tends to use adjectives (*powerful, blistering, boring, heartbreaking*) or make judgments. The trick is to turn the judgment into a question. For example, a review might state, "One minor blunder in the film, which detracts from its value, was that individuals interviewed by Morris (*The Thin Blue Line*) were not identified on screen." An *analysis* might ask, "What was gained by the filmmaker's decision not to identify on screen the individuals being interviewed?" Or, "Morris chose not to offer on-screen identification of his characters. By what other means do we know who these people are, in terms of their identities and connection to the story?"

It's important that these analyses adhere to a single focus. Rather than spend a paragraph looking closely at the role of reenactments, and then a paragraph looking at the use of title cards, and then a paragraph about the filmmaker's choice not to identify talking heads, it's much more valuable to take one thread or idea and look closely at it as it's demonstrated in a range of craft choices.

WATCHING FOR ACT STRUCTURE

As will be clear from some of the interview chapters, many excellent filmmakers don't consciously think about three-act structure when they make films. That doesn't mean that you can't utilize dramatic structure as *one* tool for looking closely at a completed film. You may do the math, look for structure, and discover that you can't find it. Or you may find some unexpected organization behind the film that's easily overlooked when the story is complex and interwoven. The bottom line is that you're doing this to see the film more clearly. You're looking for a pattern, for ideas, for insight.

So: Make note of how long the film is. To roughly see if you can find act breaks, generally divide the overall film by four. The first act is *roughly* a quarter of the way in, which means you look at what's happening in terms of the train at *around* that point, and if you can see a definitive end to one act that might push us into the second act. You do the same at the *midpoint* of the film (which is also the midpoint of Act Two), and then again about three-fourths of the way through the film, as Act Two gives way to Act Three. The train should reach a climax very close to the film's end, and then there is generally a short resolution. Remember: The act breaks relate to the film's central spine, its narrative train.

What follows is a breakdown of *Super Size Me*, noting both act structure and the train. You'll notice that once the train is under way, surprisingly little actual screen time is spent eating at McDonald's.

Instead, the train breaks up the rhythm of the overall film and makes it possible for the filmmaker to focus on a range of issues, from childhood obesity to the fast-food industry, resulting in a film that has been used in classrooms around the world.

Super Size Me

From first frame of action to closing credits, the film is about 96 minutes long. That means that I would expect the first act to end *roughly* around 24 minutes; the film's midpoint (halfway through Act Two) is around 48 minutes; and the third act should begin around 72 minutes.

Act One

The first act begins with the opening sequence, described earlier. After the opening titles, Spurlock spends time establishing a baseline for his own physical condition. Three doctors, a nutritionist, and a physiologist confirm that his health is excellent. They aren't thrilled by the experiment, but don't expect anything too terrible to happen in just 30 days. Roughly 10.5 minutes into the show, Spurlock adds a further wrinkle: Because more than 60 percent of Americans get no form of exercise, neither will he, other than routine walking. (This prompts a sidetrack about walking in general, walking in Manhattan, and how many McDonald's there are to walk by in Manhattan.)

At 12:03, we're back to the train as we meet Spurlock's girlfriend Alex, a vegan chef. She prepares "The Last Supper," one of a handful of chapters named on screen over original artwork. A little over a minute later, the experiment gets under way, as "Day 1" is identified with text on screen. Spurlock orders an Egg McMuffin and eats. (Here, as in several places throughout the film, he breaks up blocks of narration with musical interludes. These breaks are important; they add humor and breathing room, giving the audience a chance to process information.) In a quick scene, we see Spurlock writing down what he's eaten. We need to see this record-keeping at least once, because it's part of the experiment: The log provides the data the nutritionist uses to calculate his food intake. We then see Spurlock on the street, asking people about fast food. Interspersed at various points throughout the film, these interviews also add humor and alter the rhythm of the film, while providing a range of what are presumably "typical" responses.

Around 15 minutes into the film, standing in line at McDonald's, Spurlock expands on the experiment's rules (he talks on camera to his film crew, and also in scripted voice-over). After getting this additional exposition out of the way, he bites happily into a Big Mac (gray area—he enjoys some fast food). At 15:47, another piece of artwork, another title: "Sue the Bastards." We see Spurlock again on the street conducting interviews, this time about the lawsuit. All three of the people consulted think the lawsuit is ridiculous—which at this point in the film may also be the attitude of the audience. Spurlock interviews John F. Banzhaf, a law professor "spearheading the attacks against the food industry" and advising the suit's lawyers. Spurlock gives Banzhaf's work a bit of credibility (to counter the man-on-the-street responses) by noting that people thought Banzhaf was crazy when he was going after tobacco companies, too—"until he won." Banzhaf adds an important detail about why McDonald's is a particular target: The company markets to children.

Another man worried about the children, Spurlock says, is Samuel Hirsch, lawyer for the two girls in the lawsuit. But look at the gray area in this interview. Over a shot of Hirsch, we hear Spurlock ask, "Why are you suing the fast-food establishment?" The shot continues, unedited, as Hirsch considers, smiling. "You mean motives besides monetary re—, compensation? You mean you want to hear a noble cause? Is that it?" The lawyer seems to consider a bit longer, and then Spurlock cuts away from him, and that's the end of Hirsch's time on screen. It's funny, but perhaps more importantly, this willingness to paint various sides of the argument in less-than-flattering light is part of what makes this film engaging. Audiences have to stay on their toes and be willing not only to see complexity, but figure out for themselves what they think.

David Satcher, former U.S. Surgeon General, introduces the problem of "super sizing," which allows Spurlock (and other experts) to explore the issue of portion size. In other words, Spurlock is building an argument and letting one idea flow to the next. Finally, it's just under 21 minutes into the film and we've been away from the "train" for about five minutes, so Spurlock drives up to a McDonald's, and text on screen announces "Day 2."

Act Two

In the second act, the experiment really gets under way. Fortunately for Spurlock, he was asked on Day 2 if he wanted to super size, and by the rules he's established, he must say yes. (There might be a temptation, in a film like this, to let Day 4 stand in for Day 2, if it provided an opportunity like this. You can't. You don't need to give each day equal weight——some days are barely mentioned—and you don't need to show all meals each day. But the timeline of these meals needs to be factual, as does the timeline of Spurlock's health.) Watch how Spurlock condenses time in this scene: He starts out laughing, kissing his double quarter-pounder, calling it "a little bit of heaven." The image fades to black, and white lettering comes up: "5 minutes later." Fade up: He's still eating. (The visual point, underscored by the card and by the screen time given to the scene, is that this is a lot of food, and for Spurlock, it's an effort to eat it.) Fade to black again: "10 minutes later." Spurlock says that a "Mcstomach ache" is kicking in. To black, then: "15 minutes later." He's leaning back in his seat. To black, then: "22 minutes later." He's *still* forcing the food down. A cut, and we see him leaning out the window and vomiting. A meal that lasted at least 45 minutes has been effectively compressed into a sequence that's 2.5 minutes long.

At about 23:18, we see a new illustrated chapter title, "The Toxic Environment." Experts and Spurlock introduce the problem of "constant access to cheap, fat-laden foods" and soda vending machines, compounded by a reliance on cars. After a brief health concern on Day 3, he cuts to Day 4 and takes a detour to further compare obesity and tobacco use, including marketing to children. This sequence is followed by another "meadow" (or musical interlude), in which we see Spurlock enjoying a McDonald's play area.

At 28:21, a new chapter, "The Impact," explores the lifelong health implications, including liver failure, of obesity in children. At 30:38, Spurlock cuts to a 16-year-old, Caitlin, cooking in a fast-food restaurant. Here again, his ambivalence seems to leave some of the work to the audience. In an interview, Caitlin talks about how hard it is for overweight teenagers like herself because they see the pictures of the "thin, pretty, popular girls" and think "aren't I supposed to look like that?" As she's talking, Spurlock fills the screen with images of thin young women, until he's covered Caitlin's face. Just before she disappears, she concludes: "It's not realistic, it's not a realistic way to live."

Is Spurlock implying that Caitlin is letting herself off the hook too easily? This may be the case, because the scene is immediately followed (32:07) by a sequence in which motivational speaker Jared Fogle, who lost 245 pounds on a Subway diet, gives a talk at what appears to be a school. An overweight eighth grader argues, like Caitlin, that weight loss isn't realistic: "I can't afford to like, go there [to Subway] every single day and buy a sandwich like two times a day, and that's what he's talking about."

As if to offer a contrast, the film then cuts to a sequence about a man who did take personal responsibility for his health: Baskin-Robbins heir John Robbins. According to headlines on screen, he walked away from a fortune because ice cream is so unhealthy.

Robbins, a health advocate, runs through a litany of health-related problems involving not only his own family but also one of the founders of Ben & Jerry's ice cream. (This sequence, like the many shots in the film of fast-food companies other than McDonald's, helps expand the argument beyond one company to look at larger issues of food choice and health.)

At 35:09, it's Day 5 of the experiment. We see Spurlock ordering food but don't see the meal; instead, we follow Spurlock into his nutritionist's office, where we learn that he's eating about 5,000 calories a day, twice what his body requires, and has already gained nine pounds. Hitting the streets again (about 37:00), he asks a range of people about fast food (they like it) and exercise (only some do it).

About a minute later, Day 6 finds him in Los Angeles, ordering chicken McNuggets. This meal motivates another look at the lawsuit and McDonald's statements about processed foods; Spurlock augments this with a cartoon about the creation of McNuggets, which he says the judge in the case called "a McFrankenstein creation."

Back to the experiment, Day 7, and Spurlock isn't feeling well. Within 30 seconds, it's Day 8, and he's disgusted by the fish sandwich he's unwrapping. Less than 30 seconds later, it's Day 9, and he's eating a double quarter-pounder with cheese and feeling "really depressed." He's begun to notice not only physical but also emotional changes. The following sequence, with an extreme "Big Mac" enthusiast, doesn't add to the argument but is quirky and entertaining.

With that, we return (at 43:00) to an idea raised earlier, the notion of advertising to children. An expert offers data on the amount of advertising aimed at kids, and how ineffective parental messages are when countered with this. Another expert points out that most children know the word "McDonald's," so Spurlock—in a scene set up for the purposes of the film—tests this out, asking a group of first graders to identify pictures of George Washington, Jesus Christ, Wendy (from the restaurant), and Ronald McDonald. He also uses a cartoon to demonstrate how much money the biggest companies spend on direct media advertising worldwide.

At 46:34, we're back to the experiment: "Day 10." But once again, we leave the experiment quickly. By 47:02, a new illustrated chapter title appears, "Nutrition." This sequence doesn't actually look at nutrition, but at how difficult it is to get nutrition information in stores. As John Banzhaf argues, how can people exercise personal responsibility if they don't have the information on which to base it? At 49:20 (roughly midway through the film), we're back to the experiment, as Spurlock gets his first blood test. He now weighs 203 pounds, 17 more than when he started.

Around 50:30, a new chapter: "It's for kids." Spurlock takes the essay even wider, with narration: "The one place where the impact of our fast-food world has become more and more evident is in our nation's schools." This is a long sequence in which he visits three schools in three different states. In Illinois, the lunch staff and a representative for Sodexo School Services (a private company that services school districts nationwide) seem willing to believe that students make smart food choices, even though Spurlock shows evidence that they don't. In West Virginia, Spurlock visits a school served by the U.S. federal school lunch program. Here, students eat reheated, reconstituted packaged foods, with a single meal sometimes exceeding 1,000 calories. Finally, Spurlock goes to a school in Wisconsin, where a company called Natural Ovens provides food for students with "truancy and behavioral problems." The food here is not fried or canned, and the school has no candy or soda machines. (It's almost a shock at this point to see fresh vegetables and fruit and realize how brightly colored they are.) The behavioral improvements in the students here, administrators tell us, are significant. And, Spurlock notes, the program "costs about the same as any other school lunch program. So my question is, why isn't everyone doing this?" (56:02).

Over footage of the Wisconsin lunch line, we hear a phone interview in which the founder of the Natural Ovens Bakery is allowed to answer Spurlock's question: "There's an awful lot of resistance from the junk-food companies that make huge profits off of schools at the present time," he says. To me, this is a misstep in an otherwise powerful sequence. Unlike several of the experts who've been interviewed, this man's ability to speak for or about "the junk-food companies" hasn't been established. (I'm not saying it doesn't exist, just that it's not set here.) The information he conveys may be fact checked and 100 percent accurate, but to me, a better way to convey it might be through facts, such as how much money per year the fast-food companies actually make in the nation's public schools. (That companies resist being removed from schools is a point made, effectively, in the following scene, when the Honorable Marlene Canter talks about the Los Angeles Unified School District's ban on soda machines.)

At about 57:08—roughly 60 percent of the way through the film—Spurlock returns to the experiment. It's Day 13, and he's in Texas, home to five of the top 15 "fattest" cities in America. Day 14 finds him in the #1 city, Houston, but he quickly goes into a new sidetrack: a visit with the Grocery Manufacturers of America, a lobbying firm based in Washington, D.C. The group's vice president says the issue is education, teaching good nutrition, and teaching physical education.

It's a bit of a thin transition, but this leads Spurlock to explore the fact that only one state, Illinois, requires physical education for grades K–12. Returning to the Illinois school, he films an exceptional program, and then for contrast, shows an elementary school in Massachusetts where physical education involves running around a gym once a week for 45 minutes. At 61:00, Spurlock suggests a reason for the issue, the "No Child Left Behind" education reforms of President George W. Bush, which an expert says explains cuts to "phys ed, nutrition, health." This, in turn, motivates Spurlock to ask students in a ninth-grade health class what a calorie is. They struggle to answer—but so do six out of six adults interviewed on the street.

At 63:02, it's Day 16, "still in Texas," but in about 20 seconds, it's Day 17 and he's back in New York. We learn that the experiment is getting to Spurlock; his girlfriend says he's exhausted and their sex life is suffering. The following day, the doctor says his blood pressure and cholesterol are up and his liver "is sick." He's advised to stop. We see him talking on the phone to his mother; they're both concerned. She's afraid the damage he's doing will be irreversible, but Spurlock reassures her that "they" think things should get back on track once it's done. Act Two ends here.

Act Three

At 69:26, Act Three (and again, as with the other films, this is my analysis, not the filmmaker's) begins with a look at the "drug effect" of food, with input from a new expert, a cartoon about McDonald's use of the terms "heavy user" and "super heavy user," and an informal phone survey. Spurlock learns that his nutritionist's company is closing, and uses this as an opportunity to explore the amount spent on diet products and weight-loss programs compared with the amount spent on health and fitness. This motivates a transition to an extreme weight-loss option, gastric bypass surgery, filmed in Houston (74:03). Note that this sequence may have been filmed anywhere during this production; its placement here in the film makes sense, because things are reaching their extremes.

The stakes for Spurlock have also continued to rise, which helps to make this third act strong. At 77:33, in New York, Spurlock wakes at 2:00 a.m.; he's having heart palpitations and difficulty breathing. "I want to finish," he says, "but don't want anything real bad to happen, either." More visits to doctors result not only in specific warnings about what symptoms should send him immediately to an emergency room, but also the realization that these results are well beyond anything the doctors anticipated. But at 81:20, Spurlock is back at it: Day 22. In short order, he sets out to answer a new question that he's posed: "How much influence on government legislators does the food industry have?" He visits again with the Grocery Manufacturers of America, before finally (at 83:26) attempting to contact McDonald's directly.

These efforts, ultimately unsuccessful, will punctuate the rest of the film. Spurlock gets through Days 25, 26, and 27 quickly. At Day 29, he's having a hard time getting up stairs. By Day 30, his girlfriend has a detox diet all planned out. First, there's "The Last McSupper"—a party at McDonald's with many of the people we've seen throughout the film. Then it's off to a final medical weigh-in. Fifteen calls later, still no response from McDonald's.

Resolution

At 89:34, Spurlock is nearing the end of his film, and essay. He returns again to the court case. "After six months of deliberation, Judge Robert Sweet dismissed the lawsuit against McDonald's," he says. "The big reason—the two girls failed to show that eating McDonald's food was what caused their injuries." Spurlock counters by tallying up the injuries he's suffered in just 30 days. He challenges the fast-food companies: "Why not do away with your super-size options?" But he also challenges the audience to change, warning: "Over time you may find yourself getting as sick as I did. And you may wind up here [we see an emergency room] or here [a cemetery]. I guess the big question is, who do you want to see go first—you or them?"

Epilogue

Before the credits, the filmmakers do a quick wrap-up, including information about how long it took Spurlock to get back to his original weight and regain his health, and the fact that six weeks after the film screened at Sundance, McDonald's eliminated its super-size option. At 96:23, the credits roll.

SOURCES AND NOTES

There are several resources for close reading, including Francine Prose's *Reading Like a Writer* (New York: Harper Perennial, 2007). Information about Goddard College's MFAW program is available at www. goddard.edu/academics/master-fine-arts-creative-writing-2/program-overview/. Information about documentary box office can be found at www.documentaryfilms.net/index.php/documentary-box-office/.

PART II

Working with
Story

CHAPTER 8

Research

Good documentary storytelling, with some exceptions, depends on good research. This is true for what may seem like a surprising range of filmmaking styles. In an interview with Jason Silverman, filmmaker Alan Berliner describes working on his personal documentary *The Sweetest Sound*, in which he invites 12 people with his name to dinner: "I began where I always begin, with a tremendous amount of research, with a passion to understand the total landscape of whatever subject I'm entering." Susan Froemke and assistants at Maysles Films, the noted vérité company, spent about six months researching poverty and looking for potential stories in several states, including Wisconsin, Maine, Iowa, and Missouri, before they settled on the stories and characters of *Lalee's Kin*, filmed in the Mississippi Delta. Filmmaker Jay Rosenblatt creates unusual documentary stories from bits of old films and "found footage." In press material submitted to the San Francisco Jewish Film Festival, Rosenblatt says that it took about eight months to do the research for *Human Remains*, a half-hour film about the banality of evil. In it, he presents black-and-white footage of five of the twentieth century's most notorious leaders—Hitler, Mussolini, Stalin, Franco, and Mao—over reminiscences voiced by actors but scripted from actual quotes and/or factual biographical information.

Do all documentaries require research? No. Liane Brandon's memorable and deceptively simple film *Betty Tells Her Story*, while evoking powerful themes, began when the filmmaker heard something of interest in a colleague's story and asked her to tell it on camera. Not everything has to involve experts and advisors and location scouting. But many films, if not most, do involve research to some degree. With that in mind, here are a few suggestions.

Main and Redman, from *Lalee's Kin: The Legacy of Cotton.*
Photo courtesy of the filmmakers.

ASK QUESTIONS, DIG DEEPER

Whether you're looking for a story or finding the best way to tell it, a good film is one that surprises, challenges, and, often, informs. This means that the information going into that film needs to be surprising. All too often, documentaries just repeat information that everybody (allegedly) knows. The easiest way out of that trap is to stop and challenge yourself. "Energy equals mass"—what does that mean? The *Apollo 13* space mission—why was it named *Apollo*? "Everybody knows" that Rosa Parks was the tired seamstress who didn't feel like giving up her seat on that bus in Montgomery in 1955, right? It's a nice story, this downtrodden woman who has reached her breaking point. What if you found out that she was an active member of the Montgomery chapter of the NAACP, a group fighting for civil rights? Suddenly she's not so much a victim of oppression as an activist who sees an opportunity to fight it. You're telling better history and bringing fresh details to an old story that everybody thought they knew.

DO YOUR OWN RESEARCH

One of the problems of faster and cheaper filmmaking is that original and up-to-date research is often beyond the scope of a project's resources and budget. It's much easier for producers to rely on a few articles or books rather than explore what's new in a field, who's doing innovative work, or what a more diverse group of storytellers might add to the audience's understanding of a familiar topic. The same tired experts are approached time and again to speak about the same subjects, in part because the producers have already seen them on TV and know both what they look like and how well they speak on camera. But why tell the same story again, particularly if you could explore a newer or more complex angle?

DON'T BE AFRAID TO ASK BASIC QUESTIONS

Although you should gain a thorough grounding in your subject, you can't possibly, in a few days or even a few months, become an expert. Don't, in the interest of appearing "professional" to your advisors or experts, fake an understanding that you don't have. If you're confused, speak up. Your expertise is in knowing how to communicate a complex subject to a general audience.

DO GENUINE RESEARCH

A historian I know received an email from a company seeking what they said, at first, were "his thoughts" on the U.S. temperance movement. In the next sentence, they made it clear that what they actually wanted was his help plugging a hole: they envisioned a story of a twentieth-century trial involving a married woman abused (or murdered) by an addicted husband, a case that influenced activism, and were hoping he could identify such a case.

There are two problems with this. First, if their research (and historical advisors) were telling them that such cases played a significant role in the discussion of temperance, why hadn't multiple cases and names already been suggested? Second, although they seem to have identified the general area of this particular historian's expertise, they clearly had not read his work or they would have known that had he been asked, his expertise would have led him to suggest a different approach.

Although the resulting project may have worked out fine, what might these researchers have done differently? More homework could have led them to a clearer and more specific understanding of the issue they were trying to illustrate and to specific stories and scholars. Alternatively, if they were still fishing for stories that would illuminate the temperance movement, they might have contacted a range of scholars, whose work they had familiarized themselves with beforehand, and asked for help in identifying stories that the experts believed best represented the history, rather than vice versa.

WHEN DO YOU RESEARCH?

The amount of research you do, and when you do it, varies from project to project and depends, to some degree, on your chosen topic, your approach, and your strategies for fundraising. Some public funding sources, as well as some private foundations, require that your grant application include evidence that your film project is built on solid and current academic research. Projects that are funded "in house"—by public or commercial broadcasters directly—may be less rigorous in their up-front requirements, but producers will still need to do at least some research in order to effectively pitch their ideas and make their programs. Research generally is ongoing through the development of outlines and shooting treatments, and continues as needed until the film is complete. A flurry of fact checking often occurs in the last weeks of editing.

ADVISORS

The input of academic and nonacademic advisors can be crucial to a project. These people offer their insight and experience behind the scenes; some of them may also be asked to appear on camera as experts, if that fits the program's style. On any film that's intended to be the least bit authoritative about a subject, advisors can help tremendously by getting you up to date quickly on current research in the field and directing you to people, places, and content to be explored. They can help you to see how your film might contribute to the public's understanding of a subject and who, beyond a general audience, might be able to use the film (in classrooms, for example). It's important to seek out advisors and experts who represent a variety of viewpoints.

Good advisors—and they are often extraordinary—understand that they are advisors and you are a filmmaker, and that their job is to push for content and inclusion and yours is to try to tell the strongest and most accurate story you can. What a film can do best is excite viewers about new and complex material; it's up to library and web resources to satisfy the hunger you may create for extensive detail. You won't and can't do everything the advisors want, but if you have truly considered their expertise and understood their concerns, chances are you've found a way to address the concerns that also serves your purposes as a filmmaker.

When do you approach advisors? As filmmaker Jon Else summarizes:

> You read the ten most important and widely respected books about the subject, and then you read the two fringe books at either end of the subject. Then you do the basic primary research; you figure out who are the ten important living people and what are the ten important available documents or pieces of stock footage. And then you call the experts.

As mentioned, some of the people you'll be contacting as advisors may turn out to be people you want to interview. It's good to avoid confusing these roles initially, because what you need at first is background help. If someone asks whether or not he or she will also be asked to appear on camera, you can honestly say that it's too soon to tell.

Advisors' Meetings

On some larger-budget documentaries and documentary series, funds are raised to enable at least one in-person gathering of filmmakers, advisors, and invited experts. These meetings might take place as the funding proposal is taking shape, and maybe again as production gets under way. With *Eyes on the Prize* and other major series produced by Blackside, Inc., production began with what was called "school." Production teams, researchers, and others joined invited scholars and other experts in panel discussions that continued over a period of several days and were invaluable in setting out the work ahead. If you can afford them, in-person meetings spark an exchange of information and ideas that isn't possible when the filmmaker speaks individually to this advisor, then that one. Valuable information can result from their interaction not only with you but also with each other.

TELEPHONE RESEARCH

Some of your research, whether searching for people, fact checking, or just trying to get a handle on a subject, will inevitably be done by phone. Be as prepared as possible for these calls. Knowing as much as you can (within time limitations) about the person you're calling and his or her area of expertise will sharpen your questions and make the call more productive. Be careful to use a professional tone and respectful manner.

FACT CHECKING

Fact checking means being able to footnote your film. Any fact stated, whether by you as the filmmaker or by someone on camera, needs to be verified through not one but at least two credible sources. Even authors of highly reputable sources make mistakes, and bias (information that is unfairly skewed) and inaccuracy can be found in both primary and secondary sources. Have you ever been at a rally that seemed packed, only to hear it described on the news as a "small number" of protesters? Or sat through an afternoon in which the majority of speeches were credible and coherent, and the radio coverage featured a couple of speakers who clearly had no grasp of the issues? The reports may be factual, but they don't accurately represent the events.

Another example: A writer profiling an anti-poverty activist might point out that the activist grew up in a town that, she notes, is "a wealthy suburb of New York." The fact may be true, but 50 years earlier, the town was still quite rural and had not yet become a bedroom community for the city. And even then, the activist was from a family living well below the means of other townspeople. Yet the reporter has used factual material to create a false impression, whether intentionally or not, that the activist grew up wealthy—an impression that has a direct bearing on the portrayal of the activist's current work.

Suppose you're making a film about this activist's life. Because you're using multiple sources, you should realize that the picture being painted by this reporter doesn't match others that you're seeing. You should also be doing your own reality checks: Is it really possible that the description of a town in 2016 also applies to the same town in 1976? Furthermore, even if the majority of townspeople were mega-wealthy back in 1976, do you know that the activist's family was also wealthy?

Suppose you've pushed ahead without considering this, however, and have become attached to the idea of using the man's childhood in a wealthy town as a motivating factor behind his work on behalf of the poor. Maybe you've even talked to experts (unfamiliar with the activist in question) who explain that growing up wealthy can have this type of impact on children. So the information and motivation end up in your narration, whether they are accurate or not. This is a situation in which having advisors on your side can be invaluable. A biographer of the activist, if given a chance to read a treatment of your film or screen a rough cut, will respond to narration such as "He grew up in the wealthy community of X," and cry foul. This doesn't mean that you have to remove the fact; it does mean that you will need to put it into a more accurate context.

THE TELLING DETAIL

Facts are not just something to ensure accuracy; they can also be the lifeblood of the "telling detail" that will enrich and inform your storytelling. Facts can be a source of humor and irony; they can illuminate character, heighten tension, and underscore themes. As you do your research, begin to keep track of the details and tidbits that strike your fancy, as well as the ones that answer questions essential to your storytelling. Make sure to note the source material as completely as possible, so that you don't have to track it down again, *or* so that you could track it down again if necessary.

STATISTICS AND OTHER FORMS OF DATA

Statistics must be scrutinized and put into context. It's always a good idea, when you come across a statistic you want to use, to trace it back to its source. Suppose you find an article in a magazine that says that a certain percentage of teenagers smoked in the 1950s. Somewhere in the article you may be able to find the source of that information, such as "according to the National Institutes of Health." You should always question someone else's interpretation of raw data, meaning that if you really want to use this statistic, you need to go back to the NIH data yourself. Maybe it was x percent of all 17-year-olds who smoked, or maybe it was x percent of 17- and 18-year-olds in Philadelphia. People often misinterpret statistical information, whether intentionally or not. The interpretation may satisfy your story, but don't trust it until you can get it corroborated by someone with sufficient expertise.

CHRONOLOGIES

Chronologies are one of most helpful and least utilized tools of storytelling. A good and careful chronology, started early on, can be of tremendous benefit throughout preproduction, production, and editing. It can help you "see" your story in new and unexpected ways, and can open up possibilities for nonlinear structure while providing a key tool for ensuring that you remain honest. The level of detail and the range of information needed depend on the type of film you're creating. For a historical film, a good side-by-side chart that looks at your specific story in the context of its times can be handy. They can be created as a table in Microsoft Word, with a header row that repeats on each page. Take care as you input information; if you develop a habit of accuracy when you first note names, places, dates, statistics, and such, fact checking will be that much less onerous. It can also be useful to annotate your notes, even roughly: "Bennett p. 44," for example, so that you can return to the original source either to get more details or to check facts.

Chronology Format

There is no one format for a chronology. We did several for the six-hour PBS series *I'll Make Me a World: A Century of African-American Arts*. The initial chronology was a grid, containing 10 columns, left to right (one for each decade of the century), and then six rows down (one each for literature, theater and dance, music, the visual arts, African-American political history, and American social and cultural events). As the series developed, separate chronologies were made for each story. The lives and vaudeville careers of Bert Williams and George Walker, for example, were charted by month and year alongside events in American history.

The example shown is an excerpt from a research chronology (one page out of about 10) that puts the Miss America competition into context, at roughly a page per decade. For some projects, a more detailed breakdown is needed. To keep track of the many complicated strands of the history conveyed in Douglas A. Blackmon's *Slavery by Another Name* during its development as a documentary, I created an extensive chronology with seven headers: Date; Story; Trials; Letters/ Documents; Photos; State Law and Action; US Law and Action. The rows were broken down by year, and in some cases by months and even (during the peonage trials of 1903) by days.

As mentioned, within chronologies it's a good idea to keep track of where the information is from, even if it's in a shorthand you'll understand (e.g., "Blight p. 32") in case you need to go back for clarification or more details. But these can be rough; they're for in-house use, and are not shared with outside readers.

Why Bother with Chronologies?

A chronology helps you to keep track of a story, look for a structure within it, and find some telling details that might enrich it and prevent mistakes. A song commonly believed to have been popular among soldiers during World War I may, in fact, have been written in 1919— which a good chronology will show you is after the war's end. By listing the major events in your story in chronological sequence, you can sometimes see possible points of attack—places to begin the story— that come late in the chronology but are the strongest focus for your film. From there, you can think about what else the audience needs to know from the overall timeline and when they need to know it.

Table 8.1 This research chronology (which covered a century) puts the Miss America competition into general context, at roughly a page per decade. From *Miss America: A Documentary Film*, courtesy the filmmakers.

	U.S. History	Women's History	Social/Cultural	Miss America (story)
1920–1929	Jan 1920: 18th Amendment (Prohibition) goes into effect	August 1920: The 19th Amendment is ratified (women's suffrage)	Post-war spirit and disaffection characterizes era that will be known as "The Jazz Age"	September 1920: The Fall Frolic—which will become the Miss America pageant—is conceived by businessmen in Atlantic City. No beauty contest, but a Rolling Chair Parade and a masked ball.
		1920: National League of Women Voters is organized	"Bobbed" hair on women, symbol of political and social emancipation, popularized by film stars—Garbo's "page boy," Veronica Lake's "peek-a-boo," Louise Brooks' "Prince Valiant"	
		1921: American Birth Control League is incorporated, with Margaret Sanger as president		September 1921: The 2nd Fall Frolic includes 2-day "Inter-city Beauty Contest" in Atlantic City—16-yearold Margaret Gorman wins
			1922: Emily Post's "Etiquette" column debuts	1921: A number of children participate in the Bather's Revue—including a professional child actor named Milton Berle
			1923–28: The era of blueswomen—Ma Rainey, Bessie Smith, etc.	1923–24: Women's and religious groups protest the pageant
			1926: The "permanent wave" (hair care) is invented by Antonio Buzzacchino	1927: The powerful Federation of Women's Clubs demands that the Pageant cease
	1929: Stock market crash and subsequent economic Depression	1928: Amelia Earhart is first woman to fly across the Atlantic	1927: Al Jolson stars in first "talkie," The Jazz Singer	1928: Largest pageant to date, 80 contestants, but ongoing protest over scandal, loose morals, etc. Atlantic City Hotel owners withdraw support, and the Pageant is discontinued.

The other thing a chronology gives you is an opportunity to see the bigger picture, allowing you to offer your audience points of reference ("the Berlin Wall would come down the following month"), and a sense of the world surrounding your characters. For example, the first Miss America competition was held in 1921. Prior to that, according to scholars, beauty contests were held in the pages of America's newspapers. But this wasn't possible until the photographic halftone was invented—in 1880, I find out when I look that up. What else was happening between then and 1921? A flood of immigration and migration was increasing the ethnic and racial diversity in America's growing cities, sparking differences of opinion about what constituted an American feminine "ideal." Add to all of this the emergence of mass media and a consumer culture, and the stage is set for the first official Miss America pageant in 1921. But note the date. A year earlier, in 1920, American women had finally won the right to vote. Is this relevant? The truthful answer is, "Not necessarily." So while you can note the interesting dateline, you can't draw any conclusions about it. Cause and effect is a slippery slope; the fact that two things happen in succession does not mean there is a link. This is an excellent example of the kind of question you explore with your advisors, which is just what the production team of *Miss America: A Documentary Film* did.

Chronologies for Present-Day Films

Not every film is historical, but even a personal or diary film may benefit from some sorting through of what happened when. For example, the table shown is a fictional chronology in progress. Imagine a film in which a young man, Jeff, decides to document himself as he tracks down and perhaps reunites with a father he last saw when he was 11 years old. By the time this chronology is coming together, Jeff has begun to piece together some of his father's life after he left.

Note that not every detail is tracked, just a few key ones. Putting them in order on the page can be revealing: Lucy left Jeff's dad the same day his mom got remarried, for example. It can suggest ways of establishing time and the passage of time. Most importantly, it can help suggest nonlinear ways to tell this story. In this case, having located his dad and begun to communicate with him, Jeff decides he wants to see if he might be a match to donate a kidney. That suggests a stronger potential train than simply, "I want to reunite." Will Jeff's father accept his son's offer of a kidney? Will the son even be a match? Will his mother or someone else in Jeff's life talk him out

Table 8.2 Personal film, vérité (example; not from an actual film).

Date	Jeff/Filmmaker (son)	Father	Other
1987		Father and mother meet—first date, mother thinks it was *Moonstruck*; dad *thinks it was The Untouchables*	Microsoft releases Windows 2.0; Prozac is put on the market
January 2, 2000	11 years old; parents sit him down, dad is moving out		Y2K proved to be a lot of nothing
May 2002	Unaware that his father is remarrying	Marries Lucy	
		Began driving trucks long distance	
Fall 2003	Mom remarries	Lucy leaves Dad	
March 2005		Begins treatment for kidney disorder; loses his job soon after	
Sept 2006	Starts college		
Sept 2009	Decides to make a film about his father for a senior project		
November 2009	Tracks his father down	Father needs a kidney	

of it? In answering those questions, the film might go back through the course of these relationships, and the chronology will be a useful reference.

Take the Time to Do It Right

I've seen many filmmakers, including student filmmakers, try to rush through (or avoid) making chronologies. They'll jot down a few details that are so vague they're essentially useless: *Nineteenth century, Ellis Island opens, thousands of immigrants.* This is usually a big mistake: If you don't take a little bit of time to be more specific in the beginning, it's almost certain that you'll be taking a *lot* of time to figure it out later, going back to those same sources over and over and adding to your chronology in bits and pieces. But beyond fact checking, the chronology can be an important tool for finding, shaping, and sharing your *story* from preproduction through post.

PRINT AND INTERNET RESEARCH

The internet puts unbelievable amounts of information into your hands, but use it carefully. Keyword and subject searches on the internet are limited by your ability to come up with the right combination of words, spelled correctly (or the way they were misspelled by someone else), to find what you want, and if you don't come up with those words, you'll wind up empty-handed. Perhaps even more frustrating, web searches can—and often do—land you at sites that are not sufficiently credible. Wikipedia may be a place to start—*Waterloo, what was that referring to?*—but as a crowd-sourced site, it's not a place to stop.

Whether web-based or print, it's important that you know who wrote the material, based on what research, for what purpose and audience. Either online or at a library, you can get access to refereed journals, which are publications to which scholars must submit their work to other scholars for content review before they're accepted for publication. Even those articles, though, should be vetted and double-checked. Who is the author of that article about the effect of oil spills? Where does the author work? What other works does the author cite in the article or in the bibliography? Obviously, scholarly journals are not the same as brief blurbs in a popular magazine. Articles written for young readers are not the same as articles written for other scientists. Print material with no byline should be regarded with skepticism.

On the web, too, you want to know what person or agency is responsible for the specific information on which you're relying. Are you exploring the official site of U.S. Environmental Protection Agency, or a site hosted by a group that's politically opposed to the science of climate change? If you're not sure about a site, try to see if you can find out who created the site, who hosts it, and/or who funds it. Don't let official sounding names fool you; plenty of groups hoping to misinform you sound legitimate. You should know if the site is funded by a political action group or a progressive think tank, or if the information on which you're relying was the result of a third-grade science class or a college student's senior research seminar.

Don't underestimate the value of going to a bookstore or library for yourself. Browsing online has its benefits, but in person can be useful as well. For example, suppose you know you're interested in making a film about music, a musician, something along those lines. But what? Wander through the stacks of a library or bookstore and see what catches your eye.

Another obvious argument for library research is that you can find material, such as magazines and newspapers, that hasn't yet been digitized or uploaded to the web. And whether you're working online or in person, it's always useful not just to see the content of an old article but also the context—to see the article as it looked on the page back then. Along with your article on early twentieth-century performer Bert Williams, for example, you might see the price of shoes and mattresses at the time, read reviews of that week's popular entertainment, and look at how a mainstream paper discussed issues such as race, immigration, and gender. Best of all, not only do you get a better sense of the period, you also get ideas for visual storytelling and narrative context.

Be Organized

You'll need to keep track of the material you're citing. If you are taking notes on published text, make it clear in your notes that you are copying someone else's work. Note the source, put it in quotes, make the font purple—do whatever it takes to make sure that six months from now, you don't go back to this material, think that you've written it yourself, and incorporate it into narration, only to find out that you've lifted entire sentences from someone else. This is also true of material you cut and paste from the web. It is never permissible to use it without attribution.

A few other tips:

- *Note the source.* An article or web page that's not referenced is a waste of everyone's time. On the copy of the document itself, note the bibliographic data. It's also useful to note which library you found it in and even write down the call numbers, or the specific page as well as the website. Otherwise, you may very well find yourself having to look it up again.
- *Be sure you've got the whole article.* If you're downloading an article, photocopying it, or printing it off a microfilm reader, check to be sure that the entire piece is actually readable. If an article is footnoted, be sure you have a record of those footnotes. Often

the best research is in the footnotes, and no producer wants to ask a researcher to retrace steps.

- *Don't editorialize.* Do not, as the researcher, take it upon yourself to annotate the research you're compiling, unless you're asked to do so. Pages and pages of underlined and highlighted material can be annoying. Steer the production team to relevant passages, but let them form their own impressions.

- *Alphabetize.* Do your best to keep bibliographies in alphabetical order by *last* name; it will save you from looking up the same source more than once, by mistake, as you go down the list. In fact, alphabetical order is useful for all kinds of lists, and/or order by date, etc. (If you're alphabetizing by title, it's helpful not to include "A" or "The." As in, *Thin Blue Line, The.*)

- *Make use of file folders*, whether on the computer or on the desk, so that you don't end up with a massive stack of unsorted information. Things get messy enough quickly enough. Come up with a system, be clear about it, and keep on top of it. It will save you and your team sorting through data over and over again.

- *Give computer files relevant names.* There is nothing as useless as "France.docx," even if you think you'll remember what it is. "France_locations_scoutJan2015.docx" will tell you, six months from now, what's in that file and that it's different from "France_transcript_Henry5-17-15." A good file name is also essential if you're going to search for the file on the computer.

- *Neatness counts.* Research is a lot of work, and everybody gets tired. But you must take the time to write legibly, or at least to copy any scribbled notes within a short period of time, before you can no longer decipher them. And if you're keeping a research notebook, keep it current.

- A plea on behalf of libraries: *Never mark up a library-owned book or magazine.* Never bend the pages down, and if you must spread the book face down to photocopy or scan, do it gently.

- *Go a step further.* If you're doing research for someone else, get the material you've been asked to retrieve and then look through it. As mentioned, keep a record of footnotes if they accompany an article. But then look through those footnotes to see if there's additional material you could pick up while you're at the library. Does a more current book by the same author come to your attention? If there's a reference to a primary source within a secondary source, can you dig up the original material? Come back with these unexpected treasures and you will make the producers very happy. Primary sources, especially, tend to be wonderful finds that take more than internet digging.

- *Be skeptical of sources, internet and otherwise.* An impressive-looking history of the civil rights movement might turn out to have been produced by Mr. Crabtree's eighth-grade social studies class; a scientific-looking report on the "myths" of global warming might have been produced both by and for the oil industry. Read everything with a skeptical eye.

VISUAL ARCHIVES

Depending on the story you're telling, you may or may not need to explore what's available in terms of stills or motion picture footage in the archives, whether public (such as the National Archives in Washington, D.C.) or private (such as Corbis). Extensive visual research is most commonly done once a film is at least partially funded; the visual research becomes part of the overall research and development leading to a shooting treatment, and often continues as needed (or begins again) as the story takes further shape in the editing room. As with the print material, organization of your visual research is everything. Also remember that archival stills and motion picture footage, no less than print materials, should be subject to scrutiny in terms of its veracity and completeness. Even newsreels, which are often used by filmmakers as historical evidence, were at times heavily propagandized and even staged.

MOVING FORWARD

Research of every sort will be ongoing for most of the film's production, but there comes a point when the filmmaker has to decide that it's time to move to the next stage—production. This can be difficult: There's always more to learn, and the more you learn, the more you want everybody to know what you've found out. As Alan Berliner said about working on *The Sweetest Sound* (in the same interview that started this chapter), "one of the hardest things I had to do was let go of everything I knew—to accept that the film could not possibly contain everything I had learned about names."

SOURCES AND NOTES

Jason Silverman's interview with Alan Berliner can be read at www. pbs.org/pov/thesweetestsound/interview.php; see also www.alanber

liner.com. The Jay Rosenblatt press material and other information about the filmmaker can be found at www.jayrosenblattfilms.com. The discussion of *Miss America* comes from my own involvement with the film's development. The U.C. Berkeley Library offers some guidelines for evaluating web pages; see www.lib.berkeley.edu/TeachingLib/Guides/Internet/Evaluate.html.

CHAPTER 9

Planning and
Pitching

You've decided on the film you want to make and done enough research to determine that it seems feasible. Now what? This chapter is very broadly called "planning and pitching" to describe a range of activities that includes pitching, outlining, and casting your film.

PITCHING

A pitch is the core statement of your film's story, stated clearly and succinctly. It confirms to you and to others that you not only have a good subject, but you have a good *story*, one that you can tell in a way that will interest others. You'll be pitching your film, revising your pitch, and pitching it some more from the moment the idea begins to take shape until you are out in the world with a finished product that needs promotion. The good news is that pitching is the single best way to determine that you actually *have* a clear, coherent story as discussed in Part I of this book. If you can't pitch your story concisely—on an elevator, say, after you've discovered yourself by sheer luck riding up four floors with the head of acquisitions or a well-connected celebrity—then chances are you're still muddling through and will be spending time and money on film elements you don't need. The ability to pitch your story effectively and briefly does not suggest that it's a simple story or a commercial one; it simply means that you have a handle on it.

On Pitching Well

An ineffective pitch introduces the topic but not the story, as in "This is a film about the ethics of genetic testing and about how some people face hard choices." An effective pitch does both: "This is a film about genetic testing in which we follow an executive making the tough decision about whether to be tested for the disease that claimed her mother's life." The pitch works because it compels the listener to ask follow-up questions: What will she do if the test is positive? Will she let you follow her through the process? What if she doesn't take the test?

Here's another example of a weak pitch: "Four years ago, Vietnam veteran Martin Robinson decided he would scale the heights of Mount Whatsit at the age of 63—with one leg. He succeeded, and in the years since has inspired veterans' groups across America." Where's the story here? There *was* a story (his efforts four years ago), but unless you have some plan for telling it now, what's holding the film together? A 67-year-old man standing before various groups of veterans. Not coincidentally, the problem with this pitch is that it does not suggest a train (Chapter 4). Your train is the skeleton on which you hang your story and by which you hook and hold your viewer; your pitch articulates the train.

In other words: *If you don't have a grasp on your train, you probably don't have a grasp on your story—and you won't be able to make an effective pitch.*

With that in mind, a better version of this pitch might be: "Four years ago, Vietnam veteran Martin Robinson became the first amputee to scale the heights of Mount Whatsit. Now, he's going back—and bringing two Gulf War veterans, amputees who thought their best athletic days were behind them, along with him." Not a bad pitch, especially if you can follow it up with good access to these people and some information about your own skills as both a filmmaker and a mountaineer (to show you'll be capable of following them up the mountain). In many cases, the pitch will be even stronger if you show a tape that introduces your main characters, allowing people to see that they're appealing and will work on camera.

On some projects, producers pitch their stories at in-house development meetings, not once but several times as the film or series take shape. We did this during the planning of *I'll Make Me a World: A Century of African-American Arts*. Rather than survey a hundred years' worth of dance, theater, visual art, literature, and more, the six-hour historical series presented two or three stories per hour arranged in a way that moved forward chronologically. The century's thematic arc, revealed in our research, helped producers and project advisors decide which stories best exemplified a particular era, and we were careful to include a range of artists and art forms. Here is the pitch for one of three stories, called "Nobody" for the purpose of quick reference (but not titled on screen), that was to be included in the series' second hour, *Without Fear or Shame*:

> "Nobody" follows Bert Williams as he teams up with George Walker and they head for the Broadway stage, where they face an audience

whose expectations of black entertainment have been shaped by 60 years of minstrel traditions. Can they reject these stereotypes and still attract a mainstream audience? This story continues through the death of George Walker; we end with Bert Williams performing with the Ziegfeld Follies alongside stars including W. C. Fields, Will Rogers, and Fannie Brice—and yet, as actor Ben Vereen portrays him on stage, still facing intense racial hostility.

The other two stories in this hour were related thematically. One was about Edward "Kid" Ory and the rise of New Orleans jazz, and the other was about early filmmaker Oscar Micheaux. Each story was conceived of as having its own three-act dramatic structure. In the editing room, they were interrupted at key moments and interwoven with the other two stories, but in the planning stage, they were kept apart in order to see more clearly that they each had a beginning, middle, end, and arc. It's worth noting that this was also possible because these were historical stories to be built of archival material and interviews, so the structure could be significantly anticipated in advance. Our research, including pre-interviews, had made it clear which emotional moments we were driving toward, so that we knew which elements of an overall biography or history we wanted to emphasize and where we were driving to at the end of each act.

Pitching Out Loud

Giving a pitch in person can be tough. Too often, filmmakers load their pitches with parentheticals about all the information you need to know or they should have mentioned: "Okay, well, it's about this guy (well, okay, 20 years ago he won this amazing award for scientific research, but then he thinks someone ripped off the idea), so this guy was trying to (actually someone *did* rip him off, which sort of explains his motivation but I'm going to get into that later in the film), so this guy has been working to . . ." And so on.

The point is, if you're pitching out loud, it's a good idea to practice beforehand. Your pitch needs to be clear, focused, brief, and attention-getting.

OUTLINES

Most filmmakers go well beyond the pitch when planning their films. The next step is an outline which, like the pitch, will continue to be revised and honed over the course of production and editing. The outline is where you begin to flesh out your train, by anticipating and sketching out the *sequences* and the order in which they'll appear. If you're using an act structure, that also will be made apparent.

An outline helps you to see, on paper, the film as you imagine it. It should begin where you think the beginning of the film is, as opposed to the beginning of the underlying chronological story. It drives to key moments that you anticipate driving to, and it ends where you anticipate the film ending up. It should begin to introduce the characters, scenes, and materials you will need to tell your story.

Why Write an Outline?

An outline is both a planning tool and a diagnostic tool. It lets you see clearly what job a sequence is doing in your overall story and what storytelling role your characters are playing. If there is redundancy or if there is a gap, you will likely be able to see it on paper. Be careful to write the outline in a way that mirrors the film as it's currently envisioned, beginning to end, focusing on the film's story rather than its subject. Is the story about the expedition leader or about the group of retirees on the expedition? The parents waging a legal battle against commercialism in the public schools or the budget-starved principal actively courting soft-drink contracts?

As mentioned, the key difference between an outline and either a pitch or simply a research report is that an outline breaks your film into sequences. This helps you to clarify, in story terms, *why* you're filming one event and not another, one individual and not another. Trust me: It's worth doing. And frankly, you'll revise this outline (or sometimes, to get a fresh eye, start over entirely) before, during, and after you shoot and well into editing. As a consultant, one of the first things I do if I get involved with a film while it's being edited is to write an outline of the film that exists, which I use to help the filmmakers figure out what's working and what's not. This works because an outline can clearly show that two or more sequences are doing the same job, or that the first act runs for half the film, or that the film doesn't really get going until halfway through the second act.

What's a Sequence?

As discussed in Chapters 4 and 7, a sequence in a documentary is akin to a chapter in a book. It should feel somewhat complete by itself, but push you to the next sequence. It should add something unique to the story and the film: *this* is the sequence about force drift, *this* is the sequence about shock of capture, *this* is the sequence about "changing the rules" in the wake of 9/11. This doesn't mean that "force drift" doesn't get mentioned elsewhere, but that in one sequence in particular it will be introduced and looked at more closely. The single best way to understand sequences is to watch a number of documentaries and look closely at how filmmakers break stories into distinct chapters. Sometimes these chapters are labeled ("A Few Bad Apples" and "Shock of Capture" are examples of sequence titles in Alex Gibney's *Taxi to the Dark Side*, also discussed in Chapter 15). Even if you don't identify your sequences on screen—and most filmmakers don't—it can be useful to give them titles as you work, to summarize the unique *job* the sequence is doing in your overall film.

In watching films that don't have sequence titles, you can often identify a sequence through visual and storytelling cues. The film fades to black and then up again, for example; a sequence about getting the children to the beach and back gives way to a sequence about something completely different. A shift in rhythm, a change in music, the loud emergence of sync sound all may signal the start of a new chapter. You should also sense that the previous sequence has reached a natural end, and at the same time, it tips the overall story forward.

You anticipate and sketch out a sequence during the planning of your film by thinking like a storyteller. You "watch" the film in your head and listen to your gut. What *feels* like it should come next? What questions do you want to have answered now, rather than at some other time? What window does a character suggest opening up?

Those of you who are editors or have worked closely with editors will recognize that this is also how you often work when assembling and shaping footage into an edited film. In fact, outlines come in handy throughout the editing process. It's much easier to play with alternative structures on paper to quickly see them than it is to recut the whole film, only to find the flaw in the logic of the restructure. Does the fact that it seems to work on paper guarantee that it will work in the editing room? Unfortunately—and emphatically—no. But often, the exercise helps you and your team move toward a solution that *will* work.

Thinking about Sequences

What follows is a *very simple* version of an outline for a straightforward documentary, entirely invented for the purpose of illustration. The film is called *Zach Gets a Baby Sister*. The outline presumes that because this event was very contained, shooting was under way before the outline was written (i.e., the vérité scenes were filmed, but not many of the interviews).

Synopsis: This short video (estimated 20 minutes) follows a five-year-old boy, up to now an only child, as his entire world changes: His parents bring home a baby sister. The film views this event through the lens of childhood, and is intended to be both humorous and thought-provoking.

Sequence 1: Tease

(My first sequence will be the tease, which I anticipate being no more than 1–2 minutes long and highlighting maybe 3–5 enticing "bullet points"/highlights from the film to come, without giving the best stuff away.)

FILM TITLE: Zach Gets a Baby Sister

Sequence 2: "On the way"

Zach's getting ready to go to the hospital to meet his newborn sister. He's almost five; so far he's an only child; he's not sure what to expect, according to his parents, but they've been preparing him as well as they can. He climbs into his grandmother's car (this footage was shot) and sets out for the hospital. In the car, he talks about the baby and the fact that classmates of his have older and younger sisters and brothers. We use this discussion to cut to his classroom, a couple of weeks earlier, and the scene with the teacher talking about brothers and sisters; also, words of advice from some of Zach's classmates, vox pops. We return to the car just as it pulls into the hospital parking lot.

Storytellers in this sequence (other than Zach): his teacher, his classmates, possibly his grandmother.

Sequence 3: "Hello, baby"

We are in the hospital room with Zach's parents as they wait for Zach and his grandmother to make their way to the room. Zach's parents talk briefly about the baby, the delivery, their memories of Zach's birth. . . . Zach enters, and everybody makes a fuss over him. Then they settle Zach on his mom's bed. The nurse enters with a bundle wrapped in pink. Matt's dad is in tears as he looks at his son, and we follow his gaze: Zach taking in this odd little creature and then holding her, amazed, as she is set carefully across his lap. He is very, very serious. His mother asks if he has anything to say to her; his response is a whispered, "Hello, baby."

Storytellers in this sequence: Zach's parents, his grandmother

And so on. This is not breathtakingly good filmmaking. But something to notice: Each sequence is a chapter. Each has a beginning, middle, and end. Sequence 2 thematically is about anticipation: We see that Zach has no idea what to expect, and the primary voice in the sequence is Zach's; we also see his school and his classmates. In terms of plot, the sequence gets him to the hospital, where he's going to meet his sister.

In contrast, Sequence 3 is about Zach's parents, how they have tried to prepare him for the baby, how they have concerns. The primary voice in this sequence is theirs, whether or not the interviews are conducted in the hospital room or, more likely, at some other time. The point of view in this sequence is theirs, too, as they watch their son hold his sister for the first time. In terms of plot, this sequence begins with Zach at the hospital, and drives to him meeting his sister. In a 20-minute film, chances are good that this meeting is the film's midpoint.

Looking at these two sequences, I can anticipate what the next sequence should be. It does not need to do the job of getting Zach home that day, nor do we need to see his parents checking out (with the new baby). We can cut to the next best scene that tells the story we're telling. And our story is "Zach Gets a Baby Sister"—*not* "Zach welcomes a new baby home from the hospital."

So, for example, if the parents are planning a party, I might decide to film that. I can anticipate (and will be flexible if I'm wrong) that Zach will be excited that it's a party, and perhaps upset to discover that the attention is on his noisy, red-faced sister. This sequence would be about making adjustments, told from Zach's point of view.

Again, this is just an illustration. Take the time to look at successful documentaries and identify the sequences within them. Watch a range of films and film styles, from historical films to social issue films (compare the use of sequences in *Taxi to the Dark Side* and *The War Tapes*, for example) to traditional vérité. Sequences, also known as chapters, are structural devices that enhance, rather than limit, presentation.

How Many Sequences Should a Film Have?

There is no fixed number of sequences. If a film is 20 minutes long and your sequences run between, say, three and six minutes each, that's maybe five sequences. Also, to make your life a little more complicated, sequences sometimes have sub-sequences. You're in the midst of a sequence about a World Bank protest and you want to make a brief diversion into backstory, that's a sub-sequence. Just remember to get back to the main sequence you started, and finish it.

Historical Stories

Some funding agencies and commissioning editors require scripts—or at least detailed outlines/treatments—so that they can get a sense of the film's approach and focus. Although these are possible for any type of film, they're easier to create in greater detail for films about events in the past. For example, here is a description of the first sequence in a short, three-act story about the transformation of boxer Cassius Clay into world heavyweight champion and political activist Muhammad Ali. Because this hour-long film had three stories in it—which were not interwoven—the opening sequence (the tease) was thematic, setting up the film overall. This example, then, describes the second sequence, the first in the story of Muhammad Ali. It was written prior to filming.

Sequence: "I Shook Up the World"

We begin the first act of our first story: Olympic champion Cassius Clay challenges world heavyweight champion Sonny Liston. Rumors are spread that Clay is spending time with Malcolm X, spokesperson for the Nation of Islam. Fight promoters want Clay to deny the rumors; he refuses, and after he defeats Liston, he publicly announces his new Muslim identity: Muhammad Ali.

PEOPLE: Edwin Pope, sportswriter; Kareem-Abdul Jabbar, student; Angelo Dundee, trainer; Herbert Muhammad, son of Elijah Muhammad.

FOOTAGE: archival of Muhammad Ali, Ali with Malcolm X, the Liston fight.

Notice that people are identified by who they were at the time of the story; this is an excerpt of a sequence from *Eyes on the Prize*, in which the storytellers were witnesses to and participants in the stories unfolding. In this sequence, basketball legend Kareem Abdul-Jabbar is speaking from his perspective at the time, as a student. Angelo Dundee was Ali's trainer in this period.

Present-Day Stories

For films of events that will unfold as you shoot, it's still possible to draft an outline based on what you anticipate happening. If you intend to follow an eighth grader through a summer at basketball camp, you can do research to find out what the experience is typically like, and what scenes or sequences offer possibilities for meaningful interaction. Do the students board at the camp or go home at night? Do they tend to form close friendships? Are there one-on-one sessions with coaches? Is there much pressure from parents? Knowing these things can help you begin to think about what a sequence will *do*, as opposed to the specifics of what it *is*. If research has indicated, for example, that you want a sequence that you're tentatively calling "The end of innocence"—a sequence that looks at the commercial pressure on young phenoms—then you arrive on location with that focus in mind.

The same is true when considering the people you want to film. As you're doing the outline, you'll begin sketching in the names of people you need to tell your story, from those you "have to have" to those you'd ideally like. Sometimes, as you develop present-day or historical films, you won't know whom you want specifically, in which case they can be described. For example, "We need someone who was at the dance with her," or "We want to talk to people who keep the physical plant operating." An outline can help you see if your story or argument is building and if you have enough variety in casting and sequences, or if too much of your film is doing (and saying) the same thing. Over the course of filming, decisions about story and structure are bound to change, but for now you're taking the first steps in organizing your story into a workable film.

Whether or not your film is historical, present-day, or some combination of the two, this exercise forces you to think about your film's approach. If you want to follow a production of Wagner's *Ring* cycle, for example, will you do it, as Jon Else did, from the perspective of union workers backstage? Or would you see the production from the point of view of its director, or a children's group trying to make sense of the opera as part of their efforts to stage a condensed version of it on their own in school? Is your point the many months it takes to mount a production, or the tension of running such a grand show over the course of a day? Each *approach* decision should be carried through in your outline, so that someone from the outside who reads it will have a sense of the film that you are making: its themes, plot, point of view, arc.

CASTING

Not all documentary filmmakers would call it "casting," yet all would agree that the people you see on screen—whether they're interacting with each other, talking to an off-screen interviewer, or acting as narrator or host—need to be researched, contacted, and brought onto the project with care. Decisions about who will be filmed and what they're expected to contribute to the storytelling are important. Even the people who appear through archival means, whether in archival footage or through a reading of their letters, diaries, and other artifacts of the past, are important to the overall casting of a story. In fact, how you cast your documentary is so important that some executives want to see footage of your main characters before they'll approve or commission a project.

When to Cast

In general, you begin thinking about casting even as you're considering a topic and story to film; it's part of the conception of a film's style and approach. If there are specific people whose involvement is critical, you'll need to cast them (or at least know that they would be available and amenable) prior to your inclusion of them in any pitch. After that, casting takes shape as the outline and treatment do, and you begin to know whom or what type of people you're looking for and why.

Whom to Cast

For a film that requires experts, it's wise to cast a range of viewpoints. This means that instead of just shooting "five experts" on a subject, you know how each of the five differs from the others in expertise and outlook, offering a means of adding complexity and balance to the overall film. There are only so many people an audience can follow in a half-hour or an hour, and you don't want all of those people talking about the same issues from the same perspective.

One way to think about casting is to regard each individual who appears on screen, whether as a character you're following or as someone you interview (or both), as having a *job* to do in the overall film. Sometimes they stand in for a particular aspect of an argument; sometimes they represent an element that you could not otherwise film. For example, you could get three people to talk in general about Title IX legislation in the United States, but it might be stronger to find a lawyer who fought for its enforcement, a female athlete who got a college scholarship because of it, and an athletic director who opposed it out of fear that it would limit resources for his school's football program. They may each know a little bit or even a lot about each other's areas of expertise, but it muddies the storytelling if they don't stick to the parts of the story that they best serve.

Along the same lines, if you're creating a historical film, you might want a biographer to stand in for Martha Washington, for example. He or she would be asked to comment specifically and only on your story as it relates to Martha. Without attention being called to it, the audience will learn this cue. When they see that expert, they'll know that—in a way—Martha, or at least her proxy, is now on screen.

Do Your Homework

A significant part of casting effectively is doing some research before you start indiscriminately calling around looking for experts or "types." The less generic the casting is, the stronger the film will be.

Casting Nonexperts

Sometimes you're not looking for experts but for real people willing to give you access to lives and situations that embody themes and ideas you've set out to explore. For their production of the 2005 film *Building the Alaska Highway*, Tracy Heather Strain, Randall MacLowry, Katy Mostoller, and "an army of interns" set out to locate men who'd helped to build the highway as part of their military service during World War II. Military records about the highway's construction had been among materials burned in a fire several years earlier, making the job of finding the men more difficult. The producers wrote down any lead they got, whether from program advisors or from names mentioned in books about the highway project, a feat in which more than 10,000 workers, often working in intense cold, constructed 1,500 miles of highway in just eight months.

Once they had names, they began poring through telephone directories. The producers gave the interns a sheet of questions to ask, reminding them to address these elderly veterans by their proper names. "They would do a preliminary pre-interview, and then Randy, Katy, or I would follow up with the real pre-interview," Strain, the

A stretch of the Alcan Highway, from *Building the Alaska Highway*.
Photo: Library of Congress.

film's producer and director, says. "One of the problems was that people thought we were selling something, so sometimes we got hung up on. We had to come up with a strategy for saying *Alaska Highway* early." The storytellers chosen—a diverse group of men whose memories of that long-ago time are clear and poignant—are a strong element in the film. Strain estimates that they ended up filming interviews with perhaps a tenth of the people contacted.

On-the-Fly Casting

A popular device in television advertising these days is to put a group of young people into a car with a camera and portray them as making a documentary, apparently winging it. They pull up in unfamiliar places, shout questions to strangers, and then move on. There are circumstances in which you might want to do this, but in general, this isn't an effective use of time, unless of course it's part of a thought-out film design. In *Super Size Me*, Morgan Spurlock effectively conducts a number of these "person-on-the-street" interviews. While not a random sampling, these people seem to represent the average person and his or her knowledge of fast food, nutrition, and in one case, the lyrics to a McDonald's jingle. This can be fun and effective.

Casting Opposing Voices

How do you get people to participate in a film when it's likely that the viewpoint they hold is contrary to yours or the audience's? A primary way is by making it clear that you are open to what they have to say, intend to treat them fairly on screen, and believe that their point of view, while you might disagree with it, is important to the subject at hand and the public's understanding of it.

Don't misrepresent yourself or your project just to gain someone's cooperation. If you want to explore the notion that the 1969 moonwalk was faked, don't imply that your film is a look at manned space flight. Does this mean that you can't approach credible experts on subjects that strain credibility? No. It means that you need to bring them with you, not trick them into participating. Give them the option of adding their credibility to the project, and then use their credibility responsibly. (If you are an expert and are approached for a documentary, do some homework before saying yes. A quick web search should tell you a bit about the producer and/or the series that will be airing the interview.)

Casting for Balance

Balancing the point of view of a film does not mean simply presenting opposing sides. In fact, it almost never means that. Two opposing sides talking past each other do not advance anyone's understanding of an issue. When the opposing sides are actually very uneven, such as when a majority of credible experts takes one position and a small (and often fringe or invested) minority disagrees, then giving these two views equal time and weight creates a false impression that the issues are more uncertain than they actually are. This is not balanced; it's inaccurate. Instead, you should look for people who can offer shades of gray, complexity, within an issue.

Note that casting for balance also means letting the appropriate people present their own points of view. This doesn't mean that individuals can't speak to experiences outside their own; a French historian whose expertise is Native-American education at the turn of the last century, for example, might be well qualified to discuss life on a particular Oklahoma reservation in 1910. It's more of a stretch to ask a biology major who happens to be protesting foreign sweatshops to tell you what goes on in an overseas sneaker factory, unless you limit your questioning to a frame of reference relevant to that person: "Why am I here? I'm here because I read an article that said. . . ." If your film storytelling requires that you convey conditions in the factory, you'd be better off trying to find someone who has witnessed those conditions firsthand (as a worker or owner, for example, or as someone who toured the facilities on a fact-finding tour) and/or a labor expert who has studied those specific conditions.

As noted, when you hear someone on camera talking about "them"—for example, "The people living in government housing thought we were being unfair to them"—it's likely you need to find individuals from within that community who can speak for themselves, or experts uniquely qualified to speak on their behalf.

Genuine Casting

During the closing credits of Robert Greenwald's *Iraq for Sale*, he and his production team are shown trying to get interviews with representatives of Halliburton, CACI, Blackwater, and other companies. They state that between June 8 and August 4, 2006, they sent out 31 emails and made 38 phone calls. But listen to the phone calls, and see if you think you'd respond. The timeline is indicative: According to the filmmakers, they had not started the film before the end of April 2006, when they raised funds through an email campaign. They were finishing production by August, which leaves little time for research or the kind of relationship building that is sometimes necessary when handling complex and controversial topics.

In addition, the phone calls do not come across as questions, but rather indictments. Greenwald tells one company, "We've discovered frankly quite a bit of very troubling material," and argues, "I thought letting people know that we found something critical would be fairer than just kind of trying to sucker punch them." In letters, he writes of wanting "their side of the story," and so on.

Compare the casts of this film and Eugene Jarecki's *Why We Fight*, which was on a comparable topic. Jarecki's cast is far more diverse in terms of points of view and organizational affiliation. The difference, I think, reflects each filmmaker's approach and intent. Both films are successful, but they speak in very different ways to different (if at times overlapping) audiences.

Expanding the Perspective

It's very easy, when casting (and especially when casting quickly), to go after the people at the top, the leaders and figureheads. Often, they are known to be charismatic and articulate. But they rarely represent the whole story or, often, the most interesting part of it. Dig deeper, and ask yourself who else might add perspective to a story. If you're talking to policy experts for a film on education, you might want to explore what a second-grade teacher would add. If you're doing a film about corporate scandals, an interesting perspective might come from a real estate agent trying to sell the homes of some former executives who are now in prison.

Be careful, also, to avoid perpetuating misconceptions about gender, ethnicity, or nationality. It would be incomplete and inaccurate in today's world (or yesterday's, for that matter) to portray it as less diverse and complex than it truly is (or was). You should reflect that complexity in your casting.

Paying Your Cast

The general rule in journalism is that if you start paying for stories, people will come up with stories for which they want to be paid. Some filmmakers may decide to pay subjects indirectly, whether through buying them groceries or making a contribution to a charity. Scholars and experts who appear on screen (and are not also advisors) are not paid by filmmakers, although this is currently under debate and some new precedents are being set.

Casting Hosts and Narrators

There is a wide range in how and why people use on-camera hosts for documentary films. Sometimes a broadcaster will want the producer to use a celebrity, such as an actor, sports figure, or politician. With celebrities known to be involved in particular political, social, or health issues, for example, this can give the project added credibility. A celebrity's reputation—as a humorist, for example—can set the tone for a project. Finally, the involvement of a celebrity can help boost a project's promotion and raise audience interest.

Narrators (heard in voice-over but not seen as hosts) may also be cast for their celebrity, or they may simply be individuals with strong voices that carry, even when placed against music or sync sound. Remember that the narrator's voice also sets a tone for the film. Will it be male or female, or have an identifiable accent? How old do you want your narrator to sound? How do you want this person to come across to the audience? As an expert or a friend? Sounding humorous, somber, remote, or warm? Even an unseen narrator is part of the overall balance of voices that are heard.

TREATMENTS

Many projects, if not most, progress from an outline to some form of treatment prior to shooting. Information on what these are and how they're used can be found in Chapter 10.

Treatments and Proposals

In many cases, you will need to flesh out your outline into a more detailed *treatment*, whether to share with collaborators (to ensure that you and they are clear on the story you're telling), to run past an executive producer in order to get a "green light" (and resources) to start shooting, or to submit to a funding agency. Often, especially when submitted in support of a request for funding, these treatments are part of an overall fundraising *proposal*. This chapter talks about both of these documents, with the caveat that every situation is different. Before submitting a treatment or a proposal to outsiders, find out what form is preferred by the organization to which you're submitting.

TREATMENTS

A treatment is essentially a prose version of your film, playing out on paper as it will play out on screen. In some cases it's a short document written to ensure that the entire production team is on board with a film's story and concept. Even if it's only a few pages long, a treatment should demonstrate that the producer has a sense of the film's train and how it will be realized on screen. Even more than an outline, a treatment may be required by outsiders as a condition for providing funding. In that case, it should be polished, like a smart, high-quality magazine article. You can't expect outsiders, especially non-filmmakers, to decipher an outline, and many outsiders are also not good at reading film scripts. A prose version of your film, though, can be a strong selling tool.

What Does a Treatment Look Like?

Usually, a treatment in documentary is analogous, in form, to a treatment for a dramatic screenplay. You don't talk *about* the story: You tell it.

A treatment for an hour-long film might be five pages or 25, depending on what you need. (For some examples, see the end of this chapter.) They should be double spaced, for ease of reading, and written in the present tense—a film story moves forward in time, even if the story is set in the past. The structure of the treatment should mirror the structure of the film. If you plan to start at the grave of a soldier killed in Iraq, for example, your treatment will also start there. If the film is driving toward a meeting between siblings who only recently learned of each other's existence, your treatment should also drive to that point, and not "give away" the drama of that moment by referring to it earlier. If, in your thinking about the film, you envision a three-act dramatic structure and the reunion as being a culmination of Act Two, the reunion should probably not appear until *roughly* three-fourths of the way through your pages.

People, places, and events should be introduced in screen order (meaning the order in which you think they will appear on screen), including a description of how information will be presented. For example, if you plan a sequence about the New York City marathon, it should be clear in the treatment when and how it occurs in your film. Does it start the film, or do you drive to it? If you're going to explore the history of the marathon, will you do so with archival material, interviews, or something else? There's a bit of a balancing act involved—a treatment is *not* a script, nor is it the finished film. You are merely trying to convey not only your story but also your approach: "We take this journey with Nils, sitting with him in libraries as he searches through old microfilm, traveling with him to interview elderly relatives and neighbors. Finally, we accompany him to the Venice airport, where the meeting with his long-lost brother will take place."

WRITING TREATMENTS FOR OUTSIDE REVIEW

When writing a treatment for outside review, you need to engage readers who may not be as familiar with your topic as you are. For example, a shorthand line intended for the in-house team might read: "Washington crosses the Delaware; military historians explain; Smith reviews the mythology." More careful and detailed prose might read:

> Over Emanuel Gottlieb Leutze's famous painting, *George Washington Crossing the Delaware*, we learn through narration of Washington's triumphant crossing of the Delaware River on the stormy night of December 25, 1776. As our historians make clear, all had seemed lost for the Americans. Now, Washington and his army of 3,000 surprise Britain's mercenary forces at Trenton and capture one-third

of the men. They also gain a foothold in New Jersey that puts a halt to the British offensive. It's a decisive moment in the war for independence. We return to the painting, as art historian Jane Smith compares the history to the mythology. The painting was completed in 1851, a full 75 years after the event.

Note that this example, which happens to be for a historical film, hasn't said what images you'll be weaving into and out of between historians; hopefully by this point in the treatment, it's clear how you're handling the war history. Nor does it list all of the specific historians who'll be talking about this particular event, because by now the reader probably has a sense of which historians you've involved. You can't describe every image and every voice-over and every anticipated sync bite, or you might as well write the script. What you're doing is making the story and progression of events clear, and including the most important details: in this case, the use of the painting and the art historian. The same would be true if you were imagining a modern-day story for which you were seeking support.

Story, Not Images

Your focus is on story, not photography, which means that you don't want to spend time describing spectacular sunsets or what you're going to achieve with a helicopter mount. With that said, you can write a treatment that is (occasionally) cinematic. For example, "Work-worn fingers moving rapidly under the sewing machine seem to belong to someone other than the lively 14-year-old operating the machine." That sentence clearly is a close-up that widens out to reveal the person sewing. Or this, from *The Milltail Pack* (see sample pages at the end of this chapter): "The pack [of red wolves] is heading to a corn field just at the end of the road. In the brown, dry stalks of last month's corn live mice, rabbits and voles—tasty appetizers for the Milltail Pack." This is enough of an image to carry the reader through the exposition that follows. Using a different style, here is the first sentence of the treatment for *You Could Grow Aluminum Out There* (for the series *Cadillac Desert*): "In California we name things for what they destroyed. *Real estate signs whiz by the windshield. . . . 'Quail Meadows,' 'The Grasslands,' 'Indian Creek,' 'Riverbank Estates,' 'Elk Grove Townhouses,' 'Miwok Village.'* Before the Spaniards came, 300 tribes shared the Central Valley of California."

Note that there's a difference between writing to describe what you *know* you can see, and inventing it as if you were writing the treatment for a dramatic feature. A treatment for a dramatic feature might set a scene like this: "It's late at night. President Truman and his cabinet sit in a smoke-filled room, deliberating their next move." If this is how you're writing a treatment for a factual, historical documentary, either you're aware of stock/archival footage or stills of this scene, or you're planning to recreate it, based on historical evidence that supports your visual interpretation—who was in the room, how late at night it was, what was being discussed. In either case, it should be clear in your treatment how we'll be seeing what we're seeing. For example, "We recreate an impression of this meeting as we hear an actor reading from the president's own diary: It's late at night. He and his cabinet sit in a smoke-filled room. They are deliberating their next move." Or, "In black-and-white-footage shot by the president's niece, a young art student who happened to be with her uncle that fateful day, we see the late-night meeting, the smoke-filled room. A weary president and his staff, deliberating."

If this is a scene that you're *anticipating* for a present-day story—for example, you've gotten permission to film a corporation as it unveils a new product—then imagining a scene is permissible, if it is based on research and reasonable expectations. For example, "Our cameras accompany Heather Bourne as she strides into Gotham Towers and rides an elevator to the penthouse, where we'll see her present the new, and somewhat radical, ad campaign to the company's famously traditional board of directors."

Introduce People

You need to let readers know who people are. "Webster describes the carnage at the battlefield" is not enough for outside readers not already steeped in your subject. "Historian Victoria Webster, an expert on World War II military . . ." Then, if you don't mention Professor Webster for another 10 pages, remind us briefly who she is, for example, "Historian Victoria Webster disagrees."

Quoting People

Suppose you know whom you want to interview, but you haven't spoken with that person yet, either in a pre-interview or a filmed interview. You should never make up quotes based on what you hope someone will say, even if you have a good idea of what it might be. Instead, there are a few options for sprinkling in quotes from sources you haven't spoken with directly. First, you can simply describe what someone will be asked about, for example, "Dr. Hunter offers an introduction to photosynthesis. . . ." Second, you can quote from the individual's published writing. Third, you can quote from interviews that others have conducted with the person. However, if you do any of these, you need to be clear that you have not yet contacted the person directly, and that he or she has not yet agreed to participate in the film. You might say, "Except as noted, quotes are taken from print material published elsewhere." *Suggestion: If you decide to do this, write a version of your treatment with footnotes, so that you can go back to this source if necessary. Remove those footnotes in copies for outside review; they're distracting and unnecessary for readers who are "seeing" your film on paper, not reading a research report.* Another possibility would be, "We have gained the cooperation of Dr. X and Reverend Y, but have not yet spoken with Mr. Z and Dr. P, who are also quoted here." In any case, quotes should be used sparingly. This is your treatment, not your script.

Unknown Information

Even the most polished treatments are written before all of the pieces are in place; you don't know what you'll discover during the film shoot or what terrific visuals you'll find in somebody's attic. Most importantly, it's often the case that you're writing the treatment to raise money to do necessary research; you're doing the best you can with the resources you have, but you know that there's a lot more you need to learn before you can go out to shoot. One solution is to acknowledge these gaps by describing, in general terms, types or scenes that you believe you'll need. For example, "A trainer describes what it's like to work with thoroughbred horses and takes us through the paces of an early-morning workout." Or, "We are searching for an expert in queuing theory who can apply his or her theoretical work to the design of amusement parks, and we will find parents who know from experience that there is a limit to how long their children, and they themselves, are willing to wait in line."

Reflect the Work You've Done

Surprisingly, one of the most common problems I encounter when reviewing treatments intended for outsider readers (in particular, funding agencies) is that a treatment will seem to be based on an afternoon's worth of research, when in fact the filmmakers have spent weeks or even months on the project and, in some cases, have shot a significant portion of the footage. Your treatment should sell your project and play to its strengths. Add the details that will make your efforts show. For example, "In an interview filmed last May on the steps of her home in Leeds, author Celia Jones offers her perspective on the housing crisis." Or "Our crew follows Mr. Smith down spiral stairs leading to a dusty basement filled with old newspapers, magazines, and a rare collection of photographs that he offers to show us." Provide enough detail to make it clear that you know your subject inside and out, even if you also know that there is a lot more you need to learn.

Tell a Good Story

An important trick of writing treatments is to convey your passion early on. You think you've found an excellent subject for a film—convince the reader. A good story, well researched and well told, goes a long way. As someone who's reviewed proposals, I can say from experience that many submitted treatments are little more than research documents, or, even worse, ideas that haven't progressed much beyond a basic topic. Treatments that attract attention are those that set up and deliver a compelling story, one that's informed by research and enlivened by something different—an unusual perspective, a new angle, unique access to people or places.

Tell a good story as best you can. Then run your treatment past someone who knows nothing about your movie, and preferably is not related to you, so that you get impartial feedback before you send your material to the people you're likely to need most at this stage—financiers.

THE SHOOTING TREATMENT

A shooting treatment, if you create one, is the culmination of your work prior to shooting. If you did a treatment to raise development and scripting funds, a shooting treatment reflects the research and creative thinking that those funds enabled. Usually, a shooting treatment is for use by the filmmaking team; if a preliminary treatment got you some development funds from a commissioning editor or executive producer, a shooting treatment may be required to get the go-ahead to head out into the field with a crew. It's the baseline guide to the elements you need to tell the story that you anticipate telling, a document that can be shared (as discussed by Boyd Estus in Chapter 11) with cinematographers, sound recordists, and others to help ensure that opportunities aren't missed.

SCRIPTS

Documentary scripts tend to evolve over the course of production. In the case of programs that are significantly driven by narration, the script may begin to take shape during preproduction, only to be significantly revised and rewritten during editing. In the case of scripts driven by character voice-over, or entirely composed of sync, a script may be derived from what is essentially a transcript of the finished film, in which case the "script" refers to the storytelling of the overall film. See Chapter 12 for more details.

Scripts for Fundraising

Some funding agencies require a "script" as a condition of granting production money. If you are already editing, you will be able to submit a draft of your script in progress. If you are still seeking funding for production, however, what you submit may be more akin to a very developed treatment or a document that is part treatment, part script. As mentioned, I find that for many reviewers, a treatment that adheres to the description above—meaning that it is not a research report, but clearly presents on paper the film as it will appear on screen—may be more effective as a "script" submission. When in doubt, always consult with the person requesting the materials. (Better yet, ask if they have samples of successful proposals and use those as models.)

TREATMENTS AS A CLASSROOM EXERCISE

The exercises in Chapter 7 are set up to help readers deconstruct and understand the craft choices made by filmmakers. For students, it can also be really useful to ask them to make some of these choices themselves. One low-stakes way to do this is on paper only, assigning them to outline and then write a treatment for a documentary that they won't actually film.

There are a few ways to do this. One is to assign a good, long-form narrative nonfiction article, one that's well structured, with a hook, a train, and a reasonable amount of complex supporting information, such as historical or scientific detail. (This can also be useful for demonstrating that the basics of good narrative storytelling cross genres.) Ask the students to work individually or in small teams to come up with a different narrative structure, one that doesn't simply mirror the article, in order to tell the same story on screen. They need to identify a clear train and sequences, drafting a story that would motivate audiences to want to keep watching while also creating opportunities for building in the article's more complex information.

It's interesting to see how many different approaches and points of view students take on their own. Alternatively, a point of view and preferred story train can be assigned. So, for example, students all read an article about the 1851 uprising in Christiana, which tells the story of a stand-off involving runaway slaves, one that led to violence and ultimately a trial. Some students might be assigned to create a film that follows the story of the runaways; others might follow the story from the point of view of the slave-owner, coming to reclaim his runaways; others might be asked to structure the film around the trial. Each resulting outline, no matter the train, still needs to find ways to incorporate the balance of the article into the film—details about the Fugitive Slave Act of 1850, for example—but the points where the detail is motivated will be different.

If you're reading this book on your own, and not with a class, this is still a useful exercise. Find a good, long, narrative nonfiction article about a subject that interests you. It should be a well-crafted, authoritative, long-form authored piece like those you'd find in *The New Yorker*, *The Atlantic*, or *Smithsonian*. First, read the article closely not only for its content, but also to see how the content is shaped. Then, see if you can come up with three completely different but equally valid approaches to telling that story on screen. (Identifying multiple approaches can also be a useful strategy when you're in the midst of developing or even editing a film. As an exercise, see what happens if you choose a completely different point of view—or come up with a few options. At minimum, it may help you to see new possibilities in the train you're working with; you might also discover a stronger version of the film you want to make.)

A Semester-Long Project

A more complex version of the exercise above is to spend a semester researching and writing individual treatments (maybe 15–25 double-spaced pages, roughly, on paper only) for an hour-long documentary film. Because of time constraints, this is much easier to do if the students start by choosing an authoritative, well-written secondary source that is already narrative and that is focused on the subject of the student's film. For example, a student wanting to do a treatment about Mary Mallon, the woman known to history as "Typhoid Mary," might work with historian Judith Walzer Leavitt's book *Typhoid Mary: Captive to the Public Health*. This book would prove much more useful as a source for the student than would a general history of public health in the twentieth century, or a brief *New York Times* obituary of Mary Mallon, or a webpage about Mallon. (In fact, this book was the basis for director Nancy Porter's *The Most Dangerous Woman in America*, which aired on the PBS series *Nova*.)

Generally, I also ask students to use at least one additional secondary source and a couple of primary sources, but for the most part this is not a research exercise: it's a creative writing assignment. The challenge is to find a compelling way to turn the nonfiction material into a film that can appeal to a general audience without losing its rigor. In a classroom setting, it's useful to have a common set of ground rules (style, length, etc.), and to assign this work in graded stages (e.g., pitch, revised pitch, summary and outline of secondary source, chronology, film outline, revised outline, first draft treatment, revised treatment, final treatment).

Additionally, the assignment works well in a workshop environment, rather than with each student interacting only with the instructor. As invested as all of us get in our own topics and research, it's useful to see problems and strengths in a pitch or outline that we *haven't* written: to see in someone else's work what happens when a film takes too long to get under way, or there's no hook, or it's just a series of "and then this happened, and then this, and then . . ." There's also a value in developing the skills needed to give and receive constructive feedback.

PROPOSAL WRITING

As discussed in Chapter 9, some funding agencies require outlines, treatments, and/or scripts as part of a request to them for support. In most cases, these are submitted as part of a fundraising *proposal*. With the caveat that fundraising is an area of expertise beyond the scope of this book, what follows are some tips for addressing the questions often asked by funders in their requests for these proposals. As it turns out, the process of thinking these questions through, and answering them, is often very helpful in the kind of planning that can strengthen storytelling.

What's a Fundraising Proposal?

Proposals are the documents you submit in order to request funding from grant-making agencies, whether public or private. In general, the following are stages at which financial support might be available prior to the completion of your film: planning, scripting, production, postproduction, and finishing. The first two fall under the category of "development" and can be difficult funds to raise. The easiest, arguably, are finishing funds, which are awarded at or after the rough cut stage. At that point, the financier can see your film, there are few surprises, and there is a higher likelihood that you'll be able to complete the project. There are also sources of funding for public engagement, teacher training, website development, and other related endeavors.

Before offering an overview of the information that funders tend to want, be aware that every proposal you write should be tailored to the funding agency you've identified. It's very easy to get caught up in what you need, and forget that when it comes to funding, it's more about what they're looking for. It's up to you to honestly determine if there's a good fit between the two, and then to make a clear argument so that the connection is easy for the funder to see.

Each funder has its own guidelines. Some may want an initial letter of inquiry; others will have online forms to be filled out or will expect a 25-page narrative. Some may also want a sample reel, which is not covered in this book. In terms of print material, they may want some or all of the following.

Nature of the Request

Who you are, what your project is ("a 90-minute program to be shot on digital video on the history of the can opener and its impact on American cuisine"), how much you're requesting at this time from this grant maker ("$X,000 for scripting" or "$XXX,000 for production of one hour of this four-part series"), what activities are to be supported for the amount requested, and what the end result of the grant will be. (For example, if you ask for a scripting grant, you should end up with a script or, in some cases, a production-ready treatment.)

Introduction to the Subject

A general grounding in the subject matter to be treated on film. In other words, this is not your film treatment and does not have to include detail about how you will treat the subject on screen. It's an overview of the subject, presented clearly and concisely, and written in a way that will hopefully bring the reader to share your conviction that the subject is interesting, relevant, and worth a commitment of resources.

Rationale

A more focused opportunity to convey the significance of the project and, in particular, its relevance to the financier. Another way to look at it is, "Why this project now? How will it advance public understanding and awareness of the topic? Why is it useful for this topic to be presented on film? In what way will audiences be served by this project?" A few carefully chosen facts often speak volumes when making the case for a film.

Goals and Objectives

What your project is designed to accomplish. There will be a handful of these; for example:

Goal: *To explore the historical context in which Title IX legislation was originally passed and the inequalities it sought to address, and to evaluate the law's impact, intended and unintended, in the context of current efforts to repeal it.* **Objective:** *Viewers will better understand the complexity of Title IX legislation beyond the issue of school sports, and appreciate the social and political processes by which legal change is brought about.*

Related Projects

What other films have been made on the same or related subjects? How does their success (or lack of success) inform your approach to your story? How does your story build on or differ from these projects? As mentioned previously, the fact that a topic has been covered is not necessarily a deterrent, given all the different ways a topic can be treated and the different venues available. But you should demonstrate that you know what's out there.

Ancillary Projects

These are sometimes also called "related projects," which makes for confusion. An ancillary project is something that you're developing to bolster your film's shelf life and reach. These might include web-based materials, radio broadcasts, material for educational outreach, and/or material for community engagement, which uses media as the catalyst for action and discussion within and between community groups. At a time when the television landscape is cluttered with choices, including documentary choices, it's becoming increasingly important to financiers, especially those who support public television programming, that you demonstrate ways in which you will extend the impact of a broadcast.

History of the Project

Some information on how the project got under way and on the financial or institutional support you've received to date. Your passion for the project and your connection to the story are likely to come through here, because this is where you tell people how you got involved in the project, why the story appealed to you and/or seemed vitally important to tell, and what you've done, so far, to tell it.

Audience and Broadcast Prospects

Information on your target audience(s) and how you intend to reach them.

Organization History

Information about the organizations involved in submitting the proposal, including the production company and possibly the fiscal sponsor. As elsewhere, you may want to highlight those areas of your expertise that mesh with the interests of the potential financiers.

Project Staff

Information on the media team and academic advisors (where appropriate). If you or your media team aren't experienced in the kind of production you're proposing, consider taking on other team members who will add to your credibility. If it's your idea but your first film, figure out what you need to get out of it, personally and professionally, and then determine what you might be able to give up in the interest of getting it made. It's very difficult to get anything funded these days, so you need to do what you can to be competitive. (Alternatively, if you can afford to do so, you might work to get farther into the production before requesting funds, so that you have a film in progress that demonstrates your ability.)

Plan of Work

A detailed description of the work that will be done, and by whom, with the funding requested. Be sure that this plan of work doesn't exceed the scope or length of the grant period; if you're asking for scripting money, your plan of work generally shouldn't continue through production and editing (check with the individual agency).

Appendices

Résumés, letters of commitment, research bibliography, lists of films on this or related subjects, description of materials to be used, if appropriate. For example, for a film that will rely on archival footage, a list—even a preliminary one—of archival materials pertinent to the subject should be included.

Treatment

Many financiers want to see some form of written treatment in order to consider a request for scripting or production funds.

Budget

Financiers often want to see a breakdown of how you'll spend the money you're asking them to provide. They're also likely to want to see your entire production budget, to get a sense of how funds will be allocated overall.

A Few Extra Pointers

Much of the advice for proposal writing can be applied to the entire production, including the editing. From my own experience as a consultant and proposal writer and my experience as a proposal reviewer, here are a few tips:

- *Accuracy is important.* It's standard practice for potential sponsors to send proposals out for review by people who know the subject well. If you spell names incorrectly, get titles and dates wrong, or misrepresent factual information, it will (and should) be held against you. The proposal and the quality of work that goes into it are indicative of the film to come. Besides, the fact checking you do now, if filed carefully, will be useful later.
- *Do not invent what appears to factual material.* I've encountered proposals in which the writer either invented or augmented quotes from scholars. This immediately raises flags, because it indicates that someone asking for significant money to create a documentary program is unaware of basic ethical guidelines. You don't put words in people's mouths; you don't invent sources; you don't make up statistics. (As when writing a treatment, if you want to give the reader an impression of a talking head and you don't have actual interview material from which to draw, you talk about what you'll ask. "Dr. Adams will be asked about her efforts to restore habitat essential to the . . .")
- *The storytelling matters.* The people reviewing your proposal, whether they're scientists, historians, mathematicians, or teachers, are as aware as you are that audiences don't watch a film because the topic is important; they watch because they're interested in a story. So while reviewers will be on guard to see that you don't cut academic corners, they'll also be checking to see that you know how to attract and hold an audience's interest.
- *Good writing goes a long way.* Beyond the basics of spelling and facts, the proposal should present a coherent argument that flows from paragraph to paragraph. Be concise. Your readers are

likely to be plowing through several proposals, and you don't want to trip them up with writing that's unedited, unclear, or ungrammatical.

- *Be your own first audience.* Ask yourself if you'd be interested in the film you're pitching, and if the answer is no, work on it some more.
- *Anticipate resistance.* If you are going to propose a history of the American soap opera as a way to look at important themes in American cultural and social history and women's history, be prepared for the reviewer whose first instinct is to laugh. Get some experts on your side and, with them, make your case. Answer the naysayers with solid research. Producers have gotten funding for films on all sorts of subjects that might not, at first glance, have seemed "suitable."
- *Arm people with what they need to know in order to understand your proposal.* A producer can sometimes get so close to a topic that he or she forgets that other people aren't immersed in the subject and may need either to be reminded or introduced to key characters and events. Assume that your audience is smart, but seed information throughout your proposal in a way that brings readers along with you. A one-page overview chronology can be useful, for example, or a brief summary of a particularly difficult scientific concept.
- *Passion is important.* It comes across in the presentation of a proposal in subtle ways, but mostly it shows in the quality of the work—how thorough the groundwork was, how creatively the ideas have been transformed into a story, and how well that story is presented on paper.
- *Avoid overproduction.* Teachers are known to be wary when they receive papers with fancy, multicolored covers that clearly took hours to design and execute, because they doubt the same effort went into the actual paper. The same is true of proposals.
- *Avoid unfounded hyperbole.* "This is the most amazing story that the XYZ foundation will ever help to produce, and nothing that XYZ has done to date will have the kind of impact this film will have." This kind of language is always a turn-off for readers.
- *Avoid paranoia.* "While we are pleased to share this proposal with you, we ask that you keep it in strictest confidence as we are certain that others would grab this idea the minute they got wind of it." Foundations keep proposals in confidence unless or until they are funded and produced.

WORKSHOPPING PROPOSALS

Once you've identified potential sources of funding, you might ask if they can send you samples of successful proposals, or see if examples are posted on their website. Some agencies will share, others won't.

Another suggestion, whether you're in school or out, is to create a workshop-like setting for proposal writing. Ask workshop members (or friends/colleagues) to share examples of successful proposals, and study them closely, making sure to go back and see what the original guidelines were so that you can see how the proposal followed them. It's useful to look closely at how a successful proposal was constructed. At what point, for example, does the filmmaker state what he or she is requesting, and for what purpose? How detailed is the budget? And so on.

It's also useful to read and respond to each other's works in progress, along with links or handouts so that they can help you to evaluate the source of funding, what they're looking for, and how effectively you've answered their questions and positioned your project in terms of their interests and mandates.

SAMPLE PAGES FROM DEVELOPMENT MATERIALS

In the pages that follow, I've included some sample pages from treatments created during the development of for programs that have since been broadcast. The treatment for *Getting Over* (an hour of the six-part series *This Far by Faith*), for example, was part of the materials submitted to funding agencies including the National Endowment for the Humanities. Every project is different; these are just examples.

SOURCES AND NOTES

For a discussion of artistic license with fictionalized drama based on real events, see for example Linda Seger, *The Art of Adaptation: Turning Fact and Fiction into Film* (New York: Henry Holt & Co., 1992).

Not fact checked/interview subjects not confirmed   4

ACT I, THE CENTRAL VALLEY PROJECT

FIRST CAUSES

In California we name things for what they destroyed.

Real estate signs whiz by the windshield...."Quail Meadows," "The Grasslands," "Indian Creek," "Riverbank Estates," "Elk Grove Townhouses," "Miwok Village."

Before the Spaniards came, 300 tribes shared the Central Valley of California...Maidu, Miwok, Patwin. A few weeks of flooding each winter fed the great marshes and seasonal lakes, but for most of the year—the seven month dry season when Indians moved to the cooler surrounding foothills—the Great Central Valley got, and still gets, less rain than North Africa. It was the American Serengeti.

Spanish maps.

Richard Rodriguez, or perhaps Maxine Hong Kingston or Jesse De La Cruz pick up the story.

The wet winters and dry summers unique to California had gone on for a hundred thousand years before Europeans came. A rich, complex ecosystem had evolved with such intelligence that the great condors, elk, delta smelt, cougars and bunch grass could survive in the natural cycles of drought and flood. Each carried genetic information for the next generation to thrive in arid land, and the next and the next. Bidwell saw 40 grizzlies in a single day, and Central Valley salmon ran in the millions. Muir, standing on a hill south of San Francisco looked 100 miles east toward the Sierra and saw "...a carpet of wildflowers, a continuous sheet of bloom bounded only by mountains."

---

[1] Program produced, directed, and written by Jon Else; page 4 of 40, episode three of *Cadillac Desert*, broadcast as *The Mercy of Nature*. © 1995 Jon Else, reprinted with permission.

<u>HOUR THREE:</u> *Getting Over* (1910–1939)

Tell me how we got over, Lord;
Had a mighty hard time, comin' on over.
You know, my soul looks back in wonder,
How did we make it over?

Tell me how we got over, Lord;
I've been falling and rising all these years.
But you know, my soul looks back in wonder,
How did I make it over?

"How I Got Over" (gospel song)

<u>THE PRESENT</u>:

"Where is hope? Hope is closer than we know!" declares the Reverend Cecil Williams, pastor of the Glide Memorial United Methodist Church in San Francisco.

> I want you to know this morning that this is Bethlehem! The rejected are here. The wretched of the earth are here. Poor folks, rich folks, middle-class folks. You can be yourself here. You don't have to run from yourself here. You don't have to put yourself down here. You can embrace love here. Where is hope? Hope is here! Amen!

Glide Memorial Church in the Tenderloin district of San Francisco, an area of tenements, crack houses, and shooting galleries, lies at what Rev. Williams calls "the intersection of despair and hope." Williams took over the church in 1966, when the congregation included about 35 people, nearly all of them middle-class whites. Today, it has 6,400 members and a reputation, as *Psychology Today* reported in 1995, as "an urban refuge for the spiritually disenfranchised…a faith steeped more in heart and soul than in scripture."

Powerful and influential visitors like Oprah Winfrey and President Bill Clinton speak of Glide as a model religious institution. Poet Maya Angelou, a parishioner for nearly 30 years, calls it "a church for the 21st century." Glide is San Francisco's largest provider of social services, offering recovery centers for substance abusers, domestic-violence workshops for batterers and victims, anger management classes for youth, job skills and computer training for the unemployed or those wishing to further their education. Its tradition of outreach is a hallmark of African-American religion, especially as it developed in the decades following the Great Migration.

3-3

On a Sunday morning, we watch as Rev. Williams evokes the past in his demands for the future:

> Faith and resistance are the fuels that power the train of freedom and transformation....
> The train of freedom and recovery chugs on daily. Claim your place on this train. The
> freedom train is passing you by. Catch it. Then listen. Listen carefully. Those on the
> train are singing. Can you hear the voices of a New Generation? They are singing and
> shouting with unchained abandon. Lift your voice, raise your fist. You sing, too.

We will return to Glide throughout this program, as its ministry informs the historical events in this hour.
For now, we cut to:

THE PAST:

A train rushes by, seen in grainy black-and-white footage reminiscent of the early years of this century. A
woman can be heard singing softly, unaccompanied, as if comforting a sleeping child on board: *Plenty of
good room, plenty of good room in my Father's kingdom.* A few cars back, we catch a glimpse of a
window, the curtain drawn. Inside, a man's hand sets words to paper:

> I am writing on board a Jim Crow car...a horrible night ride.... Why does the negro
> leave the South?... You feel a large part of that answer on this train...and share for one
> night the longing of the people to reach the line...which separates Dixie from the rest of
> creation.

<u>Everyone Is Welcome</u>

The third hour of THIS FAR BY FAITH begins with the onset of the greatest internal population shift to
have yet occurred in the United States. In 1910, more than 90% of African Americans live in the South.
Between the turn of the century and 1930, nearly two million will make their way north in a mass exodus.
They are "led as if by some mysterious unseen hand which was compelling them on," reports Charles S.
Johnson, an African-American sociologist in Chicago at the time. A group of nearly 150 Southerners,
crossing the Ohio River, a divide "between Dixie and the rest of creation," kneels together and prays.

3-4

---

[i] Treatment written by Sheila Curran Bernard and Lulie Haddad; episode three of THIS FAR BY FAITH, broadcast as
Guide My Feet. © 1998 Blackside, Inc., reprinted with permission.

Sample treatment, *The Milltail Pack*[i]

The Milltail Pack

At the edge of a dirt roadway which runs along a thick wooded area, three red wolves appear as dusk begins to fall. The leader of the pack is an old male in his twilight years with a thick auburn coat and a long nose. Though he's not as fast as he used to be, his gait remains quick, his eyes and ears alert. Close behind are two noticeably smaller wolves. They are siblings, a male and a female just turned three years old. The pack is heading to a corn field just at the end of the road. In the brown dry stalks of last month's corn live mice, rabbits and voles–tasty appetizers for the Milltail Pack.

At nine years old, the aging male is raising, in all probability, his last offspring. He's seen a lot of change over the years, and he's survived to tell the story of how a species on the brink of extinction came to be saved by a handful of dedicated humans and a branch of government. Known to biologists at the Alligator River National Wildlife Refuge in North Carolina as #331, this old male is living proof that predators and people can live together and flourish. The only remaining red wolf that was born in captivity and reintroduced into the wild, his life parallels the timeline of a unique government initiative.

In 1980 the red wolf was declared biologically extinct–in the wild. In answer to this, the US Fish and Wildlife Service implemented the Red Wolf Recovery Plan–an all-out effort to save the species using captive wolves. This was the first re-introductory program of its kind for any carnivore in the world! Against overwhelming odds and after countless setbacks, the program has managed success.

In 1987, a red wolf breeding pair was reintroduced into the Alligator River Wildlife Refuge, and by the next year their first litter of pups was born in the wild. Since then wolves have been introduced on three island sites, three wildlife refuges, a national park, and a number of privately-owned properties in North Carolina, Tennessee, and South Carolina. But it wasn't easy. The recovery plan had to insure genetic diversity, hope the wolves tolerant of people in a captive setting would shy away from them once wild, and enlist public support for reintroduction of a predator in their neighborhoods. And the ultimate goal of the plan, not yet realized, is to have a total population of 220 wild red wolves.

Today there are about 70 wolves living in northeastern North Carolina, and all but one were born in the wild. Number 331 and his brother, 332, were released when they were just under one year old. Running together they sought out a home range that was occupied by a resident male. They killed the wolf and began consorting with his mate, 205. Together the young males shared the area with 331 mating with 205 and 332 taking up with 205's daughter. But 332 was killed by a car leaving 331 the leader of the Milltail Pack. Like gray wolves, red wolves mate for life, but 331 lost his first mate several years ago. He then mated with his step daughter, 394, who was mother to the siblings he takes hunting today. Last year, she died leaving him without a mate and the youngsters without a mother.

The Milltail Pack ranges through farmlands, wooded areas, public roadways and along the banks of Milltail Creek in search of food. They mainly eat white-tailed deer, but their diet also consists of raccoons and small mammals like rabbits and mice. Similar to gray wolves, they tend to shy away from people and stay close to woodlands or farm edges that provide cover. In their home in North Carolina the habitat ranges from farmland to wooded areas including marshy wetlands, and even a military bombing range!

Before becoming extinct in the wild, red wolves populated the southeastern United States, but as man began clear-cutting areas for wood, drainage and farms, wolves and men came into closer contact. Fear and misunderstanding led to indiscriminate killings and bounties. In addition, as coyotes adapted stretching their habitat from western states into the southeast, they interbred with red wolves, threatening the wolves' genetic purity.

The Milltail Pack has lived through the successes and failures of the Red Wolf Recovery Plan and now stands on the threshold of a new debate. Can man use this program as a model for other species and can we learn from our mistakes? Despite the success of such re-introductory programs, there will always be opponents of predators. In 1995, gray wolves were reintroduced into Yellowstone National Park and today their fate is questionable because opponents to the reintroduction have waged a court struggle to have them removed. In North Carolina opponents to the Red Wolf Recovery Plan still threaten to shut down the program with lengthy court battles. Last year 11 Mexican wolves were released in Arizona after 16 years of planning, and today they are all dead—most were shot by angry ranchers. For conservationists and biologists these programs represent a chance for society to learn from our mistakes. Without the existence of top predators, prey animals go unchecked and often overpopulate areas. And not only is it important to save wolves because of their role as predators, but they are a leading symbol of wild nature.

Because red wolves were virtually extinct until 1987, little was known about their behavior. But biologists are learning that their social structure, feeding and breeding habits are similar to gray wolves. Ten years after reintroducing the first red wolves into the wild, their numbers are growing—evidence of their adaptability, strength and stamina. The leader of the Milltail Pack has survived to sire 4 litters and he and his offspring have a unique story to tell.

Wolves have been in the news for the past few years and are a hot topic. But little has been said about the red wolf or this recovery project. Most of the national press has focused on the gray wolves and their reintroduction to Yellowstone. While there has been regional press about the Red Wolf Recovery Plan, this film is the first documentary to offer an in-depth look at these beautiful animals and the circumstances that have brought them back into the wild.

Film Approach

This film offers an opportunity for a rare glimpse into the lives of a fascinating species, and the film's goal is to tell a success story. Using the Milltail Pack we'll chronicle the program from the early days of life in captivity, move to life today in the wild, and finally speculate about the future of the recovery program and these amazing animals. We have access to footage of wolves in captivity, footage of animals being released, and filming in the wild today. {In order for the biologists to monitor the health and movements of released wolves, most of the animals are radio collared which makes it easy for us to locate packs and differentiate between them.}

This film will take the viewer on an odyssey of survival through the eyes of an aging red wolf. Filming will include captive animals at the Alligator River National Wildlife Refuge, wolf capture and tagging, wolf release, and behavior of family groups in the wild. In addition, interviews with biologists who have been working in the program for 11 years as well as area farmers and townspeople will help illustrate how these wolves came to be accepted on both private and refuge land and how they've managed to survive. While the focus of the film is the red wolf, we'll round out the piece with a look at what's happening to the Mexican wolf and the grays in Yellowstone.

---

[i] Treatment written by Holly Stadtler; film broadcast on EXPLORER WILD as *America's Last Red Wolves.* © 2000 Dream Catcher Films, reprinted with permission.

CHAPTER 11

Shooting

Shooting with the story in mind means being prepared to get all the visuals you need to tell the story you think you want to tell, and being prepared for those surprises that are likely to make a good documentary even better. Who shoots, how, and with what, depends on a host of variables. Are you shooting on your parents' farm or in the middle of a political campaign in a foreign country? Is the event you're covering something that happens every day, or is it a once-in-a-lifetime opportunity? Are special skills or equipment needed to get the shots you need?

CREW SIZE

The actual configuration of a documentary crew can vary widely. At one end of the spectrum, a filmmaker as renowned as Spike Lee might set out with the kind of crew more likely to shoot a Hollywood feature than an independent documentary. Sam Pollard, who edited and co-produced *When the Levees Broke* with Lee, says:

> Normally when you shoot a doc, it's you as the producer, camera, an assistant (if you're shooting film), sound, and maybe a production assistant. But when we flew out of Newark the day after Thanksgiving [in 2005], it was Spike, me, a line producer, three cameramen, four assistants, and six graduate students from NYU. Then, when we got to New Orleans, we got a location manager with his four location people, five vans, five drivers, a camera loader—I mean, it was like an army.

Filming the spectacular footage of birds crossing exotic skylines in *Winged Migration* took five teams of people, according to the film's press material, including 17 pilots, 14 cinematographers, and the use of "planes, gliders, helicopters, and balloons." (The DVD's bonus material includes a look at how this film was made. Most significantly, birds were raised from birth by humans upon whom they imprinted, and their flight is actually in pursuit of the "parent" bird riding, with a cinematographer, in an ultralight airplane. In some cases, birds were transported between locations.)

At the other end of the spectrum are two- and even one-person crews. In general, working alone is not ideal, although there may be situations in which a project or scenes of a project can benefit. In making their film *So Much So Fast*, for example, Steve Ascher and Jeannie Jordan worked as a team, with Ascher shooting. But Ascher says they discovered that when Jamie Heywood (who'd been diagnosed with ALS) was alone with one or both of his brothers, "it worked out better if it was just me alone. If we were both there, Stephen's focus would get split." So Ascher shot these scenes alone, eventually wearing a mic as he engaged the brothers in conversation.

Jon Else, who has served as a cinematographer on hundreds of films, says that with "very few exceptions," a minimum of a two-person crew is the way to go. "Working as a one-person crew involves such incredible compromise, you only have so much brain power, you only have so much muscle power," he explains.

Are you under significant time constraints? Vérité filmmaker Susan Froemke had just one day in which to film the making of the cast album for the Broadway hit *The Producers*, and her work could not interfere with the album's production. "We could have used four cameras, but we only had the budget for three—two in the recording studio and one in the control room," Froemke explains, adding that she hired

The aftermath of hurricane Katrina, from *When the Levees Broke: A Requiem in Four Acts.*
Photo credit David Lee, 40 Acres & A Mule, courtesy of HBO.

three very experienced vérité shooters, Bob Richman, Don Lenzer, and Tom Hurwitz. She added, "You had to go in with people who are also filmmakers in their own right, because you couldn't be everywhere at once and there was almost no way to have a communication system because it would interfere with the recording process."

SHOOTING WITH THE STORY IN MIND

You want to go into the field with a clear sense of your film's story and approach so that you can maximize the quality and impact of what you get, and so you'll be better able to recognize and take advantage of those moments you couldn't possibly have anticipated beforehand.

Some films require more visual planning than others. As mentioned, watch the "making of" documentaries on the DVDs for *Winged Migration* and *March of the Penguins*, about the challenges of making those films. Read interviews with Nathanial Kahn as he discusses *My Architect*, and how important it was to him that his footage capture the power of the buildings that his father, a world-renowned architect, had designed. Each film demands its own type of preparation.

Thinking Visually

Will your film be dependent on interviews and narration, or can scenes and sequences be played without sound and still convey story? With live-action filming, unless a member of the core team is shooting, the best way to ensure visual storytelling is to involve your cinematographer and not to simply use him or her as a "shooter." Being able to frame images beautifully is not the same thing as being able to frame *meaningful* images beautifully. Boyd Estus, a director of photography whose credits include the Academy Award-winning *The Flight of the Gossamer Condor*, has shot both documentary and drama for broadcasters such as the BBC, PBS, Discovery Channel, and National Geographic. When a documentary producer calls him about shooting, Estus always asks to see an outline or treatment in advance, something that gives him an idea of the big picture—not only what's being filmed, but also why.

In cases where a crew is filming an event, the sound recordist, too, should be in on the story, in part because he or she is often better able to anticipate, through listening to the conversations of key players who've been miked, where the action is going next. "They often will hear things that nobody else hears," Estus says, adding that when he shoots vérité, he also wears a headset so that he can hear the radio mikes directly. This can pay off in unexpected ways. For example, Estus worked on a series called *Survivor, M.D.*, which followed seven Harvard Medical School students over a period of several years as they became doctors. He was filming a student assisting in a heart operation when the patient, an elderly man she'd grown close to, died. Estus watched as the student walked off by herself, to the back of the operating room.

"By then, I knew her well enough to know she would have trouble [with the loss]," Estus says, and because he was wearing a sound monitor, he could hear that she was crying. He stayed in the distance but continued to film as the senior surgeon approached the student and consoled her, but also reminded her that as a physician, she had to balance her own feelings with the family's need for her professional guidance. She nodded, and together the doctors went to speak with the patient's family. Since the story was about the making of a doctor, the emotion shown by the tears was important, but not as important as the lesson—another step on the road to becoming a physician. The moment feels intimate despite the fact that Estus stayed several feet away (he shot the scene handheld until a tripod was slipped underneath the camera as it was rolling). "Normally I'm right on top of people, especially for that kind of shooting," he says. "But I didn't want to break the spell. And also, I felt the perspective was appropriate, the two of them meeting." Estus notes that, although at times like this he can be afraid to move a muscle for fear of interrupting the moment, at other times he's proactive in ensuring that he gets the coverage he wants.

What you shoot and how you shoot it involves more than simply documenting an event; it's a way of contributing to the story. "Think about what the scene is supposed to say, as much as you can, both before it and during it," says Steve Ascher, who coauthored *The Filmmaker's Handbook* (with Edward Pincus). He adds that the same applies "to the broader structure, in terms of how you go about deciding what to film, how much of it to film, and whom to film." In many cases, you may be filming a scene or sequence without knowing exactly how it will come out or how the overall story will ultimately be structured. "But you should be asking yourself, what seems important, who's compelling, how might the story be structured?" Ascher says. He notes that first-time filmmakers often have trouble projecting ahead like this. "They haven't done it enough to think about, *what is a narrative spine, what is structure, how will scenes get distilled?* They tend to overshoot and at the same time not shoot in a focused way that makes themes emerge."

If your crew understands what your storytelling needs are, they can help when the unexpected occurs. When Karin Hayes and Victoria Bruce left Colombia after their first shoot for *The Kidnapping of Ingrid Betancourt*, they left their second camera, a small digital recorder, in the care of their Colombian cinematographer. (His own camera had been stolen during the kidnapping, and they wanted to be sure that if anything important happened, such as Betancourt's release, he would be able to film it.) Unexpectedly, Betancourt's father died, and the cinematographer's brother covered not only the funeral but also the visit of Betancourt's two children, who'd been sent for safety to live with their father (Betancourt's ex-husband) in France. "That was the only time they were back in Colombia," Bruce noted. "So it was great that we'd left that camera there." The funeral sequence is one of the film's most powerful.

SHOOTING WITH THE EDITING IN MIND

It's important that footage be shot in a way that it can be edited. There needs to be sufficient coverage to give you options, and to let a scene play. You are not shooting news, where one shot per scene might be enough. Think of shooting your documentary the way you would shoot a dramatic feature: Within any given scene, you want wide shots, medium shots, close-ups, and cutaways, making sure that shots are long enough and steady enough to use. You want to be able to create visual scenes that give context and other story information. For example, if someone is talking or performing, you want shots of the audience, to let viewers know where the speech or performance is directed and how it's being received. You'll want exteriors of the performance space—is it a vinyl-sided church in the middle of a rural area, or the Kennedy Center in Washington, D.C.? You'll want identifying markers, if they exist: the marquis, a handwritten sign introducing the speaker, a cutaway to a program. You want to see what people are looking at, the angles at which they see each other, their points of view as they look at the world. (Look at *Murderball* for an excellent example of this; the film was frequently shot from the point of view of those in wheelchairs.)

Note that you're not randomly shooting everything possible; you're making sure that you have visual information that conveys basic narrative information: what, where, how. You want to establish the time, place, and people, looking for visuals that might let you cut back on verbal information. Look for the telling details that reveal character, whether it's the cigarette burning untended or the pile of liquor bottles in the recycling bin. Look for shots that show how people behave in relationship to each other and how skillfully they handle the tools of their work. You might want to look for humor. And as mentioned, you need to be sure that you have a sufficient range of angles, shots, and cutaways that your editor can condense hours of material into a final film that tells a coherent and visually satisfying story.

Cinematographers try to "cover scenes to leave as many storytelling options as possible open," Jon Else says. "I have kind of written on the inside of my eyelids a list of basic storytelling shots that I have to have coming away from a scene, about a half dozen shots." These include the widest possible angle of a landscape or cityscape, a proscenium shot in which all the figures involved in the action are in the frame and large enough that their faces and actions can be seen, several angles on any process being filmed, and close-ups "on every single face of every person, both talking and not talking."

If there's a sign saying, "Joe's Orchard" or "The Henry Ford Motor Company," Else says, you want to get a "nice picture of the sign, preferably one picture with something happening in the foreground or background and one picture without anything happening." If there are time markers such as clocks, you want to get a shot of them. "A lot of it's cliché stuff, and 90 percent of the time you don't use it," he says, "but that one time you need to show that time has passed, the clock is invaluable." And finally, he notes that you want to be sure to shoot simple indicators of direction. "If you're next to a river," for example, "you want to make sure that you get a shot that's close enough that you can see which way the current's going."

For those who shoot in film, the cost of stock and processing seems to mandate careful shot selection. Ascher, who shot *Troublesome Creek* (1996) on film and *So Much So Fast* (2006) on digital video, says:

Wendy, Alex, and Stephen Heywood, from *So Much So Fast*.
Photo courtesy of the filmmakers.

I used to joke that there should be a dollar counter in the view-finder instead of a footage counter. In film you're really thinking ahead about each camera move, how you can it cut with the others, what will it mean. "I'm now doing a close shot, I'm now doing a move from character A to character B." People who learn to shoot with video often shoot more continuously, and it's a real problem. They don't stop the camera, they're not thinking about where shots begin and end, and sometimes that results in uncuttable footage.

Shooting Scenes

On location, as in the office and the editing room, film storytelling means thinking not only in terms of shots but also scenes and sequences. "We're trying to make scenes, because we're trying to make nonfiction films . . . just like a feature film director makes a film," explains Susan Froemke, one of the leading vérité filmmakers in the United States. "I've got to get cutaways, I've got to get an end point of the scene, and I've got to get into the scene some way."

Froemke says that with observational filmmaking, it's not unusual to miss the beginning of the scene. "Often you're sitting waiting and something happens and you just miss that first line," she says. Froemke and Albert Maysles were in Mississippi filming *Lalee's Kin* when they discovered that Lalee was very upset, but they didn't know why. Froemke and Maysles began filming, and realized that a neighbor had informed Lalee that her son had been taken back to jail. "I knew that I didn't have a beginning to the scene. I had to get a beginning, but I didn't want to just ask Lalee, 'What's going on?'" Froemke says. At the time, there was no plan to narrate the film (eventually a few title cards were used), and so Froemke had to figure out how to nudge Lalee to get the opening line.

Froemke explains:

That's, to me, a real skill that you develop after you've shot a lot of vérité and you know what you need to bring back to the editing room for the editor to be able to craft a scene together to tell a story. Lalee didn't know what [her son] had been taken to jail for. So what I did is, I asked Jeanette, Lalee's daughter, "Why don't you call the police, to find out?" As soon as I said that, Lalee said to Jeanette, "Why don't you call the police?" That allowed Jeanette to talk with them and then tell Lalee [as we were filming] what had happened. So that we did have a beginning to the story.

Capturing Backstory

With vérité filming, there is also the challenge of telling backstory. "Often over the course of shooting I'll just throw out a question," Froemke says, adding, "Especially if there's someone else around, and some comment about the past goes into a discussion about the present. You throw out a thought and let the subjects bounce that around and see where it goes."

CREATING VISUALS

Not all film ideas are inherently visual, especially those that concern complex or technical issues. If you haven't found a sufficiently visual story through which to explore these issues, it's likely that you'll try to find general visuals that will at least put some images on screen as your experts and/or narrator speak. For a story on educational policy, for example, you might spend an afternoon filming at a local elementary school; for a story on aging, you might attend a physical therapy session at a local hospital. This material is often described as "wallpaper" because the visuals themselves are generic, in that they're not linked to any particular character or story.

Generic or not, created visuals are often necessary to a film project, and the more creative you can be with them, the better. In developing a film on the controversial diagnosis of multiple personality disorder, for example, filmmaker Holly Stadtler and her co-producer came up with a variety of visuals. To demonstrate the concept of dissociation, they filmed a child in her bedroom, on the bed, playing near the bed, standing and sitting, and then combined these images in the editing room. The result is a portrait of the child surrounded by "alternate" versions of herself engaged in a range of behaviors. Stadtler also mounted Styrofoam heads (wig forms) on turntables and had them lit dramatically. "I wanted to have some footage I could cut to that wasn't specific and wasn't someone just sitting in a park or something," she says. To further explore dissociation and compare it to the common phenomenon of "highway hypnosis"—losing track of where you've been while you're driving—they combined point-of-view shooting from within a car (including a car going through a tunnel) to a more dizzying "drive" through corrugated steel pipe, shot with a lipstick camera.

Demonstrations may also be devised to advance your story or themes. Morgan Spurlock's *Super Size Me* is built around a demonstration, a 30-day diet that occurred only for the sake of the film. Spurlock interweaves this with a range of shooting styles. He travels to several different schools and school districts to investigate approaches to diet and physical education, for example. He films a man before and during gastric bypass surgery. He interviews people on the street, asks a family in front of the White House if they can recite the pledge of allegiance, and finds a man who's fanatical about Big Macs. All of these scenes had to be planned, and each element of the film had to be weighed against the other elements. It costs money to shoot, so you don't want to waste time filming scenes or sequences that duplicate each other, whether literally or emotionally, because if they do, as discussed in the following chapter, they're likely to be cut.

Visual Storytelling in the Wild

Creating visual stories out of nature and wildlife footage can be very expensive and time-consuming, but the results, as evidenced by the blockbuster hits *March of the Penguins* and *Winged Migration*, can be spectacular. These productions took considerable time, money, and technology. But what about the relatively lower-budget natural history documentaries that are popular on television?

Filmmaker Holly Stadtler produced *America's Last Red Wolves*, a half-hour film for the series *National Geographic Explorer*. Her approach to wildlife films comes, in part, from her experience filming a documentary about the making of *The Leopard Son*, a Discovery Channel feature produced several years ago by noted naturalist Hugo Van Lawick. "*The Leopard Son* started out being called *Big Cats*," she says, "a story about lions, cheetahs, and leopards in the Serengeti." Filmed on 35mm over a period of a year, the story evolved on location and in the editing room; the final film focuses on leopards, and the real-life drama of a young leopard coming of age. Stadtler spent several weeks on the Serengeti with the production crew and saw how Van Lawick captured natural behavior by "getting the animals used to his presence, staying with it and persevering, and not manipulating things in the environment. And so I became this purist," she says, "'This is the way to do it.'"

With the growth of cable and the decrease in the amount of money available for production, however, filmmakers must often find ways to make quality wildlife films that don't require the time needed to fully habituate animals to a film crew's presence. This can be a tricky business due to ethical issues involved in wildlife shooting. Concern has been raised over such practices as tying carcasses (or worse, maimed animals) down so that animals will come to feed at predictable spots. Stadtler also notes that some people object to filmmakers using vehicle lights at night because it can affect the outcome of a kill. She says:

> What I try to do is find a happy medium. For instance, there's no way you can get 25 feet from wolves feeding in the wild—they're going to take the carcass and go—or that you could get that close to a den site. We had a lot of discussion about setting up remote cameras that could be tripped by sensors, which I had done on *Troubled Waters* (a one-hour film for TBS), but you get a shot or two and the animal leaves.

Red wolves were once extinct in the wild; they were bred in captivity by the U.S. Fish and Wildlife Service and then reintroduced into the wild at the Alligator River National Wildlife Refuge in North Carolina, beginning in the mid-1980s. Some wolves remain in captivity, however, and Stadtler took advantage of this to get the close shots she needed. She and the crew masked the fencing behind the wolves; the camera operator stood about 25 feet away from the wolves on the other side, poking his lens through the fence and filming as a deer carcass was put out for the animals. Stadtler says:

> That's how we got some beautiful images, close up, of wolves. The only other way we could have done that is if we had, in essence, habituated the wolves in the wild to our presence, which would have required months of being there—and even then, I'm not sure how close they would have allowed our camera people.

TONE AND STYLE

Visual storytelling goes well beyond what you shoot: How you shoot, how you light, and how you treat the material in postproduction are also critical. Tone (Does the light convey something harsh and cold or warm and familiar?), point of view (From whose point of view is a scene shot? Is it from a first-person point of view, or is it omniscient? Is the camera shooting up at the subject or looking down?), and context (Does the subject fill the frame, or does he or she appear small and overwhelmed by the surroundings?) are all important considerations. Knowing at least some of the answers in advance can help you plan your production needs, including lights, lenses, and filters; whether or not to use special equipment such as dollies and cranes; and how specialized (and experienced) you might need your production crew to be.

SHOOTING FROM THE HIP

It can takes months, if not years, to raise enough money to do films the "right" way. Unless you're a name filmmaker, chances are that the path between you and that kind of movie will be littered, as discussed in previous chapters, with proposals, rejections, more proposals, more rejections, and the occasional but still too small grant. At least that's the way it is in the United States, where a relatively quick timeline for a higher-budget independent project to move from idea to broadcast can be three to five years. Some very worthy films and series have taken considerably longer, and some equally worthy projects have never made the final hurdle to production. (This isn't full-time attention; it's not unusual for projects to go in fits and starts as producers intersperse development on one or more programs with additional, paying work on other films.)

So what do independents do if the story won't wait but early funding is likely to be difficult to raise? The answer depends in part on the filmmakers. Those who have significant experience and some resources may simply develop the film outline and start shooting. Their financial investment is limited to their time and out-of-pocket expenses such as equipment rental and travel, but since they themselves are experienced personnel, the resulting film is likely to be professional in quality. Those without significant shooting experience may choose to teach themselves quickly or do what they can and hire professionals to help. A powerful story, told well, can often overcome some cinematic rough edges. The converse is not true: A weak story shot spectacularly well is still a weak story.

INTERVIEWS

Before shooting, look at films that contain interviews and decide what you like or don't like about an approach and what you want to do in your own film. Do you plan to appear on camera along with your interviewees, as Judith Helfand did in *Blue Vinyl*? Do you want your interviewees to appear to be addressing the audience directly? Do you want to take a less formal approach to interviewing, asking your subjects questions as they go about their lives or filming them as they discuss specific subjects with each other?

Your answers to these questions will affect how you conduct and shoot your interviews. If you're not going to appear on camera, and your questions won't be heard as voice-over, you'll need to frame the question in a way that elicits a full answer, not just, "Yes. Sure. Oh, yes,

I agree with that." You might want to ask the person being interviewed to incorporate part of your question in his or her answer, as in, "When did you know there was trouble?" Answer: "I knew there was trouble when . . ." In any case, you'll need to listen carefully as the interview is under way to make sure that you're getting something that will work as the beginning of a sentence, thought, or paragraph. If necessary, ask the question again, maybe in a different way.

Go into the interview knowing the handful of specific story points the interview needs to cover, and then include other material that would be nice to have or questions that are essentially fishing—you're not sure what you're going to get, but the answers could be interesting. Note that if you've cast the person you're interviewing in advance, you probably already know what ground the interviewee can best cover. It's rarely productive to ask everyone in a film the same 20 questions.

Conducting Interviews

Everyone approaches interviewing differently. Some people work to put the subjects at ease, starting with more "comfortable" questions before easing into material that's more touchy. As mentioned, filmmakers whose style is more confrontational may show up with the cameras rolling. Sometimes you're asking someone to relate an event he or she has told many times, and the story's taken on a polished quality that you want it to lose; it may take getting the person riled up, or challenging something about the story, to accomplish that.

Another strategy for interviewing, notes Boyd Estus, "is for the person asking the questions not to look at the interviewee as a source of information but to get them involved in a conversation, which often involves playing devil's advocate. 'I really don't understand why this is better than that. Can you explain that to me?'" Estus explains, "So the person's engaged, as opposed to spouting a pat answer."

The Interview Setup

Only rarely is an interviewee asked to speak directly into the camera, in part because few "regular" people can do it comfortably. (Filmmaker Errol Morris achieves this effect through an elaborate setup he devised, called an *Interrotron*™, in which the interviewee speaks to an image of Morris on a screen placed over the camera lens.) Most filmmakers, instead, sit opposite the person (or people) being interviewed and just slightly to the left or right of the camera lens. The person looks at the interviewer, and so appears to be looking just slightly off camera. Although some cinematographers work further away, Boyd

Estus likes to position the camera fairly close to the interview subject, within five feet or so. "It does two things," Estus says. "If the person moves, they change size in the frame, which makes it more three-dimensional, whereas if you're on a long lens they're plastered against the background." More importantly, he says, this puts the interviewer in comfortable range of the questioner.

This kind of intimacy may also be enhanced by conducting the interview over a table. If both parties lean forward, they're very close, and their hand gestures will be in the frame. Estus notes that wooden chairs with arms can be especially good, because the arms tend to be higher than normal. "The gesture's in front of your face, and if you're leaning forward you look more energetic." You don't want the chair's frame or headrest to show behind the person, and as a rule, try to avoid chairs that swivel or rock.

Another decision to make is whether the interviewee should be looking slightly to the left or to the right. If, for example, you know that you want two people to be "answering" each other on film, you might want them to be facing different directions. This isn't always possible to do, but if it's a style you like, you'll need to plan for it in advance. You and your crew also need to think about the other visual content in the frame. "Part of the job is to sell the person so that the audience really wants to hear what they say," Estus says, adding:

> My approach is to try to make an environmental portrait, so that the setting the person is in and the way they look tells you something about them and the subject matter. In wide screen (16:9) television that's much more important because no matter how tight you are on the head, there's half the screen hanging there empty, and a wall of books doesn't tell you anything.

Additional decisions, stemming from the style of film and approach to storytelling, include how you light the interviews and whether you strive for some kind of consistency in look throughout the film (or series). How do you want the interviewee to come across? There are ways to light that will flatter someone's face and minimize the distractions that could leave viewers focusing on the appearance of an interviewee, rather than his or her words. What are your subjects wearing? For more formal interview setups, some producers ask subjects to bring a few clothing options. (For some films, a stylistic decision might be made to ask interviewees to dress one way or another; Estus did a series with gothic themes in which the interviewees were asked to wear black.)

The visual context of an interview and the visual cues contained within it can be very important to the storytelling. How tightly do you frame the interview? Some cinematographers will stay wider for expositional information and move in closer as the interview gets more intimate and/or emotional. What do the interview setting and subject's clothing convey? In *The Thin Blue Line*, Randall Adams and David Harris are interviewed in a setting that suggests confinement, and in fact both turn out to be in prison. Law-enforcement people are all filmed indoors, in suits and ties. David Harris's friends are filmed outdoors, in casual clothing. Because Morris uses no lower thirds (on-screen titles) to identify speakers by name, these visual cues serve as a form of identification.

If you've filmed someone at work or at home, you probably have captured footage that advances our understanding of the character (we can see that she is confident as she works very complex machinery, or that he is devoted to his children) even as we hear who the person is. But it's still common to see typical and uninformative introductory shots of the interviewee—"Walking into the Building" or "Entering the Office" or "Working at the Computer." Even some films that are otherwise excellent resort to these shots. In general, there are almost always better alternatives.

Interview Styles

Interviews need to have an energy and immediacy about them, as well as credibility. They also need to serve the story being told. Watch a range of interviews and you'll see that they can be very different. Is the interviewee talking about a subject from a distance of time, or is he or she speaking as if the event is ongoing? It's not only experts who talk about subjects; people often shape stories after the fact, especially if they've told them before, and it creates a kind of distance between the storyteller and the story, which is sometimes desired, but not always.

SOURCES AND NOTES

Information about *Winged Migration* is available at www.sonyclassics.com/wingedmigration/_media/_presskit/presskit.pdf. Filmmaker Nathaniel Kahn shares scenes from *My Architect* in a TED talk given in 2002, www.ted.com/talks/nathaniel_kahn_on_my_architect?language=en. Additional information for *Betty Tells Her Story* is available through its distributor, New Day Films, www.newday.com. For more information on Errol Morris's *Interrotron*™, see Morris's website, www.errolmorris.com.

CHAPTER 12

Editing

Many of the storytelling issues covered elsewhere in the book come into play again in the editing room. On the majority of films, story and structure do not truly come together until the editor begins to assemble and pare down filmed material. Several versions of the film may be cut before the best point of attack is identified; you may be cutting toward one ending for weeks before you realize that, in fact, the film ends on an even earlier and stronger note.

Although every project is different, the basic editing process is that you screen everything and make a long assembly of your footage, which is then honed into a rough cut, a fine cut, a picture lock, and, finally, a script lock. The assembly includes the material you've shot to date as well as archival material, if any. (Often, you're working not with original archival footage but with "slop" dubs, such as preview reels or stills you might have shot quickly in the editing room. Later, when you know what images will stay in the film, you negotiate for rights to use this material, order broadcast-quality duplications, or arrange for broadcast-quality filming of still material and artifacts.)

As the editing progresses, you work toward a rough cut. This is a draft of your film that is significantly longer than the final show will be. But your general story and structure are in place, and you have some, if not all, of your elements on hand. The rough cut stage is often the best time to reassess major issues of story and structure and experiment with alternatives; this becomes more difficult as the film is fine-tuned. By fine cut, the film is almost to time. You may notice at this stage that there are interviews or important scenes missing that you really need to get, because you have a clearer sense of what your final film is about, what the train is, and what the themes are. If there is narration, this is the time to begin polishing it. And for the movie as a whole, this is the time to make sure that the information you're conveying is accurate. It's not a bad idea, at this stage, to consider showing the edit to someone outside the project, to see if what you *think* you're communicating is what's being received.

Finally, picture lock means that all the images are in place and to time, and script lock means that any outstanding issues of narration or voice-over are resolved and that the material can be recorded and laid in without further changes. The edited project is ready to be packaged for release.

GETTING TO ROUGH CUT

The interaction between producer, director, writer, and editor (or some combination of these) differs with each project. Some teams watch the rushes (the raw footage) all together and discuss which interview bites work, which scenes are strong, and how material might be assembled. Some editors screen the footage alone because they want to evaluate the material without being influenced by the producer's ideas of what worked or didn't work on location. "I really like to just look," says Jeanne Jordan, of her work as an editor on films that others have directed. "I don't want people to even tell me 'This was a difficult interview' or 'I didn't get what I wanted.'" Observational filmmaker Kazuhiro Soda (Chapter 21) says that even though he has shot his films himself, he tries to begin the editing process without any pre-formed ideas. "I try to look at the footage and listen to what this material is saying to me," he explains.

As you screen the footage, you're watching for moments that affect you in some way, whether emotionally or intellectually. You may be looking for scenes and sequences that can play on their own, interview bites that seem strong and clear, material that has the potential to reveal themes and issues, or the special moments that you hope audiences will discuss with each other at work the next day. Sam Pollard, whose recent editing credits include *Sinatra: All or Nothing At All*, which he co-produced with director Alex Gibney, says:

> I'm looking for emotion, that's always my first thing. Then I'm looking for some tension and opposition, because that's going to always make those sequences work the best. And if I feel none of those elements are in there, then I figure I've got to convey another type of feeling. Maybe this is a moment where you just sit back and listen to some music; maybe it's a moment to be somewhat reflective. You've got to know what the material says.

Each person will come away from a first screening with his or her own favorite moments; this memory of what was strong in the raw footage will be useful as you shape and trim the material into a coherent story, all the while working to retain the energy it held in its raw state.

Some editors work from a written outline of scenes and sequences, especially if the film consists primarily of live action, such as cinéma vérité. If there is a significant amount of interview material, whether or not there is to be narration, the producer and/or writer may also take transcripts of the interviews and cut and paste selected bites into a "paper edit." If the project was shot to a script or a script-in-progress, that working script will be adjusted to reflect the actual material on hand. In either case, rough narration (if it's to be used) can be written to seam together disparate elements, make a transition clear, or hold a place for a sequence that's still to be shot. In many editing rooms, "scratch" narration is recorded and cut in against the picture, to better evaluate its effectiveness.

As previously discussed, what works on paper won't necessarily work on film. The juxtaposition of two interview bites and two filmed sequences might read very well, but there may be something about the way a phrase is spoken or the scene plays out that makes it less than powerful on screen. This doesn't mean that you shouldn't do paper cuts; they can be a faster and easier way to "see" an edit before realizing the changes physically. But since a good portion of the paper editing won't work on film, it's also useful to know why you're suggesting a particular change, in addition to what it will be. Perhaps you pulled a bite because it conveyed two specific points; if your choice doesn't work, the editor might be able to satisfy those points in a different way, either through a different bite, a combination of bites, or perhaps through a scene that he or she has just edited that makes the interview bite unnecessary.

The editor, meanwhile, may be assembling scenes, whether from live action or archival footage, shaping them individually, and putting together the strongest beginning, middle, and end possible before sequencing them into the overall film. The editing process tends to be very collaborative. A producer, director, or writer coming into the editing room to watch a cut in progress can often see links and transitions that the editor may not have seen, or he or she may see something in what the editor has assembled that will spark a realization that additional material—a piece of artwork, a fragment of music, a different interview excerpt—is needed. It's a give-and-take process, with everyone in the editing room putting themselves in the role of viewers as well as storytellers. Ultimately, there has to be a single person who makes decisions, usually either the producer or director.

Transcripts

If you've conducted interviews or filmed scenes with a lot of relevant discussion, you should get them transcribed, accurately and thoroughly.

Not a summary ("Dr. Fisher talking about gravitational forces . . ."), but an exact transcription of what is said, including the "um, um, he said, he said, um, well, let me back up by saying that what gravity is not, is . . ." This will save you a lot of time later, because you're likely to go back to these transcripts repeatedly during the editing process in search of story solutions, and an inaccurate or incomplete transcript can mean that you assemble a scene based on what you think someone said, only to find out that it's close but not what you need, or that it's great but the answer took forever. Some filmmakers will also transcribe scenes that have a lot of dialogue, such as a meeting, press conference, or conversation.

In the case of foreign language interviews, filmmakers in the field often rely on quick translations to get a sense of what's being spoken. In the editing room, particularly if no one on the team is fluent in the interview language, it's good to get an accurate and detailed translation as soon as you can, but no later than rough cut. You don't want to fine-tune a film to interview material that doesn't say what you think it says.

When viewing the interviews, make notes on the transcripts to help you remember what someone's energy level is like, if there are problems such as flies or a microphone in the frame, or whether someone sneezes. Some portions of the interview may be usable but only as voice-over; others may be useful as information only. Better to write it down once than to go back to the same bite three times in the course of the editing session because you forgot that there was a reason you didn't use it in the first place. (You're also writing down time code that corresponds to the transcript, so you can find material quickly.)

Another reason to transcribe interviews is that it's unfortunately very easy to cut up someone's words, assemble them with other interviews, and eventually lose track of what the original answer was. I always try to make a point of rereading the transcripts as the editing nears completion (or if I'm hired to help on a project late in the editing stage), for three reasons: to make sure the interviewee is not being misrepresented; to make sure that some terrific material wasn't overlooked earlier when the story was somewhat different; and to look for color and details that might be helpful to narration, if there is narration.

The Paper Edit

There's no need to buy a commercial screenwriting software program; these are designed specifically for dramatic feature films and serve that function well, but they're of little use for documentaries.

Many documentary filmmakers use Word or similar software to create scripts that can be formatted in either one or two columns.

If two columns are used, one is for visuals, the other for audio. With a single-column format, visuals, if mentioned, are put in parentheses or italics. In either case, narration and interview bites should stand out from each other; for example, the narration might be in bold, or the interview bites indented. On films with significant interview material, whether or not there will also be narration, it can be helpful to create a separate block (whether you're working with one column or two) for each interview bite that's pulled, so they can be quickly moved around. Some filmmakers also use the outlining function to keep sequences intact, again, so they can be quickly rearranged.

The first paper edit is usually an *assembly script*, in which you put all of your selected scenes and interviews into the order in which you think they'll appear. The next target draft of the script is a *rough cut script*, in which you're honing everything down and fine-tuning structure. Every team has its own way of working, but often the director, producer, editor, and writer (if there is a separate writer) are collaborating, so that changes made either on paper or on video are communicated back and forth.

Editing Interviews

As you trim sync material, be careful to mark the script in some way so that you know an edit was made. Not only will this help to ensure that you remember which parts of the statement were constructed (in a way that remains truthful), but it will also help if you go back a month later hoping that the entire statement is on camera, only to discover that it has three different cuts in it. For example, here's a pull as it appears in the assembly script, with no edits:

> CHARLIE: (beginning v/o) He was selling auto parts, used auto parts. Besides, embezzlement's a white collar crime, he's a blue collar guy—well, not really, he's not working with the auto parts, he's more the manager of the store, driving to work in his, oh, what was it, Tercel, his blue Tercel, shirt and tie and all the while I guess he's thinking nobody above him would miss that thirty thou.

The edited bite as it might appear in the rough cut script, with the excision noted:

> CHARLIE: (beginning v/o) He was selling auto parts, used auto parts.// and all the while I guess he's thinking nobody above him would miss that thirty thou.

Juxtaposition

The juxtaposition of two shots, or two sequences, adds meaning that is not necessarily contained in either of the elements alone. This works to your advantage, but it's also something to guard against if the juxtaposition creates a false impression. If you cut from someone saying, "Well, who was responsible for it?" to a shot of Mr. Smith, you are creating the impression that Mr. Smith was responsible, whether you mean to or not.

Entering Late, Exiting Early

As you edit, try to enter a scene at the last possible moment and leave at the earliest possible moment. This doesn't mean chopping the heart out of a scene or losing its context, but it does mean figuring out what is the most meaningful part of that scene, and what is just treading water on screen. Suppose you've filmed a sequence in which a mother goes to the grocery store, chats with a neighbor or two, fusses with the butcher over a choice cut of meat, waits in line at the checkout counter, drives home, prepares a meal, calls her college-age daughter to the table, and then watches with dismay as her daughter storms off, angry that her mother has not respected the fact that she is a vegetarian—a fact that the mother says she didn't know.

Where you enter and exit this scene depends on what the scene is about. Is it about the mother going to tremendous lengths to make her daughter feel welcome at home, perhaps because of a recent divorce or the daughter's expulsion from school? Or is it about a chasm between mother and daughter and their inability to communicate even basic information? If it's the former, the scenes in the grocery store help to establish the mother's efforts to please; if the latter, the grocery store scenes aren't really relevant. You could convey their lack of communication with the following shots: the mother puts the steak on the table; the daughter refuses to eat it and storms away; the mother is left looking at the steak.

Where do you end the scene? Again, it depends on where your story is going. If the story is about the fuss the woman made to please her daughter, you might end it with the reversal: the daughter rejects the food and storms away from the table. But if it's about the communication between mother and daughter, you might want to go a bit further and see what happens next. Will the mother try to find some other way to reach the daughter, perhaps by cooking a vegetarian meal?

Again, you don't want to cut scenes to their tightest in terms of the action; you want to focus them so that their meaning and their emphasis in your film's narrative are clear.

Sequences

Review the discussion in previous chapters about sequences, because construction of these is an important part of getting to rough cut. You want to be sure that each sequence does a unique job in the film, advancing the overall story while also varying the rhythm, tone, and emotional level of the film. Be sure to let each start properly and come to a satisfying close. These are your chapters, the breadcrumbs that entice people to keep watching.

Anticipate Confusion

In general, audiences are willing to do quite a bit of work to figure out what the story is and where you're going with it—that's part of what makes viewing a good documentary an active rather than passive experience—but eventually, if they become too lost, they'll give up. A good storyteller anticipates the audience's confusion and meets it in subtle and creative ways, skillfully weaving information in where and when it's needed and not before. It may take some effort to bring a general audience up to speed on what those gadgets actually do or how certain laws of physics work. But armed with that information and an understanding of how it furthers or frustrates the efforts of the protagonist to reach a goal, solve a mystery, unlock a secret, or prove a theorem, the audience can be one step ahead of the story. Those moments when the audience "gets it" just before you—as the storyteller—give it to them, are enormously satisfying.

Just as you want to present information at the moment it's most needed, you also want to be careful not to clutter a story with too much detail. Many film stories get diluted by details that the filmmakers are convinced are "important," although they are not directly relevant to the story at hand. If you're telling the story about a candidate's political campaign, for example, you might not want to spend a lot of time looking at his business career. If there's something about his career that he's promoting on the campaign trail—he wants to bring his cost-cutting strategies to the job of managing a state budget, for example—then it might be relevant. Otherwise, it's taking up space that you need for your story.

Be careful, though, that you don't "cherry pick" your information, selectively using only those details that support your argument or "take" on a story and ignoring those that contradict you. It's possible to be factually accurate and still create an overall story that is fundamentally dishonest. Choosing some details from a person's life as a means of focusing a story is not the same thing as selectively leaving out information you don't want the audience to know. Ultimately you'll be found out, and it weakens your film and credibility.

ROUGH CUT TO FINE CUT

As the film moves toward completion, footage is dropped and hard decisions must be made. Is the story working as filmed, or is new material needed? Does the story that was set up at the film's beginning pay off at the end? Is it being told for maximum audience involvement? Is this the kind of film that people will talk about? Will it keep an audience watching? If the filmmaker hopes to convey important but difficult concepts, are those concepts being communicated accurately and well? To get the film to a broadcast length, would it be better to delete an entire scene or subplot, or should time be shaved off a number of scenes?

One way to begin answering these questions is by showing the film to an impartial audience. Often this is done at rough cut and, schedules and budgets permitting, again at fine cut. You want to invite people who don't know the story and aren't necessarily interested in it, as well as people who know the story better than you do. If, in previewing your

Convicts, North Carolina, 1910, still from *Slavery by Another Name.*
Library of Congress, Prints & Photographs Division, FSA/OWI Collection [reproduction number, LC-USF344–007541-ZB].

film, you discover that the message you think you're sending is not the message being received, there's a problem. As simple as this seems, it's not uncommon for filmmakers to simply decide there must be something wrong with the audience: "I've said it clearly; I don't know why they're not getting it." Or they fear that if they "pander" to an audience, they will be toning down their "message." It doesn't work that way. If one person doesn't get your film, maybe it's just not that person's cup of tea. If two people don't get it, fine. But if a significant portion of an audience has missed your point, your point isn't being made.

Screening Tips

You want to invite a manageable number of filmmaker colleagues, scholars, and a general audience of "others" to these screenings. If you have a very small screening room, it may be necessary to show the film more than once to get an adequate cross-section of reactions. Before the screening starts, make sure everyone has paper and pencils for note taking. You or an appointed moderator should explain what stage your film is at, mentioning, for example, that it's running several minutes long, that narration is provisional, and the footage has numbers and other information printed on it that will be gone by the time it reaches broadcast or it plays at an upcoming festival. In other words, it's a work in progress, and their input and help are extremely valuable to you. Make it clear that you will be asking for their reactions, both positive and negative. Ask them to please stay in the room for a few minutes immediately after the film ends. Then dim the lights, but not so low that people can't see to scribble occasionally in the dark. As the film plays, notice the audience's reactions. When do they seem intent on the story? When is there a lot of shuffling and coughing? Is there laughter? Are there tears?

After the film ends, ask people to jot down their first impressions, anonymously if they'd prefer. Then start the discussion, with you or the moderator asking for broad impressions—what worked, what didn't, what was surprising or confusing or fascinating. After a while, move on to specific questions agreed on by the production team, such as: "Were you confused by the transition to France?" "If you had to cut eight minutes out of this film, what would you cut?" "Did you understand that Dan was more concerned about Marcie's health than about his job?" Concrete responses can be very helpful.

Two important points. First, during a feedback session, the members of the filmmaking team should be quiet. Don't answer questions, offer explanations, or defend any aspect of the filmmaking. You are there to receive information, period. It will waste the opportunity afforded by this valuable audience if you take 15 minutes to explain why it was important to keep the sequence with the demolition derby in, or to explain the backstory that left this audience mystified. Even if it kills you to sit there and listen to people debate subjects that you know the answer to, restrain yourself. You're not there to educate this audience on the topic or show them that you do know more than was up on the screen; you're there to get a good sense of what actually was on screen and where it needs work.

Second, take any and all suggestions, say thanks, and keep going. You know, and your entire production team knows, that you can't possibly afford to shoot another four interviews, as the guy in the corner suggests, or that cutting out the trial sequence would make your entire film irrelevant. After this audience goes home, however, consider *why* these suggestions were made. Nonfilmmakers don't always know how to articulate a problem, and they can't be expected to know how to fix it. You can and do. If your audience thinks that you're missing significant interviews, is there information that those interviews would add that you could convey in some other way? If you believe the trial sequence is critical and they think it's disposable, what's wrong with it? Is it edited badly? Is it in the wrong place? Is the narration not effectively setting it up so the audience can see its relevance?

You don't have to take anything that anyone says as marching orders. But you do need to pay attention to which elements of your film are working and which will send your audience racing for the remote or the door.

With that said, it's your film. Know when to trust your gut. Understand that there will be a degree of criticism that is not about your filmmaking but about your ideology. Someone doesn't understand why you would even give the skinheads a chance to speak. Someone else thinks it's invasive to stay focused on the woman sobbing because her son has blown his mind on inhalants. This is useful information to have, because it anticipates some of the criticism the final film might receive. But if the issue is not one of fact or clarity but of style, the choice is yours to make. Hear that people don't like it, but decide for yourself what makes you and your team comfortable.

The same is true of scholarship. Tell an accurate story, but don't feel compelled to tell everything. It's sometimes difficult for scholars who care deeply about their subjects to see that the entire section on primate behavior is only six minutes long or that you decided not to include a certain letter that Albert Einstein wrote. Accept the criticism and really consider whether or not it would enrich the story you have chosen to tell on film. If not, file this information away for use later in the companion book or website, if you're creating these, or for the teachers' guides and other educational and community engagement components of the project. Your film is successful if it appeals to a wide audience with a strong story and motivates part of that audience to go to the library or the web for more information.

FINE CUT TO PICTURE LOCK

The process as you get down to the wire is more of the same, looking backward as well as forward. It's often very helpful at this stage to go back and reread initial outlines and treatments to see if you've lost a story thread along the way that might prove useful. You might also reread transcripts to see if the changes that you've made to the structure are better served by interview bites you didn't pull because you were looking at a very different film back then. It's even useful to look back into research files, to make sure there aren't details and other tidbits that might speak volumes. And, of course, you are by now immersed in the task of making sure that everything that will end up on screen has been fact checked, not once but twice.

Fact Checking

Fact checking means going through your script line by line, finding the information that needs to be verified through at least two credible sources. If you can't confirm a fact—and it happens—find a way to write around it. Maybe you don't need to say that 25,000 bikers rode into town. If your sources all agree that it was "over 20,000," then say that instead.

What needs to be checked? Pretty much everything:

- "Brilliant and fearless, Admiral Marks now seized command of the troops." *Brilliant* and *fearless* both need corroboration, as does *seized command*. You don't want to find out after broadcast that Marks was widely considered a coward, or that command was thrust upon him when the admiral before him came down with food poisoning.
- "The senator was *exhausted* and *frustrated*, convinced now that the bill she'd *authored* would not be passed." Exhausted and frustrated need to be confirmed, and you should have solid evidence that at this point, she truly was convinced of the bill's failure, and that she had authored it and not simply supported it. (Confirming an emotional state depends on reliable reports from reliable eyewitnesses, recorded as close to the event as possible.)

You need to fact check interview and sync material as well as narration. For example, an auto manufacturer says, "Forty percent of the tires we got in had the problem. They all had to go back." He's the expert, but you find out that in fact, 25 percent of the tires were sent back because of the problem. You can't hide behind the argument that "He said it, I didn't." As the filmmaker, you are incorporating the statement into your film and, therefore, it will be your statement as well. In this case, the line has to go. Of course, if the falsehood is deliberate, and that's part of your story, or if it's clearly a lie and therefore reveals character, you don't need to cut it. But when it is presented as significant evidence to support the argument you're making, then it must be accurate. However, there is also some room to maneuver. For example, if you've confirmed that 38 percent of registered voters in Millville voted for a rise in property tax, and the mayor says, "I don't know, about a third of the voters wanted it," that's probably close enough to use.

FILM LENGTH

If you're creating a film for which you have a specific venue in mind, length is something you want to plan for from the beginning. A theatrically released film will tend to run around 80 to 90 minutes or longer. A film for broadcast has to meet the length requirements of the programmer, leaving time as needed for series credits, packaging, and, in some cases, commercial breaks. The subject and story, too, will suggest appropriate length. When I'm helping people to develop ideas, one of the questions we ask ourselves is, "How much time would it take to tell this well?" If a subject seems to demand three hours, do we reasonably think we could raise money to produce it (and convince programmers to give us a three-hour television slot), or do we want to narrow the focus and try to create an hour-long film that might appeal to the commissioning editors of an existing series?

It's usually better to resist the temptation to leave your film long. Filmmaking is about making choices, and among the most important choices you face is what to include and what to leave out. If your story feels complete in 45 minutes, padding it with extra footage won't make it a longer story; it makes it a 45-minute story that took an hour to tell.

THE OPENING SEQUENCE

The opening sequence is also sometimes called a tease. By tease, though, I don't mean the trailer or brief advertisement for the film that may run in advance of the actual broadcast program ("Tonight on *Frontline* . . ."). I mean whatever comes up at the very first frame of the film and runs through an opening sequence that generally sets your film's story, themes, and creative approach in motion, and includes the film's title. How you open your film, as discussed in Chapter 7, matters a great deal, because you are setting forth the terms of your engagement with the audience: "*This* is what this film is about, *these* are the storytelling tools I'm using, *this* is why it's worth your time." Don't forget that the story you set up in these opening minutes must be the story you resolve at the film's end. Your opening minutes should not be didactic—they should be creative and inspired, which is in part why they're so tough to do, and are often the last piece of the film's storytelling to fall into place.

NARRATION SCRIPT

When it comes time to record narration, your narration pieces are generally numbered and then isolated into a script of their own—a *narration script*—which is often a single-column, double-spaced document, with very wide margins to the left and right for ease of reading. Don't put the narration in all capitals, because this makes it more difficult to read.

PROBLEM SOLVING

Every film has its own problems, but the following ones seem fairly common.

No Story

You have scenes and sequences that are interesting but aren't adding up to a coherent whole. One reason for this may be that there really wasn't a clear story to begin with. What you can do at this point is take a step back and return to the earlier stages of the process. Looking realistically at what you have and what you know, do you now see a truthful story in the material? Do you have enough footage to support that story? You may need pick up material to fill in the gaps, but you also may be surprised to find that you are heading in the right direction and just need to do a bit of housekeeping. You also may need to drop favorite scenes because they don't serve the story that you've now identified. If a shot or a scene or even a sequence is a distraction rather than an addition, it's got to go, no matter how expensive it was to shoot or how difficult it was to get. The same standard should be applied to interview material. If you didn't plan ahead but instead simply shot a few available experts, it's very possible that there will be redundancy and somebody's interview will be dropped. (If you end up cutting people out of a show, do them the courtesy of letting them know before the program is aired.)

You Start One Story and End Another

A related problem is that the film starts one story and then drifts onto a different track. As previously discussed, creating a new outline can help you to decide which of the stories you want to tell and have the footage to tell. Be careful not to bend material to tell a story other than the one for which it was originally shot. Footage of Sally's graduation party should not be substituted for the engagement party you didn't film. Find a way to use the party footage to make a more generic point, if need be.

Too Many Characters or Story Threads

You didn't want to give up the incredible research you did or the wonderful people you found, so now you find yourself telling the stories of eight people, all with different goals but perhaps a common thread—maybe they're all recent college graduates looking for work. But your film is only an hour long and everybody is getting short shrift, or audiences can't keep track of which person was having trouble with his neighbors and who was being investigated by the Immigration and Naturalization Service and which one was going to move her business to Seattle. You may need to make choices as to which people best embody the themes you are trying to convey or the policy issues or areas of discrimination you want the audience to know about. You can also get distracted by too many details within an overall story. No matter what style film you're making, you need to keep track of the one primary story you're telling, folding in additional threads (or subplots, backstory, etc.) as they serve that one story.

Too Many Beginnings or Endings

The film opens with a look at the farming industry and the cultivation of wheat. The narration offers some information as to what's being presented, and the audience thinks, "Oh, it's a documentary about farming." Then it seems to start again with a look at the processing of wheat into bread. "Oh, it's a film about food as big business." But then it starts again, and gradually it becomes clear that your film is really a look at the health issue of wheat intolerance or sensitivity. An unfocused opening is a fairly common problem, so it's good to watch out for it, asking yourself as the story unfolds, "What do I think this story is about at this point?" The primary story you're going to tell should start soon after your film begins, and it should be possible, from the way that story is launched, to anticipate—not to know, but to anticipate and be curious about—how it will end. In this case, the remaining details of wheat farming and the baking industry can be folded into that overall story.

Where you end your film is also very important. Appearing to end it, and then ending it again, and then ending it again can dilute a film's overall power; furthermore, there's generally just one ending that will truly bring a satisfactory resolution to the story you set out to tell. Resolution does not mean things are resolved; it means that you've reached a conclusion that satisfies the questions and issues initially raised in your film's opening moments.

Not Enough Breathing Room

In the rush to cut a film down to time, to get everything tight, and to make every point, it's possible to trim interviews or scenes into oblivion. The production team doesn't necessarily notice; they've been looking at this guy day after day and week after week, so they know what he's going to say, they've heard it before, and the joke is no longer funny. Or they realize that they can say in two lines of narration what that scene takes nearly two minutes to convey. It's important to resist this—you need the energy that real people bring to a film and the enthusiasm they bring to their storytelling. While radio and television news reports may cut interviews or scenes into fragments, you generally want to let material play for a reasonable period of time.

Insufficient Casting

You may discover, in editing, that an important voice is missing, or that someone you've interviewed is filling a storytelling role that would be better filled by someone else. If possible, you might shoot an additional interview, trying to match its tone and look to your film's style. Otherwise, you need to find another way to bring this point of view forward, such as through archival voices or the way a scene is edited. It's also possible, as your story becomes more focused, that you've neglected to ask someone important story-related questions. Depending on how significant the problem is (and the size of your budget), you can either do another interview with that person, intending to either replace one with the other or somehow use both (although cutting directly between them may prove difficult), or you can work to match the audio enough so that you can use the pick-up material as voice-over.

Occasionally, an entirely new sentence can be crafted from some-one's existing interview, a sentence the person never uttered but one that you think he or she would agree with. If you really want to do this, and it's your only option, you must run this new sentence past the person and secure permission to use it.

GETTING UNSTUCK

Even the best creative minds get tired. You try six ways of cutting some-thing and it still doesn't work, or the editor thinks it works one way, the director hates it, and the producer is thinking that now might be a good time to get that law degree. Assuming that you have at least something strung together in sequence, take a step back and try throw-ing all the pieces up in the air. This is easier done at rough cut than fine cut, but it's a useful exercise in any case. You've got a story and structure that maybe aren't great, but they're fine. Open the door, for a short period, and let everyone throw out the craziest ideas they can think of, without anybody becoming scornful or arguing about why it won't work and that it's already been tried. "What if we started where the film now ends? What if we held off on the fireman's story until after his wife is in the accident? What if we told the story from the child's point of view, and not his parents'?"

Just throw it all out there and then try a few things. Maybe none of them will work. But in the difference between what was boring and safe and what is outrageous and stupid, you might see new opportu-nities. In other words, two wrong answers may lead you toward one that's right. You can't do this indefinitely, and at some point whoever's in charge has to make the final call. But what you end up with might be really interesting.

BE YOUR FIRST AUDIENCE

A mark of a good storyteller is the ability to look with fresh eyes—the audience's eyes—at material each time a new cut is available, and to honestly assess its weaknesses. If you see problems, don't ignore them. Audiences are uncanny in their ability to see that one flaw you thought you could gloss over or the transition whose absence you thought you'd masked with some fancy music and images. At the same time, you can't cut a film or tell a story with a critic on your shoulder. Don't sec-ond-guess yourself; that's not what this process is about. Instead, ask yourself every step of the way, "Is this interesting? Would I keep watch-ing? What do I care about here? Who am I worried for? Am I confused? Where do I need more information?"

SAMPLE PAGES

In the pages that follow, I've included some sample pages from outlines and scripts in progress during editing, and pages of final scripts, for programs that have since been broadcast. Every project is different; these are just examples.

Sample editing outline, *Lalee's Kin*[i]

AUGUST
A NEW SCHOOL YEAR BEGINS

LLW AND KIDS ON PORCH

    Intro kids

    Main flunked first grade

BOYS BATH – before school

LOST CLOTHES (night before school)

TELEPHONE GAME

FIRST DAY OF SCHOOL – LW brushes Redman's hair

PARKING LOT ADVICE – LLW and Redman

REGISTRATION – LLW and Redman

SAN'S HOUSE

    Supplies

DON'T NOBODY KNOW

SUNSET

    Praise Jesus

GRANNY CRIES ON PORCH

    No pencils

KIDS GET ON SCHOOL BUS/ARRIVE AT SCHOOL

REGGIE – If kids don't come to school first day we're not going to solve anything

    We have a test Oct. 1 and instruction begins now

    Someone has to be Level 1, but we don't want to be it

GRANNY IN SCHOOL

SADIE DILLS

COTTON FIELD

LALEE AND REGGIE RE COTTON PICKING AND PLANTATION MENTALITY

    R- Closed schools

---

[i] © 2002 Maysles Films, Inc., reprinted with permission.

Narration: For the first time, freed people could choose their work. Some chose to work in the home, raising children. Others chose to be farmhands, furnace workers, laundresses, teachers, laborers, working for others or, ideally, themselves. "I am as much at liberty hire a white man to work as he is to hire me," vowed a black soldier, shortly after the war.

> JAMES GROSSMAN 14:07:04.08 They were willing to work very hard. They were willing to work a lot longer work day than I do, and that most Americans do right now. They were willing to exploit themselves in the same way that small business people, immigrants who have come to this country, have exploited themselves and their families with small– with long work days. They were willing to do that. But they wanted to own their own land. They wanted to control those hours. They wanted to be the ones to decide.

WE SEE JOHN DAVIS, EARLY 20S, WORKING A PLOT OF LAND—PERHAPS HE IS POSED, STANDING WITH A HOE OR CULTIVATOR IN HAND, AS HE LOOKS OUT AT THE LANDSCAPE.
Narration: John Davis was born a dozen years after the war. He grew up in freedom, on a farm rented and worked by his father. His goal, like his father's before him, was to someday own the land on which he toiled.

> ADAM GREEN: 12:12:23.07 there was a really strong sense of trying to create some basis of sovereignty for black people. //13:51:02.16. They're trying to gain title on land. They're trying to transform their occupations. They're seeking to farm sustenance crops rather than cash crops, and take care of their own plot. They're seeking to use mobility in order to find out where they might get the best terms: from a white landowner or from somebody that has a kind of small proto-industrial space.

WE SEE GREEN COTTENHAM, EARLY 20S, LEANING AGAINST A BRICK WALL, MAYBE SMOKING A CIGARETTE. PERHAPS HE PUTS THE CIGARETTE OUT AND REACHES FOR A PAMPHLET OR NEWSPAPER IN HIS POCKET, SOMETHING APPROPRIATE TO READ.
Narration: Green Cottenham's father, too, was a farmer, and his mother looked after a handful of children, with Green the youngest of the boys, born more than 20 years after emancipation. By the time Green was a teenager, public schools—serving black children equally with whites—had been established in the South, and Green was among those who attended.

> DAVID LEVERING LEWIS 14:45:45.09 People marched to small schoolhouses in great numbers to learn to read and write and count. They took their civics lessons very seriously. The enthusiasm and the discipline in order to . . . make citizenship a reality is reflected in the statistics that within a decade's time, the rate of literacy achieved by this population was simply quite-quite remarkable.

BACK TO EZEKIAL ARCHEY, writing.

Sample editing script page, *Slavery by Another Name*.
[1] Written by Sheila Curran Bernard, based on the book by Douglas A. Blackmon. © 2012 Twin Cities Public Television, reprinted with permission. The material in bold (in blue in original) describes re-enactments yet to be filmed.

Sample page, _Slavery by Another Name_ editing script (March 2011, page 4 of 55)[1]		
		White text on black: The words spoken by the actors are based on original documents, including sworn testimony.
Title: Georgia, 1903		ACTOR/KINSEY (begins v/o): Mr. President, I have a brother, about 14 years old. A man hired him from me and I heard of him no more.// He went an' sold him to McRee, an' they has bin working him in prison for 12 months. I asked him to let me have him, but he won't let him go.
		Narration: For a period of nearly 80 years, between the Civil War and World War II, black southerners were no longer slaves, but they were not yet free.
		In one of the most shameful and little-known chapters of American history, generations of black southerners were forced to labor against their will.
		RISA GOLUBOFF: From almost the first moment, white southerners were responding to try to put African Americans back into a position as close to slavery as they possibly could.
		KAHLIL MUHAMMAD: 09:00:55.29 The Old South and what was quickly becoming the New South, could not proceed without the work of African Americans.
		MARY ELLEN CURTIN: But you know // if you've had something for free in the past, you don't necessarily want to pay for it now.
		ADAM GREEN: 12:09:24.07 It was a straight, simple, exploitative system.// 12:09:58.18 There was only power, there was only force, and there was only brutality.
		DOUGLAS BLACKMON: 09:02:46.02 What happened in that period of time was so much more terrible than anything most Americans recognize or understand today: the depth of poverty, // the inability of African Americans to access any of the mechanisms of wealth achievement and growth, // they're all rooted in this terroristic kind of regime that-that existed in so many places.
		BERNARD KINSEY: 01:10:06.24 Their ability to have what we call the American dream. // That is what has been stolen from black folks all through the South. And that legacy has to be understood so that people will be able // to speak to it and give our ancestors voice.
To black Title:		**Slavery by Another Name**
		Narrated by Laurence Fishburne

Sample page, final script, _Slavery by Another Name_.
[1] Written by Sheila Curran Bernard, based on the book by Douglas A. Blackmon. © 2012 Twin Cities Public Television, reprinted with permission.

VOICE 001: It is odd to watch with what feverish ardor Americans pursue prosperity – ever tormented by the shadowy suspicion that they may not have chosen the shortest route to get it. They cleave to the things of this world as if assured that they will never die – and yet rush to snatch any that comes within their reach, as if they expected to stop living before they had relished them. Death steps in in the end and stops them, before they have grown tired of this futile pursuit of that complete felicity which always escapes them.

Alexis de Toqueville

TITLE: THE DONNER PARTY

NARRATOR: It began in the 1840s, spurred on by financial panic in the East, by outbreaks of cholera and malaria, and by the ceaseless American hankering to move West. When the pioneer movement began, fewer than 20,000 white Americans lived west of the Mississippi River. [Ten years later the emigration had swelled to a flood, and] Before it was over, more than half a million men, women and children had stepped off into the wilderness at places like Independence, Missouri, and headed out over the long road to Oregon and California.

In places their wagon wheels carved ruts shoulder-deep in the rocky road.

The settlers themselves knew they were making history. "It will be received," one Emigrant wrote, "as a legend on the borderland of myth." But of all the stories to come out of the West, none has cut more deeply into the imagination of the American people than the tale of the Donner Party high in the Sierra Nevada in the winter of 1846.

INTERVIEW HS24: Human endeavor and failure. Blunders, mistakes, ambition, greed – all of the elements. And if you call the rescue of the surviving parties a happy ending, it's a happy ending. But what about those that didn't make it. Terrible, terrible.

Harold Schindler

INTERVIEW JK1: We're curious about people who've experienced hardship, who have gone through terrible ordeals. And certainly the Donner Party, you know, 87 people went through a crisis the likes of which few human beings have ever faced. And we're curious about that. It can tell us something

1

---

[j] Written by Ric Burns. © 1992 Steeplechase Films, Inc., reprinted with permission.

Sample page, script (two column), *Lift Every Voice*[i]

SERIES TITLE	***I'LL MAKE ME A WORLD: A CENTURY OF AFRICAN-AMERICAN ARTS***
NAME OF SHOW	***EPISODE 1: LIFT EVERY VOICE***

Lower third: **Melvin Van Peebles** **Filmmaker**	**Van Peebles**: People always talk about the—the down side of racism. There's an up side, too. The up side is that nobody thinks you're smart. They don't even know why they don't think you're smart. Don't woke 'em, let 'em slept. Just go ahead and do the deal you have to do. Racism offers great business opportunities if you keep your mouth shut.
clips of Bert Williams – *Nobody*	(hearing a few bars of *Nobody*) *When life seems full of clouds and rain* *And I am full of nothing and pain* *Who soothes my thumping, bumping brain?* *NOBODY.*
lower third: **Lloyd Brown** **Writer**	**LLOYD BROWN**: Bert Williams combined the grace of a Charlie Chaplin, imagery and all, and at the same time with a very rich voice too. And so he—he was...wonderful comedy.
lower third: **James Hatch** **Theater Historian**	**HATCH**: He has a...(laughing) song where he's obviously explaining to his wife who the woman was that he was seen with. And the refrain chorus line is "She was a cousin of mine." He has that line, I would say, six or seven times in the song: "She was just a cousin of mine." Every time it's different. Every time it's a new interpretation. (v/o) The man was a genius.
Stills of Bert Williams	**NARRATION 1: In the earliest years of the 20th century, Bert Williams was the most successful black performer on the American stage. But each night, he performed behind a mask he hated: blackface.**
Lower third: **Ben Vereen** **Performer**	**VEREEN** (v/o): Bert Williams didn't want to black up. But socially during that time, he had to. And he realized that. He was a very intelligent man.... We have to hide our identity by putting on this mask, in order to get things said and done. (o/c) But we did it. We did it. And today we don't have to do it. But we cannot forget it.

---

[i] Written by Sheila Curran Bernard; episode one of *I'll Make Me A World*. © 1998 Blackside, Inc., reprinted with permission.

CHAPTER 13

Narration and Voice-Over

Narration is not the worst thing to happen to a documentary, but bad narration might be, which might explain why so many filmmakers want to avoid it at all costs. We've all seen films that were talky, preachy, hyperventilated, and dull. But there's also narration (or extensive voice-over commentary) that makes films funny, sarcastic, spare, poetic, and elegant. *Enron, Super Size Me, Grizzly Man,* and *Born into Brothels,* among many recent films, have effective narration. *Enron's* narration is the most traditional, in that it's spoken by an unseen person, the actor Peter Coyote, who has no identity in the film other than to provide information that moves the story along. *Super Size Me,* narrated in voice-over and on screen by filmmaker Morgan Spurlock, is packed with what would be considered traditional narration: facts and figures about nutrition, health, the food industry, and more. *Grizzly Man* is narrated in the first person by filmmaker Werner Herzog, whose voice-over tells of his journey to explore the legacy and death of naturalist Timothy Treadwell. *Born into Brothels,* although narrated by Zana Briski, does not refer to her role as the film's producer and director (with Ross Kauffman), but to her involvement in the story, as a photographer helping a group of children in the brothels of Kolkata.

Narration or voice-over, if done well, can be one of the best and most efficient ways to move your story along, not because it tells the story but because it draws the audience into and through it. Narration provides information that's not otherwise available but is essential if audiences are to fully experience your film. It can be especially useful when a film delves into complicated historical policy or legal and legislative issues. Filmmaker Jon Else explains: "Something that might take 10 minutes of tortured interview or tortured vérité footage can be often disposed of better in 15 seconds of a well-written line of narration."

POINT OF VIEW

When crafting narration, it's important to choose the point of view from which to tell the story. For example:

- First-person narration is when the narrator speaks of him- or herself. *I needed to find out.* This point of view is generally limited to what the narrator knows at a given point in the story.
- Second-person narration may be found more often in print than on screen. It has the narrator addressing the audience as "you," as in, *He asks if you want a soda, and you say yes.*
- Third-person omniscient is the most commonly used form of narration; it is written using "he" or "she," and the narrator can slip in and out of anyone's thoughts or actions. For example, *The mayor was well aware of Smith's plans. And from his campaign headquarters, Smith knew that the mayor's response, when it came, would be fierce.* Most often, this narration is described as "objective," meaning that it is limited to factual information that can be observed or verified. However, as discussed in the first chapter, it still has a point of view, no matter how balanced or neutral it seeks to be.
- Third-person subjective uses the "he" or "she" form, but is limited to the same point of view as first-person narration. In other words, I might describe the writing of this chapter as *She sits at her desk and types, wondering if she'll meet her deadline.*

Beyond the narrator's point of view, there is also a point of view in the words being spoken. Even if you've chosen an omniscient narrator, you want to be careful not to jump back and forth between points of view, but instead situate the viewer. For example, if you begin to narrate a Revolutionary War battle from the point of view of the advancing British, you don't want to suddenly switch to the American side without signaling to the audience that you've done so. In other words, the following (imagined) scene is confusing: *British forces prepared their charge as the Americans assembled near Boone Hill. General Washington ordered his men, a ragtag group of 300, to stand firm. The soldiers advanced, a force of nearly 2,000 in territory that offered little resistance.*

Told from the American point of view, the scene might go like this: *The Americans were assembled near Boone Hill when they got word that British forces were advancing. General Washington ordered his men, a ragtag group of 300, to stand firm, as nearly 2,000 British soldiers advanced toward them.*

From the British point of view, it might go this way: *British forces prepared to charge on the Americans who were assembled nearby. A force of nearly 2,000 men, they had little difficulty with the terrain as they approached Boone Hill, where General Washington was waiting with a rag tag force of about 300.*

Obviously, your writing should fit the visuals. But it's very easy in a case like this to quickly lose track of who's fighting whom or who's advancing where. One way to help, as the filmmaker, is to maintain a consistent point of view.

VARIETY IN NARRATION

At times, filmmakers "narrate" films without speaking, through the use of text on screen. This usually means using either title cards (text on a neutral background) or lower thirds (text over a scene) to add information that's not otherwise evident. This technique is generally used in films that are strongly vérité (action unfolds on screen) and is always used sparingly. Filmmakers who use title cards generally use them to set up the film and then, on occasion, to establish time and place or to bridge sequences.

For example, the documentary *Spellbound*, about a group of children who compete in the National Spelling Bee, sets up the story with a brief series of cards that immediately follow the film's title. The cards come on in the following order (numbers are added here for clarity and do not appear in the film): 1, joined by 2, both off; 3, joined by 4, both off; 5, joined by 6, both off:

1. *Across the country, 9,000,000 children compete in school and city spelling bees.*
2. *Only 249 qualify for the Nationals in Washington, D.C.*
3. *Over two days of competition 248 will misspell a word.*
4. *One will be named champion.*
5. *This is the story of eight American children*
6. *who, one spring, set out to win the National Spelling Bee.*

These effectively set up the story to come; later, text on screen briefly introduces the protagonists, for example: *Perryton, Texas* (over an establishing shot of the town) is followed shortly after by *Angela* (over an establishing shot of Angela).

When to narrate, how to narrate, who should narrate—these are important storytelling decisions, driven in part by the content of the film and the style and tone adopted by the filmmakers. Compare the narration in *Enron* with the lack of narration in a film like *Spellbound*.

Enron, Alex Gibney's film based on the reporting of *Fortune* magazine's Bethany McLean and Peter Elkind, seeks to give general audiences an understanding of a corporate financial scandal that was enormously complex. The narration is relatively spare, but it helps the filmmakers weave together a complicated body of evidence derived from interviews, news reports, audiotapes, video coverage of hearings, and more. In contrast, *Spellbound* does not set out to provide a wealth of complex factual data, but instead seeks to let viewers inside the homes and lives of selected children as they prepare for a national competition, and then follows them there to see how they do.

As mentioned, Werner Herzog's voice-over in *Grizzly Man* is an important part of the film's story. The film begins with an intriguing excerpt of Treadwell's footage. Then, like the title cards at the start of *Spellbound*, the first words we hear from Herzog set up the premise of the film to come:

> *All these majestic creatures were filmed by Timothy Treadwell, who lived among wild grizzlies for 13 summers. He went to remote areas of the Alaskan peninsula believing that he was needed there to protect these animals and educate the public. During his last five years out there, he took along a video camera and shot over 100 hours of footage. What Treadwell intended was to show these bears in their natural habitat. Having myself filmed in the wilderness of jungle, I found that beyond a wildlife film, in his material lay dormant a story of astonishing beauty and depth. I discovered a film of human ecstasies and darkest inner turmoil. As if there was a desire in him to leave the confinements of his humanness and bond with the bears, Treadwell reached out, seeking a primordial encounter. But in doing so, he crossed an invisible borderline. . . .*

Herzog plays a number of roles as the film's narrator. Sometimes he provides basic exposition: *Timothy grew up with four siblings in Long Island . . .* or lends his expertise as a filmmaker: *Now the scene seems to be over. But as a filmmaker, sometimes things fall into your lap which you couldn't expect, never even dream of.* Perhaps most interesting are Herzog's challenges to Treadwell. At times, these are simple statements of contradiction, for example: *Treadwell saw himself as the guardian of this land and stylized himself as Prince Valiant, fighting the bad guys with their schemes to do harm to the bears. But all this land is a federally protected reserve. . . .* But Herzog also argues directly with the Treadwell we see on screen, as when Treadwell mourns the killing (by other animals) of a bear cub and then a baby fox. Treadwell says, in his footage: "I love you and I don't understand. It's a painful world." In voice-over, Herzog responds: *Here I differ with Treadwell. He seemed to ignore the fact that in nature there are predators. I believe the common denominator of the universe is not harmony, but chaos, hostility, and murder.*

WHEN IS THE NARRATION WRITTEN?

When you write narration varies from project to project. In general, if you are using narration to seam together visual images, interviews, and perhaps archival material, the final narration (or voice-over) won't come together until you're editing. You may assemble other elements first, such as filmed footage, archival material, or interview bites, and then rough out narration as needed to help move the story along. Sometimes you need to write "into" a talking head, which means that your words are needed as a kind of setup, to make the meaning of the upcoming interview bite more clear. Sometimes you need narration to set the stage for a scene that can then play out on camera without interruption, or to make a transition from one sequence to the next.

WHO WRITES THE NARRATION?

Film writing is a different skill than magazine or book writing. While some prose writers make the transition successfully, not all do. Writing to picture—writing words that will be heard rather than read—and structuring a film story within the confines of the time allotted, whether 30 minutes or eight hours, are specialized skills. Just as a great poet might be a terrible screenwriter, a great print journalist might not write a good movie.

On many documentary projects, the film's producer and/or director is also the writer (meaning the individual responsible for story and structure, regardless of whether there is also narration), and in that role also writes narration. At other times, a person identified as the writer may be involved in the project through development, production, and editing, and will therefore take primary responsibility for narration. It's also not uncommon for an editor to rough out pieces of narration as he or she works, which will then be polished in collaboration with the film's writer(s).

Occasionally, a writer is asked to join a project solely to write and/ or polish narration and make it stronger. This kind of wordsmithing can make a positive difference if the film is otherwise in good shape. But keep in mind that polished narration cannot mask underlying structural and story issues. If there isn't a strong writer on the team, consider bringing one on, even part time, much earlier in the process.

Note that if you plan to hire an actor or other celebrity to narrate your film, you may also need to fine-tune narration to suit their unique voices and identities.

WRITING TO PICTURE

The camera pans across a sepia-toned still photograph of a wagon train on a dusty road. To the side, an old farmer stands, watching as the wagons pass. The shot ends on a hand-painted sign tacked to the back of one of the last wagons: *Califna or Bust.* As you watch this shot on screen, which line of narration would be more useful to you?

- *The wagons set out along the dusty road.*
- *On August 4th they set out: four men, five women, and eight children determined to find gold.*

Which narration breathes life into the photograph, and which just states the obvious? Narration should add information to picture, not simply describe it. Above all, narration should advance the story.

Here's a second example, from a film that follows a group of college friends as they face their first year in the job market. In a live-action scene set in a private home, a group of young women sits down to a fancy dinner. One of them, dressed in an expensive-looking suit, sets a roasted turkey on the table. Which narration is useful?

- *Donna is the most vivacious of the group, and the most fashion-conscious.*
- *Donna, who graduated from Harvard Law School, hopes to pursue a career in advertising.*

Obviously, what you say depends on what the audience needs to learn. But we can tell from watching the scene that Donna is vivacious and well-dressed. We can't tell from looking at her that she went to Harvard Law School. That narration adds to picture.

Here is another approach that people sometimes use, believing that it will create a sense of tension:

- *Donna, the organizer of this gathering, would soon learn that her life would change in ways she couldn't imagine.*

What exactly does this add? Are you on the edge of your seat wondering how Donna's life will change? No. This sounds like it's intended to build tension, but it's just words. Tension comes from the story, not a narrator's hints.

Just as you should write to picture, you should never write against picture. A common mistake people make is to write in a way that sets the film up to go in one direction, when in fact the images are going somewhere else. Here's an example. We see a group of executives sitting around a table, talking. Narration: *The board decided to hire a consultant, Jane Johnson.* Cut to a woman talking. Wouldn't you assume it's Jane Johnson? If it's not, it's going to take a moment to readjust your thinking, to figure out, well, if it's not Johnson, who is it? By then, you'll have missed at least part of what this woman has said.

Suppose the woman that we cut to is on the board of directors, and she's explaining why they're hiring Jane Johnson. The edit makes sense. But the narration gets in the way. Try again. We see a group of executives sitting around a table, talking. Narration: *The board decided that a consultant was needed.* Cut to the woman from the board, who explains, "We were spinning our wheels. And so . . ." It's a minor difference but an important one.

Words and picture should work together, each adding to the build-up of your story. Words should also accurately identify the picture. This can be frustrating to filmmakers when the visual record is limited. Suppose, for example, that you are telling the story of a man and woman who met in Ohio at a USO dance, the night before he was shipped off to fight in World War II. But the family only has photographs that were taken five years later, after the man returned from the war and the couple, now married, had a child. No footage exists of that particular USO dance or even of the club in which it was held. Can you use footage of another USO dance, from another state and another year?

Of course you can, but your narration should avoid creating the false impression that the audience is seeing the real thing. For example, suppose the editor cuts in footage of a USO dance held two years later in a different state. The narration says, *On February 2, 1942, at a USO dance in Columbus, Ohio, Tim finally met the girl of his dreams.* The audience may think, "Gee, isn't that amazing, there was a film crew there to capture it." I think it stretches credibility, and if the audience assumes that this couldn't possibly be the USO dance on the night in the city, they will see your footage for what it is—wallpaper. From that point on, the archival value of the footage is diminished, and the rest of your material becomes a bit suspect, deservedly or not.

There is an alternative, using the same scene, with the same footage. Open the narration wider, as in this example: *USO dances were held in gymnasiums and hospitals, canteens and clubs throughout the U.S., and it was at a dance like this that Tim met the girl of his dreams.* You're not writing as closely to that one particular image; at the same time, you're offering a valuable reminder that your characters are just two people caught up in a time and a situation that's bigger than both of them. The footage is no longer generic wallpaper, but illustrative of an era.

Writing to picture also means that the words you choose work in tandem with the visuals. Here's an example. You are making a film about a team of cyclists competing in the Tour de France. You need to introduce Ralph Martinez, riding for the Americans. In the scene you're narrating, it's early morning and the cyclists are gathered in a village square, drinking coffee or juice, eating pastries, and psyching themselves up for a day on the Tour. The specific shot starts close on a croissant. A hand wearing a bicycling glove reaches in and picks up the pastry; the shot widens and pulls back as we follow the pastry up to a rider's mouth, and see that it is a young man (Ralph) perched on his bike, sipping coffee as he laughs and talks with teammates. Some narration options:

- *Pastry and coffee start the day for Ralph Martinez and his American teammates.* Too "on the nose"—we can see the pastry and coffee for ourselves.
- *Ralph Martinez, getting ready for his third tour, is riding with the American team.* This won't work, because the words "Ralph Martinez" will fall too soon, probably when we're still looking at a big glob of jam on a croissant. You want your narration to roughly mirror the picture and to arrive at Ralph when the visuals do.
- *Riding with the Americans is Ralph Martinez, in his third Tour de France.* This might work—it's hard to tell until you see and hear it against picture. Note that you don't need to say "team" because it can be assumed. Chances are that by this point in the film you also won't need to say "de France." You want to be as economical in word use as possible. Better to have a moment for natural sound than to keep yammering away at the viewers.

Writing to picture can be difficult, especially for those who resist rewriting. While a film is being edited, nearly everything is subject to change. A scene needs to be cut down to give another scene more time. An archival shot needs to be changed because the rights to it aren't available. A sequence is moved from the last half of the film to the first half and therefore needs to be set up differently. From the assembly through to script lock, narration is a moving target. You must be willing to make changes. When enough changes pile up, the editor or someone else on the production team will record a new scratch narration track and lay it against picture. As you'll discover, at least some of these revisions will need further revising. Eventually, though, the script will be locked, the picture will be locked, and the narration will be finished.

WRITING NARRATION TO BE SPOKEN

Narration scripts are, by design, written to be spoken out loud. Every word counts. Important words should stand out in a sentence or paragraph. Sentences should be short and written in an active voice. Phrases should be reviewed to ensure that they don't create a confusing impression, such as *Mark left Philip. Underneath the house, a skunk was waiting.* Reading it, the meaning is clear. Hearing it, you wonder if Mark left Philip underneath the house, or if the skunk is going to catch Mark unaware. *The remains were sent to the local anthropology lab. There, they believed Dr. Smith could provide vital information.* The remains believe something about Dr. Smith?

You also need to avoid tongue twisters and quotation marks; audiences can't hear the irony when a narrator says, *Eleanor was "sorry," but no one believed her.* On paper, a reader could reasonably figure that Eleanor had made an apology but it was taken as false. To the listener, it sounds like the narrator has determined that Eleanor is in fact sorry, but no one believes her. There's a small but important distinction. (For the same reason, you need to be wary of words that sound alike but have different meanings, and of conjunctions, such as "shouldn't," which may be misheard as "should.")

The solution is very simple. Read your narration out loud, even as you're writing it. You will find it far easier to hear the rhythm, feel where the strong words are falling, and get a sense of what's hard to say or where words are superfluous. Then read it aloud again (and again, and again) against picture.

If you are the film's final narrator, at some point you'll have to record the actual voice-over. As you watch documentaries, pay attention to the narrator's tone. Morgan Spurlock's upbeat energy pumps up the narration of *Super Size Me*. Al Gore brings two separate tones to his voice-over in *An Inconvenient Truth*: one is the public voice that lectures on climate change, and the other is a more private, intimate voice in which he talks about his life and family. Actors hired to record voice-over for films tend to aim for clarity and neutrality in their tone.

SOME GENERAL GUIDELINES FOR NARRATION

Reapply the Rules of Grammar

As with proposal writing, narration writing must be grammatical. Common problems include dangling and misplaced modifiers, dangling participles, a confusing use of pronouns, a lack of parallel form, incorrect or inexact use of common words (such as *fewer* and *less; but* and *and; since, like,* and *as;* and *might* and *may*), and use of nonsequiturs. Some excellent style books are available, including *The Elements of Style,* a classic by William Strunk, Jr., and E. B. White; *The Associated Press Stylebook and Libel Manual,* edited by Norm Goldstein, and *The New York Times Manual of Style and Usage,* by Allan M. Siegal and William G. Connolly.

Use Anticipation

Narration needs to follow the arc of the story, not lead it. In the film's opening minutes, you want to set up the questions that will drive your story forward. You then want to anticipate the audience's needs and almost intuitively seed information in, just as—or just after—the question or confusion begins to flicker in the viewer's mind. Pay attention as you watch a well-made film, and you'll notice this happening. You turn to a friend and say, "I don't understand; I thought she couldn't run for governor," and seconds later, the narration answers your question: A loophole in electoral law had worked to her advantage.

Avoid Stereotyping

Use the most gender-neutral terms available (e.g., *firefighter* rather than *fireman, police officer* rather than *policeman*). This is important for two reasons. It more accurately represents the world in which we live, and it's a step toward acknowledging (and involving) an audience of diverse backgrounds.

Avoiding stereotyping also means being careful of "code" words (saying "suburban" when you mean white or middle class, for example) and watching out for an overlay of judgment based on stereotypes, such as "She was pushing 40, but still attractive." Whose point of view does a statement like this reflect? "Pushing 40" implies that this is an unbelievably ancient age, and the "but" is a dead giveaway that nobody on the production team could imagine anyone over 25 being worth a second glance. Stereotypes—dumb jock, dumb blonde, little old lady, "not your grandmother's store"—have no place in documentary narration. Mothers-in-law run corporations and countries; "geezers" set foreign policy and rob banks.

Watch Out for Anachronisms

If you are telling narration from a point of view within a story, stay within the boundaries of that point of view. This means respecting the limitations of your character's frame of reference, including time and place. An example of narration that fails to do this comes from *When Dinosaurs Roamed America*, an animated series from the Discovery Channel. Narrator John Goodman is speaking from the point of view of a dinosaur, trying to size up a new beast he's encountered. *The raptor's never seen a dinosaur like this before*, Goodman says. *Is it a predator, or is it prey? No other creature in the world looks like a half-plucked turkey and walks like a potbellied bear. Still, an oddball can be dangerous.* This narration has the dinosaur comparing what he sees to animals he has no knowledge of, since they won't exist for several million years. For the audience, the comparison may be valuable, but its use here pulls us out of the story. To use the comparison, the producers should have acknowledged the leap in time by moving—even briefly—outside the raptor's point of view, for example: *The raptor's never seen a dinosaur like this before. Scientists today say it probably looked like a cross between a plucked turkey and a potbellied bear. To the raptor, it just looks odd—and oddballs can be dangerous.*

You also want to be careful, when speaking of the past, not to impose your twenty-first-century values, assumptions, and knowledge.

Limit the Number of Ideas in Each Block of Narration

Your narration should convey only the story points needed to get to the next sync material; if you go too far or include too many points, your audience will lose track of the information and will be distracted or confused by what follows. For example, here's a piece of narration from *Not a Rhyme Time*, a program from the *I'll Make Me a World* series: *In the spring of 1967, Amiri Baraka was scheduled to address the Black Writers' Conference at Fisk University in Nashville, Tennessee. Gwendolyn Brooks was also on the program.*

The tension in the film comes from the fact that Baraka represents the new Black Arts Movement, and Brooks—a Pulitzer Prize-winning author who publishes with a large, mainstream publisher—represents the "establishment." The interaction of the two will help to spark Brooks's transformation, which is the focus of the story.

Look at what happens if we go too far and turn the corner with this narration: *In the spring of 1967, Amiri Baraka was scheduled to address the Black Writers' Conference at Fisk University in Nashville, Tennessee. Gwendolyn Brooks was also on the program. She had prepared to read her poem "The Life of Lincoln West."* Suddenly the focus is on this one particular poem, and the power of the narration is lost.

This is probably one of the most common and most serious narration mistakes people make. Say less, say it better, and say it in the best possible way to advance your story, including the one being told by the pictures.

Foreshadow Important Information

The American troops battling the British in the Revolutionary War were promised in July of 1776, when the fighting broke out, that they would all be discharged by December 31. Don't wait to tell the audience this until it's December 31 in your film's chronology. Tell them in July, when they won't think it matters; remind them in September, when the war is dragging on. That way, when winter sets in, it will be on their minds—just as it must have been on General Washington's mind—when the troops are tired and demoralized, and there's no way that Washington can keep his word.

Understand the Different Roles Played by Narration and Sync Material

It's all too common for filmmakers to use talking heads to do work that is better done by narration, and vice versa. Sometimes, this happens because the casting is weak; everybody talks about everything, nothing is differentiated, and they all might as well be narrating.

Ideally, your interviewees should be advancing the story through the lens of their own expertise, experience, and point of view. This is information that is more valuable, in some ways, than narration, and it's certainly more personable. Using these characters to convey information that narration could convey just as well is something of a waste. Conversely, if you replace too many of your talking heads or too much of what they say with narration, you risk pulling the heart and soul out of your film. Even people who are resistant to talking heads would prefer a good visit with an enjoyable character to narration.

Except in films where the filmmaker's investigation, at least in part, drives the film, narration is generally not the best way to contradict an interviewee. The subject says, "No one knew about those documents," and a disembodied voice interrupts, *No one knew? It seemed unlikely.* So how do you contradict people on screen? You find another interviewee to offer a rebuttal, or you film scenes that contain evidence contradicting the interviewee's statement. Let the individuals, facts, and story speak for themselves, and trust that audience members can decide the truth for themselves.

Use Words Sparingly and Specifically

Screen time is a precious commodity, and you want your narration to be as spare as possible. Don't waste good airtime on words that are little more than filler, such as: *Salinas. A town of working people, it hardly seems the place for a murder. But on January 14, 1998, the owners of a house discovered something that would change that impression forever.* A quick check shows that Salinas is a city of around 123,000 people, and that in the 20 years before the homeowners discovered a body buried beneath their house, a total of 218 people had been killed in Salinas, including 18 in 1997. The narration pumped emotion into the story, but it's not useful or even accurate.

The perceived need for hype—most often on commercial television—often seems to lead to imprecise writing. *In rural Michigan, a search for a missing man ends in cold-blooded murder.* Well, actually, it doesn't. If the search ended in cold-blooded murder, then someone involved in the search would have ended up dead. What happened is that a missing-person case is revealed to be a murder case—the search for the missing man leads to a corpse. Why not say that?

Along the same lines, you want to avoid writing that is passive and vague, especially if the result is generally inaccurate. Early in *Jonestown: Paradise Lost*, the narrator says, *By the late 1960s and early '70s, the streets of America erupted in violence and civil strife. The war in Vietnam, civil rights marches and political assassinations played out on television. Out of this turmoil thousands of Americans flocked to hear the sermons of a charismatic preacher named Jim Jones. A fiery orator, Jones's early speeches were a mixture of socialist ideals and Christian redemption.* If you consider how valuable the real estate of broadcast time is, why waste a block of time on such generalities? As importantly, why *tell* us that Jones is charismatic or fiery, rather than allow us to witness it, either directly or through the eyes of his followers? And if it's important to state that the speeches mixed "socialist ideals and Christian redemption," those terms need to be teased apart and clarified.

Using words sparingly also means choosing the best word to describe what you mean, being careful of nuances. Does a teenager walk across the room or saunter? Does a CEO say that he doesn't have numbers for the fourth quarter, or does he admit that fact? Has the world leader made an impassioned speech or launched into a tirade? Was a nation's capital liberated, or did it fall? Was it a conflagration—a term that has specific meaning among firefighters—or simply a bad fire? Choose your words carefully, and be sure the meaning you want is not only the most exciting, but also the most accurate.

Along these lines, try to avoid the slogans of others, whether you agree with them or not. For example, rather than adopt the phrases "pro-life" or "pro-choice," state that someone is either for or against abortion rights.

Use Telling Details

A well-placed detail can convey a tremendous amount of story information. If there were any doubts about the need for a campaign to register voters in Selma, Alabama, they were dispelled in *Eyes on the Prize* by this fact: *More than half of Dallas County citizens were black, but less than one percent were registered* [to vote]. Details can set a stage where visuals are insufficient, as in *The Civil War* series: *Sherman began his march. Sixty-two thousand men in blue were on the move in two great columns. Their supply train stretched 25 miles. A slave watching the army stream past wondered aloud if anybody was left up north.* And details can convey tone and wit, as in *Troublesome Creek: A Midwestern*, narrated by filmmaker Jeanne Jordan: *Like a lot of families facing a real crisis, we immediately stopped talking about it.*

Put Information into Context

Your narration needs to move the story along, which means it should not only impart facts, but also make it clear how they are relevant to the story you're telling. *The 390 people in the club now fought their way to an exit* is interesting, but I have no way of knowing if that's a lot or a little. If the club is Madison Square Garden, it's a very small crowd. In contrast, *390 people—nearly twice as many as the club could legally hold—fought their way to an exit* tells you that laws were broken even before disaster occurred. The same is true for motivation. *The mayor called a late-night meeting* may not advance your story as well as *Hoping to avoid the press, the mayor called a late-night meeting.* Motivation must be fact checked, however. Never guess at what someone was thinking or feeling, unless your narration makes clear that it's speculation, as in, *She might have been concerned not to hear from him; perhaps that's why she got into her car that night.*

If quantity is important to convey, offer it in terms that are comparative, rather than giving specific numbers. *From head to tail, the dinosaur would have been half as long as a football field.* Comparisons and context are also useful when discussing quantities from the past. It's common for filmmakers to imply that someone "only making $5 a day" in 1905 was being exploited, without finding out what this amount meant at the time, what it might buy, and how it compared to other incomes at the time.

As you add this context, keep in mind that you're building toward story events. You need to remind the audience occasionally (not constantly) what's at stake, what information we know, and where we're going. *The board will stop hearing testimony at 9:30. At that point, their vote will decide the future of this regional school system.* Offer gentle clues about the outcome as we move forward. *He had gambled everything, and he had lost. As Ransom's troops trudged wearily north . . .*

Get off the Dime

Like the story itself, narration needs to keep moving forward. It's surprising how often narration repeats the same information over and over, especially to remind viewers that they're seeing something for the first time, or that it's very dangerous, or that no one knows what's around the next corner. If you've told us once that a particular military unit is untrained and untested, don't tell us again; build on that information as you move the story forward.

Don't Drop Names

If people are worth mentioning, they're worth identifying. The first time someone's name comes up in narration, let us know who the person is, even if you think that we'd have to be living under a rock not to know. You don't have to go into a lot of detail, just enough to remind those who know and inform those who don't: *Noted composer Leonard Bernstein once said . . .*, or, *He was filmed in performance by cinematographer Gordon Parks . . .*

Along the same lines, try to anticipate words that your audience may be unfamiliar with, whether they're spoken by the narrator (and a more familiar word can't be substituted) or spoken by an interviewee or someone on camera. If the word's meaning is not clear in the context, you may need to set it up. For example, suppose the historic artifacts you're presenting on screen include a bill of sale for a frigate. You might set it up as, *That day, the general placed an order for a new sailing ship, one outfitted for war.*

Put Lists in an Order that Builds (or Descends)

This is fairly straightforward. You want your paragraphs to pack a punch. Look at the following line of narration from the series *Liberty! The American Revolution*, describing the British invasion of New York in 1776: *30,000 troops. 10,000 sailors. 300 supply ships. 30 battleships with 1200 cannons. It is the largest seaborne attack ever attempted by England until the twentieth century.* What's great about this is that the build is not by number but by power; in fact, the numbers decrease from 30,000 (troops) to 1 (attack). But the power goes from men to supply ships to battleships, and news of the force that's about to hit the newly independent states is delivered with a sentence that jumps the chronology and lands us, very briefly, in the present. It's very effective drama.

Use an Active Voice

You want your narration to be as active as possible. For example, *A decision was made to allow Coca-Cola to advertise on school property.* Who made the decision, and how? (I don't remember where I encountered this tip, but if you can insert the phrase "by zombies," the sentence is passive.) A more active way to say this is, *By a vote of 4 to 1, the school board decided to allow Coca-Cola to advertise on school property.* With this said, remember that you're writing to picture, so if we're watching a scene where we know it's the school board, and can actually see four hands up and one down, you don't want to say this. But if we're seeing a shot of the hallway with soda vending machines all lined up, you want narration that helps that shot along.

Help to Differentiate among Similar Things

Narration can play an important role in getting a viewer through a succession of battles, or medical interventions, or political gatherings. Since you've been careful to film a series of events that build on each other, and not just three or four examples of the same thing, your narration may be needed to simply make that build a little more clear or fill in the details. *The operation on Bill's knee had only improved mobility. Now Dr. Fishman needed to add cartilage . . .*

Do the Math

If you write narration that says, *Born in 1934, she was 18 when she met Mark*, there are viewers who will be so distracted trying to figure out the year she met Mark (1952) that they'll momentarily lose track of your story. Whether it's calculating profits or age or elapsed time, it's best to write it in a way that doesn't make the viewer do the work. This is not an issue of involving the audience in the story, it's a matter of not wanting to distract them from it.

Avoid Hype

If a story is truly astonishing or an event is truly chilling or a person is really sinister, that fact should become evident through the story or character or event and the way you present it. The cheapest and worst way to try to pump emotion into a piece is through adjectives and hyperbole. Frankly, audiences become skeptical when narrators begin to sound like over-caffeinated salespeople. If your story is really good, it will sell itself.

Know When to Stop Narrating

Prepare the moment, and then let it play. If you're building toward the battle of Waterloo or a lifesaving operation or a statewide volleyball tournament, get us there and then let it play for a bit. Audiences need a respite from the talking; they need time to feel those moments of humor or pathos or fear. Anticipate those moments and build them in, whether it means a moment of silence or a moment with music or just action and sync sound. This is also true when the information is very complex and needs to be processed, or when it's very funny and the audience needs time to laugh.

CHAPTER 14

Storytelling: A Checklist

Here's a list of questions to be asked at each stage of production, and especially as you near the end of the editing process:

- Given a choice between your film and the latest sitcom or indie drama, which would you choose? Are you telling a compelling and dramatic story and giving the viewer a reason to watch?
- Does your film involve the viewer in a story unfolding on screen, rather than talk at them?
- Are there interesting questions being asked and answered throughout, offering mystery, intrigue, and suspense?
- Are you offering new information and an unusual perspective, or just rehashing tired, unchallenging material?
- Have you established your story and themes sufficiently, so that viewers can anticipate where you're going and will be surprised and engaged when you take unexpected turns?
- Are you in the driver's seat of your film, steering toward emotional and intellectual highlights? Have you created moments of discovery for the audience, allowing them to reach their own conclusions before having them confirmed or denied?
- If there is backstory in your film, have you gotten a story under way that motivates the audience to want to go there?
- If your subject is complex or technical, are there points in the forward-moving story that motivate viewers to want to understand that complexity?
- Have you "cast" the film carefully, with a manageable group of characters who fairly represent the complexity of an issue and not just its extremes? Or, if your focus is the extremes, have you made that context clear?
- Do individual characters stand out and play differentiated roles in your overall story and film, or is their presence generic?

- Does the story that was set up at the film's beginning pay off at the end? Can you articulate that story in a sentence or two?
- As creative or unusual as your film is, are the choices you've made transparent enough that the film can genuinely be considered a documentary, meaning that it truthfully reflects the factual record as remembered or reported by you and your team?

SOURCES AND NOTES

Credit and thanks are due to Steve Fayer and Jon Else, who created earlier versions of this list for the producers at Blackside, Inc., in Boston.

PART III

Talking about Story

CHAPTER 15

Alex Gibney

Filmmaker Alex Gibney founded Jigsaw Productions in 1982, and in the years since has produced films with partners including Participant Productions, Magnolia Films, Sony Pictures Classics, ZDF-ARTE, BBC, and PBS. The company's website notes that Gibney is "well known for crafting stories that take an unflinching look at the political landscape of America." When we spoke in 2010, his film *Casino Jack and the United States of Money* had just premiered at the 2010 Sundance Film Festival. Other recent films included *Gonzo: The Life and Work of Dr. Hunter S. Thompson; Taxi to the Dark Side*, the 2008 Academy Award winner for Best Documentary Feature; and *Enron: The Smartest Guys in the Room*, nominated for the 2006 Academy Award. For both *Enron* and *Gonzo*, Gibney won the Writers Guild of America award for Best Documentary Screenplay.

The list of projects completed since 2010 is extensive, and includes *We Steal Secrets: The Story of Wikileaks, The Armstrong Lie, Finding Fela*, and *Going Clear: Scientology and the Prison of Belief.*

We spoke by phone in March 2010, as Gibney was en route to catch a plane from New York to Los Angeles.

I wanted to talk particularly about Gonzo, Taxi to the Dark Side, and Enron. At first glance, these are difficult subjects: a deceased writer, torture, accounting. How do you approach a subject, and how do you begin to find a story within it?

In the case of *Taxi*, I was approached to do a film about torture, and initially reluctant because it was a very difficult subject and I wasn't sure the subject would be a film. And so I looked for a story, and Dilawar's moved me very much, the way [*The New York Times* reporters] Tim Golden and Carlotta Gaul had told it. It had a strong emotional heart, and in a peculiar way, connected up this man [in Afghanistan] with Iraq, Guantánamo, and indeed Washington, just by following the threads. The people who were in charge of Dilawar's interrogation in Afghanistan are then sent to Iraq just before Abu Ghraib. Once Dilawar dies, they send the passengers in Dilawar's taxi to Guantánamo, as if to suggest that they'd really stumbled on a conspiracy, when these guys were nothing but peanut farmers. And then you get some sense that the Dilawar story was actually heard in Washington, D.C. And so finding ways to have that central story feather throughout the film, even as we're dealing with McCain and Bush and Cheney and all of that other stuff, was critical. It's one of the reasons I picked that story.

The father and daughter of Dilawar, in *Taxi to the Dark Side*.
Photo credit Keith Bedford.

In the case of the other two, it was more about finding the themes inside the stories, and the characters are so rich. And even in the case of *Taxi*, to find the characters *around* the story of Dilawar, who was dead, that was hard. But that's where the stories, I think, get good. It's fleshing out great characters and seeing how they perform in action, just like a movie.

Are there strategies for how you do your research?

I have characters in my films who are journalists, so to some extent, I'm being introduced to subjects by people who have done a tremendous amount of research already. I want to honor that rather than pretend that I found it, when in fact they did. We also do a tremendous amount of research ourselves, so that at the end—and particularly if we're taking somebody on—nobody can say that there's anything that's factually inaccurate.

Yet I also want to take that journalistic rigor and find a visual language, when telling a story, that will create what [filmmaker] Werner Herzog called the poet's truth rather than the accountant's truth. That's why I have an argument sometimes with people in the audience who stand up and say, "Why don't you just give it to us straight? Why don't you take out all this junk?" I feel like what they're really asking me to do is to show somebody at a blackboard with a pointer, going point by point by point through a story. I don't find that very compelling. It doesn't do what film does best, which is to engage people emotionally.

In other words, the subject itself is not a good movie—or a good book, for that matter. You have to put it together in a way that tells a compelling story if you want to reach an audience.

That's right. What I do is similar to doing a nonfiction book. The best nonfiction books, in my view, are like good fiction in terms of their storytelling and their sense of narrative momentum. I lead the audience (hopefully) through some kind of unexpected emotional journey; this is where narrative issues come into play.

In the case of *Taxi*, a lot of viewers have told me that they came to identify greatly with the soldiers and liked them. And then at the end of the film, they found out they're the killers, that they were convicted. And that was a blow to viewers, but they couldn't go back to where they might have been if they had known that information to begin with, and say to themselves, "Oh, now I think they're bad guys." They couldn't do that. "No, I like these kids." That's something more profound.

Knowing when to reveal information is part of the skill of good storytelling—too soon and it's meaningless, too late and we don't need it. How do you know when to fold in new information?

It's a really hard thing. With *Taxi*, we had to discover some of that in the storytelling. The film wasn't quite working for a long, long time. One of the things we realized was that we revealed the [prison] sentences of soldiers a bit too early in the film; it was toward the end, but not sufficiently close to the end. Once we revealed the sentences, the audience felt like the story was over and we'd better wrap it up. But we still had a lot of story, and that was just dead wrong. So we had to shorten the film and also move the section of the soldiers being sentenced further down, where it made sense in terms of expectations of narrative structure: Oh, we've concluded their story, so the film must be about to end.

Do you run test screenings periodically during the editing?

Yes, particularly when we get close. I'm doing that now on a couple of films. And it's really important, because you learn a lot about what people don't get, who they like, who they don't like, obviously whether it's too long.

Where do you find your test audiences? Who's in them?

Usually it's a combination of friends and a few acquaintances or friends of friends. It's generally a reasonably friendly audience with a few strangers thrown in. But even in that audience, you can feel the room when you watch the film, and the reactions that are consistent among the viewers are the ones you most likely want to listen to.

There was a woman, Amanda Martin, who is the blonde executive [in *Enron*], and in our original cut she ended the film with a kind of confession, in effect saying, "I was human," meaning she was deeply tempted to become corrupt. But nobody wanted to accept her in that role. They're thinking, "Human? Screw you. You profited from this company." They weren't prepared to hear that from her, because they saw her, very pretty, in this very opulent house, dressed in very expensive clothes. But they *were* prepared to hear it from that younger kid [former trader Colin Whitehead]. We thought the ending was beautiful, but they hadn't seen in Amanda what we had seen in the cutting room. They could only reference what was in the film. So we took that bit out and put the kid in at the end, and people were much more comfortable with that.

Alternatively, you would have had to go back and restructure the film to get the audience to the point where they would have accepted her.

Yes, and I don't think there's anything wrong with that. Also, peculiarly, what ends up happening—and this is the hardest part to accept as a filmmaker—is that the story you create has unexpected dimensions that you never imagined. And rather than extinguish them, you're better off embracing them.

Can you give me an example?

Well, there were a lot of thematic issues I wanted to explore in *Enron*. And they were very meaningful in broader social context—for example, how the banks were complicit in Enron's fraud. We have some of it in there, but we had to take a lot of it out because it was just stopping the narrative. None of that stuff would matter if people weren't going to be riveted by the story. So it had to go by the wayside.

There is another example, in *Taxi*. There was a sequence which I love, which is now in the DVD extras. It was one of these weird side trips you take. [There was a] hunger strike at Guantánamo when we were there, and there was a desperate need to figure out how to break the strike. One of the things they were going to do was force-feed the prisoners who were on hunger strike, so they needed a way of restraining them. And lo and behold, some enterprising soldier at Guantánamo found this website called www.restraintchair.com. It turns out that there was a sheriff in Denison, Iowa, who was manufacturing restraint chairs to help calm people who were whacked out on crank, until they could reason with them, and to do so in a way that was not hurtful. So out of the blue, this sheriff gets a call from Operation Enduring Freedom saying, "We'd like to order 50 of your restraint chairs." That was a big order for this guy. I found that sequence to be funny, and I went out and visited with him, and we had a great sequence about it. But ultimately, once we got to the death of Dilawar, there was very little interest by the audience in exploring that kind of dark humor in the film.

I had other Catch-22 moments in the film that, bit by bit, I had to excise because they couldn't see—I had been immersed in this subject and had developed a kind of gallows humor that a doctor develops by being in an operating room all the time. But the audience couldn't go there. They wanted to experience the anguish without irony, and I couldn't rob them of that. So we had to eliminate a lot of that material that ultimately was distracting.

And just to clarify, that's a different kind of omission than, say, leaving out the negative side of Hunter S. Thompson's life, the pain he at times caused his family, just because you want to present a positive portrait of him.

Right. I'm not Hunter Thompson's press agent. Interestingly enough, in the case of Hunter—and we talked about this a lot in the cutting room—I think his bipolar nature, the way he would vacillate between dark and light, the way he would be wonderfully generous and also very cruel, I think that allowed him to appreciate the essential contradictions of the American character in a way that somebody who's more balanced probably couldn't.

I wanted to return to the analogy between your films and nonfiction books, because you've also noted that in your films, as in books, you can hear the voice of the author.

Yes, in terms of the style. Likewise, in a film, you have to find a visual language to carry the story. And that language should be different, in my view. There're some people like Ken Burns, whose visual language is the same no matter what story they're telling. The archival imagery may be different, but the style is exactly the same. To me, I think you find a style that fits the subject.

How do you decide upon a visual language for a particular film?

In *Gonzo*, we were wrestling with the fact that the guy's a writer. And a lot of the visual style—that scene of the motorcycle at the beginning of the film, it's overlaid with a kind of paper texture that's meant to evoke, in an emotional way, that this is a kind of written story, even though we're out there on a motorcycle with the surf. The other thing we were playing with was this blend that Hunter investigated between fact and fiction. He liked to rocket back and forth between them. He was a good reporter, at least early on. And then he would occasionally, for dramatic effect and also for thematic value, fly into fantasy. With something like the taco stand scene, we visualized it. That's a passage that's from the book [*Fear and Loathing in Las Vegas*], done in a way that felt true to their experience.

That's an interesting example, because the visuals are created to look a bit like home movies, while the audio, as you note on screen, is an "Original audio recording by Hunter S. Thompson & Oscar Acosta, Las Vegas, 1971."

Even though it's fiction, it was much more realistically shot than some of the other material we used, which was nonfiction. We were playing with that mixture of fact and fiction that Hunter liked to investigate. [That] was one of the reasons we decided to shoot his wife Sandy against green screen. [Still and motion images of their history together play behind her as she's interviewed.] She became the person that knew him the longest throughout his life. So rather than shoot her in a living room or a yoga studio—she's now a yoga teacher—or something, there was something literary to me about seeing different backgrounds behind her, as if she were a character, literally, in a fiction or nonfiction narrative. So that she didn't have her own space; she was inside this guy's story. It wasn't about, "Where are they now?" It was about, "Where were they then?"

That's a kind of visual choice you have to plan for ahead of time.

Yes, you do. Sometimes you stumble into that stuff, but you do have to think about it beforehand. In *Enron*, we thought about it a lot beforehand, and certainly in *Taxi*, too. The way we shot the interviews of everybody who was at Bagram, the guards and some of the prisoners—they were shot against a painted backdrop and lit with high-contrast lighting, where you have one side of the face in light and one side of the face in dark. That was meant to do two things: to signal the moral ambiguity of the guards, but also, in a story that's so complicated in terms of who's military police, who's military intelligence, who's the prisoner, it was meant to convey one very simple idea, which is: anybody who's photographed that way came from Bagram. And also that dark lighting had a kind of prison vibe, so that you create a sense of place. We had to think that out ahead of time, or else it never would have worked.

How much do you put on paper before you shoot? Do you have a basic narrative skeleton?

Yes, I think it's fair to say that I have a narrative skeleton ahead of time. Not too detailed, but at least a sense of the story that is going to be told. And then I go out and try to talk to people, and occasionally shoot stuff on location, as in *Taxi*, because that was a story that in some ways was still unfolding. So I went down and shot a sequence in Guantánamo, for example. And then of course the story changes, and you have to reckon with that. But if you don't at least give it some contour up front, then you don't have enough focus, I think, to really dig in.

Do you write a treatment?

We usually have a treatment, but it's not very long. It's maybe three or four pages, like a general sense of structure. And with that in mind, I go out and get stuff. And sometimes I see an opportunity to get something that wasn't in the plan, and I get it just because it seems like it might be great material.

There is a certain kind of filmmaking where you wade into an event and you just observe. But even there, it seems to me, you're being influenced by your own preconceptions—what you know, what you're hearing off camera—and you begin to focus on things that interest you. There was a lot about Enron that we could have gone into but didn't, because I had a sense of what to tackle, what would be a good story. But, that having been said, you do improvise a lot, based on material.

Early on in my career, I had a much more rigid idea about what to look at and cover, and what I was interested in. I would tend to make the material fit my idea of the story. The problem with that is that sometimes you end up using a lot of rather weak material, instead of looking at what you've shot and realizing, "Man, this is strong," and finding a way to include that material. If there's not a kind of balance between those two things, then either the film is all great material but no narrative thrust, or it's all story and theme and no heat, no passion. The key is finding the right balance.

In the case of *Enron*, we didn't know exactly who was going to talk. If Rebecca Mark had talked to me—she was the woman who, among other things, had done the Bhopal initiative, which was a big power plant they tried to make happen in India—the narrative might have taken a slightly different direction. Also, halfway through the film [production], we discovered the California audiotapes. We spent much more time on the California story than the authors of the book did, and the reason is that those audiotapes told us something about the culture at Enron that was so powerful, and something that you couldn't do on a printed page. Part of what makes them powerful is *hearing* the kind of "frat house" attitude of the people [Enron traders] laughing while the California grid goes down.

In Gonzo, the imagery is often quite unexpected. We see an actor as Thompson, for example, sitting at his desk in Woody Creek, Colorado and writing about the attacks on 9/11, as the attacks are seen—impossibly and very stylistically—through the windows in front of him. Or we're looking at a still of Thompson holding a gun, and it suddenly becomes animated.

It's looking at that in a playful way. Hunter really pushed the envelope of that kind of storytelling. As a filmmaker, I was trying to say right up front, "Beware." So when you see that photograph of him shooting his typewriter in the snow and suddenly it becomes live, and you see the typewriter jump and then it snaps back into the photograph, that was a way of saying: "Watch out. Everything is not what it seems. There's a kind of playful manipulation of reality going on here."

When Hunter does his riff in the campaign trail book about Edmund Muskie being addicted to Ibogaine, I don't think he really intended to fool his audience into thinking that "Oh my God, Ed Muskie is eating Ibogaine!" It was a playful, satirical way of saying to people, "This guy looks like and acts like he's a drug addict. That's how bad he is." So again, it's stretching the form, but in a way that, at its best, Hunter could do without violating larger notions of truth. I think later on it became sloppier in Hunter's writing. But in his prime and in some of the best pieces later, he really used that to great effect, where there was great, real, factual material, but then there was a lot of playful stuff. And I think he laid out the rules so that you as the reader could get it. We tried to play with that a little bit in the visual storytelling.

You also lay out the rules. The dramatizations (or reenactments, or recreations) are styled in a way that distinguishes them from actual archival materials, for example, and when something is real—the taco stand audio, for example, or the Enron traders on the phone—you make that *clear as well.*

I think that's pretty important. Sometimes I get criticized for recreations in my films. People say, "Why would you do such a cheap trick?" or something like that. Like the suicide of Cliff Baxter in *Enron*. I have a pretty careful explanation for why I did that. It may fool somebody at first, but then it's very quickly revealed what's happening, so there's no attempt to deceive the viewer. I think that's terribly important, because the idea of faking something and pretending it's real is really a big, big problem. [Audiences] need to have a sense of trust that the filmmaker's done their best to show you what they think the truth is.

There are different ways to the truth, and different kinds of truth. That's why every filmmaker needs to have a different kind of an approach, a different set of rules. You let the audience in on those rules right off the bat; you signal people. If you do that and you follow those rules, then everything is fine, because then the audience gets comfortable with what you're doing. The way *Enron* starts, both with the Tom Waits music at the beginning and also with that recreation, it lets people know this is not a *Frontline*, so you shouldn't see it that way. The idea of creating a film that looks and feels like a *Frontline* but then mixes artificially recreated footage with regular archival footage and pretends they're the same—that's hugely problematic.

The actor Johnny Depp "narrates" Gonzo, but only in the sense that he is reading from Thompson's work in voice-over—so he's really a stand-in for Thompson, and we know that because you also filmed Depp reading with the book in his hand.

Right. That was a play on a lot of different things. Here's the guy who played Hunter [in the dramatic feature *Fear and Loathing in Las Vegas*], now reading Hunter. It also signaled to people in a very simple and clear way—because clarity is another thing that I'm kind of a nut about—that all the narration you hear from now on will be the undependable narrator of Hunter Thompson, as read by Johnny Depp.

What are your thoughts about current efforts to articulate some sort of formalized understanding about documentary film ethics?

That's made me a little bit uncomfortable. If there's some committee that decides what's right, I could find myself on the wrong side of that committee. I think the thing to do is to make people think long and hard about why it's important not to fool the viewer. But I would hate to go back to the old days where—I did a *Frontline* a long time ago. There was a prohibition against using music; music was considered a manipulation. And of course it *is* a manipulation. But it seems to me to be a pretty good storytelling device, and part of what you're doing is telling a story. There are many fictional methods that I like to use. The key is creating a grammar so that viewers know you're doing that, and don't believe that you're showing them a *Frontline* when you're not.

The reason I put in the recreation of Cliff Baxter right at the top was because I felt that—First of all, you don't know yet that it's Cliff Baxter. It could be any executive. But you're riding alongside somebody who's listening to a Billie Holiday song ["God Bless the Child"], which happens to be very carefully chosen. It's the kind of song he might have listened to late at night on the radio, but it's also about how the rich and powerful screw the weak. You're on the seat next to this person, smelling the cigarette, hearing the water going down his throat, and then he kills himself. And that's very intimate—"Oh my God, somebody's just killed himself!" That's a very powerful human emotion. Then, when [the film cuts] to the archival footage, "Cliff Baxter was discovered dead today," blah-blah-blah, you realize, "Okay, that was just a recreation. Now we're in the real world." What I tried to give to the viewer is a sense of identification with that executive, so we're not there the whole time wagging our fingers at the Enron executives and creating too great a distance between them and us. We see the human dimension of this story in a way that's very emotional and palpable. And to me, it's perfectly legit.

That gets to a different aspect of your storytelling, which is that part of being fair as a filmmaker—not balanced in some phony way, but fair—is to allow for complexity, which includes seeing more than one side to a character or a point of view. In an interview you said, "I always take my cue from Marcel Ophüls (The Sorrow and the Pity) *who said something like this: 'I always have a point of view; the trick is showing how hard it was to come to that point of view.'" Can you explain?*

There's another quote that I like a lot, too. [George Bernard] Shaw once said, "Showing a conversation between a right and a wrong is melodrama. Showing a conversation between two rights is a drama." A political science professor of mine would say, "Embrace the contradiction." All those things to me mean that if you find some-body that you think is kind of a bad guy, and then you only show that stuff that fits your preconceptions of who that person is, or the role they're playing, [that's] a kind of melodrama. Much more powerful is a drama, in which that bad guy is actually, in person, kind of a nice guy. Or you're surprised to learn, for example with the guards [at Bagram], these guys who beat a young kid to death, are young kids themselves who, in their own way, are nice guys that have been brutalized by the experience. That, I think, shows a kind of hidden dimension that con-nects us all together, which is part of what filmmaking and storytelling is all about. It doesn't necessarily undermine the moral outrage, but it makes it tougher to point at people and say, "They should wear the black hat, and I wear the white hat."

I try not just to preach to the choir. A lot of times people will come to seeing your point of view, or at least to appreciating your point of view, if they feel that you have respect for theirs. You may not agree with it, but at least you have respect for it and have tried to reckon with it. I think that's important, because otherwise we're just in some kind of endless loop of crossfire from the left, from the right. Ugh. What could be worse?

There are a couple of very pragmatic things I want to talk about. The first is the way that you visualize scenes, creating a strong sense of place.

I like the idea of creating visual beds, particularly in a complex story. An example would be the strip club which [Enron executive] Lou Pai used to inhabit. We shot it in a way that emphasized numbers, and we cut it to music by Philip Glass. We tried to shoot a sense of the place of the California trading floor too, and find music and a shooting style that would convey the frat house atmosphere, to portray it from their point of view. So those are two examples. [Someone else] could have done it very differently.

The other is sequences, which you sometimes name, such as "Shock of Cap-ture" in Taxi to the Dark Side. *Your films are built on sequences, each of which has a unique job to do in the overall film, and each—while different from the others—moves the film forward.*

That's right. I find that helpful, and then if you vary the manner of the sequences, too, it keeps the audience fresh. You keep moving from one place to another, like you're on a journey. It's like a bus tour: We're leaving the Grand Canyon, and now we're headed for the Rockies.

And you've arrived at the airport! Thank you so much.

Delighted. I rarely get to talk about form. When you're a documentarian, the curse is, you almost always only talk about the subject, which is okay, but in terms of documentaries in the last 15 years, I think one of the great things that's happened is that the form has just exploded, which I think is really exciting.

SOURCES AND NOTES

The website for Gibney's company is www.jigsawprods.com. The official website for *Gonzo: The Life and Work of Dr. Hunter S. Thompson* is www.huntersthompsonmovie.com. Interview with Alex Gibney by Alex Leo, "The Gonzo World of Alex Gibney," *The Huffington Post*, posted July 3, 2008, www.huffingtonpost.com/alex-leo/the-gonzo-world-of-alex-g_b_110695.html. The website for *Taxi to the Dark Side* is www.hbo.com/documentaries/taxi-to-the-dark-side. For more information on *Taxi to the Dark Side*, see also Tim Golden, "In U.S. Report, Brutal Details of 2 Afghan Inmates' Deaths," *The New York Times*, May 20, 2005, online at www.nytimes.com/2005/05/20/international/asia/20abuse.html. Information about *Enron* can be found at www.pbs.org/independentlens/enron/film.html.

CHAPTER 16

Susan Kim

Susan Kim is a prolific writer of books, plays, dramatic and documentary films, and children's television. For the stage, she wrote the adaptation of Amy Tan's *The Joy Luck Club*, as well as numerous one-act plays that have been performed at the Ensemble Studio Theatre and elsewhere, and also published. A five-time Emmy Award nominee, her television writing includes more than two dozen children's series. Her documentary credits include *Paving the Way* (1997), a 60-minute film for PBS for which she won the Writers Guild Award; *The Meaning of Food* (2005), a three-hour series for PBS; and the feature-length *Imaginary Witness: Hollywood and the Holocaust* (2007), which explores the 60-year relationship between the U.S. movie industry and the horrors of Nazi Germany.

At the time of this interview, Susan Kim and Elissa Stein had recently published the nonfiction book *Flow: The Cultural Story of Menstruation* (St. Martin's Press, 2009), and she and Laurence Klavan had completed two graphic novels, *City of Spies* and *Brain Camp*, both of which were published by First Second Books in 2010. Since then, she and Klavan completed a young adult trilogy, *Wasteland* (2013); with director Daniel Anker, she wrote the feature documentary *Icebound* (2012); and she was the head writer for the new Scholastic children's television series *Astroblast*.

Susan serves on the faculty of the low-residency MFA Program in Creative Writing at Goddard College, which is where we met in 2008, as advisor and student.

The film I particularly want to talk to you about is Imaginary Witness, *which you wrote (as co-producer), and Daniel Anker directed and produced, along with Ellin Baumel. How did this project come about?*

It was back in 2001, and AMC, American Movie Classics, had a commissioned series, Hollywood and the Blank, Hollywood and Blank. So it was Hollywood and Islam, Hollywood and Vietnam. . . . How does the commercial narrative machine of Hollywood tackle complex geopolitical, historical subjects? And they approached Danny Anker to do Hollywood and the Holocaust. AMC's budgets were quite small, and I think their expectations were very much for it to be a clip show. The schedule was really tight. The budget was very small. And from what we saw of what they were doing, it was what you would expect.

I met with Danny right after 9/11, maybe two or three weeks after, and you could still smell the smoke, even in Danny's apartment near Lincoln Center. We spent half of the conversation talking about the attack, and it was sort of clear to us that—part of it was just pure emotion—this was much bigger than just a clip show, and we don't want to do a clip show. We spent a lot of time talking about, "What are the fictional movies about 9/11 going to be like?" We just immediately started thinking about [the film] in very alive and current terms, as opposed to, say, historical terms. And I think that alone made it seem very, very urgent. From the beginning, the conversation became about: "How is this a current story? What are the issues we're dealing with today? This is not just some dusty subject that happened in the 1940s. This is actually something that has relevance."

All of us were in agreement that we didn't want to do it "trash and cash," one of those quick-and-dirty money jobs. We wanted to do it carefully. And Danny became this incredible warrior of this film, because it was extremely difficult. We had a lot of conflict with AMC, because the schedule was crazy. He started raising outside money, and we just slowed down, because we all thought, okay, this needs a lot of research. We did a ton of reading, all the books and articles we could find, and a ton of screening. And we discussed and argued and screened together for the longest time before we actually started digitizing footage and talking about interviews. Also, we had a fantastic researcher in D.C., Julie Stein, who was pulling material from the Library of Congress and National Archives and feeding it to us.

One of the things that comes through in the film is a very clear evolution, a transformation of the relationship between Hollywood and the Holocaust over this 60-year period. Is that something you discovered through this research?

Absolutely. It was a very cumulative thing. Early on, I drafted a really bad, really preliminary kind of shooting draft. And it was just sort of trying out different structures. For a very long time, we thought the movie moguls' trip to visit the camps in postwar Germany was going to be the wrap-around story. That was one of our earliest structures. When Bruce Shaw, the editor, came on and he started digitizing and laying out the roughest bones, we all kept saying, "We don't want to do chronological. We want to do something more clever." We wanted to impose a sort of a brilliant structure. But the more we started filling in the chronology—I think it was understanding that the chronology was not just a simple schematic device, but that there was extraordinary complexity within the chronology. That if you take it from 1933 until 2001, it followed a psychological arc in terms of the survivor community. There was a business relationship arc, certainly, between Hollywood and Germany in the '30s and '40s. Things like Israel and identity politics in the '60s and '70s. All these things started playing more and more of a part that we could not have anticipated. The miniseries *Roots* was really important in terms of laying the groundwork for the miniseries *Holocaust*.

It took a very long time. We were sort of reading and transcribing and interviewing. There has been some good, interesting literature. Annette Insdorf has written *Indelible Shadows*. Judith Doneson—she was going to be our advisor, and then she died fairly early on in our preproduction—wrote a book called *The Holocaust in American Film*. And there's a wonderful book *Celluloid Soldiers* [Michael Birdwell], which took a look at Warner Bros. and the run-ins they had with conservatives in Congress about interventionism versus isolationism. So it was cumulative. It was sort of like a gesso, just layer after layer after layer, and going back and finding out more and more things.

And then of course the interviews, as you know, inform the direction of your research. All that material got transcribed. I would start sticking pieces of transcript into my drafts while the editor was also starting to do his assemblies. We would all get together, and he would show us what he had assembled, and I would distribute my script, and then we would argue about it, and then Bruce would occasionally take some of what I'd written and try to make it work. And then we would say, "What are we missing? Do we need another interview here?" A lot of times, the interview subjects would mention resources that we didn't know about or hadn't heard about. So we would then go back into research, or we would get more films in, or we would research another person to interview.

I think you have 21 people that you interview on screen. How did you go about selecting them?

There are the obvious people, there are the clever people you interview toward the end to stitch together, there are the people who make the points you want them to make, and then there's sort of the marquee people. You weigh all these different things. Annette Insdorf was someone we obviously wanted. Even though I would say her angle tends to be a bit more European than American, she could certainly speak about it with great authority. So she was one of those "we've got to have." We very much pursued Elie Wiesel, and came very close to getting him, but he was ill, I don't believe he was in the country, and we didn't. That was a big disappointment. But Thane Rosenbaum's a colleague of Wiesel's, and Danny had heard him speak, and we knew that he would make Wiesel's argument: that it was commercializing the Holocaust to film it, and that there's an ethical quandary involved and something obscene about fictionalizing it.

Obviously someone like Steven Spielberg was a big "get." Rod Steiger, in terms of content, he said something very actor-y, but it's really effective. Same thing with Fritz Weaver. He was in *Holocaust*; he played the patriarch in the family Weiss. They're not necessarily adding heavy academic or historical substance, but they're certainly adding the Hollywood flavor, which was also part of the film.

Neal Gabler was one of the last people we interviewed. He screened the film, and we said, "We need you to pull together some things." They really were advisors, all of these people. They came in and screened the film several times, talked to us at great length: "Well, you made that point; you could make this point." And we *really* let these people talk on camera, which was a luxury that AMC would not have allowed us to do on the original budget and schedule. I think Neal Gabler said that he's used to being interviewed for two hours for a documentary and then seeing an 11-second bite go by and that's it. That was a real pleasure about working on this film.

The team used documentary footage to convey the history itself, and the Hollywood footage only to convey the Hollywood approach to the history. Was it difficult to make that work?

I really can't speak highly enough about our editor, Bruce Shaw. Bruce is very creative and thoughtful. And of course later, the whole concept of using documentary to inform us on screen becomes a thematic point.

Such as?

Certainly with, say, *Sophie's Choice* and the use of survivor testimony to inform the detail and the verisimilitude on screen. Certainly with *Shoah*, and the detail Spielberg used in *Schindler's List*. That was very much based on testimony from survivors.

But just visually speaking, it was a lot of back and forth and playing with things. Often it would be the three of us—Danny, Bruce, and me—sitting in the edit room. And I would be writing, and Danny would be researching something online, and Bruce would be editing. And occasionally one of us would say, "Hey, take a look at this," or "Stop, stop, stop. Can we use this?" And it was just a lot of arguing.

It was kind of fractious, like the pervasive smell of Chinese food and burritos and a lot of yelling, because it was very delicate.

Because Imaginary Witness *contains both, it's interesting to compare the raw power of actual Holocaust footage with the different kind of power that comes from fictionalized accounts.*

I think you say that as a filmmaker and filmgoer, with more of an understanding of what's involved. I've seen the film many times, and I'm always intrigued to see people sobbing at *Sophie's Choice*, the scene where she has to choose between her children. I'm very dry-eyed at that point. But I am [continually] blown away by the reunion moment from *This Is Your Life* [a reality program that aired between 1952 and 1963], when Hanna Kohner [a survivor] is reunited with her brother. To me, the difference between Hollywood emotion and real emotion, documentary emotion, is just so vividly different.

One of our big decisions, something we went back and forth on, was whether or not to use actual atrocity footage. There's a very brief glimpse of a skeleton in an oven. It was from the section on *Judgment at Nuremberg* and that film's use of documentary footage. I personally thought it was obscene; I thought that we couldn't use it. But there's a sequence in the documentary where the newsreel footage is finally brought back to Hollywood for the first time. And we just have details of a film projector running, and a voice-over describing what it was like to watch it. We don't actually show the footage.

It's interesting that as the decades pass, the Hollywood dramatizations became increasingly graphic.

Yes. You can see Dan Curtis doing his incredibly graphic *War and Remembrance*, where you have piles and piles of skeletons. And then you have the Einsatzgruppen shooting all these naked people; they're tumbling into a ditch and it's extremely graphic. I think it does have a teachable value for people who don't understand the scope of it. But again, to me, knowing the production history a little bit, I know those are all extras from a nudist colony. You can tell these are plastic skeletons. You can see the show business to it; I think I can. But at the same time, I see the value of it. You need to use strong tools to tell a story.

With such a wealth of material to choose from—60 years of Hollywood moviemaking, plus all the documentary material and interviews—how did you decide what to leave out?

Ultimately—and this is something getting back to dramatic writing— you want everything to serve the story. There are times when something is really fascinating, but it sort of spirals off into [another] direction. For example, when I think of films that I wish we could have included, there was a screwball comedy called *Once upon a Honeymoon* [1942, with Cary Grant and Ginger Rogers], where the couple accidentally go into a concentration camp because they're mistaken as Jews. And it's done as a wacky comedy. I really wish we could have used that. There was a really good film with Kirk Douglas called *The Juggler* [1953]. But you get these clips, you screen the film really carefully, and it doesn't support the structure of the act. Perhaps there's a larger point you're trying to make, and it does not support or challenge it in a way that moves the argument forward.

Documentary film, although I think any good film or any piece of art, frankly—the greatest work is ultimately interactive because it causes you to think and argue, and it doesn't necessarily give you a sealed package. I think anything good has complexity to it. But at the same time, you should be telling a story; you should have a point of view. And it's always that delicate balance about: "Are we sealing this too hermetically? Is there no air in this beat? Are we giving this moment the complexity that it needs, and the detail and the ambiguity it may demand? Or is it just amorphous?" And that's a really difficult thing. It's like: "Is this contributing to the ultimate shape?" There should be a sense of cohesion and vision, or point of view, in the finished piece, whether it's a marble sculpture, a documentary film, a play, a nonfiction book, or a magazine article.

Imaginary Witness looks very critically at its subject. With a film like this, how do you avoid it somehow coming across as a celebration?

The most important thing that we were trying to do in *Imaginary Witness* was pose larger questions. If you do that, by definition, you're not going in a celebratory direction. Celebration implies catharsis, closure, finality, that something has been won. And I think the themes that we were trying to explore are ones that are still active and alive, even when applied to other atrocities and other things that Hollywood attempts, on occasion, to grapple with.

You've described Imaginary Witness *as coming together very organically, and at the same time, it's built on a three-act structure. To me it sort of illustrates a basic point about structure, which is that it's a tool for understanding and shaping the film that exists, as opposed to a formula imposed from without.*

And it's funny because "structure" itself sounds so rigid. It sounds like everything has to fit to a T-square. But of course that's not true. Beautiful structure is like anything. Every great thing has its own structure that works, and it's not necessarily something you can apply to every film, but it makes sense within that film. So you're right. You can look at something and say—for example, with me when I'm working on a documentary, I will write something that to me makes great sense on paper; it's beautifully structured on paper, and we start putting it together, and it's so boring! It doesn't work. So then you start ripping it apart and asking those questions about: "Do we subvert the structure? Do we play with the chronology? Do we shift the perspective so we're not looking at it from this point of view, we're looking from that point of view? Have we misidentified the central event? Is that not the real point of this? Is there something else going on subtextually that we have not been aware of, and that is slowly starting to emerge?" Anybody who understands structure can argue this a lot of different ways. You can give the same raw footage to 10 different filmmakers and they can come up with 10 terrific films that are quite different, which is something that always fascinated me.

You've written a lot of television for children, some of it nonfiction, or at least with documentary elements. Do you approach storytelling differently when you're writing for young audiences?

I've written a lot of *Reading Rainbows*, [which] is a magazine format but often has documentary elements. And I also wrote and produced several episodes of *Really Wild Animals*, a natural history series for children that was produced by National Geographic for CBS. It's a little different because you can't assume that the attention span is there to follow these long, twisting threads over the course of a half hour. You're not necessarily going to have the same kind of setup and payoff, and stories cross-cutting the central story. With children, I tend to be much more modular; more basically educational. Like: "These are the different layers of a rain forest; these are the animals that live in the—." You basically say what the structure is going to be, and then you take them through it. And obviously the bells and whistles are a little more vibrant with kids: humor, animation, songs, jokes. Also, comparative visuals if you're working with young kids. Film editing is hard enough for a very young child to follow, because sudden visual juxtapositions are confusing.

You and Laurence Klavan have two graphic novels coming out this year, both written for middle school children. They're fiction, but one, for example, is inspired by a real-life story, the discovery of a Nazi spy ring in New York City. For documentary filmmakers whose work is sometimes compared to creative nonfiction, or nonfiction novels, the graphic novel seems like another creative model—*certainly as we saw with Ari Folman's* Waltz with Bashir, *an animated documentary memoir.*

Some of the most successful and effective graphic novels are [grounded in] nonfiction. A lot of them are memoir. I'm thinking of *Palestine* by Joe Sacco, and *Persepolis* obviously has documentary elements, but it's still a memoir. And *Stitches, Epileptic, A Drifting Life* . . . They're so strongly drawn and so heightened, it's interesting for documentary filmmakers to take a look at them. They're like storyboards; they're so visual.

What do you say to filmmakers or dramatists who resist the notion of story as being contrived?

I'm always intrigued by people who don't have a taste for it. I have a student this semester who was attacking narrative, attacking theater as being fundamentally conservative. "Why do we have to read the stupid *Poetics*? I am sick of plot. I am tired of character. Why can't we explode them?" She said that all other art forms have transformed radically since, say, the ancient Greeks. She said you cannot look at painting today and say that it's at all based on the same precepts of, say, a Renaissance painting, even though of course they're using the same tools—color and composition and subjects and brush stroke. The rules have been completely exploded, and it's fine. She said, "Why can't drama have the same revolution? When people bend theater"— someone like Richard Foreman or Lee Breuer and Mabou Mines—"it always gets ghettoized."

My argument is, that while much of *The Poetics* is not germane because we live in a different era, there is something about the power of tragedy to effect catharsis. Drama is a really effective form, a really ancient form, and a powerful one. One of the first things children do is play act. They respond to fairy tales—the good guy, the bad guy, the antagonist, the ending—really strongly. The unconscious mind attempts to make narrative every night when we sleep. If we are very bothered, we will have dreams that are rife with subtext and symbolism and thematic development and conflict and strong emotion. I think that's just the way we as humans are neurologically and culturally structured. So I think there is something inherent in the dramatic form that's really powerful. And I think that's why, as storytellers, as people who want to make documentary or write plays, it behooves us to understand the potential of that structure.

I was thinking about *Hands on a Hard Body* yesterday, and I was thinking I don't particularly like marathons or dance-a-thons or endurance things. I would not last holding on to a truck for 48 hours. But that movie has stayed with me. The story actually was very simple: You had a very clear sense of character; there was a real beginning, a real dramatic action, and a real ending. And a surprising person wins, and people flame out. And even though, going into it, I wouldn't have necessarily thought that was an exciting story, I was really captured by it.

Spellbound *is another example of a film like that. I'm going to spend 90 minutes watching kids spell?*

Exactly, exactly. Or *Man on Wire*. These films where you're thinking, "Okay, I could see watching that for 20 minutes." And then 90 minutes later you're sobbing or applauding or jumping back because you want to see something again.

So how would you explain how that's done?

I think part of it is, if you love the story—if you really are emotionally and intellectually compelled by the story—then you start finding the complexity and the nuance. It's all specificity and stakes. Whether you're writing dramatic fiction or doing something that's nonfiction, the more specific you are—and if the specifics serve the dramatic action, and it's a good story to begin with—that, by definition, puts you ahead of nine-tenths of the pack.

People don't want to see a statement. They want to see action. And action is a fight; it's people fighting for what they want, and you don't know who's going to win. This is why people watch sports. For example, *Man on Wire*. We know that Philippe Petit is going to successfully walk across the World Trade towers, but if you break that into the separate battles of his achieving that, you don't know how each thing is going to turn out. And each step is full of surprises. You don't spoon-feed the information to the audience. You let it develop, so that there is suspense: Is he going to get up the stairs or not? Is the guard going to wake up or not?

How would you articulate that in terms of Imaginary Witness?

That there are real setbacks. Each act has different things going on that are very high stakes. Certainly during the 1940s itself, you could argue that thousands and thousands of Jews were being killed every day in the concentration camps, and was the United States going to do anything? Unless you're a historian or you've read a lot about the period, you don't necessarily know what's going to happen.

I think a lot of it has to do with narration; it's a heavily narrated film. I can understand why a lot of documentary filmmakers veer away from narration, because I think at its worst, it is what I'm talking about, a filmmaker spoon-feeding the audience. In an ideal world, it's merely giving you just enough to keep you up to speed with what's going on in the film. It should not stand apart from the film. It should not be imposed on the film. It really should be part of the film. And we phrased each of our acts as a question. For example, the question of, "What was going to happen to the tales of the survivors?" People were dead. Germany was trying to rebuild. Liberal voices in the Hollywood Jewish left wing were being silenced because of HUAC [the House UnAmerican Activities Committee]. So you pose those questions, and you don't answer them until you earn the answer.

SOURCES AND NOTES

Imaginary Witness is currently (2015) available on hulu, www.hulu.com/watch/532445. Susan Kim's Amazon.com author page is at www.amazon.com/Susan-Kim/e/B002MA0V78. The segment of Hanna Bloch Kohner on *This Is Your Life* (aired May 27, 1953) can be viewed online at the Internet Archive, www.archive.org; the segment is at www.archive.org/details/this_is_your_life_hanna_bloch_kohner.

CHAPTER 17

James Marsh

James Marsh directs both documentary and dramatic features, most recently including *The Theory of Everything* (2014), featuring Eddie Redmayne as physicist Stephen Hawking, and *Shadow Dancer*, a thriller featuring Clive Owen and Gillian Anderson. Other dramatic credits include *The King*, a theatrical feature based on a script he wrote with Milo Addica, and *1980*, the second film in the dramatic trilogy *Red Riding*, which aired on Channel 4 in 2009.

In 2010, Marsh spoke with me about his work as the director of *Man on Wire*, which won the Academy Award for Best Documentary. Based on the book *To Reach the Clouds* by Philippe Petit, the film tells the story of how Petit, at the age of 24, conspired with a group of friends and strangers over a period of eight months to plan and carry out an illegal and astonishing high-wire performance: On August 7, 1974, Petit spent nearly an hour walking, dancing, kneeling, and even reclining on a wire that connected the north and south towers of New York's World Trade Center, 1,350 feet—nearly a quarter of a mile—above the ground.

At the time we spoke, Marsh was completing *Project Nim*, about a 1970s language experiment in which a chimpanzee was raised as a human. The film received many honors, including the 2011 Directors Guild of America (DGA) Award for Outstanding Directorial Achievement, and selection as Best World Documentary at the 2011 Sundance Film Festival. Marsh's other nonfiction credits include *Troubleman*, a look at the last years and death of singer Marvin Gaye; *The Burger and the King*, based on the book *The Life & Cuisine of Elvis Presley* by David Adler; and *Wisconsin Death Trip*, based on a book of the same title by Michael Lesey, which looks at the strange fates that befall residents in a small Wisconsin town during the economic depression of the 1890s.

How did your collaboration with Philippe Petit come about?

Most of the documentary films that I've made have been inspired by existing books, and *Man on Wire* is no exception. The way into the story for me was through this very personal, very idiosyncratic, very detailed memoir that Philippe had written. That gives you quite a strong sense of his character and what you're going to be faced with when you begin to start collaborating. So I read the book very carefully, and I had a very awkward phone conversation with Philippe, who's not the best approached on the phone; he's much better when you meet him in person. But we agreed to meet on the back of that awkward phone conversation.

What I gleaned from the book is that he is an absolute control freak—and would have to be, to be doing what he's spent his professional life doing. So in our first encounter, I just wanted to offer this idea of him being involved in the making of the film. It was his story, and I needed to entertain the ideas he had about how the film was going to turn out. Now, that was pragmatic on my part. To invite input would be much better than for it to be negotiated in that first meeting. So it was a long lunch with lots of wine and conversation, and then he called me just five minutes after I'd left the meeting, saying, "Let's do this together." It was a very spontaneous act, which is the best part of Philippe's character; he just trusts his instincts and feelings and goes with them.

And so that became a very long, intense, and often quite antagonistic collaboration, which ended up with a piece of work that I think reflected both the story and all the ideas that the story threw up, but it wasn't an easy process. Philippe, like many people, had seen lots and lots of films—he loves films—and there's a sense that if you've seen a lot that somehow you can make them. And that's quite difficult, when you're dealing with someone who's very beholden to their own opinions and ideas. When we didn't agree, I had—as the filmmaker—a greater responsibility to the film to do things the way I thought were best.

With the subject of the film so involved in its creation, there is the risk that it will become a vanity piece, but that doesn't seem to be the case here. The portrait of Philippe that comes through is complex and not always flattering, and of course the film is much more than just his story. It's also the story of his many collaborators and their relationship to Philippe and each other.

It was a very slow process of trying to, stage by stage, suggest that I felt the film needed to have elements of reconstruction and evocation. It wasn't generic reconstruction, but was based very specifically on the recollections of people that were there. Philippe quite vehemently resisted that for quite some time. That was particularly true of two Americans who got involved late in the adventure, both of whom bailed on him, in a certain kind of way, as it unfolded. He was violently against them being in the film. Of course, as a director you ought to tell the story with all the available voices you have, and the very fact that they betrayed him, as he would see it, made them very interesting to me. They were there, they saw things, they were part of the team.

So those were quite difficult obstacles that were overcome through dialogue and time. And to be honest with you, I just persevered to get my own way, and that feels like part of the job of a director in this kind of project. I do feel there's a responsibility to tell the story, the narrative, as well as I can. My job is to make a story that fascinates me as available to people as possible. And Philippe, to his great credit, saw that I had to make the film that I was seeing and to pursue the things I needed to pursue—even though he didn't necessarily agree with them, even when the film was finished.

So you're expanding on characters who may have been mentioned in the book, but aren't front and center.

These characters are referred to in the book, often in very disparaging terms. But it felt to me that what I needed to construct was a kaleido-scope of narrative. To give you a good example, there are two teams involved in getting the equipment into each tower, and then up each tower, and then across each tower. And therefore if you eliminate one team from that, you're losing half the story. Just on that very basic level, you need these other points of view. The drama that plays out in the tower where Jean-Louis is, in a sense, equal if not more striking than what plays out with Philippe. And of course, therein lies dramatic conflict as well: you've got a group of people who aren't necessarily friends—there is lots of disagreement—going on this venture where a man's life is at stake.

It felt to me very obvious that people needed to represent them-selves and be allowed to have their recollections, even if they were in conflict with other people's recollections. What's interesting about *Man on Wire*, as is often the case in documentaries, is that the most unlikely and preposterous details—that you think, "That could never have happened that way"—checked out! And everyone agreed on the most unlikely things that happened. It's very pleasing to confirm the most outlandish facts of the matter. That's what makes documenta-ries so special; you can't argue with something that happened. It hap-pened. There are facts here. And when people agree on those, those really unlikely ones, it just makes the documentary almost transcend fiction.

Do you have a general approach, as a filmmaker, when you start with books? Wisconsin Death Trip, for example.

That was a much more imaginative interpretation of a book that, in its own way, doesn't look like you can even film it. There was a film I made in the '90s called *The Burger and the King* that was also based on a book, *The Life & Cuisine of Elvis Presley*, an Elvis Presley cookbook. And that was a starting point for a very detailed, written treatment.

Philippe Petit, in *Man on Wire*, a Magnolia Pictures release. Photo courtesy of Magnolia Pictures.

That was also true of *Man on Wire*. I had a 60-page outline for that film, which organized the structure of the film, which for documentary is quite unusual. It has various timelines and you're flashing back and overlapping them, which is quite difficult to pull off in a documentary film, so I thought it was good to organize it on paper. And that feels sort of antithetical to the practice of documentary as some people see it—that you're writing out the story before you've discovered it—but for me, it's very good to have. If you've got written source material that appears to be quite reliable, there's no reason why you shouldn't try and organize it as a narrative and lay it out for yourself and the people who are going to invest in film.

And, of course, in the course of making the film, you have to be very alive to new discoveries, things that might change the architecture that you've already created. I'm doing that now on a film I'm working on, called *Project Nim*—I'm not sure that will be its actual title. It's the story of an experiment to try and make a chimpanzee human, and based on a book as well [*Nim Chimsky: The Chimp Who Would Be Human*, by Elizabeth Hess]. And in this case, I found that the book is only half the story. By reaching out to people who didn't speak to the author, I'm finding a very different story. We've gone quite a long way away from my written script or outline.

I do find books, generally, a very good source material for the kind of work that I like to do. I'm not an observational filmmaker, or a filmmaker who wants to follow a story as it unfolds. Would that I could. I think it's actually quite a lot harder than what I do.

Given different types of source materials and subjects, how do you decide what approach you'll take, or what genre it might be? Man on Wire, *for example, is something of a heist film.*

I think it's not so much a genre, but a question of the *tone* of the film that you're doing. In Philippe's case, the tone is set by the protagonist, the main character, and how he sees himself, how he presents himself. It's a very important part of the story. So *Man on Wire* does have this heist movie kind of structure, and indeed elements that feel more fictional than a conventional documentary but that emerge from the theatricality of Philippe's personality. It felt like a very good extension of how he told the story, to construct the film that way.

The story that I'm seeing in *Project Nim* is about mothering and female nurturing. The chimpanzee has a series of human mothers that look after him; each one has a bad ending with him. To me, the essence of the film was the struggle to nurture and mother this alien life form, and to project onto it lots of human emotions that the chimpanzee doesn't either understand or will exploit in some way. So that sets a tone for a film that's about the experiences of these women, emotionally. That's what the focus is. And so the genre, for me, is same as the tone: What level do I play this at?

Would "theme" be another word for what you're calling "tone"?

To some extent, yes. But tone is the amalgamation of how you cut the film, how you score the film, how you emphasize humor over sadness, or whatever—where you put the emphasis. I think the scoring of film is perhaps the crudest part of that. You can see documentaries where the score feels very generic. It doesn't feel that it has its own personality; it feels like it's meant to grease the wheels. Scoring—or not scoring, which is equally important and equally a part of what you're doing in a film—is something that some documentaries do in a way that doesn't feel thought out. I'm very mindful of what score can do. And that's the crudest expression of this idea of tone that I'm getting at.

But theme is part of that, too. In *Man on Wire*, the ideas of the film were ones that I can't even control, because of the response that people are going to have based on later events. [The destruction of the towers in 2001, which is never mentioned in the film.] That's also probably true of the film I'm doing now on the chimpanzees. I think men and women will respond to this film very differently. So it's something you're trying to be mindful of, how it might be perceived, without making that the main thing that you're doing. You have to ultimately create something that you can stand to watch and that addresses your curiosities about the subject matter. That feels to me to be the first thing that all good documentary films have: You feel like the person who's made that film has pleased themselves, to some extent.

You're credited as writer on some of your documentaries, but there's no writer credited on Man on Wire, *and yet you just talked about writing a 60-page treatment.*

I wasn't allowed to have one, nor do I see [the need]; I feel it's somewhat of a vanity. And I don't understand how anyone who's directing a film would hire a writer to then write it, but you see it a lot on documentary credits and clearly that works for certain filmmakers, but would never work for me. I assume that as a director of a documentary, you're very actively involved (although of course that's not always the case) in the treatments for a film, the way a film is constructed before you shoot anything, and also you're very, very actively involved in the editing, where you're, in a sense, writing the scripts for it after you've shot it. I co-edit, essentially, although I don't take a credit for that either. It's because I feel like it should be implicit. The words are given to you by your contributors, but you're definitely, in some real sense, authoring and writing the film in the cutting room.

You hear stories of directors who don't come to the cutting room that often. I'm there every single day for the whole duration of the edit. And before I do the edit, I would've done a first cut myself at home, and worked on the structure. And that's not in any way to diminish the role of my editor [Jinx Godfrey], who's someone I've worked with for 13 years on practically every project I've done.

When it comes to dramatizations, how do you decide which moments in a story should be dramatized, and how?

Because of the nature of this kind of filmmaking, everything—every shot, every scene—has to be intentional. In certain documentaries that isn't the case at all. Clearly, the moment you make an edit, a documentary ceases to be real, whether it's an observational film or a film like the films that I make, which are very constructed. I think that the way to use reconstructions is to make them incredibly specific. In *Man on Wire*, they're written scenes. They're not just illustrations or generic shooting of locations or wallpaper imagery to get you across the talking heads or provide a cutaway. In this kind of filmmaking, you can and should be very precise about the images that you're going to use to tell the story.

In *Man on Wire*'s case, [the dramatizations] were evoked by the dialogue, by the interviews. I shot all the interviews first, and then spent three or four months editing them together before I shot anything else. When we had a structure that worked in the cutting room (and was very much like the structure I had worked out ahead of time), we had a fairly tight film; it was an hour and 45 minutes at this point. It was a little loose, but not very loose. I scripted and shot the reconstructions very specifically around the evocations of the words that were used by the contributors. So it was completely sourced on their memories, but of course it was my imaginings that ended up on the screen, very much tied to and informed by the dialogue. And throughout those reconstructions, you'll be hearing voice-over from the contributors, because that's where they came from: They were inspired directly by them. And I think that's important, in this kind of filmmaking. One isn't looking just to shoot general shots to toss into a film, to cover up the absence of imagery or archive. They should have a different and more singular purpose than that.

Some audiences weren't able to separate the reconstructions from the archive. I found that to be both flattering and utterly baffling at the same time, because it felt to me there was a clear feel and texture to them. And also, there's a progression in the way the reconstructions are organized, so that they start being reasonably realistic and they become much more abstract as the story unfolds, as if the characters had gone to some other place—and indeed they had: They'd gone to the top of the world, the World Trade Center. And I thought that was pretty clear, but it wasn't to some people, and I wasn't troubled by that. I think as long as the film is working on a narrative level, then how they reflect upon the elements you've used doesn't really bother me one way or another.

A.O. Scott of The New York Times *described your reenactments as "witty," and I thought that was a great word for them. But is that something a filmmaker can aspire to, or do you need to be born witty?*

I think it's perhaps the same point. The tone of those reenactments was based on the tone of the interviews, and the recollections were often quite witty, particularly Philippe's. They were flamboyant and sometimes self-parodying and sometimes self-aggrandizing. Philippe's story is playful, but with the most profound dimensions to it: questions about the nature of beauty and art, testing your personal limits, the absence of the Twin Towers, and so on—there are big, big ideas in this story. And that tension between the fanciful nature of the quest and the objective, and the fact that it is on one level totally pointless and on the other level totally profound—the idea of walking between those Twin Towers, why would you want to do that? Well, that's not a question I would ever ask him or myself. The "why" is completely the wrong word to use for that.

Other than the presence of Philippe himself on screen, were there other reasons that you felt this should be a documentary rather than a drama?

I never thought of it as a feature. Firstly, it wasn't what I was invited to do. And secondly, it felt to me that because of the nature of the story and because of the nature of the people involved, it would be vastly better as a documentary. Once [I met] Philippe, there was no question in my mind that this would be much better expressed as a documentary.

We'll see whether that's true, because there may well be, as we speak, an attempt to make Philippe's life story, and indeed that part of his life story, into a very expensive movie. But it feels like it's very hard to improve on the real people telling you the real story in this particular case.

A lot of documentary work in the past few years—not only your work, but also Waltz with Bashir *and* Gonzo *and other films—strikes me as pushing against the boundaries of the form while also striving to remain truthful. What is your take on the balance between creativity and truthfulness?*

I'm not sure I'm the best person to resolve that argument, not that you're asking me to. My responsibility with *Man on Wire*, with that subject matter, was to make the best possible film experience out of that, because it was such an experience for those involved. Here's this completely blank, empty canvas for a hundred minutes and you need to fill that canvas in the best way you can, tell the story as you see it. Now, another filmmaker would have made a very different film out of *Man on Wire*; they could have seen very different things in the narrative or very different emphases. So for me, it's obviously a very personal interpretation of the story. And that's true of the film I'm making now. It's, in a sense, my version of the story. By definition, it's selective. It ignores certain things and stresses other things, but that's true I think of any documentary film.

My issue with something is when it isn't true and you're trying to make it true, then that's wrong. But if you've established something as best you can to be a fact or the truth, and you dramatize it or you visualize it in a certain way that isn't completely literal-minded, that's fine. *Waltz with Bashir* is a very good example. It's an extraordinarily good film—it's one of my favorite documentaries of the last decade—and I think it truly is a documentary because it's based on a series of collective and personal experiences of a very extraordinary moment in history, and the events themselves. That film seems to critique the very notion that everything is subjective: This is how I remember it; it might not have been that way. That I think is a brilliant example of a documentary truly pushing against the form, both in its visuals and methods.

Can you talk about rhythm, and the role it plays in successful film storytelling?

I think the key to all good filmmaking—whether they're documentaries or features, and I've made both—is to understand the rhythm. How the story unfolds, when you stop and breathe, when you gallop forward, when you bombard with information, and when you have one single striking fact that you want to expose. And that comes, I guess, from really knowing the subject matter inside out. You know where the emphasis should be and what the real story is, the dramatic story.

With *Man on Wire*, I read everything I could read—I read all the newspaper reports, I had preliminary interviews with all the people involved—to really understand the story. And then when you do the interviews, you have to construct them really, really carefully. I don't just randomly sit down and ask questions. I'll spend a day planning out an interview, where I will very carefully work through the questions and when to ask what, when to ask the difficult questions. So the rhythm of the film gets established at that very point of the interview. Awkward ones will have their own rhythm, where you feel like you're leading the person through their memories and recollections, trying to give them space to reflect, trying to occasionally almost ambush them with questions that are going to throw them—all those kinds of things that you organize at the point of interview. That's certainly even more true with the film I've just done, *Project Nim*, the chimpanzee film, which is a much more complicated story and therefore I have to know it much, much better.

You're trying to be a conduit of what really happened, and looking to establish the ebb and flow of a story and the turning points. If you get it right, then the film is going to work. It's that simple. I've gotten them wrong; I know what a film looks like when you haven't got the rhythm right and it doesn't quite hang together.

In terms of the footage that you discovered that Philippe had shot but not processed—that was the footage of training out in the fields?

A film crew spent a week with him at his parents' home in France, as he was preparing for the World Trade Center break-in and walk, and documented some of these preparations. There were nine or 10 rolls of film that were shot over two or three days. And Philippe had kind of hoarded the negative of that film. So we processed it, and that's when I realized that I might have something a bit more extraordinary on my hands.

Why?

Because I saw in that footage—You can see the essence and spirit of what this is all about. A group of young people who know no fear, or know a little fear, but not enough to stop them doing something reckless and dangerous. And just the playfulness of that footage. And also, you're seeing some of the real solutions being found for real problems. That footage, for me, became the emotional center of the film: I felt I could anchor the film in spirit with what it was really like to be part of Philippe's merry band of ne'er-do-wells at that time. That footage gave me that, in a beautiful way. The sun is shining, people are galloping in meadows, and everyone is there who needs to be there. You see them all looking handsome and attractive as young people. It was just an amazing gift, that footage.

And it gives an arc to these relationships, adding depth especially to the stories of Jean-Louis and Annie—

And it shows you how much they care about what they're doing. It's not just some frivolous game that's being played. There's a lot of focused discussion and obsession from people like Jean-Louis and Annie, who know what the stakes are: It's their best friend whose life is potentially at risk by doing this. You get to glimpse the stakes as well, because of the intensity of the relationships that you see in that footage.

In storytelling terms, when did you first find out about this footage and how did it change what you were already doing?

Philippe alluded to it very cryptically as we were discussing the project initially, and then didn't really let me see it for quite some time. It was almost as if I had to prove myself to him before he'd let me see it. It came after we'd started shooting the film. He finally let me—We went to his garage and there it was. And then it was processed, and I remember watching it at DuArt as they were grading the negative transfer, my heart leaping, and thinking, "Oh my God! This doesn't change the film but it enriches it and illustrates it in ways that I could never have expected." At the moment, I knew that the film had become profoundly better. You could see things that, up until this point, I thought we'd have to somehow create or verbalize in order to evoke. Even better still, what I was seeing really sunk up with what I felt the film was about. Had it been different, I would have had to change my views and ideas about making the film the way I was making it. But there it was.

Looking at the list of documentaries you've done, it's very eclectic. I'm curious about how you pick a topic and how you find a story within that.

It's an interesting question, not one you ask yourself very often. It feels to me that I'm just looking for subjects that personally fascinate me. When I was younger, I did specialize in films about rock music and the rockumentary. But I always try to get involved in something that I haven't quite seen before, at least in the way I'm seeing it. You want to do something that feels like it's going to be an original contribution to the form, if you like, both by virtue of subject matter and [that] you've got a potentially original way of telling that story. Something that intrigues you and draws you in on a very personal level, and you feel that you can do that for other people too: You can draw them into what's made you so fascinated in that subject matter.

Also, you have to know that you're going to live with something for a year or so, and so you need to find subjects that open up and open up and open up, so that the ideas that lurk around them and beyond them and are activated by them feel strong and substantial. For *Man on Wire*, you've got the whole future tense of the buildings [the Twin Towers] to reckon with, and how what Philippe does has interesting tensions with what is going to happen later on. In *The Burger and the King*, a preposterous story about Elvis Presley eating himself to death, I felt there were really interesting stories about what it's like to grow up in the Depression, what that does to your mentality, what it's like to be able to have anything you want whenever you want it.

I read that you started out as an assistant editor and have said that editing is a good way to learn about directing.

Yes, I think it really is. When I worked at the BBC, I'd make little five- or 10-minute films for an art show, and you had to edit those yourself as well. It's a great way of seeing and having to reckon with your mistakes as opposed to passing them off to somebody else to deal with. That's a good way—and a painful way—of not repeating your mistakes.

Also, I think it makes you very mindful of what a film actually is. A film is a constructed piece, even if it's the best Frederick Wiseman observational film—and he's the best practitioner of that kind of filmmaking. His films are remarkably and brilliantly constructed to be the way they are; they're heavily constructed in the cutting room. I think he calls them "reality fictions," which is a great title. Even though you would think that his work transcends all those accusations about documentaries being pure, and being about real experiences, and not [shaped] with other elements and reconstructions and on and on, he's the first person to admit that that's not the way they are.

I'm surprised that more editors don't become directors. Personally, I always wanted to be a director; I was trying to find a way in, and that's the way I did it. Editors tend to be, I think, quite private people. I'm a much more gregarious person, and so editing would not have been what I wanted to do, but it was a brilliant way of going to film school, if you like. And editing is the thing I find most rewarding about the filmmaking process.

You recently directed 1980, *the middle film in Channel 4's* Red Riding *series of three feature-length films set in Yorkshire in the 1970s and '80s. I'm wondering whether your documentary work influences your approach to fiction?*

It does. And in fact that film opens with what is essentially a documentary montage of news footage that has very clear and overt references to a real-life case in England. But I think what documentaries have given me is a really good sense of structure, because in a documentary you often have to find that structure, to find how the story's going to work in a dramatic way. Structure is a thing I'm absolutely obsessed with in documentary filmmaking. Is the structure working? Do things lead to other things the way they should? Is there cause and effect in my narrative or in my characters' actions? And that's enormously beneficial when you analyze a film script. It means that you can approach a film with a better sense of what it's going to be like, because documentaries are so slow to come together in the cutting room and you always try to figure out how to be more efficient and get to the end point more quickly.

Also, in documentaries, there's the constant frustration of low budget; you're quite restricted on what you can do and how you can do it. So that's why I love making [dramatic] features, is that you get to play more. You can use more complicated film grammar, in terms of what shots you can do and the time you're given to do them. So I find that quite liberating.

You have such an international perspective on documentary—you're from Cornwall, you lived for many years in New York City, and now you're in Copenhagen. How are the storytelling approaches different across boundaries, or the same, and how are they changing?

That's a very intriguing question; I wouldn't know where to begin on that. I grew up in the U.K. and became a documentary filmmaker within the BBC, essentially. Many filmmakers from England have worked for the BBC or worked within the BBC. So definitely the U.K. tradition of documentary filmmaking is the most important part of my earlier career. And I was fortunate enough when I was younger to work on *Arena*, an arts film series where you had an hour to make a film about a famous artist or some kind of artistic phenomenon. The series had absolutely no ground rules and it was run by crazy people who would let you do almost anything if they felt it was going to be a good film. They would encourage you to experiment. And that, to me, was the most formative part of my career, working for two very maverick producers. It was a completely anarchic environment, but so much brilliant work came out of that, much more so than if you were in a locked-down office and made to do a nine to five job with a film.

So I was sort of steeped in British TV; every week you could see two or three really good, very well-made documentaries. And within that, there were many great directors who you would be able to imitate initially, and then find your own voice. It was only later on I discovered the great masters of American documentary filmmaking: the Maysles brothers, and Pennebaker, and particularly Wiseman, who's so far away from what I do and yet the filmmaker that I almost most admire in the world, because of the rigor of what he does. He gets something that I think no other filmmaker has gotten so regularly and consistently in his work. His portraits of institutions and people within them are just breathtakingly profound and beautifully edited. And so that became a later influence on me.

I think that the feature documentary in the last 10 years has really emerged as a very credible form in world cinema. In American cinema, I think documentaries are way more vigorous and exciting than what's going on in independent [drama] at the moment. There's a whole movement in American documentary filmmaking, that may be because journalism itself has been so poor in the last 10 years. We've been through a period of time where questions needed to be asked on a very basic level and documentaries have been doing that.

But not only that. You can see a film like *The King of Kong*, which is about something altogether nonpolitical. I love that documentary. You can see *Waltz with Bashir*. It feels like a very, very good time to be making documentaries. And increasingly, feature films—the Bourne films [*The Bourne Supremacy*, *The Bourne Ultimatum*] are taking some of their energy from documentaries. And [director Paul] Greengrass is a documentary filmmaker, lest we forget. We're blessed to live in a time where documentaries are very much part of the culture and are having an impact on the culture. And people are doing very interesting things with them, [which] wasn't true so much in the '90s. It's definitely over the decade that this movement has emerged and can be defined clearly for what it is.

Is there anything that I haven't asked you that, as you're thinking about storytelling or you mentor younger filmmakers, you try to convey?

The thing that should be thought about most in any film is the structure: how things relate to each other. We talked about that and it's my big obsession; I'm just obsessed with it.

So with a film like Man on Wire, *that has a very complex structure built around multiple story lines and flashbacks, are there strategies for keeping track of it all?*

You can't play with structure until you've really got a grip on the story that you're telling. That's true with a narrative film as well. I think some of it came, for me, from making *Wisconsin Death Trip*. What I'd liked in the book [is that] it had no given structure—it was completely formless and chaotic. But a film *has* to have some kind of structure, even if the structure is terrible—and there are films that have terrible structures and usually they're terrible films. That was such a struggle to make that film work, if it works, to flow and to feel like an experience that you could watch and lose yourself in. It was that film, by its very formlessness, that made me really conscious of structure and how important it was to good filmmaking.

If you're going to try a structure that isn't linear or isn't just one big long recollection, you have to really know your story inside out. And also, the structure has to serve the story. With *Man on Wire*, it was very clear to me that most people who were going to see the film would know the outcome—or would guess the outcome. And therefore, one had to structure it that way, to create suspense and live in the moment, [to invite] the audience into the gripping unfolding of this unlikely story. It was all worked out on paper, ahead of time, that it should have this structure. Not in the cutting room.

Feature films can be very helpful, if you watch, as I do, feature films all the time and you enjoy the structure. I just watched *Citizen Kane* again. It has an amazingly good structure, that. It's been imitated endlessly, but it's a brilliant, formal piece of filmmaking, so beautifully structured. I admire that more than anything else in a film: a well-structured piece of storytelling. It's about telling a story the best way that you can.

SOURCES AND NOTES

The website for *Man on Wire* is www.manonwire.com. A.O. Scott's movie review, "Walking on Air Between the Towers," was published in *The New York Times* on July 25, 2008, and can be viewed online at http://movies.nytimes.com/2008/07/25/movies/25wire.html. Information about the Channel 4 *Red Riding* trilogy can be found at www. channel4.com/programmes/red-riding. The HBO website for *Project Nim* is www.hbo.com/documentaries/project-nim.

CHAPTER 18

Cara Mertes

Since 2013, Cara Mertes has been director of the Ford Foundation's JustFilms, a global social justice initiative supporting independent film and digital storytelling projects, as well as the organizations and networks that sustain and disseminate them. Founded in 2010, Just-Films builds on Ford Foundation's many decades of support for documentary film as a social justice tool, and has supported more than 80 projects, including the Academy Award-winning *CitizenFour* (Laura Poitras); *The Look of Silence* and Academy Award-nominated *The Act of Killing* (Joshua Oppenheimer); *3½ Minutes, 10 Bullets* (Marc Silver); *Through a Lens Darkly* (Thomas Allen Harris); *Gideon's Army* (Dawn Porter); *The House I Live In* (Eugene Jarecki); *How to Survive a Plague* (David France); and *The Black Panthers: Vanguard of the Revolution* (Stanley Nelson). To strengthen the projects and speed their completion and impact, JustFilms has also been a major supporter of a global network of organizations that provide creative, technical and leadership training opportunities, including Sundance Institute, Tribeca Film Institute|New Media Fund, BritDoc|Good Pitch, and ITVS.

Mertes reports that new for JustFilms under her leadership is "a focus on artists-as-leaders fellowships; supporting an emerging global social justice film/digital network; building up regional hubs that support creators locally in the Middle East, India, Indonesia, China, and Africa; networking movement and community leaders with filmmakers; and expanding impact-producing resources as well as other needs in the field around safety and security of artists, subjects, and information."

Prior to JustFilms, Mertes served for eight years as director of the Sundance Institute Documentary Film Program and Fund, where she and her team expanded the Documentary Labs, tripled re-grant and funding resources, and spearheaded global creative partnerships, including the Sundance-Skoll Foundation "Stories of Change" initiative, Sundance-BritDoc Foundation's "Good Pitch" initiative and the Sundance-TED Prize Film Award.

Mertes is a former executive director of American Documentary, Inc, and executive producer of the acclaimed PBS documentary showcase *P.O.V.*, where her work was recognized with numerous honors, including multiple Emmy, Peabody, and DuPont awards, and several Academy Award nominations. She received a Webby Award as creator and Executive Producer of PBS's first online series, *POV's Borders*, and has been honored with the ACLU Freedom of Expression Award and International Documentary Association's Pioneer Award. Mertes has also taught, written about, and curated independent film, and produced/directed her own work. Early in her career, she received support from NYSCA and NYFA, and has received numerous fellowships and grants to pursue her work as an artist, an advocate for, and a funder of independent film.

We spoke by phone in June 2015 and continued a collaborative conversation in print, online.

According to the website, projects submitted to JustFilms for content grants are judged on the basis of several criteria, including alignment with Ford Foundation priorities, contemporary relevance, the potential for strategic impact, and a focus on marginalized and vulnerable populations. The criteria also include artistic excellence and "creativity and innovation" in form. From your perspective, why do these last two matter?

I think that we're understanding more and more how telling visual stories that support and accelerate the kind of change that we want to see—progressive change, reduction in inequality, the kinds of work that hopefully makes societies, communities more just and equitable—is really key. We are globalized. We are connected. Many more have access to technology. And we are increasingly living with vast inequality; a growing gulf between those who have opportunity and those who have virtually none by comparison. All of this creates an imperative for innovative, compelling visual storytelling and the kinds of experiences and impacts it can provide.

As you evaluate projects, what are your criteria for good stories?

We're looking at stories that are often from outlier perspectives; perspectives that we haven't heard before or heard often enough. We want them to aim for transformative storytelling, in terms of helping people understand a new reality, or a new understanding of events or characters or patterns in our communities, in our societies.

Also, we privilege artistry. These are not didactic infomercials, or built-to-order advocacy tools; we want creativity and imagination to be in play. So we're combining creativity and artistry with this question of—I'm hesitating from using the word "impact" because that's such a loaded word right now in our field—but we're trying to combine creativity with the notion of intentionality. We are always asking the question: As an artist, what do you believe is your responsibility to your subjects, their communities, and to your potential audiences? It's a different way to frame the question of a story's impact that doesn't lock it into an instrumental, static, and predictable function.

Narrative is dynamic, it circulates, it evolves, and its meaning is completed by its engagement with other humans. It is stifled if it is bound by outputs and outcomes, though at the same time, we certainly should understand the realm of what's possible in terms of our stories and social change. As social justice storytellers and those who support and facilitate them, we are people broadly engaged in contributing productively to our current realities. My belief is that we need to be inspired and audacious in our roles as funders, artists, and stakeholders, but also accountable and disciplined. Rigidity and narrowness in our approaches will undermine the imaginative and the authentic faster than soap dissolves in water. We need to hold the tension between creativity and change productively, in a way that impels possibility rather than limits it.

Is there a particular style or structure you're looking for?

We don't have a format that we look for. We've funded films that run the gamut from experimental all the way to traditional, character-based, multi-act structures. We seek new forms and new approaches. We want [projects] to meet the goals of the artists and the needs of an audience. This question of style and structure is even more open because we're focusing not just on linear cinematic storytelling, but also multi-platform nonlinear storytelling. With the new technologies, this is going to be a very robust space, especially for younger creatives and those from the Global South and so-called developing economies. The new structures of nonlinear storytelling are being invented as we speak. It's as if we are living in the 1900s, when the fundamental rules of cinema—framing, montage, pacing, character, animation—were all being invented, only now we are talking about nonlinear approaches like virtual reality, augmented reality, web-based interactivity, and apps.

Can you talk about that a bit more? How have you made that expansion from linear to nonlinear forms of digital storytelling?

At a meta-level, I think about these projects as visual storytelling projects which encompass moving-image-based content creation and deployment for multiple screens in various formats. And that content can take different forms depending on the intentions of the artist, the needs and desires of the audience, and sometimes the imperatives of the topic at hand. Increasingly we're looking for projects to manifest in many different ways: a short-form video, a long-form documentary, an interactive web series, an application, a game—one or some or all of these things. We have examples, like *Revolutionary Optimists* and *Logs of War*, where the app that derived from the film content has a broader reach than the film itself. I think this will not be unusual in the future. In the social justice or contemporary issue cinema space, we're going to see many more multi-platform iterations, and in interactive storytelling, my hope is that independent artists can lead the way with new forms of socially aware interactive narratives.

New technologies have afforded pathways into an incredible array of structural and presentational possibilities. There is real urgency around these issues, and the way in which the conversation can become global very quickly—or certainly national or regional, through our social networks—demands that the story be fluid; that creators be able to move among all of these different modalities wherever possible.

Is there any kind of mandate to involve communities not only as subjects and participants but also as storytellers?

It's a great question. There's not a mandate per se, but interestingly, the stories that we're supporting through a social justice mandate inevitably involve community in some way; there are myriad narrative paths to follow for storytellers, but at the deepest level they all lead to questions of justice and human dignity. And we're finding that when story, artist, and community intersect, the different avenues to reach different generations and multiple populations can take many forms, each powerful in their own right. And so we're supporting our artists to be as strategic as possible in reaching and galvanizing each of those audiences.

I have found that the best storytellers build into their process not only a feedback loop, but what I think of as a participatory loop. For example, think of the characters who are protagonists on screen. Because these people are being observed and asked to reflect by the filmmaker, often over a long period of time, because they are acting as witnesses in a certain way in their own lives, their own transformation and change process accelerates. Often they become spokespeople for the issue, or their profile is greatly heightened.

In effect, the very process of storytelling creates new leaders, new leadership in community, and sometimes even new communities of belief and practice. This can be extraordinarily powerful. And when you see that play out with individuals who are protagonists in their own communities—this can actually change what happens in the community because of the act of telling the story. They might find solutions to a particular issue or they might learn to advocate better. They become better organizers. They become better speakers. They become more effective at calling attention to an unmet need in a community, whether that's social services or criminality or lack of educational opportunities—whatever the issues are—those subjects of the stories become the link between the communities and the audience. This is the heart of what I am thinking about as a social justice cinema practice. It's a term which has not been defined and perhaps it's a field which may not even really exist, but I hope to continue to explore what it might consist of at JustFilms.

At times, filmmakers with access to technology use it to document marginalized or vulnerable populations without, it seems, adequately understanding the limits of their own perspective or the privilege they hold as media makers. There's a risk of taking advantage. Do you encounter that with works submitted?

I think one will always encounter that question. As an artist becomes more experienced and more skilled at what they do, they have to address that balance of who's telling the story, who's enabled to tell the story, what are the power dynamics inherent in the relationship, and how is the story being told. What values and beliefs are being activated? How is the story intervening in or transforming a regressive or damaging narrative? This is a form of media literacy that the artists need to be versed in. We will tend to work with filmmakers that are conscious and intentional about this, whether they use these terms or not.

For me, it's less about what the filmmakers say about their work, and more about what is happening on the screen: What is the material telling us? I have found that there is often a distance between what the filmmakers think they're achieving and what they're actually achieving on screen. The process of editing is the process of closing that gap. And while we do see artists who are not really thinking about these things, and just dipping into a community and "story snatching," these projects will not rise to the top in terms of our priorities. You can see that dynamic played out in the film through a lack of authentic access, discomfort in front of the camera, mutual manipulation and playing to the camera, and so forth. And we also have extensive conversations about how the film team is building trust with characters and in the community. We ask whether or not they're able to be responsive to the subjects' changing needs or interests over the course of time, and whether they're being transparent and up front about their intentions and their process.

These ethical questions are foremost at JustFilms, and that's really a conversation with the filmmakers and the stakeholder groups as well. We find ourselves often working with artists and their teams to build a sort of stakeholder base, and so NGOs and other groups can enter the picture and create another set of needs or interest that are brought to bear on the story. But they also often bring access and deep knowledge into a situation. And so this is a very dynamic, iterative space to be in now, the story-building space. Filmmaking is no longer staged and linear; the story creation process can be multi-dimensional, involving overlapping timelines, processes, and releases, each evolving with changing context and information before, during, and after the stories are completed.

How do you handle filmmakers who are so steeped in an issue that they run the risk of preaching only to the choir, to those who already agree, or how do you advise those who hope to reach and influence a broad constituency?

This storytelling process is deeply psychological; it's the very essence of being human. I think as we understand more about conscious and unconscious behaviors, and how narrative works on people in their minds and in their hearts, we will understand better how to answer that question. What are the deep value structures that people hold—and sometimes they don't even know they hold them, as with the phenomenon of implicit bias. Knowing some of what we do is consciously driven, and some is subconscious, how do you motivate people? Do you do it through advocating directly? Do you make a debate-like argument? Do you do it using the kinds of tools that poetry might use? How does the imagination function in the building of belief systems? How do you keep someone engaged? How do surprise, fear, and humor operate in narrative? These questions are just the beginning.

The question that we ask is, "What's going to be effective in your particular case?" as opposed to starting with restrictions like, "You simply can't use argument. You can't have an opinion. You can't use interviews as background," etc. We don't have a perfect formula. Different things work in different situations with different audiences. Like snowflakes, the stories are as complex as the human beings that are going to both participate in making them and receiving them. One thing I will say: It's crucial for filmmakers to become adept at screening their material for others during the making of the project, so you can understand if you are preaching to the choir, creating new choirs, or—ideally—both.

Are there challenges involved in trying to speak to a global audience, when both storytellers and audiences come from such diverse backgrounds in terms of culture, religion, and more?

Certainly in narrative there's a lot of discussion about finding the universal in the particular. Being human, the human condition, is the baseline. We have more similarities than differences in the big scheme of things. And so our projects start from that place, and trying to come up with a story framework that is going to engage people in their imaginations, engage people where they're at in their life experiences, in their value sets. And often they ask them to expand their thinking, to grapple with something that [they] hadn't understood well or [had] actively rejected.

I think that visual storytelling is particularly apt for a global justice agenda. It works through love and language; through emotion and intellect. It transcends difference and invites a visceral response. Vision is our primary sense and we tend to trust what we see, even if we know it's inaccurate in some way. The visual represents "the truth" at some level, and in an inauthentic world full of lies and manipulation, the hunger for authenticity has never been more profound. This is the gap our stories can fill.

Engaging with this kind of storytelling is a full body experience and our stories, as I have said before, are ultimately about human dignity. It can be healing. It can reveal truths that have been kept hidden. This is the very essence of what justice is. So visual storytelling is a natural ally to bring to bear in conversations that revolve around, "How do you restore dignity, or even establish it as a baseline for populations or communities that are living without it?"

How do you think about this work and its place in the discussion of whether documentary is art or journalism or something else? What would you say are the parameters that keep a project within the realm of "documentary"?

I think that there is a profound change going on in the definition of what we used to understand as journalism and its traditional function as the Fourth Estate. The internet has created new networks and new information sources, including bloggers (sometimes referred to as the Fifth Estate), and there are other non-traditional, non-profit and independent information sources, most crucially the independent film movements. We're seeing this disruption in part because of the collapse of the commercial journalism business model, and in part because of the changing ways in which we're understanding how stories can be told and disseminated, how information is gathered, how it's analyzed, and what the perspective is. Journalism's classic definitions of balance, objectivity, fairness, and accuracy are under examination. What is balance, and is it a useful concept, or does it obscure truths? When do we understand something to be fair enough? What constitutes accuracy? How do we achieve objectivity in a world of stories that all have a perspective of some kind or other? All of the standard definitions of what journalism has been are evolving.

We emphasize accuracy and fairness with our filmmakers. Balance and objectivity are not as useful in creative storytelling. And our artists, our filmmakers—our nonfiction filmmakers in particular—are leading this redefinition. They're performing journalistic functions in an age where we're having an increasingly difficult time having access to multiple and diverse perspectives, or perspectives that disrupt dominant narratives.

In this context, JustFilms supports documentaries and multi-platform work that often functions like long-form journalism. Sometimes our filmmakers are journalists, often journalists are characters. *CitizenFour* is an extraordinary example of this confluence. At the Ford Foundation and Sundance Institute, we supported it because it spoke to so many issues of importance, [including] privacy, surveillance, and whistleblower protections. The filmmaker [Laura Poitras] identifies as an artist, has become a journalist who's independent, and is now leading the team that has exposed one of the biggest twenty-first-century [issues] at *The Intercept*, a new digital journalism platform inspired by the Snowden revelations. [A publication of First Look Media, *The Intercept* was founded by Poitras, Glenn Greenwald, and Jeremy Scahill. See https://firstlook.org/theintercept/.]

But it comes with responsibility.

It comes with responsibility and accountability. Often what passes for news today is highly ideological, and we are finding more nuanced conversations about current events in comedy, documentary, independent film, and even serialized drama.

There seem to be ongoing issues with critics and the public not recognizing the level of creativity in documentary, or understanding that documentaries can be enormously varied, quite different from what they were in the past.

I think that that used to be true more than it is now. I think people are catching up to how creative and powerful documentary can be. More and more [documentaries] are being released theatrically in a commercial marketplace, and digital platforms have provided some level of revenue for certain films. Now, when Netflix launches *The Square* and *Virunga*, when HBO, Participant, CNN, A+E, and other platforms are competing for titles that fit their brand and audience, when PBS broadcasts *The Act of Killing*, these are all indicators of the broad sweep, scope, and ambition of nonfiction filmmakers today. They are in demand, and the form is celebrated critically and in mainstream discussions more broadly. Of course there are templates; the illustrated overview film with an agenda, the expert talking-heads argument with lush graphics, the character-based three act structure, but there are also exceptional break-outs that stand the cinematic form on its head.

In your view, at what point do the boundaries get pushed too far, and a project moves from nonfiction to fiction? For example, when is it all right to set something up for the purpose of filming it, as is often done on reality TV?

Transparency of intention is paramount for our filmmakers. There are exceptions to that, for instance, undercover footage for the purposes of investigation as in *Virunga*, or reenactment, which has developed a whole vocabulary of its own in nonfiction. *The Act of Killing* is an example. The conception of the filmmaker was to create scenarios wherein his characters would behave in certain ways, though he never knew exactly what they were going to do [and] he was very upfront about the fact that he was doing that. [For this 2012 film, director Joshua Oppenheimer asked former members of an Indonesian death squad, active in the mid-1960s, to dramatize their experiences.]

There are a number of films that use the form itself to leave the viewer wondering whether they are watching something that actually happened, or a construction of some sort. This can create a really interesting dynamic, and these films seem to function more like fiction, and can be highly manipulative, even to the point where they have been reclassified as fiction rather than documentary. All of these attributes are worth exploring; the question I would ask is to what end? How does it elucidate the key thesis of the film? Does it contribute to the ongoing dialogue in a useful way?

Interestingly, in Europe, there is far less of an emphasis on the distinctions between fiction and nonfiction. It is first and foremost cinema, and both modes of storytelling borrow tropes and tools from the other. In the U.S., this is a constant topic. In some sense we are very concerned with what we can believe in—who is telling us the truth.

I do think that artists that engage in nonfiction have a responsibility toward a set of truths and toward accuracy, as we have talked about. But narrative has a function, and that is to distill the realities we experience and provide a story form that can be understood by audiences. There's a quote I like, "Lives are led and stories are told." A story is not what happened; it is about what happened, and it needs to maintain a tie to reality to be called nonfiction. If there is no real referent, or it is substantially a work of the imaginative, it moves away from documentary on a spectrum. If the film makes a claim to representing a reality, it moves closer to nonfiction.

JustFilms supports endeavors that it believes will "encourage civic dialogue and active community engagement," among other goals. At what point in the production process do you encourage media makers to begin planning for impact? Is sooner better than later?

For us, it's up to the filmmaker to decide how and where they're going to engage in that conversation as they're building the story, but I am a supporter of the idea that the construction of the narrative can be mirrored by the process of constructing the future audience and begin at the same time if needed. With crowd-funding, audiences can now financially support films from the start. NGOs and other stakeholders have entire networks of potential audiences. Audiences can provide new characters, unknown information, and powerful networks for dissemination. Engagement early can lead to changes in the story itself since they generally take place over several years and context can swiftly change. The production process for contemporary-issue cinema is not necessarily linear and chronological; it can happen in waves, in spirals, and in multiple arenas and on different platforms simultaneously.

What sorts of questions are they considering as they go about this?

"Who am I trying to reach? What do I want this story to do? How do I want people to understand this particular story, in terms of how I'm representing it? What are the different layers that I'm building into my narrative?" One of my favorite examples of that is *The Revolutionary Optimists* [a 2013 film by Nicole Newnham and Maren Grainger-Monsen]. It started out being a story of a non-governmental organization in India bringing education and culture to an off-the-grid community outside of Kolkata, a story about attorney Amlan Ganguly and all the art, sports, and education that he was bringing to this community that was very, very deprived of even basic services like water.

What ended up happening, in the course of the filmmaking and conversations with him and with other stakeholders, is that the filmmakers found that the young people in the community were actually being empowered to become advocates for their own communities through Ganguly's work. These 11-, 12-, and 13-year-olds were working on behalf of the community to do things like make a map to identify where the water systems were down or polluted, to document when garbage was not being picked up, to document when there were [newborns] who had not been vaccinated. So they became the center of a story that was about living in this informal community, but what you understand about that community is that it's absolutely *not* without dignity. In fact, it was quite highly organized socially. And while there was severe deprivation, there was a lot to understand about how everybody in this community was coping with this deprivation and there were very strong family ties. It was the young people that became the way into that, in a way that I think even the filmmakers felt was very surprising. And in the end, because of the film, the young people became nationally and internationally known, the Indian government built a water infrastructure to the community, and the app they created is now supported by the Gates Foundation and Google—all because of a film.

And so as an artist you constantly have to be open to the story evolving and changing radically in front of you. What you really want to stay with is: "What am I really talking about here?" Not, "Who are my lead characters," because that could change, but "What am I really trying to get at?" And in that case, they ended with a story about young people being leaders in their community—very different than the one that they set out to do.

[Print] authors will talk about the moment when their characters take over from them and write their own trajectories, and the author is almost *organizing* all of these different things as opposed to being the creator of them. I think that filmmakers often play the same role. They have a sense that there is an injustice or a challenge or something dramatic that they want to capture, and they set out with one set of ideas and end up in a very, very different place. The trick for the artist in that case, both writer and filmmaker, is to stay true to—or always be excavating for—what the original, the deepest intention is, and then tying however the story evolves to that. You have to do that on a pretty consistent basis or you find that you lose the story.

That sounds a bit like what happens at the Sundance Institute's Documentary Edit and Story Labs, where filmmakers work with mentors on story editing, character development, and dramatic structure. Can you explain how that process works?

As it is with all labs at Sundance Institute from the time when Robert Redford began them, artists and their relationship to their work was the central focus. I organized the labs around the belief that caring for the artists' well-being is key to creating the strongest story possible. So we removed all external concerns for the duration of the lab. Everything was supplied; food, lodging, community, focus, expertise, camaraderie, a deep understanding of the process in technical, narrative, and human terms, and even some of the healing arts like blessing ceremonies, knowing that art comes from the deepest places inside us as humans, and the work of creation can be both joyous and painful. Everything was organized around accelerating and supporting the process of integrating the artists' view of their creation with the community of experts and practitioners that we had gathered around them. Generally we had about 40 people in a lab; five to six film teams together for 10-day periods; each team supporting the others. We inaugurated assistant editing fellowships and brought full teams of producer/directors, not just directors. It was comprehensive and also served to build strong professional networks that would continue long after the lab itself, often in the form of jobs.

There was a lot of time spent trying to mirror back to artists what their footage is saying, helping the makers understand that play between what they want to achieve and whether that is reflected on the screen. As subjective beings, formed by our own histories and experiences, we sometimes forget that the distance between what you mean and what I understand can be vast. I'm constantly surprised by how complex humans are, and how visual storytelling—what we actually see and respond to with film—is as close to a full human experience with all our senses as we get through the arts, because all of our dimensions are in play: It uses sight and sound and, in a certain way, space, because of how you're watching.

You can't just say, "I know what everybody's getting out of this film." In fact, very often you know maybe a fraction of what people are seeing, unless you sit there and you listen to people giving feedback and you engage in this process of mirroring and iterating, mirroring and iterating. And that improves the film exponentially. We had an estimate, based on talking with filmmakers that went through the lab, that we were speeding up their process by anywhere from six to eight months. So they would be doing this [on their own], but they'd be doing it at a much slower pace without the concentrated focus on just that feedback loop.

That's interesting, because it also addresses another ongoing challenge facing filmmakers, which is having the time and support system to get these films done.

Exactly. I think one of the great lost opportunities in the U.S. is the current lack of support for the arts generally. We should have residencies like this all around the country, not just at Sundance Institute. This notion of a residential, immersive, very intensive laboratory of support isn't supported, and it builds community, capacity, skills, networks, knowledge, and great stories which get done faster and better.

Given the diversity in documentary work and the creativity involved, how do you think about issues of truthfulness, and what that means? The sense that all documentary work is subjective, edited, manipulated, but at the same time works that are seeking to make a difference need to do so honestly and accurately.

I do think that nonfiction film of the kind we support is an art form first and foremost, and art is all about excavating and experiencing truths, whatever those might be. However, the definition of what is or isn't a documentary is not fixed, hence the ever-present dialogue about the relationship between fiction and nonfiction. Narrative, by its nature, is not simply about repeating all of the facts and creating a picture of something exactly as it happened—that's documentation, not documentary. Nonfiction is about understanding some aspect of the human experience, and presenting it in the hopes that it will have a resonance for others. That perspective can be regressive, or it can be progressive. Sometimes this is an experiential impulse—the experience of beauty or awe. Sometimes it is about information and experiences that have been hidden or silenced. Sometimes it is highly manipulative, and successful in that manipulation. Cinema performs this function almost like memory, synthesizing and producing a set of truths; the ones we [at JustFilms] support are ones from which we hope to learn and advance rather than stories that promote a lack of information and perception, which can lead to violence and despair.

Can you explain that a bit more?

I find visual storytellers are drawn to nonfiction because it is a particularly powerful format. It provides an emotional and intellectual experience that seems to fulfill a need for authenticity as well as understanding; we seek greater understanding, and these films are often about finding a resolution to a universal human experience. This can be very dramatic and affirming of our eternal hope that, for instance, justice will prevail, or that seemingly impossible odds can be overcome. Nonfiction teaches us lessons about how others have lived, the values they had and the decisions they made, and it has the weight of reality behind it. This is very compelling, particular now, when our twenty-first-century experience of the world is impossibly complex, connected, overwhelming, and chaotic.

What advice would you have for newer filmmakers entering the world of nonfiction?

There are so many top-ten lists full of pragmatic advice that I won't repeat the basics. I think from my own work and work with others, I would say it's critical, especially in nonfiction, to know your intentions and to also build a community of support as you move forward. It's not important that you know at the end what you're going to say, it's important that you know *why* you're saying it, why you're engaged in this process. What are you as an artist trying to understand? Instead of giving yourself the challenge of saying: "How perfect can I make this film? What do I want it to look like at the end?" it's much more about, "What's your motivation? How does that motivation get articulated to the other people that you want involved in the process?" Because filmmaking narrative is by its nature a participatory process. You're working with other people, both on their stories [and] also in the making of it. Making visual stories that engage with contemporary reality is one of the most difficult jobs I know, and also the most satisfying. To work in collaboration when you really know why you're there in the first place as the artist and as a person makes the road easier to travel.

SOURCES AND NOTES

The website for Ford Foundation's JustFilms is www.fordfoundation.org/issues/freedom-of-expression/justfilms/strategy. The site for the Sundance Institute's Documentary Film Program is www.sundance.org/programs/documentary-film.

CHAPTER 19

Stanley Nelson

Filmmaker Stanley Nelson has been awarded five prime-time Emmy
Awards, two Peabody Awards, a 2002 Fellowship (often called the
"genius" award) from the John D. and Catherine T. MacArthur Foundation, and a National Medal in the Humanities, bestowed in 2013
by President Barack Obama. Eight of his films have premiered at the
Sundance Film Festival: *The Black Panthers: Vanguard of the Revolution*
(2015); *Freedom Summer* (2014); *Freedom Riders* (2011); *Jonestown: The
Life and Death of Peoples Temple* (2007); *A Place of Our Own* (2004); *The
Murder of Emmett Till* (Special Jury Award, 2003); *Marcus Garvey: Look
for Me in the Whirlwind* (2000); and *The Black Press: Soldiers Without
Swords* (Freedom of Expression Award, 1999).

In 2000, Nelson and his wife, Marcia Smith, an award-winning
writer and philanthropy executive, founded the independent production company Firelight Media. In 2008, they expanded the company's
mission, creating the Firelight Producers' Lab, a mentorship program
for emerging diverse filmmakers. In 2015, the Lab was one of nine
nonprofit organizations worldwide to receive the MacArthur Foundation's Award for Creative and Effective Institutions, a one-time grant of
$500,000 to help ensure the Lab's sustainability.

When we spoke in February 2015, *The Black Panthers* had just premiered at Sundance and Nelson was moving forward with two new
films—*The Slave Trade: Creating a New World* and *Tell Them We Are Rising: The Story of Historically Black College and Universities*—that are part
of *America Revisited*, a trilogy that includes *The Black Panthers*.

How you think about story as you approach your films?

Every film is different. I'm always looking for a beginning, middle, and
end to stories. What's the throughline? What's the story about, aside
from the obvious A to B to C? I'm looking at all those different pieces.

*When making films about topics that are likely to be somewhat familiar to
audiences, like the American civil rights movement, what is your process for
finding new information or new insights?*

Many times, the stories that I've worked on, for one reason or another, have not been fully told, or are not known to the general public. So a lot of times, just in the telling, it's a fresh story. But when I look at the films I've done as a whole, I tend to try to find the people behind the scenes who were part of the story, who aren't the famous people necessarily, and then to try to tell the story from as many different angles as I possibly can.

So in *Freedom Riders* [the story of a campaign, May to November 1961, in which black and white Americans rode together on buses throughout the U.S. South to protest racial discrimination], we interviewed the Freedom Riders, we're interviewing the governor of Alabama, we're trying to interview people that had the federal government's point of view, and also people who can talk about the local people, to try to get as many different sides of the story as we can. Why would somebody burn a bus just because people are trying to sit together on that bus? By and large, people make decisions that are at least rational to them at that time. So what rationality would make somebody burn a bus, or attack people with lead pipes, just because they're sitting together?

And then just visually, we're trying to tell the story in a different way. People have seen footage of the civil rights movement before. So we're trying to find new pictures and footage to tell the story in a different and new way.

How do you explain to students or new filmmakers why it's important to seek out alternate points of view?

I think it only makes the story stronger if you show that there are other opinions. We can see through those opinions today. It doesn't make it any more sensible, that they attacked these riders on the buses. It just illustrates, in a lot of ways, how wrong they were.

As I'm talking, I'm thinking about something like the Black Panther film, where you hear from the cops. They seem very rational, and it makes sense. I think it really helps the film, because you see it as a viewer, and part of you is saying, "What about the other side?" Even if you're not consciously thinking that, I think unconsciously you are. And so by giving the other people a say, you head that off a bit.

It also seems to help if you're not only telling a story but also building an argument and presenting evidence. By presenting multiple viewpoints, you're letting the evidence speak for itself.

Yes. I think that's partially what we try to do, is to build a case, build an argument, tell a story.

And of course in practice that's not as easy as it looks—good structure tends to feel inevitable, which is one of the reasons I ask students to closely watch multiple films on the same story.

Your hour-long film The Murder of Emmett Till, *for example, has a very clear structure. [Till, a black teenager from Chicago, was murdered in 1955 by two white men in Money, Mississippi. They were acquitted by an all-white jury, but later admitted their crime to a reporter for* Look *magazine.] The film's opening minutes include a newsreel story about the murder. Can you talk about deciding to launch the film that way?*

The newsreel was great because it gives the whole story, but it didn't really work to use it [later], to describe the actual kidnapping and murder, because it didn't have the drama we wanted. And so we had cut it from the film. But then I thought of just using it—I call it the *Citizen Kane* moment—where we can have him tell the whole story, and then go back and retell the story in detail. That's why the film starts as it does.

Structurally, the opening minutes are also critical to the film because you go beyond teasing the murder. Through quick interview excerpts, you set out the bigger themes and the "why" of the overall story: This was a final straw that helped to ignite real change.

We always felt that the story was in some ways about the clash of cultures between Mississippi and Chicago. If he hadn't been from Chicago, his mother would have never left the coffin open. His mother would have never been able to marshal newspaper and magazine coverage of his murder. It would have just passed, one of those murders down south that are not even covered in the news. And also that he didn't understand the culture of Mississippi; that he whistled to this white woman and thought it was kind of a joke. He didn't really understand it. And there was this unwritten agreement between the North and the South, that the South would do what it wanted and the North would ignore it. That was at the heart of the whole Emmett Till case: Mamie Till made it so that the North couldn't ignore the South.

From there, the forward moving story of the film gets under way, and you start with two distinct sequences. The first establishes the racial climate of rural Mississippi at the time. The second introduces Till and the very different world he's from, urban Chicago. The result is that when he heads south to visit relatives, we know enough to be afraid for his safety, but he doesn't. And we suspend our disbelief—we're in that moment with him, hoping for the best.

I think that that is really important, that you bring the audience on a journey with you in the film. One of the clearest examples is in *Emmett Till*, where we talk about Chicago, and the woman says, "We used to dance to rock 'n' roll. The girls wore these pleated skirts. The boys wore these rubber shoes." And then near the end of the film, as the murderers describe what they've done to *Look* magazine, they say, "We burned his clothes to the shoes, but the shoes wouldn't burn because they were rubber." And we don't say anything more about it, but hopefully, as a viewer, you make the connection, so that there's a moment of discovery. And so that it puts you into the story a little bit.

How do you decide what material to reenact?

In general, I've tried to keep the reenactments down to a minimum. One, that's just my feeling; but two, I think it's very hard to do reenactments. They've got to be perfect. They can't seem like, "Oh, those are actors," or "Where'd they lift that bus from?" It has to be organic in the film, so we try to keep it down. But sometimes there are just no visuals. In *Emmett Till*, there was nothing of the night he was kidnapped. In *Freedom Riders*, we really wanted you to [feel like you were] on that bus or on that journey, so we shot a lot of buses, and wheels on the road, to help put you there.

Part of good storytelling is making choices about what to include or not include. How do you make those choices while remaining truthful to your subject?

I think the first thing is that you have to draw limits on when the story begins and ends. Sometimes it happens on paper before we start. Sometimes it happens in the edit room, and those are sometimes the hardest decisions to make.

In *Freedom Riders*, we wanted to do a long piece about nonviolence and the legacy of nonviolence as it comes down from Gandhi and goes into the movement. When we did interviews, we talked to people about how they were influenced by Gandhi and the Indian struggle. Gandhi had said that the true test of nonviolent civil disobedience would be in the United States, because African Americans were the minority [rather than the majority, as in India]. So how do you change things if you're a minority? But as we got into the film—and so many times this happens—as we got into the editing, a lot of the background stuff had to fall by the wayside because we've got to get into the story. You don't want to start the story in India in 1947 or something. And it's hard, once you get into the story, to get back and talk about those things. It's much easier to do in a book. You can always write another chapter in a book.

So a lot of times, the first thing you have to do is say, "Okay, what are the parameters of the story?" And look, in some ways we're making those up. *The Black Panthers* could have gone on to 1982 or so, when the Panthers actually disintegrate. They spent a long time disintegrating, so we could have gone on. We had thought about starting the film out with a guy named Robert Williams, an African American who advocated defending yourself with guns. Or we had a whole piece on the Watts riots, or Watts rebellion. Then once we got into cutting, we just couldn't do it. So one of the first decisions is: Where does the story begin and where does it end? That's really central to how these stories are told.

And then within the film, there are different sequences, obviously. We want a sequence, as much as possible, to lead to something else.

Panthers on parade at Free Huey rally in Defermery Park.
Photo: Stephen Shames, used by permission of the filmmakers.

So you might choose between possible sequences on that basis.

An example of that is, in the Freedom Rides, they stopped somewhere in the northern part of the South, and they got [attacked], but then they get back on the bus and kept going. And finally we said, "This story doesn't lead anywhere." You know what I mean? There are other attacks that happen later that are much more important. You don't want to have this series of attacks to where it wears you down.

I describe sequences as chapters. They're unique in themselves, and then they advance the overall story.

Right. That's what they do. You really want them to advance the story, or else it's just kind of there. And I think as an audience you might not, in your mind, connect and say, "Wow, that was a nice story but it didn't really go anywhere," but part of you does feel that. You really want each sequence to push the whole forward.

In the Black Panther film, we look at the LA shootout [an early-morning police raid on Panther headquarters in Los Angeles, December 8, 1969]. There are a lot of different shootouts, but we picked the LA shootout to use because there's a lot of video—it lasted for five hours, and the press had a chance to get there, and for whatever reason, the police let them get close enough to film it—and it's a very important shootout. But we could have done others.

A clearer example is in *Jonestown*. Everybody had a story of some crazy sexual thing on Jim Jones. Just everybody. But we couldn't have ten stories of Jim Jones' craziness, and so we had to pick a couple of stories to illustrate that. You try to pick stories that stick in your mind, that illustrate it best. And who knows why that is, why some stories resonate and some don't? And sometimes it's a matter of visuals, that you have visuals to back it up.

Let's talk a bit about Jonestown. *[In November 1978, more than 900 member of the California-based Peoples Temple, founded and led by the Reverend Jim Jones, died in a mass murder/suicide in Guyana.] Some films about this event present Temple members as an undifferentiated group of crazy cultists. Your film brings the audience along with Temple members as they spiral downward, toward Guyana, and the line of "normal" keeps changing. Was that a goal, to put the members back into the historical narrative, as people?*

Yes. The way we came to the Jonestown story is that my wife and I heard some former members of Peoples Temple on the radio. It was some kind of anniversary of the Jonestown murders, and we heard them talking about it, and they sounded so sane. They talked about how they joined this progressive church that did all of this great work, and it was about loving each other, and it was such a great thing, and it all turned bad. And it started us thinking about it in a different way. The way the story's always told is that these 900-and-something crazy people commit suicide. But how do you get 900 crazy people? You couldn't gather 900 crazy people if you tried. So these people were in some ways rational, up to a point. And so we really wanted to take you on this journey. How did a rational person join this thing and stick with it for years? What was that all about?

Do you consciously use three-act dramatic structure?

No. I do not. I do have to say that. I know what it is, and maybe it's in the back of my head in some ways, but no, I don't.

My theory is that it's hard-wired. If you do an analysis with three-act structure of Jonestown, *for example, the acts seem to shift on the theme of suicide. It's really interesting.*

Yes, I think that three-act structure is ingrained in us. I look at it as beginning, middle, and end. Any story has to have these pieces to it. So that's what I'm looking at. I'm looking to try to tell this story. But I'm not consciously thinking of what's the first act, what's the second act, what's the third act, in that way. Look, you have to begin. You have to have a beginning. Then something has to rise up in the middle. Something has to change. Something has to happen in the middle, and then there's got to be some kind of resolution to it. So I think it's natural, but it's not something that I think about as I'm going forward.

What is your process? Do you write an outline or treatments before you film?

It really depends on the project and who the project is for, in some ways. *American Experience* [a PBS series that's presented seven of Nelson's films] wanted a written treatment and then a written script. So I think that that has really helped me, because at first it seemed like "Why are we writing this thing out?" But I think as a discipline, it really helps to have a script, even though you kind of throw it away as you go. We tend to have a first treatment, then kind of a written script that guides me in terms of interviews and interview subjects, and in some ways puts some limitations on how many interviews we do and what we're asking and where we're going. It's kind of a roadmap. One way to look at it is like if you're going on a summer trip and you say, "I'm going to drive from New York to California," you have to have a map so you don't end up in Canada somewhere.

How do you work in the editing room?

In the edit room what we do, nuts and bolts, is we take the interviews and lay out an assembly, which is basically to lay out the story of the film from beginning to end, with all the bites that we've got that we like. So I think one of the keys for me in the editing process is, I'm constantly cutting the film down. And I think what saves me is that once I cut something, I'm really pretty sure that that's out. So it's a constant whittling down. And we lay the film out in terms of all the bites that we like, in a very, very, very rough form, based on the script from beginning to end. And the first time through, we're not making hard choices. We might have three people talk about the same exact thing, but we're not making a choice of which one we use.

We're trying to keep in any kind of humor, anything anybody says that is in any way humorous, because so many times these subjects are so serious. Or we just like it. So for whatever reason, "I just like this." Because again, I'm trying not to go back, which is central. I'm trying not to go back and say, "Oh, what about when he said this? I really liked that." You know what I mean? So everything is kind of in. And then we just keep cutting down, cutting down, cutting down.

The thing that we've done recently, because so many of the films that we've done in the last couple years have not had narration, is we'll save maybe a third or fourth of the interviews to do after we've gotten some kind of cut to look at. And a lot of time they're central interviews. So we didn't interview Ray Arsenault, who wrote the book *Freedom Riders*, who was central to the film, until very late in the process, because he could fill in holes. I could talk about anything because he had written the book.

I try my best to save historians 'til later, because I'm trying as much as I can not to interview historians. You don't want the story of the Freedom Riders or the Panthers to seem like it's being told by historians; usually you [just] need a couple. *Jonestown* is probably the film that needed the least historians, because so many of the people in Jonestown had already written books, and they served as their own kind of historians. But we're trying to hold back and do the interviews with the historians last.

So for the rest of the casting . . .?

We talk to a lot of people on the phone. A lot of times there'll be a co-producer and they'll do pre-interviews, and write up what was said and what they liked. And one thing that we'll always do is, if somebody says something that we really like, word for word, we'll write that down and put it in quotes, so that we can try to get it out of them again. In *Emmett Till*, Wheeler Parker—who's Till's cousin—describes the night they took Emmett Till: "It was as dark as a thousand midnights; you couldn't see your hand in front of your face." When he said that in the pre-interview, I put that in quotes; I want to try to get that.

So you're not coaching them, but you're asking questions in a way to elicit that?

Right. We're trying our best to get them to repeat what they said. And it may get down to reminding them that they said it. I don't feel bad about that, because it's their words. It's not like I'm saying, "Say this." It's like, "You said this before."

Given a choice, you would prefer not to use narration?

Look, I love great narration. I think that narration is great. But given a choice, yes, because I think people connect in a slightly different way to a film with no narration. It does make the degree of difficulty that much more, to try not to have narration. There are things that you just can't say, because the people never said it or they never said it clear enough or quickly enough. And there are films, I think, that are just much better with narration.

We've been very fortunate in the last few years to make films about the civil rights movement, and about Jonestown, where there are vibrant people who are around, who were part of it, who are alive and who can really talk about it. And so we've been able to say, "Let's try this without narration." I think it's harder if you're doing a film about Harriet Tubman. If there's nobody alive, you never get that perspective.

To get back to the roadmap, have you ever had a situation where you started a film, thought you were pursuing one particular take on it (beginning, middle and end), and then along the way discovered something that shifted the film significantly?

Not that I can think of. Shifted the whole idea of the film? No. Because by the time we're writing the script, we've already talked to a number of people. We're pretty much there, especially with the historical docs. The personal film that I made, *A Place of Our Own*, that film totally shifted.

Can you talk about that?

The original idea was to do a film about black resorts—and there were different black resorts all over the country—and the idea of the history of these black resorts, and why black people would still go to these resorts. By and large, most of them started in the twenties, thirties, forties, whatever, during segregation, and these were safe places. But now people could go anywhere. "Why do people go to Oak Bluffs when they can go to the south of France?" was kind of the idea. And we couldn't raise the money to get that done.

Then we found out about this program that ITVS had, an experiment, actually. They wanted to see if somebody could make a film, start to finish, for $125,000, every single penny. You weren't supposed to raise any more money or anything like that. We couldn't go to five or six different resorts for $125,000, so we shifted the film to be about

Martha's Vineyard. And that's when *A Place of Our Own* became a film about Martha's Vineyard, because that's a place that I've gone to all my life. We realized that we could go there and put everybody up in my house, and do the film that way.

And then as we got the money, my mother passed away. And we kind of shifted a little bit to make a film about my mother and what happens when the matriarch of a family, who's held the family together, passes, and what happens there. And then we shot that film and it just wasn't working, wasn't working, wasn't working. We had to hire a new editor, and the new editor said, "Let me just look at all the footage that you shot." And she said, "Well, I think there's a film here, but it's not really about your mother. It's about your father." And I said, "I think you're out of your mind." She said, "No, give me a week and let me just try to start putting some stuff together, and then let's look at it." And she did, and we said, "Wow. There is a story here." Now, it took a long time to get this story to work and make this all make sense, but we did.

So that film went through a lot of different iterations, from being a film about black resorts in general, to being a film about Martha's Vineyard, to being a film about my mother's family in Martha's Vineyard, to finally being a film that's much more about my father and Martha's Vineyard and family, all those things.

Your historical films are often very moving, because of the way they're told and what they convey. A Place of Our Own *was also very moving, but it's a different kind of emotional storytelling. It's obviously much more personal. What was that like for you as a filmmaker, to shift gears and do something so intimate?*

First of all, it was an incredibly difficult film to make for me personally. This was the first and last personal film I ever made. There are a few documentary filmmakers who mine that territory; that's what they do, and they're good at it. But it was just totally a different process to make that film. And I can say that I had a lot of help. I needed a lot of help from the associate producer, from the editor, from Marcia (my wife), who wrote the film. It's just really hard to judge. It's very different to make that kind of film than it is to make, let's say, *Emmett Till*, where Emmett Till gets on a train, goes down south, gets killed, they have a trial—all of those things have to be part of the film. Within *A Place of Our Own*, there was probably a time where every single theme that you see in that film was, at one point, out of the film. What has to be in the film and what doesn't have to be in the film are very different.

You've worked with writers, co-producers, and editors. I'm curious about how you collaborate, and what the process is in terms of storytelling.

It really just depends. Usually the producers have certain tasks that are not so much the storytelling tasks, if that makes any sense. Their job is to find the people, put people in front of me, find footage, put footage in front of me, to know the story as well as I do, or even better than I do in some ways: to know the timeline, the dates, what comes first, what comes second, to know all those things. But usually it's myself and the editor in the edit room. I just find that everything in the edit room is very, very, very fragile. Having someone else in the edit room changes the dynamic, changes the decisions that are made. But I try to be open to ideas from everybody who's part of the process. So like in the Panthers, the assistant editor, who started as an intern, found footage of the Chi-Lites singing "Give More Power to the People" on *Soul Train*. And he said, "Hey, look at this." That's great; it's actually how the film starts. So I try to be open to everybody kicking in ideas, but it's my job to use them or not use them.

You're the decider.

Yes. And your job is to not get offended and to keep coming up with more ideas. And that's the hard part for people working on the film, is to be able to say, "I came up with ten ideas and none of them were used, but I'm going to come up with the eleventh idea." That's really important. That's what we ask of people.

Let me ask you about the Producers' Lab—and by the way, congratulations on the MacArthur!

Thank you.

Firelight Media, your company, created the Producers' Lab in 2008. On the website it's described as a "flagship mentorship program that seeks out and develops emerging diverse filmmakers." How does it work?

The Producers' Lab came out of the fact that I was getting calls and emails from random people, asking me to look at their project. Could they come in and talk about their project? And I have to say, part of it came from a film that I worked on years ago called *Shattering the Silences*, which is a film about minority college professors all over the country. And one of the things that minority college professors are asked to do, something extra that white professors aren't, is to mentor people at random. We talked to one woman who said that the first day of class, she was in her office and she heard a knock on her door, and it's like five black students who said, "We looked in the window and saw you here, and we want you to mentor us." And it's the same way, in some ways, for filmmakers of color. White filmmakers are asked to do this too, but I think there's more of a feeling like, "I'm black, you're black, I can call you up and ask you to help me out."

So I was doing a fair amount of mentoring of filmmakers. Some of it came out of working with Byron Hurt on *Beyond Beats and Rhymes*, which was Byron's first film and was very successful. Marcia and I helped him work on that film, and we just started thinking about how we could institutionalize the idea of working as mentors. It wasn't only us. Sam Pollard, Marco Williams, a whole bunch of other people were doing this. How can we institutionalize this, and can this work? And so there were two main ideas that we had. One was that there are enough filmmakers of color out there with projects that are good, and with a little help they can get done and get on the air. And the other was that we could raise money independently to support this project. And I think both of those ideas have, at least at this point, proved to be true.

But the way it works, it's really a mentoring piece. We work individually with the filmmakers and mentor them and try to provide other mentors. So we may look at their project and say, "Your sample is great. You need somebody to help you write the proposal. You may need a writer." A lot of times people are working with editors who were their college roommate, who are competent editors but they've never really cut an hour-long film. So maybe they need to have an editing mentor, a supervising editor that we could pay for. We're working with a filmmaker now who's decided to make her film from a kind of historical film to a personal historical film. So [she] needs to talk to some people who have made personal films about: How do you do that? What are the tricks to make a film move into this kind of personal realm?

It really depends on the project, how we work with the filmmakers. Each project is very different.

And the Lab itself is very selective; filmmakers apply with treatments, a sample reel, production team bios and more.

It's very rigorous. The projects that we accept in the Lab are films that can see the light of day. It may need a lot of work, but we can see this film getting done by this filmmaker.

There's a conversation now in which filmmakers describe the boundaries between fiction and documentary as being increasingly fluid. I'm curious what you say when people talk about that.

I don't know. I think in fact there's a line somewhere, and films are coming closer and closer to that line. The stakes with documentaries have just gotten that much higher.

In terms of the marketplace?

In terms of the marketplace, yes. The marketplace, your career . . . You have people going from making a documentary to going to Hollywood. You have documentary filmmakers who have ambitions that I think traditionally documentary filmmakers have not had.

But at a certain point, once you cross the line, you're actually making up stories.

Yes. Look, once the stakes get higher, it's, "Can I do this? Can I do that?" And then the line starts moving. I think it's a great thing that people are being more creative in documentaries. That's a great thing. And that's definitely happening. But there still have to be certain standards of: Is it documentary or is it fiction?

SOURCES AND NOTES

The website for Firelight Media is www.firelightmedia.tv/. The websites for films discussed include *The Black Panthers*, http://theblackpanthers. com/; *A Place of Our Own*, www.pbs.org/independentlens/placeofourown/; and *Freedom Riders*, *Jonestown*, and *The Murder of Emmett Till* can all be found at www.pbs.org/wgbh/americanexperience.

CHAPTER 20

Deborah Scranton

Deborah Scranton's first feature-length documentary, *The War Tapes*, won the award for Best Documentary at the 2006 Tribeca Film Festival and Best International Documentary at the 2006 BritDoc Festival, among many other honors. *The War Tapes* follows three National Guardsmen—Sergeant Steve Pink, Sergeant Zack Bazzi, and Specialist Mike Moriarty—during a tour of duty in Iraq that began in March 2004 and ended a year later. Scranton broke new ground by putting cameras in the hands of the soldiers themselves, training them as cinematographers, and communicating with them through instant messages and email. She and cinematographer P.H. O'Brien filmed the soldiers before, during, and for several months after their deployment, and also followed the women and families they left behind.

A New Hampshire-based filmmaker, Scranton had previously directed *Stories from Silence: Witness to War* (2003), the World War II remembrances of 47 veterans, including one woman, from the small farming community of Goshen. After *The War Tapes*, she produced, directed, and wrote *Bad Voodoo's War*, a 60-minute film commissioned by WGBH and ITVS, which premiered on the PBS series *Frontline* in 2008.

This interview was conducted in 2010, before Scranton's second theatrical documentary, *Earth Made of Glass*, about post-genocide Rwanda, had its world premiere in competition at the 2010 Tribeca Film Festival. The film, which aired on HBO, was nominated for Best Documentary Feature by the Producers Guild of America and won a 2011 Peabody Award.

To start from the beginning: In February 2004, you received a call from the public affairs officer of the New Hampshire National Guard, Major Greg Heilshorn, asking if you'd be interested in embedding, as a filmmaker, during a tour of Iraq. And you came up with a novel alternative.

My background was working in televisions sports, like the Olympics, the Tour de France, big sports events, as well as doing a lot of adventure or extreme sports. And literally, the night I got the call,

I woke up in the middle of the night with the idea: What if I could virtually embed? And what if I could cover a war as if you covered a sporting event? That sounds distasteful, but in the sense of: When you're covering a big event, one camera [isn't enough]. You can't film a football game with just one angle; you're going to have a very limited view. What if you could have a multicamera filming platform, which was the background I came from, and through that, try to tell the story of war?

And they agreed.

They gave me my pick of units, and I picked Charlie Company, 3rd of the 172nd, which is a mountain infantry unit, because infantry typically is like the "tip of the spear," as they say. And I knew that they were going to be based in Balad, in Anaconda [Camp Anaconda is a large U.S. military base near the Balad Airbase, about 40 miles north of Baghdad, located in the Sunni Triangle], and they would have internet access. Because in order for this to work, I needed for them to be able to communicate with me. And don't forget, that was in '04, so cellphone use wasn't as common for communicating data. I wanted to be where their home base would have internet access.

So I went down to Fort Dix [New Jersey], where they were training, getting ready for their deployment, and my caveat for the access was that I had to get the soldiers to volunteer. So I hopped out in front of the unit, like 130 guys, and told them what I wanted to do. And the commanding officer said, "Well, whoever is interested . . ." They gave me a day room; I went in and had a further conversation for a few hours with the guys. Because by nature, I think, people in the military are skeptical of the media. They figure you've got an agenda. And I needed to make my case that I really wanted to know what it was through their eyes.

I mean, look: The war is often highly politicized, but soldiers rarely take part in that discussion. And my intent was to try to capture the experience of combat and everything that goes along with that: the fear, the boredom, the humor. What does it mean to be a soldier on the ground in Iraq, through the eyes of the soldiers themselves? I felt that was a voice that was really missing. Their experiences are important to understand, regardless of one's political beliefs. And I think often beliefs can be a way of avoiding looking at reality. People can stand behind their beliefs, and they disconnect. One of my major reasons for making the film was to try to help bridge that disconnect between those who know a soldier and those who don't. They're there (in Iraq and Afghanistan) in our name. Soldiers swear to uphold the

Constitution of the United States. They don't swear fealty to an administration's policy.

I read in your press materials that 10 soldiers volunteered; five stayed with it for the entire year, and overall, 21 soldiers contributed. Each of those 10 was given a one-chip Sony MiniDV camera along with some microphones, lenses, and lots of blank tape. How did you prepare them to document their lives, to shoot in a way that would convey stories?

I think that's where the internet really came in handy. Before they left, my cinematographer—P.H. O'Brien, a technical whiz—and I went down to Ft. Dix, and we talked them through different things, as far as framing, and you don't want to be backlit, and everything. And we came up with all these innovative things [for] mounting cameras on the dashboard, mounting them on the gun turrets, to have steady shots. So we did chest mounts and things that would have that stability. And they understood the basics—everybody, by and large in our society, has picked up a video camera. It was important not to inundate the guys too much; it was just basically to get them filming, and then we refined it as the process went on. Tapes on average took two weeks to get from Iraq to me, so it wasn't that long. We could see what they were doing, and send emails, and talk and make suggestions.

Dust was a real factor. We had some underwater housing that we used. It was always a fight against the sand. And the cameras would get blown off sometimes, so we had to have a steady supply of cameras. We'd cycle them from Iraq back here to New Hampshire; I'd get them serviced and send them back to them. We sort of had this round-robin of cameras going in and out at all times.

In 2007, you gave a presentation at the TED conference in which you described this process, and the more than 3,200 emails, IMs, and text messages that went back and forth (and that's after you started keeping count). You talked about how you'd captured the scene in the film that follows the explosions at Al Taji, an airfield about 17 miles northwest of Baghdad. You wanted to be sure to get an immediate response—what the military calls "hot wash." Can you explain?

Yes. There's an incident in the film where there was a double VBIED, which stands for Vehicle-Borne Improvised Explosive Device (IED)—a word for a car bomb, basically. And there was a double VBIED outside the gates of Taji as Steve Pink's crew was getting ready to go out on a mission, and they responded to the call.

So how it worked was, Steve Pink had sent me an email at the end of the day, and attached still photos of the burned body that was outside the car. And in the email, Pink said that it had been a really bad day, and he told me a little bit about what had happened. I saw in one of my IM windows that Mike Moriarty was online. So I pinged Mike and I said, "Hey, Mike, I heard Pink's squad had a bad day today, and I wondered if you could go over and do an interview with him," because I wanted to get that interview within 24 hours. So what you see in the film is the actual film of the event as it unfolds, which is from Pink's camera; you see an interview done with Pink, that Mike Moriarty did within 24 hours; then you have audio from an interview that I did when Pink was home; combined with him reading his journal. (Several months after he came home, he felt comfortable enough to read his journal for me.) So it's all layered in there, this multifaceted perception of that event.

And that's what I talk about in the TED talk, [in part] because it illustrates what the process was for making the film, but also for the fact that we sometimes hear that soldiers are disappointed with the media, and that's a perfect example [of why]. Because you see the scene; it made the news; it made CNN; it was an event covered in the traditional media, but they didn't add one more line, which was: "And U.S. soldiers spent the entire day, at great risk to themselves, trying to save Iraqi lives." There were no U.S. soldiers outside the gate. Those were all Iraqis.

You've said that for you, "truth resides in contrasting ground-level narratives, and amplifying the voices of the people truly involved."

Yes. I don't like narration-driven pieces. I think when you write and you have a narration in it, you're framing it. And it's true, what I chose to edit and include, that's also a framing device. But I feel that when you write and have a narrator, you have a point of view and you get sound bites to support that point of view, versus looking for different points of view and trying to put them together to share with the viewer this multifaceted perspective, which I think is much more representational of what reality is.

When you look at Rotten Tomatoes, for *The War Tapes* we have like a 98 percent rating, which very few films do, as far as people responding to it. That was very . . . gratifying is not the right word, but it felt good because it felt like we had done what we set out to do, which was share their voices. And people listened and responded.

This also means that you, as the filmmaker, are letting the contrasting narratives speak for themselves, and trusting audience members to make up their own minds.

Right. I think you have to have more faith in people. We grow up surrounded by stories; it's how we share meaning and create meaning and share experiences and build meaning. And I think that if you communicate different visceral experiences, then, in a way, you're opening a window so other people get to meet those people, versus having an agenda. I understand auteur-driven pieces. Somebody has a point of view and they have something to say. I just think that we need to hear more voices.

In all my interviews and in all my appearances, inevitably somebody would ask what my position on the war was. And I said I would never answer it in the context of Deborah Scranton, director of *The War Tapes*. If we were having dinner and we were having a conversation, of course I'm happy to have a conversation. But for me to go on the record and to say what my views were, it would diminish everything that the guys and I had done in making that film. The whole point was to try to share what their experiences were, and to amplify their voices.

You've said in other interviews that you were impressed as a student by works such as Let Us Now Praise Famous Men, *and the idea of living journalism.*

Those photos and that type of journalism just struck me as very honest and very true, and it didn't have an agenda. It was bearing witness to what people were experiencing at a very difficult time. And those were stories and pictures that the rest of society needed to see, to hopefully empathize and better understand and be aware of what reality is. It goes back to that whole thing of: Beliefs can be a way to avoid looking at reality. This is reality.

I'm curious about the logistics of it. This is a 94-minute film, made up of about 800 hours of footage that came back from the soldiers, plus about 200 more hours that you and your crew filmed with the men and their families here in the United States. I noticed, for example, that there were a lot of people credited as "loggers."

They were college students nearby. Basically, the guys [soldiers] had to roll a lot of tape, and there was a lot of empty tape with nothing happening. But if you're not rolling—they're not going to press "record" when they get into a firefight or an IED explodes. You have to hope the camera's rolling when that incident occurs. Right? The guys would tell me, "We got this firefight. It's on these tapes." So I knew which tapes had material that I definitely needed to go through with a fine tooth comb. But I wanted to make sure that we saw everything. So we watched everything and made sure that we noted [anything] that maybe would come in handy—it could have been a funny one-liner that they had just said. So the logs didn't necessarily have a lot, but even if one tape had one one-liner, I wanted it. Some logs were just like "driving in the desert . . ." and you'd know there was nothing on it. But I didn't want the guys to risk injuring the tape or recording over something. They would often ask me, "Should I just rewind and take the tape out again?" And I said, "No, send them to me."

Your film is only as good as your database of footage that you have. Because when you make a film, you have to think of it—or I think of it—as one giant puzzle. And you have to know all the pieces that you have. It's like painting a painting. You don't just paint with primary colors. You want all of your shades. You have to know where everything is. I use a database called Filemaker Pro, which is a searchable database. So something that comes in, that at first maybe you don't think could be important, later—because of something that happened—all of a sudden becomes very important. And you want to be able to find it. So logging is crucial.

I'm curious about the various collaborators involved. You got the initial call from the National Guard in February 2004, and by March the unit was headed to Iraq. At that point, you were only working with executive producer Chuck Lacy, is that right?

I had met Chuck, [who] is a former president of Ben & Jerry's. So he helped us get started financially, to be able to buy the cameras and to do this, and was instrumental in us getting started. So, we had been working on the project for eight months before I met Robert May.

So the guys were still over in Iraq at that point?

Yes. And we had cut a little trailer. Very often, when you produce a film, you've got to raise the money to do it. And typically, when you start out, you don't have anything to show. The big question is: "Are you going to get it? Are you going to be able to do it?" People aren't necessarily willing to take that risk; they want to see that you're already succeeding and that there's something there. So we had cut a 15-minute trailer and applied to go to the Sundance Producers Conference, and [there we] met a few different producers. Robert May, one of the executive producers of *The Fog of War*, watched it and decided that he was interested and wanted to help us produce it, help us raise the additional money.

And I read that Robert May connected you to Steve James, who came on board as a producer and editor, with Leslie Simmer. Can you talk about what you look for from an editor?

An editor has to have a very good background in story structure, in finding story and coming up with how scenes will come together. Any film is a collaboration; film by nature is a collaboration. You have to find people who are willing to go on the journey with you and to bring their eyes and ears to the project.

Before I agreed to bring Robert or Steve onto the project, I vetted them quite rigorously, because I didn't want anybody involved in the project that was going to try to insert a political bias into it. That was very important to me, because I had given my word to the soldiers that we would tell the story through their eyes, and the footage wouldn't be taken and made into something that had a bias.

You edited for about a year, and as part of that, chose to focus on just three of the original 10 soldiers: Pink, Bazzi, and Moriarty. Why?

We ended up picking the three most divergent stories, in the sense of what they represented. We had done some test screenings with more soldiers [in the film], and we got audience comments that they couldn't tell the soldiers apart. It was quite disconcerting. But on the other hand, I can understand what they're saying. And I prefer to go very personal, character-driven: People really do get into their lives. So in the end, I think it served the film best. And that informed [my decision], when I made the *Frontline, Bad Voodoo's War*, to just work with one platoon [30–35 soldiers, rather than a whole unit] and one main character, the Platoon Leader SGT Toby Nunn. We had 12 cameras filming in that one platoon. I felt there would be more of a chance for these different intersections because they were all out on the same missions together. We could gang more cameras together and get an even more intimate view.

As you approach the editing, do you work at all on paper, like with an outline?

I do colored index cards. So I have different colored index cards by character, and I put it out on a wall, and I move them around.

So you've mapped out when, for example, you want to come back to the fire-fight that you opened the film with, at Fallujah.

Right. I knew it had to come in later, because it happened in November 2004; it was the second siege of Fallujah. The actual timeline of events definitely informs it. You just don't know how fast—the second act can be pretty big. And then you have to pick what your climax is, what is *the* moment of the movie. Which in the case of *The War Tapes* was the tragic scene of Moriarty's squad hitting and killing the civilian woman by accident.

Did you screen The War Tapes *for the soldiers and their families before it was released?*

We did a screening, and they could comment on their section. It's really important for me to say if you feel that you've been represented accurately. I think it's always hard for people to see themselves distilled on film; I don't think it's easy for anybody to do that. And I think it takes a lot of courage to be willing to share your story. For *Bad Voodoo's War*, for instance, the whole reason that Toby Nunn, the main character, agreed to work with me on the film was because on his prior tour, one of the guys on his squad, Jake Demand, had been killed, and no one had told his story.

Let's move on to Bad Voodoo's War, *a one-hour film that you made for the PBS series* Frontline. *The film is similar in that it is also a "virtual embed," but as you noted, it follows a single platoon; also, you're present in the film, both as narrator and as your process of directing is seen.*

The whole reason to do *Bad Voodoo's War*—the war had changed, it was around the time of the surge, and the whole reason for it was [to] see what that meant for those guys. *Frontline* was adamant that my process and what I do be part of the story. I think they were interested in the step beyond, the "2.0" of *The War Tapes*—to make it even tighter and more intimate, and to show the process more. And I came to see what their point was, because it added a layer to the story that wouldn't have been there otherwise. So in the end, I was grateful that they pushed for that inclusion, but it was not my idea.

Were there any technology changes that made a difference in how you worked?

With *Bad Voodoo's War*, we could do stuff over iChat, so that I could listen, which you see in the film. I could be listening while Toby was doing an interview of one of the guys. So it was as if I was in their tent with them, listening to the interview. I would say both of these films aren't *about* the internet, but neither of them could have been made without it. The internet allowed the soldiers (in *The War Tapes*) and Toby (in *Bad Voodoo's War*) and me to talk about what happened, and to examine how to best tell the story as it unfolds.

Which is remarkable when you consider, as you've noted, that the first live reporting from battlefields didn't occur until the first Gulf War (1990–1991).

Right, on CNN. Now, if you look at the London bombings (in 2005), that's the Nokia effect. That's on cell phones. The Green Party in Iran, with the death of Neda [Agha-Soltan, in 2009], that was all [reported] by cell phone and cameras. And I think that speaks again to the ground truth, again away from some of that narrator-driven information. It's irrefutable. This is what's unfolding on the ground right here. It's not necessarily a summation of everything, but it's like "This is true right here. You can't deny this."

Do we need to be concerned about a lack of training in ethical journalism? There are things one can do with visual images and sounds that are not honest.

Right. But I think some journalists have been doing that for years too.

So how do you impart the guidelines of what's good citizen journalism?

You have to stick to the truth. You have to decide what truth you're telling, whose truth, whose voice, what stories you want to share, and then you have to be true to it. I don't believe in objectivity. I think that we're all shaped by the experiences of our lives, and we bring all of that to it, and anybody who says they're objective, I just flat out don't believe. My personal belief is, you have to decide whose story you're going to tell.

Very often in Q&As I'd get asked, for *The War Tapes*, why didn't I tell the other side of the story. That wasn't the story I said I could tell. I could recommend other films that told the Iraqi perspective, and they're wonderful films. But you can't tell the entire story in a 90-minute film—any story.

And it's very transparent what story you're telling, whose story, and how.

I think a film can be really illuminating when you construct it in this multifaceted framework. You see these things unfold in real time; you hear their reflections and their perceptions of what the experiences were like for them within 24 hours; and then you hear the words after they've had a few months to process it out, and time has kind of weathered the edges around it. For me, that as a style is a really, really important way to see the world through someone else's eyes.

Sound plays a big role in these films. I'm thinking of The War Tapes, *especially. Before you even see the opening image of the battle in Fallujah, you hear a man breathing heavily. There's a heartbeat to the way sound and music are used in the film.*

There was a lot of audio work done on the film. Those small cameras don't have the best audio function. We re-layed every single bullet under that film, to make sure that it [was heard]. We wanted a visceral experience; we wanted it to sound like you were there. We didn't add anything artificial, putting stuff in that wasn't there. It was just making sure that when you're in the theater, [you get] the feeling of what it was like to be there. For instance, when you see the shots of the guys up in the turret, what they kept talking about to me was the wind; they kept feeling the wind. So I wanted to make sure that when you see the film, you'll [hear] the different wind tones when the guys are up in the turret, because that's what they said they heard. And it was certainly windy up there.

Can you talk about your relationship with the military, in terms of access? Don't most audiences assume you were carefully watched, if not censored?

The access that I got [for *The War Tapes*] was from the New Hampshire National Guard, and they were very committed that the story be told, so they didn't hold back. People are stunned, but that was a fact. Look, it's all based on trust and relationships. If you're not good at establishing trust and building relationships, you're never going to be a good filmmaker. You earn your trust day after day. In order for [the soldiers] to film that much, they had to trust me and not self-edit. They had to be able to be vulnerable, and know that I wasn't going to take advantage of that vulnerability and make them look stupid. We could all be filmed and somebody could cut it and make us look like bad people. So it all comes down to trust and relationships and being a person of your word. And I think it may have been helpful that I'm not, at this point in time—nothing against being New York- or LA-based, but it's not like I was some slick producer coming in who didn't know anybody. These guys are my neighbors. I live here. I'm not going to take them out of context. I understand their world, and I'm not going to make them, on purpose, look bad. On the other hand, they were very clear that I wasn't going to make them look good either. They just wanted a fair shot. They just wanted somebody to say the truth.

Production on The War Tapes *began with a basic narrative arc: the year of deployment. Beyond that, how did the shape of this film, its story, emerge from all of those hours of footage? Steve James is quoted as saying, "If the story we ended up with works, it should seem obvious and self-evident. But, believe me, it wasn't."*

The story emerges from within, and it sort of becomes obvious. You know when you look at it—as it's unfolding, when a monumental moment happens—you know for sure that that's one of your main story points. You may not know what act it's going to be in, but you know. That's where the puzzle part comes in. And the art is in how you link those, and what you butt up against each other for whatever effect you want. I enjoy that process.

Do you consciously work with act structure?

Yes. I work in scenes. You know when you have a scene: For instance, when [the convoy] hit and killed the civilian woman, that was a scene that was going to be in the movie, so we could cut that scene. The double car bombing outside of Taji, I knew that was a scene. Mike Moriarty had told me endlessly about that vehicle graveyard and how he found it so haunting. When I got that in and looked at it and heard the commentary, I knew that was a scene. So you sort of fill it out. And then you start seeing who your character is, and how you've come to know them, and make sure that you have on film the different aspects of a person that they are, that you can share with the audience their strengths, their vulnerabilities, their fears, their hope. So it's all a big hero's journey: Set up the premise, the characters, situations and relationships, the confrontation. They've got to encounter the obstacles, the dramatic need, and the resolution, which doesn't necessarily mean the end. It's got to have a beginning, middle, end. Was it Godard who said, not necessarily in that order?

For me with *The War Tapes*, probably one of my most influential films—well, there's two of them. One was a movie called *Before the Rain* by a Macedonian director called Milcho Manchevski. It won at Venice. And it tells the story in a circle, which is why I wanted to open the film up with the firefight in Fallujah and go back to it again. Because sometimes you think you see one thing, but then when you come back around, you have a different understanding and a greater context for what world you're actually in. And then the other one was *Black Hawk Down*, where I think Ridley Scott did an amazing job at showing the two different worlds: the world on the ground and the world of the U.S. soldiers, and how isolated they were from each other. As well as the *Iliad* and the *Odyssey*, the two greatest books ever written. I think all stories, no matter what, it's a hero's journey. You take a flawed hero; they're on their path, and you want to go with them on the journey and see where they end up.

I film my docs like dramatic [films]; one of my favorite books is *The Screenwriter's Bible*, by David Trottier. Without a strong story structure, you don't have a movie. For me, making a film is kind of like a diamond shape. You start out, you think, "Okay, this is where we're going," and then you'll reach a point in production (and almost every filmmaker I've talked to has this experience) where you feel, "Uh oh,

I have something here but it's not what I thought I was going to have."
At that moment, you have to trust in the story itself, that it *will* become
clear and come back down again to the other end. You can't force it,
and you shouldn't try to superimpose something on it. You just have
to listen. Just simply listen.

The story is a living, breathing thing. You have to be informed by
what you're finding; it's a constant refining process. But in that process,
you have to be aware, you have to have a structure to hang it on. So you
have to be thinking: "What are the inciting incidents? What am I going
to use for that? And then if I use this one, what am I going to need to
follow up? If I use that one, what am I going to need to follow up?"
Because what you don't want is to end up in the editing room with not
enough of the needed material to tell the story you've chosen to tell.
That's the other reason why I always start editing my films two-thirds
of the way into my shooting, so that if I find that I need something,
I'm still shooting.

*So it's flexible but not spontaneous. Before you go out, you have a suggestion
of a narrative—*

Or a question you're trying to answer, and you don't know who's going
to give you the answer. So for Rwanda it was: "What happens after war
ends?" That was my question. We still have all these areas of conflict
around the world that are locked in cycles of violence and retribution.
Rwanda charted a different path, different from South Africa, different
from anywhere in the world. And they're having success at it. So what
does that mean? What does forgiveness mean? What I found so interesting was that it's a different definition of forgiveness than I've ever
seen articulated, which was basically a decision made to stop the cycle
of violence in this generation, and at great sacrifice to themselves. That
they will not teach or perpetuate hatred to their children, regardless of
the incalculable brutal losses that they suffered. Fascinating.

But if I had gone in there saying, "Oh, I want to find someone
who has said, 'I totally forgive and love who did this . . .'" I didn't go
in with an agenda. I really wanted to find out, "What is really going
on here?" I don't want them to tell me what they *think* I want to hear.
What *really* is going on there?

So we set out to make this film about what happens after war ends,
and forgiveness. And as we're about to touch down, France arrested
Rwanda's chief of protocol, Rose Kabuye, on terrorism charges. Three
months earlier, on August 6, 2008—against the backdrop of the world's
deadliest war in neighboring Eastern Congo—Rwandan President
Paul Kagame had released a report detailing the French government's

Jean Pierre Sagahutu (l) and Gaspard Bavuriki (r), in *Earth Made of Glass*, © 2010 Sparks Rising LLC.

hidden role in planning the 1994 Rwandan genocide. Rose Kabuye was his closest aide. So all of a sudden we end up in a whole different world. And it basically was Rwanda taking on France to expose the truth about what really happened in Rwanda, which was France's active complicity in the genocide. A million people died in three months. The world was told one story, and the truth was buried.

So it's a president's search for truth for his country. And then it's a genocide survivor's search for his father's killer, a very personal story, and the choice of what he does and what he teaches his children. And we find one of his father's killers. So you see it unfold. That's what I mean when I say it's a documentary, but it's filmed as if it was a narrative, because it has those scenes. Instead of a talking head telling you what happened, it's built in scenes.

For *Bad Voodoo's War*, the story was about the dread of being attacked. It was the tension of wondering if today was the day. And the decision for *Bad Voodoo's War* was: End it with them going back [returning to Iraq after a mid-tour break]. That was really important to me, that the film end with them going back, because we're still there. I didn't want to make another film that brought the guys home, because those guys may be home but others are sent in their place. The viewer response to *Bad Voodoo* was off the charts. It crashed the server twice, as far as viewers writing in. There are some amazing comments, people's reactions. And that was really important to me, because I didn't want to let the audience off the hook. Guys are still there.

SOURCES AND NOTES

TED is a nonprofit that brings people from technology, entertainment, and design together to share ideas. The conference is held annually in Long Beach, California. Scranton's talk, filmed in March 2007, can be viewed online at www.ted.com/talks/lang/eng/deborah_scran ton_on_her_war_tapes.html. Scranton quote from an online discussion with her, conducted April 2, 2008 following the PBS broadcast of *Bad Voodoo's War*, available online at www.washingtonpost.com/ wp-dyn/content/discussion/2008/03/30/DI2008033001258.html. Rotten Tomatoes (www.rottentomatoes.com) gathers reviews from a selected pool of sources, including some media outlets and online film societies, and merges ratings and other data into a single measurement, the "Tomatometer." With 64 reviews counted, *The War Tapes* scored 98 percent on this meter. The Sundance Institute's Independent Producers Conference evolved in 2009 into the Sundance Creative Producing Summit, www.sundance.org/initiatives/creative-producing. *Bad Voodoo's War* premiered on the PBS series *Frontline* on April 1, 2008, and as of this writing (2015) can still be viewed online at www.pbs.org/ wgbh/pages/frontline/badvoodoo/. See Milcho Mancevski's website for information, www.manchevski.com. *Before the Rain* is a dramatic feature that won numerous awards at the 1994 Venice International Film Festival. The film was released on DVD in 2008; the screenplay is available at the website. For information on *Black Hawk Down*, a dramatic feature released in 2001, see www.sonypictures.com/home video/blackhawkdown/.

CHAPTER 21

Kazuhiro Soda

Born in Japan, filmmaker Kazuhiro Soda graduated from Tokyo University with a degree in religious studies before moving to New York City in 1993, where he studied filmmaking at the School of Visual Arts. With his wife, choreographer Kiyoko Kashiwagi, he co-founded the New York-based multimedia production company Laboratory X.

Soda worked in New York for many years as a filmmaker for NHK, Japan's national public broadcasting organization, before completing his first feature-length documentary, the Peabody Award-winning *Campaign* (2007). The film follows the political campaign of Kazuhiko Yamauchi, who was chosen by the Liberal Democratic Party to run for a key city council seat despite having no prior experience. (A 60-minute version of the film aired on the PBS series *POV*.) Soda returned to that story in the wake of the 2011 Fukushima disaster, observing the candidate as he ran for office again, this time without party support, for the film *Campaign 2* (2013).

Soda's acclaimed documentary *Mental* (2008) observes daily life at Chorale Okayama, an outpatient mental health clinic in Okayama, Japan. This was followed by *Peace* (2010), which follows the daily lives of people, their caretakers, and cats in Okayama.

In *Theatre 1* and *Theatre 2* (2012), Soda turns his attention to the world of live theater, observing the work of Japanese playwright and director Oriza Hirata and his company, Seinendan.

He is the author of five published books in Japan, including *The Reason Why I Make Documentaries*, and *Theatre vs. Film—Can a Documentary Capture Fiction?* We spoke in February 2015.

You've said that you do "observational" films but you don't call them vérité. Is that true?

Yes. Well, I call my style "observational" because I think observation is a key to good documentary filmmaking. Of course it implies a connection to the tradition of direct cinema. People often call documentaries without narration, "observational" style. And it's certainly true that my filmmaking method and style is a continuation of that tradition. But at the same time, I wanted to redefine what is observational cinema. I call my films observational for that reason.

What's involved in thinking about redefining it?

When I say "observational," it has two meanings. One of them is that I as a filmmaker try to observe the reality in front of me and make films according to my observation, not according to my preconceived ideas or agendas. The other meaning is that I let the audience observe what's going on in the film, using their own eyes, ears, and brains, rather than tell them what to feel and think.

The English word "observational" implies "being distant" or "not involved," but it's not about that. It's about looking and listening attentively. The Japanese word *kansatsu* (observation) literally means "looking" and "sensing."

So I came up with ten commandments of observational filmmaking, like a guideline to follow when I make documentaries:

#1: Do not do any research about the characters or the theme.
#2: Do not have any meetings with characters.
#3: Do not write script or synopsis before shooting. Shoot spontaneously without preconception or planning.
#4: Minimize the crew. Basically I roll the camera myself and I record the sound as well, because I need to be flexible and spontaneous.
#5: Shoot long rather than short.

Do you mean long duration of time, or long scene?

Well, it means I shouldn't make any assumptions. There are many moments where I feel maybe this scene won't make it to the final cut so I should probably quit shooting, but I roll the camera anyway because you never know what's going to happen. So I try to roll as much as possible.

#6: Try to go deeper in a narrower place, rather than wider and thinner coverage. Meaning, focus on a very small area, and go deeper.
#7: Do not set up a theme first in the editing room. You look at the footage and you find the theme by editing the materials.

So you're saying that although you might have a theme in mind, something that came to mind during the filming, you ignore that and try to look at the raw footage as if for the first time?

Exactly. First, when I'm shooting, I'm observing the reality in front of me. But then in the editing, I do exactly the same, because if I had a theme first, I would try to pick and choose whatever fits the theme. In other words, all the scenes would become tools to prove the theme, or prove the point. But that's boring. I try to look at the footage and listen to what this material is saying to me. So usually I discover the theme of the movie late in the process, like two to three months into the editing process. Until then, I don't really know what this movie is all about. That's number seven.

> #8: Do not use narration or superimposed titles to explain the situation, or music. It's because I want the audience to observe what's going on in the film. I'd like to minimize interference of their observation.
>
> #9: Don't chop up shots. Use longer shots rather than short shots. Leave some space for the audience to observe.
>
> #10: Pay for the production cost yourself. It's because when somebody pays for the movie, that somebody wants to tell you what to do. I welcome grants which don't tell me what to do, but basically I need to be self-sufficient financially. To be independent, you need to be independent financially.

So these are the ten commandments I have when I make so-called "observational" films.

In terms of not having a theme, when you're making choices about what to even start filming, do you have a question in mind? In other words, why make the films Campaign *or* Mental *or* Theatre, *versus some other film?*

Usually it's the person or situation which intrigues me. For example in *Campaign*, the candidate, the protagonist [Kazuhiko Yamauchi] is a friend of mine from college. We were classmates. And I learned that Yama-san—I call him Yama-san—was running for a vacant seat, backed by LDP (Liberal Democratic Party), which is the most powerful party in Japan. So I was intrigued by the situation, especially because he is a very bohemian guy, not a traditional person. And LDP is a conservative party, like a Republican Party. So I was intrigued by this mismatch, and curious to know what would happen. So that was the starting point. I didn't know what kind of movie I was making when I was starting it, or even while I was shooting it.

Of your films that I've seen, that's the most narrative, in that you have the structure of a 12-day campaign, beginning, middle, and end. And you had amazing access.

Yes. But I had no idea what kind of story I was telling. Everything was happening spontaneously. The fact that he was running for a seat, I got to know it by accident because our mutual friend sent me an email with a picture he took in Kawasaki, which was a poster of his political campaign. And he asked me, "What's happening to Yama-san?" And I didn't know. I didn't know he was running. But five days later I flew to Japan and started shooting. I had no preparation. So I didn't know what I was getting into.

The film is so rich in visual detail, like the conductors shoving commuters onto the train, or the candidate so caught up in bowing to everyone that he jokingly bows to a statue of KFC's Colonel Sanders. It seems this richness is part of what gives the film its worldwide appeal; it doesn't just speak to a Japanese audience.

Yes. Actually that's thanks to the power of observation. When I'm rolling the camera, I try to look and listen to what's going on in front of me, and try to interpret my observation to film language or actual shots. For example, the first scene where Yama-san made a speech, it was my very first experience of seeing him making a speech in public. So I didn't know what kind of speech he would make; I was following him and trying to record what he was doing. But eventually, I noticed that nobody was listening to him! So my next thought was, "How can I translate my discovery to film language?" So I decided to take the last shot of the scene where I positioned myself far away from Yama-san and I took a gradual zoom-out from him.

I'm so glad you mentioned that shot. There's a whole scene in that shot. You see the candidate close up, talking his heart out, and the camera pulls back and back, and nobody's paying any attention at all. The station's empty.

Exactly. And that kind of thing is something I discover while I'm rolling the camera. I like that because I wasn't allowed such freedom or luxury when I made documentaries for TV, especially for NHK, a public network in Japan. I made more than 40 documentary programs for NHK. Back then, I was required to do a lot of research and to write detailed scripts with the narration before shooting.

What was the subject matter of the documentaries?

It ranged. I made a two-hour documentary behind the scenes at the Metropolitan Museum in New York City, for example. I also made a two-hour documentary about a traditional festival in Peru. I made a documentary about the adoption process on the internet in America.

So they're almost like illustrated lectures? You wrote the entire script, including the narration, before you filmed the visuals?

Yes, I was required to write the narration and shot lists before I even shot. And that kind of process was necessary in a sense, because in a TV station there are many layers of approval process or bureaucracy, you know? There are many producers to go through to get approval from, and they need to know what kind of program I'm making. Pre-established harmony.

How quickly did you have to turn these around?

Sometimes it took me one year to make one program. But shorter programs—I was a regular director for a 20-minute mini-documentary series called *New Yorkers*, about people in New York—I had to make one program per month. So that had very short turnaround. The first week, I did the research and wrote the script, and the second week I'm shooting, third week I'm editing, and fourth week I was finishing it up. By the fifth week I'm already starting the next project. I did that for three years, and that gave me a lot of training. But at the same time I was frustrated because I had to write the script beforehand, and I had to kind of follow that. And if I shot something different from the script and came back to the editing room, then the producer complained to me, "Why didn't you follow the script? We have a totally different project now. I didn't give a green light to this project." They often complained and scolded me, and ordered me to reshoot sometimes.

Is that what led to the ten rules for making observational films?

Absolutely. They are basically anti-TV commandments! On TV, I had to have a preconceived idea and follow that preconception. It was very hard to make new discoveries while shooting, and even if I made new discoveries and shot that, I got complaints from the producers. But that's very strange because documentary is all about discoveries, finding out something we didn't know. That's the beauty of making documentaries, isn't it? So at first I was enjoying making those programs, but gradually I got very frustrated by this limitation. So when I started making my own, I decided: Okay, I won't do any research. I won't have any meetings with characters. And I'll try to empty my head as much as possible, and try to observe what's going on in front of my camera, and try to learn something new from that process. That's the whole motivation.

Is there any intervention at all? I'm thinking, for example, of a scene in Campaign *where a group of friends come to the candidate's apartment for* dinner, and their conversation is very helpful in making it clear what's going on politically. Did you ask them to talk about it, or did you just get lucky?

I didn't ask them; I was just lucky. I never ask any characters what to do or what to say, because I want to be open to what's going to happen. But I also respect the methods of filmmakers like Jean Rouch who tried to involve characters in the filmmaking process, so it's a matter of choice, I think.

Occasionally in your films, you can be heard asking questions.

Yes. If I have a burning question, I would ask. But I try not to ask any questions only to get the comments I want. When I ask questions, it's more like a conversation, not an interview. I only ask questions which I would ask even if I didn't have a camera. So as long as it is a conversation between me and that person, and if I'm just recording that, that's okay. But I try not to dig into somebody's mind and try to get something I want, because that way I become like a hunter and I'm kind of using that character as a tool to prove my point.

The other thing I noticed is that you sometimes include footage in which the people you're filming mention the camera or talk directly to you, behind the camera. For example, there's the scene in Mental *when the poet Naohiko Sugano says "Cut! Cut!" Is there a reason you keep that in?*

Yes, I made a conscious decision to keep that in. Actually, I'm heavily influenced by Frederick Wiseman. I love his movies. When I made *Campaign*, I tried to be like him. I tried to be invisible. I would cut off anything which mentioned my presence. But when I made *Mental*, it was very hard. I tried to be invisible but people asked me all kinds of questions while I was rolling the camera, and I had to answer them. So even though I told Sugano, "Okay, I'm not here. I'm not here, please ignore me," he didn't listen to me. He kept mentioning the camera, and he kept saying, "Cut, cut, cut," pretending he was the director! And actually, when I was shooting, I felt I was not able to use those scenes because he was saying that. But then when I was editing *Mental*, his scenes were some of the most interesting scenes I shot. So I thought, "If my method prevents me from using the most interesting scenes, what's the use of the method?" The method is to make a good documentary. The method is to make something interesting.

So I decided, okay, I have to redefine what is observation and adjust my method. Then I came up with this idea: Whatever I'm observing is changed by my presence. The observer is always a participant in the observation; it is observation of a world which includes myself. When I redefined the idea of observation like that, I felt more liberated and dynamic. I decided to include those scenes. So my concept of observation changed when I made *Mental*.

What was your initial idea in filming the Chorale Okayama outpatient mental health clinic, how long did you film, and what did you say to the patients that they allowed you into such intimate moments in their lives?

Basically, I got to know this clinic through my wife's mother.

Is she in the film?

Yes, very briefly. Actually, she's one of the protagonists of *Peace*. She works with Dr. Yamamoto as a caregiver [Dr. Masatomo Yamamoto is the elderly psychiatrist who runs the clinic], so I got introduced through her.

Initially, I wrote a letter to Dr. Yamamoto to ask for permission to shoot. I said, "I don't know what kind of film it's going to be, but I'll try to observe what's going on and make a film out of it." But Dr. Yamamoto didn't say yes or no to my letter. He wanted to let the patients decide what to do.

So there is a patients' association in this clinic, which briefly appears in the film. Remember, a bunch of people were discussing something about this change in government policy? That's a patients' association meeting. So Dr. Yamamoto gave the letter to them. They discussed it and decided to accept me with one condition, that I needed to get permission from each person. That's reasonable.

So my wife Kiyoko and I went to the clinic every day with a camera. There were a bunch of people waiting for their sessions in the waiting room, so we introduced ourselves, saying exactly the same thing: "We are trying to make a documentary about this clinic. Are you willing to be in the film? What kind of film it's going to be, we don't know." We asked every single person we saw in the waiting room. And maybe 80–90 percent said, "No, I cannot be in the film because I don't even tell my parents I have an illness," or "My colleagues do not know." Most of the time, they did not want to publicize that they had an illness. But 10–20 percent said yes. And as soon as they said yes, we rolled the camera. That's how we got access for the footage.

Campaign is narrative in the sense that you don't know how it's going to end, but you know that the candidate will either win or not. With Mental, *there's no sense at any moment in the film of where or how it will end. You're just watching; you're just there. And it's not an essay. You're not making an argument. It's almost poetic, in a sense, or a slice of life. What was your thinking in terms of how you were structuring it, how you were organizing* Mental? *How would you decide what to film?*

It's true that the structure of *Mental* is very different from *Campaign* because it doesn't use the passage of time as the driving force of the narrative. My mindset was closer to a painter than a storyteller, I guess. I tried to depict a detailed picture of this micro-cosmos Chorale Okayama. But deciding what to film was very easy, because a very limited number of people said yes to us. As soon as they said yes, I turned on the camera. I shot about 70 hours of footage. [The final film is 135 minutes, so this is a ratio of about 31:1.]

And how long were you filming at the clinic?

About 30 days, I guess, in total. It was 2005 and 2007, two separate times. And there were days when I couldn't roll the camera at all because nobody agreed to be in the film.

How do you know when to stop, when you have what you need?

It's very hard to know when to stop the camera. But when I make a documentary, I usually encounter some scenes which could be the core of the film. For example, remember the last scene of *Mental*, where one of the patients was talking on the phone, sometimes yelling, and he vanished into the darkness, cutting the red light? When I shot the scene, I immediately thought it would be one of the most important scenes in the film. I didn't know why, but I was very intrigued and I was interested in this guy. I knew I was shooting something extraordinary. And when I shot the scene with Mr. Sugano, the poet, I also felt the same: It's going to be one of the core scenes in the film. Another scene where I felt that was the scene with the mother who accidentally suffocated and lost her baby. When I was shooting the scene, I immediately felt it would be an important scene—although later on I was very concerned, and had to think so many times before I decided to use that footage. And if I acquire several scenes like that, I feel comfortable to stop shooting. And this instinct is never wrong, until now. I've never gone back to the subject and reshot.

Concerned for the mother?

Yes, because she was revealing something she would probably have never revealed to anybody.

Did you show the patients a cut before it was finished?

No, I didn't. I only showed the rough cut to Dr. Yamamoto and a few of his colleagues to seek their professional opinions as a doctor and caregivers, because I'm not a medical expert. But they didn't request any changes.

In terms of the scene with the mother, when I was shooting it, I was excited as a filmmaker. I was shooting something extraordinary. But at the same time, as soon as I finished shooting, I was kind of worried. I was not 100 percent sure if I should use it or not. But I remember that after she talked to me on camera, she was saying, "I don't know whether I should have talked about this to you, but I wanted to do that." A few days later, I even visited her place to shoot her at her apartment, and she didn't ask me to cut the scene. So if I cut the scene out because I'm worried that something is going to happen, in a sense, I'm kind of trying to silence her, and I wasn't sure if that was ethical, either. So I decided to use it. But I was also determined to avoid sensationalism.

By which I think you mean that you let the scene play long, allowing for context. She's talking, going down a rabbit hole of detail that just gets worse and worse.

Exactly.

It's all one take. She's just talking to you.

Right, exactly. The longest shot was about six minutes and 30 seconds, and she was talking nonstop. And if I let her talk, including the background of her story with her mother and her doctor and her husband, if I could capture the whole story, not only the most sensational part but also the whole story, then—

—There's a humanity to it—

Yes. In fact, listening to her story, I was able to relate to her as a human being. I felt like I could have done the same thing if I was in the same situation. So if I could let the audience feel the same, then maybe it's not unethical to use it.

Some documentarians seem to think, "I have to teach people this. I have to prove this. I have to show this." You're letting the scene play for so long that the audience reaction can be complex.

Yes. It's a complex story. I wanted to depict her complex story as it is, without reducing it to something simplistic. And as long as I could keep that complexity in the scene, I thought it was okay to use it. Anyway, without that story, we cannot understand her suffering. Her suffering is based on that incident. And if I skipped that, I couldn't get closer to her. It's impossible. If I self-censored that scene, it would be unclear why I was making *Mental*.

Why?

I mean, if I decided to cut the scene because I was afraid to show it, then why was I making this film in the first place? I wasn't sure. So I decided to include the scene.

Do you know if she suffered any repercussions after the film came out?

Well, it's quite complicated. I think she had both good effects and not so good effects of the film.

When I completed the film, she was happy to be in the film, but then when the release date of the film approached in her town, she became very apprehensive. She didn't know what would happen, so she became very, very worried about the outcome. So I got very worried, and I seriously thought about not showing the film in Okayama.

But before I made that decision, I went to Okayama to see her, and we talked, and I listened to her. Also, other patients who supported the film spoke with her, and she gradually felt okay. Also Dr. Yamamoto gave me full support about the film, and he also consulted her. My mother-in-law also listened to her. And so in the end, we kind of overcame the situation together. And in the end, she gave me a letter to read in front of the audience. She didn't come to the screening but she gave me a letter. "Please read this letter to the audience." So that's what I did.

What was the letter about?

About her tough experience and how she felt about it.

Did she ever see the film, and was she okay with it?

Yes, she did. She's okay and nowadays her condition is far better than when I filmed her, but her anxiety comes and goes. For example, she recently had a psychological crisis. Her daughter is now 20 years old, and as a mother, she's worried that the film might be a disadvantage to her.

Which speaks to an underlying issue in your film, which is stigma.

Yes, stigma. Because the characters of my film are coping with stigma, I'm coping with the same stigma too. It's kind of endless. The issues of her daughter, which I never imagined at the time of filming in 2007, come out now because they are living human beings. In a sense, we documentary filmmakers need to be responsible to our character's life until we die. It was a very short period of time when I shot those scenes, but it means I'm responsible for their images for the rest of my life. It's a tremendous responsibility to be a documentary filmmaker.

I always feel that. It's fashionable to say that there's no distinction between fiction and documentary, but they are totally different in this aspect. And if I knew all of these ordeals before I shot *Mental*, I don't know if I would have shot *Mental*, because it's a lot of work mentally. Sometimes I can't sleep, even now.

So legally you can do what you want, but morally and ethically—

Exactly. Ethically, I'm responsible. It's a huge burden. But at the same time, that's the beauty of documentary too. I think because I made that commitment, I was able to know her much better, and it's a lifetime relationship.

A documentary is kind of like a sharp knife, I think. It could hurt people, but it could be very useful, too. It can be used in a good way or a bad way.

In making Mental, *were you hoping the film might raise awareness, or bring more resources to the problem, that sort of thing?*

I didn't make the film for that purpose. A film is a film. I mean, I'm not using my film as a tool to change society.

Would you define your film as art?

Yes. It's more like art. So it could change people's mind or perspective, or it could contribute to know about human society better, but I'm not making my films for social change. If I had that purpose, probably my films would have less complexity.

For example, in *Mental* there was a lot of discussion about the last scene. If I were making a documentary to tell people how human patients are, I would probably have ended the film with the poetry scene [Sugano and other patients share poetry with each other], because that way you can feel closer to the patients. "Wow, yeah. People with mental illness have a great sense of humor, and they are poets, and they are really great. We shouldn't have any prejudice against them."

Instead, there's one final scene, about 12 minutes long, in which we see a patient on the phone, even as clinic workers try to close for the day, arguing with various agencies about benefits. And then he leaves, gets on a motor scooter, and drives through a red light. There's so much in that scene.

Exactly.

I know it wasn't your intent in making Mental, *but has that film had any effect in terms of policy or awareness?*

In terms of awareness, yes. About 30,000 people saw it in movie theaters in Japan, and DVDs are still selling. It's selling more than my recent films. It hasn't really phased out, maybe because there are so many people who have the issues. Also, it became a "must see" movie for a lot of mental health professionals; they often use it for clinical studies and education. So I think it has a significant impact. The clinic, Chorale Okayama, receives regular visits from all over Japan.

I'd like to return to the question of definitions. You're not creating just any kind of art; you're calling it documentary, which suggests that there's a truthfulness or accuracy required. Where are your journalistic boundaries, as somebody making art?

I don't consider my documentaries as journalism. It's different from journalism, I think.

But then can you define what you mean by documentary?

Yes. Journalism assumes that there is a Truth (capital T) and we can get closer to the Truth. But I don't think documentaries deal with the Truth. And also, journalists tend to try to achieve objectivity, but we documentarians think we are subjective. We don't even try to achieve objectivity. And it's okay.

But it's not fiction. It's not invented or imagined.

Right. We are aiming a camera at reality, but at the same time, who's aiming the camera? It's me, or it's somebody. So it's that person's point of view. Whatever I'm recording is my subjective view or my personal experiences. If I had been shooting *Mental* in a different time, I would have met different people and I would have made a totally different film. I visited the clinic at a certain time, and I met a certain group of people, and I left. For me, documentary is an art form to recreate my personal experience in film language and to share it with the audience. It's not about whether what I witnessed was true or not. It is about my personal, subjective experience. It's closer to diary than to newspaper or academic paper.

Are there things that you would not do in terms of juxtaposing two things, or intercutting, or taking scenes that happened late in the process and using them early on, things like that?

Not really. I do that all the time, because I need to translate my experience into cinematic language. In order to do that, sometimes I need to rearrange the chronological order and reconstruct my experience. It's kind of like when you talk about your recent travel to your friend. When you tell your friend how your trip was, you don't necessarily tell her everything in a chronological order like "First I got out of the apartment and hopped on the train and . . ." That's a bad storytelling.

How do you sequence your films? Or do you think in those terms?

First I look at all the footage, and I transcribe whatever is happening. If anybody says something, I transcribe it. So I make a full transcription of all the footage, and then I start editing whatever scenes interest me. I don't really start chronologically. I start to work on the scenes which intrigue me.

And then, after a while, I have several scenes which intrigue me, and I start assembling those. Then I have the first cut, which usually is a mess. It doesn't look like a film at all. It's just a random assortment, just an assembly of the scenes. So I start shuffling them around. I put each scene on a Post-it and I put them on the wall, and I shuffle around these Post-its.

What are you thinking about as you do this shuffling?

Well, for example, scene B needs to be earlier than scene A, because if I see scene B first, scene A becomes much more interesting. That kind of thing. And I keep shuffling them around so that I can find the right structure of the film. I do that process for quite a long time, and I often make discoveries. For example: I thought scene 1 and scene 12 had nothing in common, but when I put them together, wow—you see some connection between them. Or the other way around: If you put two scenes side by side, it's not very interesting, but if you put them apart, it's more interesting.

It's kind of like chemistry experiments. You mix and match, and sometimes the right match generates a chemical reaction. Because I don't make any commentaries, the order of the scenes is the only thing I can manipulate. It's a very manipulative process. But that's the only way I can translate my experience into film. So I do a lot of shuffling like that.

Let's talk about Peace, *which follows Toshio Kashiwagi, a retired principal, and his wife Hiroko—your in-laws, although it's not mentioned in the film— as they care for individuals who are ill or disabled, and as Mr. Kashiwagi cares for many cats. There's also a sort of poetry to the film, where you're cutting not to story shots, people caring for people, but instead to nature (turtles, birds, plants) or details on the street. Does the title relate to that?*

Yes, definitely. Also the title relates to the tobacco Mr. Hashimoto was smoking. [Shiro Hashimoto is a 91-year-old client, living in an apartment infested with ticks and mice.] "Peace" is a brand name. It's a very significant cigarette, actually. It was the first cigarette the Japanese government started selling after World War II. So it's a symbol of postwar Japan, and he's been smoking Peace for many years, and he got lung cancer from that. It's very ironical but poetic.

Can you talk more about these interlude shots? It's a technique you use in other films as well, although it's more notable in Peace.

When I'm shooting so-called "main" scenes with protagonists, I feel like I'm kind of looking at something with a magnifying glass, closely looking at the person or the actions. I feel gradually suffocated by doing that, and feel desire to see a larger world to put these protagonists (or cats) into a context. So I go out to shoot nature or the surrounding environment, to capture some shots which I feel are connected to what I'm shooting with the main characters.

When I was shooting *Peace*, obviously my eyes were drawn to people with disabilities. I never realized, until I shot *Peace*, that there were so many people on wheelchairs on the streets. And also my eyes got drawn to older people on the street, or children, or other animals, because I was shooting the cats. So my point of view got affected by these main characters, and that reflected what to shoot in the streets or in nature.

These interlude scenes serve a few purposes. One is to create rhythm to the editing. Also, the human brain cannot process all the information at one time. You need some time to digest after you've seen

Shiro Hashimoto, in *Peace*.
Photo courtesy of the filmmaker.

something thick, something complicated. So I try to place these scenes in between heavy scenes. It's like when you're eating dinner, you have *hashi yasume*. They are not main courses, but kind of like side dishes served between main courses. They also give context to the main characters.

What would you say are the main differences between documentary in the United States and in Japan, in terms of storytelling?

It's very hard to generalize, but my impression about American documentaries is that they use a lot of talking heads, and shooting documentaries is almost synonymous with shooting interviews. And what's interesting to me is, there is a world called B-rolls. Whatever images support the interviews are called B-rolls. But for me, B-roll is the main thing. So right there, my approach is pretty different from many American documentaries. But at the same time, my method and style is an extension of the tradition of direct cinema, which mainly flourished in America.

Is "story" the wrong word to use when talking about your films?

No, I don't think it's wrong. I think my films also tell stories, although it may not be a very traditional way of storytelling. Even *Mental* is storytelling. It's kind of like I tell my experience to my neighbor or to my friend: "I visited this clinic and I met those people, and I'm back now." In that sense, it's storytelling. And within that large story, there are many smaller stories. For example, the mother told her very significant life story, about her suffering. Mr. Sugano was also a storyteller. So there are a bunch of stories within the film. And as a whole, I am telling my story of visiting that clinic. All of my documentaries are like that, I think: *Peace* is also storytelling, or even *Theatre 1* and *Theatre 2*. It's telling my experience of encountering these people.

What are you working on now? What's next?

I'm working on a film about fishermen in Japan, in a region called Okayama. It's the same region as *Mental* and *Peace*, but it's in a remote village. I think I'm making two films out of the material I've got, and I'm editing the first one, which is about an oyster factory. They raise oysters, and remove the shells in the factory to sell them. But like in every city in Japan, this village is aging rapidly and they don't have enough people to work at shucking. Traditionally the industry relied on local people, especially women, but they are getting older, and they don't have enough workers. When I was there to film, coincidentally, they were about to get new workers from China. So all of a sudden it became a story about globalization. A small oyster factory became a microcosm of globalization.

That sounds really interesting. And it gets back to your sixth commandment: "Focus on a very small area, but go deeper." Which is great advice, because student filmmakers, for example, always seem to want to go very big, and tell the history of the world or solve racism in 20 minutes.

Yes, it's impossible.

You can't do it. Find a person.

Yes. Find a person. Find a situation, or encounter a situation. I didn't know this globalization thing was happening; I got to know the fishermen only because my wife and I often take a vacation in that village. The house we stay in is by the sea, so we often see fishing boats going out, going in. We became friends with these fishermen, and I got interested in shooting them because fishermen themselves are becoming scarce. Like other primary industries, fishery is slowly dying in Japan, which made me curious to know why. So I had an interest in them. And one of them happened to be an oyster farmer. So I asked him, "Can I come in to shoot your factory?" and he said yes. So we went there with a camera, and then I found out they were accepting new Chinese workers. So of course, I had to shoot that. I kept shooting until the new workers arrived.

SOURCES AND NOTES

The filmmaker's website is www.laboratoryx.us and is available in Japanese or English. Information about *Campaign*, *Mental*, and his other films, including *Theatre 1* and *Theatre 2*, can be found here at www.laboratoryx.us/theatre/HOME.html.

CHAPTER 22

Orlando von Einsiedel

A former professional snowboarder, London-based filmmaker Orlando von Einsiedel co-founded Grain Media, a TV and film production company, in 2006. He went on to direct a series of short, social issue and investigative documentaries around the world, including Afghanistan (*Skateistan: To Live and Skate Kabul*, 2010); Nigeria (*Aisha's Song* and *Radio Amina*, 2011); and Sierra Leone (*Pirate Fishing*, 2011).

In 2012, von Einsiedel began directing his first feature-length documentary, the Academy Award-nominated *Virunga*. With executive producers including Leonardo DiCaprio and Howard G. Buffett, *Virunga* premiered at the 2014 Tribeca Film Festival, winning awards there and at more than 50 other festivals worldwide.

One of the striking things about Virunga *is the complexity of its storytelling. I'm curious about your intent as you began the film.*

I cut my teeth in documentary filmmaking doing investigative films. And invariably I'd go out to developing countries, there'd be some sort of injustice, and then our role as filmmakers was to document that and ideally bring someone to account at the end of it. But I kept meeting really inspiring, amazing people doing incredible things, and I'd realize that those were stories I'd never hear about back home. So I started thinking, okay, the films I'd much rather make are not these depressing investigations, which are important of course, but positive stories. And the film which took me there to begin with is *Skateistan: To Live and Skate Kabul*, about a skateboard school in Afghanistan. And that set me on this path of trying to tell positive stories.

While I was making a film in Sierra Leone some years later, I picked up a newspaper, and there was a story about this place called the Virunga National Park. I'd never even heard of this park. It almost looked like Jurassic Park; it was otherworldly. There were volcanoes, there were glaciers, and there were mountain gorillas. The story was about the rangers of the park and these ambitious development projects that they were doing, trying to rebuild their country after 20 years of war. They were trying to create jobs and development, and they were doing that by using the park's resources. So that was a story I went out to tell, this positive story about the rebirth of the region after so many years of fighting. Look—I didn't go in blindly. I knew it was eastern Congo. I knew it was unstable. But I did not bank on finding the story which unfolded when I arrived.

Did you plan to embed yourself there for a certain period of time?

I didn't really know, to be honest. The first trip I did was for Al-Jazeera, the TV channel. They commissioned me to make a half-hour show about the park [*Tales from Virunga*, for the series *Earthrise*], so I used that as a way to fund a research trip. My initial trip was meant to be about a week. But within a few days of getting there, the park rangers told me, "Oh, you're British, right? You really should look into this oil company that's from your country [SOCO, an international energy company based in London], that's illegally exploring for oil here." So the story very quickly took this U-turn, and we realized that the skills that I'd developed in my earlier career could be used to investigate what this company was doing. And then within a couple of weeks the war started. [In April 2012, regional fighting broke out between members of the M23 rebel military group and the government.] So it became this much, much bigger story quite quickly.

How much of a baseline story do you need to have before you start shooting, or is part of your investigation just being there with a camera?

No—you definitely need an idea about what you're going in to do, because generally [you] have limited resources. There's not that much money; I know I can only afford to be there a certain amount of time. So you need a rough idea of at least the initial arc of what you think is a film. And so I normally go out with that in mind.

How do you think about that, a film's arc?

With the films I make, I always run them through narrative film structures. So I tend to structure things in three-act structures in the same way a movie is structured. I know a lot of documentarians don't, and I think a lot of people say what's so exciting about documentary is that you're not confined to those storytelling tropes. But it's worked well for me, that I've tended to set out with a rough three-act structure in my mind for what might happen. Of course you need to be very flexible, because you can't shape reality, and things happen very differently to what you expect. But I start with a very rough idea about how things might play.

And then the conflict broke out. Did you consider leaving at that point?

Every part of me was terrified. But by the time that had come, I was already in so deep—I'd made really close friends, I truly believed in this park, I was incensed about what I was seeing with this oil company—that I felt at that point I just couldn't go. And also I knew that the rangers weren't going to go. They were going to stand firm. And I figured that the small, tiny, tiny contribution I could make was to stay and document what was happening. Weirdly enough, the camera gives you a bit of protection. In a way, it removes you from what's happening around you. The scariest moments weren't the ones when I was filming. The scariest moments were when I was in a combat situation of some sort and I didn't have a camera, because the camera gives you an element of protection, at least psychologically.

You seem to have had tremendous trust from the rangers and people you were with.

Yes. Early on, they recognized that this film could be a tool to protect the park. It was a vehicle through which to investigate what SOCO and its supporters were doing, but also the end product could show the world what was happening in this park, and try and get the world to rally with the park to protect it.

So nuts and bolts, how do you plan what to cover on any given day? And is it just you?

Every film is different. But with *Virunga*, I spent the first year on my own, out in Congo, basically because we didn't have any money. I could have sat at home in the UK for months on end and tried to raise money, and probably would have missed the whole story. The alternative was to go out there and live in a tent with the rangers, with a small, fairly cheap camera, and just be there as much as possible. And that was the route we opted for.

So on a daily basis, at the beginning at least, I was following lots and lots of different storylines, lots of different characters. Generally, one day I'd spend with one character, another day with another. So on one level you're documenting these character stories, and on another level you're trying to capture the bigger story about what's playing out around them—the oil issue, the war—and you're trying to meld the meta story with the personal story.

When did you figure out that Rodrigue Katembo, Andre Bauma, Emmanuel de Merode, and Mélanie Gouby would be your four central characters? Was that an editing decision or a field decision?

That was definitely a field decision. I think initially I probably had about 10 characters, but it became clear, quite quickly, that we'd end up with Andre, Rodrigue, Emmanuel, and Mélanie, partly because of circumstance and partly because their stories all told a bigger story about Congo. I've always tried to use micro character stories to tell much bigger meta stories.

So teasing that apart, for example, you have Andre, who is caring for the orphaned gorillas—four of only 800 left in the world. You found him through that original newspaper story.

Yes, that's right. Andre's story told the story of the park and the rangers' connection to its wildlife, and of course he was a route into the gorillas. He is also one of the most amazing human beings I've ever met—extremely kind, unbelievable sense of honor, brave.

And then Rodrigue's story [Katembo is head park ranger], told the story of Congo and its wars. He's grown up as a child soldier, and his life almost epitomizes the cycle of violence which has been happening in the country for almost 150 years. He's now trying to make sure that his son doesn't grow up in a world like himself. So this is what drew me to him, as his story really roots us in what this is all about—protecting the park isn't just about saving animals, it's really about saving people. It also turned out that contractors and supporters of SOCO had approached him, and Rodrigue had already started to investigate them. He was willing to wear the undercover equipment. So he immediately became a really key character.

Initially I didn't really want to have foreign characters in the film; this was always meant to be about Congolese heroes. But I couldn't avoid including Emmanuel, because half the key decisions that are made in the park, he's involved in. [A conservationist and a descendant of Belgian royalty, de Merode has been director of the Virunga National Park since 2008.] By the fact he is from Belgium he represents Congo's colonial legacy. He is also a truly brave and remarkable man of integrity, so it became clear that he was going to be one of the main characters.

And finally, Mélanie [Gouby is an independent French journalist] was the one who wasn't planned at all, because I met her about six months into the shoot. I was filming something one day, and she was there as a journalist. And I'd always been very secretive about what I was doing because of security concerns, and so publicly I'd just say I was making a film about gorillas. At the end of this day of filming, she said, "I know some guys you might be interested in. They work for the oil company." And of course all my alarm bells went off. And then Emmanuel and I decided it was a worthy risk to tell her about what we'd been doing and ask her if she would she be interested in working with us, and she said yes.

But also, aside from her being able to [gather] all that material from a journalistic point of view, there was a storytelling bonus in having a character like Mélanie in the film. In the Q&As [that follow film screenings], she's almost always the person who gets asked about first. I think that's because she's the character that most people in the West can relate to. And that was a conscious decision at some point in making this. Mélanie was like the girl next door, whereas everyone else, they're all amazing people but they're not like someone that you grew up with, someone that you recognize from daily interactions.

Mélanie also plays a key role in advancing exposition, our understanding of who's who and what's happening, which is helpful because there's no narration.

Yes, I knew as a character she could do that, whereas the others— Andre, of course every day is changing for him, but he's not actively pursuing a story on his own. Rodrigue was of course, too [through his investigation and participation in undercover filming], but with him, we were waiting for moments to happen because we didn't want to arouse suspicion. Mélanie's a journalist. She's doggedly researching stuff, charging ahead with the story, and that's creating exposition just by the fact that she's doing it.

At one point she's printing out full-color maps, which was very useful for the viewer. Is that something you asked her to do, or is it something she actually just did?

It was a bit of both, actually. At her apartment she had notes on all sorts of things. But some of them were so intricate that they didn't really work on camera. So there were a couple of bits where we basically got her to redo, to map out in a slightly bigger form what she already had in her notepads, so we could film it. But the inspiration for that was what she was already doing at her desk at night.

Is the hidden camera footage something that your characters would have done anyway, as part of their work?

In this case, no, they wouldn't have done it anyway. Rodrigue, civil society groups, and fishermen were investigating what SOCO and its agents were doing before we got involved, but they weren't doing it with undercover cameras. I realized that I could contribute to their work with technology. Using an audio/visual device to document evidence of potentially illegal acts is a good way to build up a case. Otherwise, it's effectively your word against someone else's. We also taught Mélanie how to use the undercover cameras.

Did she get any fallout after the film came out and they saw what she had done?

Well, for safety reasons, both she and Rodrigue left Congo before the film was released. We took security incredibly carefully. Just for instance, Mélanie and Rodrigue never met, the entire time we made this film. We kept them apart. Journalistically that was really great, because they were doing independent work and started to bring back the same sorts of material; they corroborated each other. But we took security very carefully, and before the film came out both of them left Congo.

In some ways, Virunga—the park itself—is a character in the film. Would you agree, and is it the character that drives the film?

I don't know if it's the character that drives the film, but I always wanted it to be a character. It was important for me that as a viewer, ideally, you feel the presence of this living, breathing entity in the same way you feel the Andre and Emmanuel characters. Part of trying to get that across in the film wasn't just making it look beautiful, but it was also showing the life, the rich biodiversity in this park, everything from the streams running through it to ants on the ground to these enormous breathing mountains of clouds. It was really about trying to get that across.

And at some point you brought in people to do the aerial photography?

Exactly. And the reason I wanted the park to be alive was because we didn't ever want to make any obvious overtures in the film about the environmental impacts of oil. In fact, there's not a single moment where anyone says, "Oh, if there is oil there, it's going to destroy the park on an environmental level." But that, I think, comes across on a much deeper level because you see, you feel how incredibly alive this place is.

One of the key challenges of filmmaking is making choices about what to leave out. In this case, there are other threats to the park, including charcoal, deforestation, and poaching, which you touch on, but not extensively. How do you make those kinds of choices?

Andre Bauma with gorilla, from *Virunga*.
Photo © Orlando von Einsiedel, used by permission of the filmmakers.

Well, I guess, ruthlessly. The key choices have to be what's going to drive the narrative forward. And when I say the narrative, in the case of *Virunga*, I mean the oil story and the growing war story and then how elements of the two stories potentially intersect. So that meant that all those other things (poaching, deforestation), there wasn't even a place for them after the first ten minutes. We touched on poaching a tiny bit in the very beginning, but only to introduce the characters of those orphan gorillas; we didn't want to talk about poaching per se. There's a bit later on where you see a poached elephant, but it's only used with reference to the way armed groups fund themselves [black market ivory]. And [even] that's only included to explain why the oil might be of interest to them. So that was the kind of ruthless storytelling drive. How do we push forward the two main narratives in the film?

So when you're thinking in terms of three-act structure for this film, what's tipping you from one act to the next? What's the thread that's pulling you through?

This film follows quite a classic three-act structure. Act I is the slowest act; it's almost the most traditional documentary act in the way it's structured. It's introducing our four or five main characters, giving some context to the situation so you understand this pattern of resource extraction and the trouble on the ground that has come with that. And then there's—in the way a movie works—an inciting incident, in this case the introduction of SOCO International and their work in the park and the characters' decision to follow this story. In Act II, we really we see that story play out. We see how oil interests are growing, how those in favor of the oil exploration are breaking down the rule of law and how rebel groups are interested with it, and then how these elements feed into wider instability in the region. And then the war comes to a climax, and then we're finished with Act II, and then Act III is sort of the aftermath and wrapping up those storylines and looking to the future.

What are some of the other filmmaking questions you're frequently asked about Virunga?

I'll talk about some of the influences on this film. I'm drawn to films with a social issue at their heart and I'm a massive believer that if you really care about a social issue and you want to make a film about it, you need to make a film which is entertaining and exciting if you want people to watch it. Your film could be about the most important social issue in the entire world, but if it's a really difficult film to watch, because it's boring for instance, you're going to limit your audience to a very small number of people, and therefore you're going to have a lot less impact on the social issue you care about.

I was really influenced by films like *The Cove*. There is an environmental issue at the heart of that film, and what they've done is, they've taken a kind of heist-movie narrative and used that as an entry point. They've made a really exciting heist movie, which of course can bring in a massive audience, and therefore the issue gets an enormous amount of attention.

And so with *Virunga*, right at the beginning, I always felt that this needed to be a really exciting, dramatic film. Of course I didn't know that the footage would lend itself so well to a lot of that, but right from an early stage we were trying to do that because we wanted to make a film with mass appeal. And obviously gorillas played a part in that too. They really give a heart to the film, act as a metaphor for all of the animals in the park, and in some ways are a mirror onto our better selves. But they were definitely used very strategically. Of course I love gorillas, but it's no coincidence that all of the advertising for this film focuses on the gorillas, because people respond to them incredibly well.

You cut to them periodically in the film too, as a reminder: this is what's at stake here.

Yes. But they also are a metaphor for what the park is and what the park can bring in its development, all that other stuff. But you're right.

They also tug at all the heart strings, because they're innocently caught up in the whole thing.

I read that you worked with veteran feature editor Masahiro Hirakubo (Ella Enchanted, Trainspotting) to shape this film. You shot something like 300 hours (a ratio of about 180 to one, with the final film about 100 minutes).

Something like that, yes.

How long did it take to edit, and how much of the structural choices were made in the editing room?

Well, we worked with a different editor to begin with, Peta Ridley, and it was really tough, because this film was almost three separate films. There was a PBS *Frontline* investigation, there was a National Geographic film, and there was this vérité war film. And a lot of people said, "You should make this two films. It's crazy. It's never going to work, making it one film." And we struggled enormously, to begin with, to make it work, because the footage was so different for each type of film; stuff wasn't jelling. But we doggedly pursued making it one film because all those elements were interrelated. It wasn't like the oil was a story that was playing out in a vacuum. So it always felt that to tell the true story of what was happening in this park, to see how things could be interrelated and to show that everything that was happening in Virunga was a microcosm of a much bigger historical pattern in Congo, we needed to bring these things all into one film and one story.

At that point, it started to feel that we should try and work with a narrative editor who was more versed in weaving together a myriad of different storylines, themes, character stories, and sequences. We were running out of time badly, and then Joanna [Natasegara], our producer, came up with Masahiro's name, and we went to meet him. He's worked on so many big films, so we thought there's no chance he's going to be interested in working with us on a small documentary, but he was, thankfully. And it was with him that we managed to pull the film into the rough structure of what the final product was. We also worked with other editors afterwards to fine tweak things, but Masa wrestled it and made it the film that it is.

The film opens powerfully and somewhat mysteriously with the funeral of a ranger. At what point did you decide this was the place to start, and why?

That was almost one of the last decisions we made in this film, was to start with the funeral. For 90 percent of the edit, that scene was cut out.

There just never was a place for it, and it wasn't a ranger that had been in the film. But there was a point where it just suddenly felt that we needed to know, right up top, that these rangers were risking their lives for this park and they were trying to make eastern Congo a better place. So that when you then come to later scenes with the rangers on patrol, you instantly know the stakes, you know how dangerous it is, and you know how utterly committed these guys are to doing their work.

I'm curious about your approach to chronology. About 20 minutes into the film, you show Emmanuel de Merode addressing the rangers. The same scene returns about 32 minutes later, after the overall story has moved forward considerably, and we hear a different part of the address. When do you feel you can break things up and move them around, and when can't you, because it might be inaccurate or misleading?

That's a really good question. We were very constrained in terms of what we could do with playing with time or being creative with the order of events, because the film is based upon a journalistic investigation—we had to play a lot of things absolutely straight and maintain journalistic integrity. That said, with some sequences we did have a bit more freedom to compress time. The main combat sequence, for instance, obviously didn't play out over the course of 15 minutes, as it does in the film. It played out over a number of days, and then we simplified some things. As far as I see it, you always have to do that. That's all a part of making a film legible for people to understand.

But presumably you're being careful to make it bulletproof factually, so that the overall film can't be dismissed.

Totally. If there was anything in the film that was factually incorrect from a journalistic point of view, the first people to come after us would have been SOCO International, to discredit us. So we had to be incredibly careful with how we portrayed things journalistically, and we just didn't have the kinds of creative freedoms that I've had in other films, where you can be much more loose with how you mix things around, structure the story.

At what point in the process did you and Joanna Natasegara, who is also the film's impact producer, begin to plan for the public engagement/outreach component of the project? Was it from day one?

When we realized that the film could help protect the park, it became very important to build a campaign that would use the film in the best possible way to do this. I'm just a filmmaker and knew that for the film to have as much impact as possible we would need experts.

Joanna Natasegara is one of these. She devised an impact campaign with a number of strands but chief among these was getting the film out to as wide an audience as possible—this was why we were so keen to work with Netflix—and screening the film to strategic audiences in the business community, to politicians all around the world and to key influencers. We wanted to pull all of the different possible levers that might create the key pressure on SOCO to get them to do the right thing.

Did this change how you were filming? When you were editing, did you do any test screening as part of thinking about its possible use and engagement?

Absolutely. Definitely. Yes. We test screened; this is one of the problems we had near the end. We were running the film through all these different lenses. We were running it through: Is it exciting? Do normal audiences engage with it? Is it journalistically robust enough? Will this have impact from a campaign perspective? And they don't all benefit each other. Sometimes they're massively at odds with each other. I mean, even the end cards, at the end of the film. If it wasn't a campaign film, we probably would have ended the film differently. There were all these sorts of competing agendas.

How do you balance your own passion for the subject with the sometimes conflicting demands of art, journalism, and advocacy?

I guess, touching on what I was saying to you, all the investigative work had to be objective, so we had to play those things fairly. We couldn't just cherry pick soundbites to make them more dramatic. On some levels we were lucky that what some of those guys said was just crazy anyway. But we had to play those sequences as they were; they couldn't be manipulated.

So on one level, the journalistic thrust of this film is very objective. But of course, as a human being, while making this film, I sided with the park enormously, even while I had to keep an open mind journalistically. I could see illegal acts happening in front of me, and that's horrendous. You can't help but feel angry at watching enormous injustice play out. So as a filmmaker, I know where my heart lay, but we had to have journalistic hats on to make sure that what we were documenting of SOCO International was truthful, it was credible, and we weren't being unfair to them.

How was Virguna *funded? Did you go through a proposal-writing stage?*

We went through the proposal stage, absolutely. Apart from the initial money from Al-Jazeera, then I think we had about $15,000 after that, which paid for some flights and a bit of camera equipment. But then we did another nine months with virtually no money. During that whole period, I was writing funding applications all the time, but no one wanted to fund it. I'm an unheard-of filmmaker, this was a story in a part of the world that is far away, in Africa, and also making the kind of vérité film where there's no idea what will actually happen on screen. So everyone turned us down. Sundance turned us down, the MacArthur Foundation, Sheffield Doc/Fest—there must have been about 15 applications. And no one gave us money until WorldView, and the BRITDOC/Bertha foundations jumped on board. Having BRITDOC really helped turbo charge the project, as they introduced me to Joanna Natasegara, and she helped open more funding doors. We then got some fantastic support from the Arcus Foundation and the 11th Hour project and several other smaller organizations.

Did you try to get representatives of SOCO to talk to you for the film?

The way we'd normally do an investigation is that we'd go to the target of the investigation while in production and try to get an interview. But in this case, the stakes are so high on the ground in eastern Congo that the idea of going to SOCO, a company we didn't trust, and just saying "Hey, we're here. We're doing this big undercover investigation into the work of your staff, contractors, and supporters" just wasn't an option.

So what we did instead was, just before the film was finished, but near the end of filming—everyone had left Congo at this point—we wrote to them. We said, "We're making a film about you; these are the allegations we're going to make. How do you respond?"—so that we could incorporate their response within the film. They wrote us a very long legal letter basically saying, "If you go ahead with this film, we may sue you." And then they wrote to a number of the festivals we were about to launch at, and said, "If you screen this film, we might sue you." And then they wrote to some of the journalists who reviewed the film and said, "If you don't take your reviews down, we might sue you." [The filmmakers include SOCO International's written response at the end of the streamed film.]

When did Netflix come on board as the distributor?

We launched at Tribeca in April last year [2014]. We wanted the widest possible audience, to shout as loud as possible about what was happening in this park, so we were looking for the biggest distributor. Netflix saw the film at Hot Docs in Canada [about a week later], and started the conversation, and as a filmmaking team, it became clear quite quickly that they were going to be the best possible platform for us.

They go out to 60 million homes in over 50 countries, and this is growing all the time. The film lives there forever. Anyone can watch it at any time. It was incredibly powerful for us to be able to have that in our toolkit. And then on top of that, Netflix had a really great marketing plan, and they were really excited, kind of from the top of the organization all the way down, about protecting the park. So they felt like great partners to work with, and they were amazing.

You've worked a lot as a filmmaker in countries and cultures other than your own. How do you think that your educational background—an undergraduate degree in social anthropology from the University of Manchester and a master's in development studies from the London School of Economics—has helped?

I think there are two things that anthropology and development studies instilled in me as a filmmaker. The first is a real interest in other parts of the world, other ways of life. I was fascinated with how other people around the world lived. That's why I studied anthropology. I love to travel. I like to spend time in other places and learn about them and see the diversity of human societies.

I think probably the more important thing that I learned is that you can't always judge everything on your own terms and what your society believes is right and wrong, because that's just too narrow a view. Anthropology and development studies definitely taught me that. And I think if you go into situations in other countries with that, you're very open to things. It means you can be open with people. You're not judging every practice as somehow inherently less good than what you might be used to in Europe or America; it's just different. So I think that helps you have an open mind and allows you to work more comfortably in developing countries.

A more general question, because you've worked on so many shorter films: How do you decide when something merits short treatment and when it should be a feature?

Good question. How do I decide? Well, *Virunga* is my first feature so I wouldn't say I'm an expert on this, but I think it's really all to do with a combination of factors: inspiring and engaging characters, a wide range of interesting themes, a strong story at the heart of it, and the ability to follow that story over a sustained period—to actually document real change in the characters and situation you're following. High stakes also don't hurt, and I would say you also need the ability to tell the story in a cinematic way.

What are you working on now?

You know, you have to juggle lots of balls, and only occasionally they land. So there're a few doc projects that I'm excited about, if any of them actually happen, and I'm also looking at some narrative projects. For me, to do a narrative, it's really about reach. If I can find the right subject matter and social issues I care about, you've got a much bigger potential audience to hit. But I'll always make documentaries. Documentaries are where my heart is. So it's too early to say which projects I'm going to do next, but there's a couple I'm excited about.

SOURCES AND NOTES

The website for Grain Media is www.grainmedia.co.uk/. The official site for *Virunga* is http://virungamovie.com/. The site for the park is https://virunga.org/. Mélanie Gouby's website is www.melanie-gouby.com/.

PART IV

Additional Material

Films

Many documentaries, including not only recent releases but also classics from previous decades, are easily available as DVDs or streaming online, through vendors such as Amazon, Hulu, Netflix, Intelliflix, and/or through distributor websites, including the channels on which they aired (such as PBS, or National Geographic, and the National Film Board of Canada). Please do not use pirate sites.

Through the web, readers will likely be able to find official information about specific films, including press kits, teachers' guides, and public engagement plans. This is especially true for theatrically released documentaries. Otherwise, be careful of web-based information about films and filmmakers. IMDB, for example, is a user-generated site, and as such the information it contains may not be accurate, complete, or up to date. Wikipedia, for the same reasons, is not necessarily a reliable source.

Transcripts and other useful materials are available online for many documentaries that have been shown on U.S. public television, including *American Experience* (a historical series, www.pbs.org/wgbh/amex/), *Nova* (science, www.pbs.org/wgbh/nova/), and *Frontline* (current affairs, www.pbs.org/wgbh/frontline/). These can be especially useful as a reference while watching and analyzing story and structure.

The following titles include only producing, directing, writing, and editing credits when available; executive producer, co-editors, cinematographers, and the many other people critical to a film's successful completion and impact aren't listed here due to space.

20 Feet from Stardom: Produced by Caitrin Rogers and Gil Friesen; directed by Morgan Neville; edited by Jason Zeldes and Kevin Klauber.

Bad Voodoo's War: Produced, directed, and written by Deborah Scranton. Co-produced by P.H. O'Brien and Seth Bomse; edited by Seth Bomse.

Balseros: Produced by Loris Omedes; directed by Josep Ma Doménech and Carles Bosch; scripts by David Trueba and Carles Bosch; edited by Ernest Blasi.

Betty Tells Her Story: Produced, directed, and edited by Liane Brandon. This film is distributed by New Day Films, www.newday.com/films/Betty_Tells_Her_Story.html.

The Black Panthers: Vanguard of the Revolution: Produced by Laurens Grant; directed by Stanley Nelson; edited by Aljernon Tunsil.

Blackfish: Produced by Manuel V. Oteyza; directed by Gabriela Cowperthwaite; edited by Eli Despres.

Blue Vinyl: Produced by Daniel B. Gold, Judith Helfand, and Julia D. Parker; directed by Judith Helfand and Daniel B. Gold; edited by Sari Gilman.

Born into Brothels: Produced and directed by Ross Kauffman and Zana Briski; edited by Nancy Baker and Ross Kauffman.

Bowling for Columbine: Produced, directed, and written by Michael Moore; additional producers, Kathleen Glynn, Jim Czarnecki, Charles Bishop, and Michael Donovan; edited by Kurt Engfehr.

The Boys of Baraka: Produced and directed by Heidi Ewing and Rachel Grady; edited by Enat Sidi.

A Brief History of Time: Produced by David Hickman, Gordon Freedman, and Kory Johnston; directed by Errol Morris; edited by Brad Fuller.

Building the Alaska Highway: Produced and directed by Tracy Heather Strain; co-produced, written, and edited by Randall MacLowry.

Cadillac Desert: Hours 1–3 produced, directed, and written by Jon Else; based on Marc Reisner's book *Cadillac Desert*; hour 4 produced and directed by Linda Harrar; based on Sandra Postel's book *Last Oasis*.

Campaign (Senkyo): Directed, shot, and edited by Kazuhiro Soda.

Citizenfour: Produced by Mathilde Bonnefoy, Laura Poitras, and Dirk Wilutsky; directed by Laura Poitras; edited by Mathilde Bonnefoy.

City of Cranes: Produced by Samantha Zarzosa; directed by Eva Weber; edited by Emiliano Battista and Ariadna Fatjó-Vilas.

The Civil War: Produced by Ken Burns and Ric Burns; directed by Ken Burns; written by Geoffrey C. Ward and Ric Burns, with Ken Burns; edited by Paul Barnes, Bruce Shaw, and Tricia Reidy.

Control Room: Produced by Hani Salama and Rosadel Varela; directed by Jehane Nounaim; edited by Julia Bacha, Lilah Bankier, and Charles Marquardt.

The Cove: Produced by Fisher Stevens and Paula DuPré Pesmen; directed by Louie Psihoyos; written by Mark Monroe; edited by Geoffrey Richman.

Culloden: Produced, written, and directed by Peter Watkins; edited by Michael Bradsell.

Daughter from Danang: Produced by Gail Dolgin; directed by Gail Dolgin and Vicente Franco; edited by Kim Roberts.

The Day After Trinity: J. Robert Oppenheimer & The Atomic Bomb: Produced and directed by Jon Else; written by David Peoples, Janet Peoples, and Jon Else; edited by David Peoples and Ralph Wikk.

The Donner Party: Produced by Lisa Ades and Ric Burns; directed and written by Ric Burns; edited by Bruce Shaw.

Earth Made of Glass: Produced and written by Reid Carolin and Deborah Scranton; directed by Deborah Scranton; edited by Seth Bomse.

Enron: The Smartest Guys in the Room: Produced by Alex Gibney, Jason Kliot, and Susan Motamed; directed and written by Alex Gibney; edited and co-produced by Alison Ellwood.

The Execution of Wanda Jean: Produced by Liz Garbus and Rory Kennedy; directed by Liz Garbus.

Eyes on the Prize: America's Civil Rights Years (hours 1–6): Produced by Orlando Bagwell, Callie Crossley, James A. DeVinney, and Judith Vecchione; edited by Daniel Eisenberg, Jeanne Jordan, and Charles Scott; series writer, Steve Fayer; executive producer, Henry Hampton.

Eyes on the Prize: America at the Racial Crossroads (hours 7–14): Produced and directed by (in alphabetical order) Sheila Bernard, Carroll Blue, James A. DeVinney, Madison Davis Lacy, Jr., Louis J. Massiah, Thomas Ott, Samuel Pollard, Terry Kay Rockefeller, Jacqueline Shearer, and Paul Stekler; edited by Lillian Benson, Betty Ciccarelli, Thomas Ott, and Charles Scott; series writer, Steve Fayer; executive producer, Henry Hampton.

Gimme Shelter: Directed by Albert Maysles, David Maysles, and Charlotte Zwerin; edited by Ellen Giffard, Robert Farren, Joanne Burke, and Kent McKinney.

Gonzo: The Life and Work of Dr. Hunter S. Thompson: Produced by Alex Gibney and Graydon Carter, with Jason Kliot, Joana Vicente, Alison Ellwood, and Eva Orner; directed by Alex Gibney; screenplay by Alex Gibney, from the words of Hunter S. Thompson; edited by Alison Ellwood.

Grizzly Man: Produced by Erik Nelson; directed and narrated by Werner Herzog; edited by Joe Bini.

Harlan County, U.S.A.: Produced and directed by Barbara Kopple; edited by Nancy Baker, Mirra Bank, Lora Hays, and Mary Lampson.

Hoop Dreams: Produced by Frederick Marx, Steve James, and Peter Gilbert; directed by Steve James; edited by Frederick Marx, Steve James, and Bill Haugse.

Human Remains: Produced, directed, written, and edited by Jay Rosenblatt.

I'll Make Me a World (series): Produced by Betty Ciccarelli, Denise Greene, Sam Pollard, and Tracy Heather Strain; edited by Betty Ciccarelli, David Carnochan, and Eric Handley; series writer, Sheila Curran Bernard; series producer, Terry Kay Rockefeller; co-executive producer Sam Pollard; executive producer, Henry Hampton.

Imaginary Witness: Hollywood and the Holocaust. Produced by Daniel Anker and Ellin Baumel; co-produced by Susan Kim; directed by Daniel Anker; edited by Bruce Shaw.

An Inconvenient Truth: Produced by Lawrence Bender, Scott A. Burns, and Laurie David; directed by Davis Guggenheim; edited by Jay Lash Cassidy and Dan Swietlik.

Iraq for Sale: Produced by Sarah Feeley, Jim Gilliam, Robert Greenwald, and Devin Smith; directed by Robert Greenwald; edited by Carla Gutierrez and Sally Rubin.

Jonestown: The Life and Death of Peoples Temple: Produced and directed by Stanley Nelson; co-produced by Noland Walker; teleplay by Marcia Smith and Noland Walker; story by Marcia Smith; edited by Lewis Erskine.

The Kidnapping of Ingrid Betancourt: Produced and directed by Victoria Bruce and Karin Hayes; edited by Geof Bartz, Karin Hayes, and Victoria Bruce.

Kurt & Courtney: Produced by Nick Broomfield, Michele d'Acosta, and Tine van den Brande; directed by Nick Broomfield; edited by Mark Atkins.

Lalee's Kin: The Legacy of Cotton: Produced by Susan Froemke; directed by Susan Froemke and Deborah Dickson, with Albert Maysles; edited by Deborah Dickson.

Man on Wire: Produced by Simon Chinn; directed by James Marsh; based on the book *To Reach the Clouds* by Philippe Petit; edited by Jinx Godfrey.

March of the Penguins: Produced by Yves Darondeau, Christophe Lioud, and Emmanuel Priou; directed by Luc Jacquet; narration written by Jordan Roberts; based upon the story by Luc Jacquet; based upon the screenplay by Luq Jacquet and Michel Fessler; edited by Sabine Emiliani.

Mental (Seishin): Directed, shot, and edited by Kazuhiro Soda.

Miss America: Produced by Lisa Ades and Lesli Klainberg; directed by Lisa Ades; written by Michelle Ferrari; edited by Toby Shimin.

The Multiple Personality Puzzle: Produced by Holly Barden Stadtler and Eleanor Grant; directed by Holly Barden Stadtler; written by Eleanor Grant; edited by Barr Weissman.

The Murder of Emmett Till: Produced and directed by Stanley Nelson; written by Marcia A. Smith; edited by Lewis Erskine.

Murderball: Produced by Jeffrey Mandel and Dana Adam Shapiro; directed by Henry Alex Rubin and Dana Adam Shapiro; edited by Geoffrey Richman.

My Architect: Produced by Susan Rose Behr and Nathaniel Kahn; directed, written, and narrated by Nathaniel Kahn; edited by Sabine Krayenbühl.

New York: A Documentary Film: Produced by Lisa Ades and Ric Burns; directed by Ric Burns; co-directed by Lisa Ades; written by Ric Burns and James Sanders; edited by Li-Shin Yu, Edward Barteski, David Hanswer, and Nina Schulman.

Nobody's Business: Produced, directed, and edited by Alan Berliner.

Peace: Directed, produced, shot, and edited by Kazuhiro Soda.

A Place of Our Own: Produced and directed by Stanley Nelson; written by Stanley Nelson and Marcia Smith; edited by Sandra Christie and Helen Yum.

Recording The Producers: *A Musical Romp with Mel Brooks*: Produced by Susan Froemke and Peter Gelb; directed by Susan Froemke; co-directed and edited by Kathy Dougherty.

Roger & Me: Produced, directed, and written by Michael Moore; edited by Wendy Stanzler and Jennifer Beman.

Shelter Dogs: Produced by Heidi Reinberg and Cynthia Wade; directed by Cynthia Wade; edited by Geof Bartz.

Sing Faster: The Stagehands' Ring Cycle: Produced, directed, and written by Jon Else; edited by Deborah Hoffman and Jay Boekelheide.

Skateistan: To Live and Skate in Kabul. Produced by Orlando von Einsiedel and Louis Figgis; directed by Orlando von Einsiedel; edited by Peta Ridley.

Slavery by Another Name: Produced and directed by Sam Pollard; written by Sheila Curran Bernard; edited by Jason Pollard.

So Much So Fast: Produced, written, and directed by Steven Ascher and Jeanne Jordan; edited by Jeanne Jordan.

Sound and Fury: Produced by Roger Weisberg; directed by Josh Aronson; edited by Ann Collins.

Southern Comfort: Produced, directed, written, and edited by Kate Davis.

Spellbound: Produced by Sean Welch and Jeffrey Blitz; directed by Jeffrey Blitz; edited by Yana Gorskaya.

The Square: Produced by Karim Amer; directed by Jehane Noujaim; edited by Pedro Kos, Muhamed el Manasterly, Christopher De La Torre, Pierre Haberer, and Stefan Ronowiscz.

Standard Operating Procedure: Produced by Errol Morris and Julie Bilson Ahlberg; directed by Errol Morris; edited by Andy Grieve, Steven Hathaway, and Dan Mooney.

Super Size Me: Produced by Morgan Spurlock and The Con; directed and written by Morgan Spurlock; edited by Stela Georgieva and Julie "Bob" Lombardi.

The Sweetest Sound: Produced, directed, and edited by Alan Berliner.

Taxi to the Dark Side: Produced by Alex Gibney, Eva Orner, and Susannah Shipman; directed and written by Alex Gibney; edited by Sloane Klevin.

The Thin Blue Line: Produced by Mark Lipson; directed and written by Errol Morris; edited by Paul Barnes.

Troublesome Creek: A Midwestern: Produced, written, and directed by Jeanne Jordan and Steven Ascher; edited by Jeanne Jordan.

Virunga: Produced by Orlando von Einsiedel and Joanna Natasegara; directed by Orlando von Einsiedel; edited by Masahiro Hirakubo.

Waltz with Bashir: Produced by Ari Folman, Serge Lalou, Yael Nahlieli, Gerhard Geixner, and Roman Paul; directed and written by Ari Folman; edited by Nili Feller.

The War Tapes: Produced by Robert May and Steve James; directed by Deborah Scranton; edited by Steve James and Leslie Simmer.

The Way We Get By: Produced by Gita Pullapilly; directed, written, and edited by Aron Gaudet.

When the Levees Broke: Produced by Spike Lee and Sam Pollard; directed by Spike Lee; supervising editor, Sam Pollard; edited by Sam Pollard, Geeta Gandbhir, and Nancy Novack.

Why We Fight: Produced by Eugene Jarecki and Susannah Shipman; directed and written by Eugene Jarecki; edited by Nancy Kennedy.

Winged Migration: Produced by Christophe Barratier and Jacques Perrin; directed by Jacques Perrin; written by Stéphane Durand and Jacques Perrin; edited by Marie-Josèphe Yoyotte.

Wisconsin Death Trip: Produced by Maureen A. Ryan and James Marsh; directed and written by James Marsh; edited by Jinx Godfrey; adapted from the book *Wisconsin Death Trip* by Michael Lesy.

Workingman's Death: Produced by Erich Lackner, Mirjam Quinte, and Pepe Danquart; directed and written by Michael Glawogger; edited by Monica Willi and Ilse Buchelt.

Vietnam: A Television History: Produced by Judith Vecchione, Elizabeth Deane, Andrew Pearson, Austin Hoyt, Martin Smith, and Bruce Palling; edited by Eric W. Handley, Carol Hayward, Ruth Schell, Eric Neudel, Glen Cardno, Paul Cleary, Mavis Lyons Smull, and Daniel Eisenberg; chief correspondent, Stanley Karnow; executive producer, Richard Ellison.

Yosemite: The Fate of Heaven: Produced and directed by Jon Else; written by Michael Chandler and Jon Else; edited by Michael Chandler; executive produced and narrated by Robert Redford.

Index